Walking the Tight Rope

Informal Livelihoods and Social Networks in a West African City

Ilda Lourenço-Lindell

Abstract

The study addresses the way processes of informalization looming large in the world today take shape in the West African city of Bissau, Guinea-Bissau. These processes are analysed in a historical perspective, whereby the historical imprint on current forms of informality and the forces that have shaped them through time are uncovered. The picture that emerges is that of a multifaceted process involving a wide variety of agents and relations that earlier analyses of informality have often failed to recognise.

A central concern in the study pertains to how disadvantaged groups who rely on informality for survival are faring in the context of wider contemporary changes, including those related to structural adjustment programmes. This is done by studying the informal livelihoods of these groups in a neighbourhood of Bissau, both their informal income-generating activities and the social networks in which they engage to sustain both incomes and consumption. The study challenges assumptions in the neo-liberal literature that these informal activities and networks provide the poor with sufficient incomes and welfare in an environment of economic liberalisation and state withdrawal from welfare responsibilities. Firstly, a share of small informal operators in Bissau were found to be experiencing a deterioration in their conditions of operation. Small businesses collapsed on a frequent basis, which is captured in the popular expression 'falling off balance' that has inspired the title of this book. Secondly, the study illustrates how widespread economic hardship is undermining collaborative efforts among the poor. While some people could count on wide and diversified networks of support comprising resilient ties and egalitarian relations, others were found to be quite isolated, unable to enforce their perceived rights to support and to occupy subordinate positions in support systems. Among relatives, norms of assistance were changing in a way that left a share of people to fend for themselves and that increased the burden particularly of women, including elderly women. People who were disadvantaged in these respects acted to improve their positions in networks, to influence norms of support and to disengage from oppressive relations of assistance. I refer to these power relations in informal support systems as 'the politics of support mobilisation'. This differs substantially from current notions of 'social capital' that neglect issues of exclusion, subordination, power struggles as well as the weight of wider structural constraints. Finally, the study has uncovered how informal forms of regulation influenced the conditions of small informal actors and has pointed to the variety of ways in which informal relations are regulated, contrary to widespread notions of informality as 'non-regulated'.

The study is based on qualitative methods including interviews with households, traders, food producers, a variety of key informants, government officials, as well as on a household survey in the studied neighbourhood.

Key words: social networks, social capital, informal safety nets, informal sector, informalization, livelihoods, urban food, regulation, social change, structural adjustment, Guinea-Bissau, West Africa, African cities

Department of Human Geography
Stockholm University

ISBN 91-22-01968-5
Printed by Akademitryck AB, Edsbruk, Sweden, 2002.

Contents

List of maps

List of tables

List of photos

List of figures

List of abbreviations

CFA	Communautée Financière Africaine
FAO	Food and Agriculture Organisation
INEP	Instituto Nacional de Estudos e Pesquisa (National Institute of Research)
NGO	Non-Governmental Organisation
PAIGC	Partido Africano da Guiné e Cabo Verde (African Party for the Independence of Guinea and Cape Verde)
PG	Pesos Guineenses (Guinean Pesos)
USAID	United States Agency for International Development

Glossary

abota	rotating savings groups
bentaninha	small size and low cost fish
djilas	male (itinerant) traders
grumetes	African boat hands who assisted European traders
lançados	European traders prior to colonial rule
lumos	rural rotating markets
manjuandade	social clubs for recreation and material assistance
surni	casual work

Currency exchange rates

January 1995: 1 French Franc = 3,000 Guinean Pesos
June 1999: 1 French Franc = 100 CFA Francs

Acknowledgements

While I alone am responsible for the words written in this book, many have contributed to its content in a variety of ways. To begin with, I would like to thank the population of the neighbourhood of Bandim in Bissau for tolerating a curious stranger in their midst. Particularly my respondents always showed me kindness and were generous in sharing their experiences with me. Even when their lives had been shattered by an unnecessary war, they took time to talk to me, for which I am infinitely grateful. This is not just because they enriched the substance of this study. Their stories and their endurance taught me many lessons. I developed close contact with many local residents, too many to mention them all. But I would like to thank at least those who showed me hospitality each time I returned to Bandim. These include António Vieira and Sábado, Tasso and Rosa Dju, Julieta and Nônô, Dona, Natália and husband, Dina, Sábado and Giro Gomes, and Daniel and Mama. Particularly the compound headed by João Baptista and the Arriaga family within it became my home in Bandim. Rafael Barbosa, Pinto Marques, João Baptista and Tasso Dju were tireless in sharing with me their long experiences from Bandim and Bissau. I am indebted to my fieldwork assistants João Arriaga and Domingos Nanque who never tired and who provided enjoyable company. Albino Biai and Elsa Gomes were also dedicated when they assisted me with my household survey.

The Health Project in Bandim (Projecto de Saúde de Bandim) facilitated my work in Bandim by giving me access to office equipment and by making available their data and reports. At the Project, I would like to thank especially Peter Aaby and Anita Sandström. The National Institute for Research (Instituto Nacional de Estudos e Pesquisa) also supported me during my stays. At the Institute I would particularly like to thank Carlos Rui Ribeiro, Faustino Imbali, Mamadu Jao, Uco Monteiro and Raul Fernandes for their interest in my work. Among Guinean colleagues, I want to mention Julieta Barbosa and Nina Aimé (and Mamadu Jao) who guided me around in the rural areas and shared their knowledge of Guinean society with me. Still in Bissau, I want to thank the Swedish Embassy, in particular Johan Sundberg, Tom Abrahamsson and Lena Rupp, for facilitating my stays in Bissau in various ways. Christer Holmgren made possible my last fieldwork by helping with transportation between Dakar and Bissau in the aftermath of the war.

A number of colleagues around the world have been a source of inspiration and advice at different points in time during the project. These include Jonina Einarsdóttir, David Smith, Lars Rudebeck, Ulrick Schieffer, Jacob Songsore, Arne Tostensen, Paule Moustier, Patrick Gervais and Jan Vretman. I am grateful for the comments that I received on the manuscript or parts of it from AbdouMaliq Simone, David Simon, Anders Sjögren, Mariken Vaa, Gunnel Forsberg and Bo Lenntorp.

I want to express my gratitude to the Department of Human Geography for the support that it has provided me through the years. The research group People, Provisioning and Place has been a stimulating environment. Still at the Department, Lars Wåhlin, Katarina Strömdahl and Johan Cederström helped with the graphic and practical work surrounding this publication. Andrew Byerley worked with perseverance on my English. I am grateful to moral support from Agnes Andersson, who submitted her doctoral thesis at the same time as I. My thanks also go to Kjell Lundgren for his work with the cover of the book and to Patric Lindell with the layout and maps. Helena Neves Abrahamsson helped with translations into Creole.

I am greatly indebted to my supervisor Gunilla Andræ for her endurance, her dedication and for encouraging me to take one step further. This thesis would have not come through without the support and patience of my family, Patric and Leonard. My son was deprived of considerable time with me. My gratitude also goes to my wider family in both Sweden and Portugal. This research has been financed by the Hans W:son Ahlmann Foundation, the Axel Lagrelius Foundation and The Nordic Africa Institute.

Agradecimentos

Gostaria de agradecer à população de Bandim por me terem feito sentir bem-vinda no seu meio. Agradeço em particular ás pessoas que participaram no estudo por terem sido generosas com o seu tempo, mesmo quando as suas vidas se encontravam de rastos devido a uma guerra desnecessária. As suas experiências enriqueceram tanto este livro como a minha própria vida. Estou muitíssimo grata à família Arriaga e ao 'homem grande' João Baptista e sua 'morança' por terem sido o meu lar em Bandim. Agradeço também a hospitalidade de Tasso e Rosa Dju, Julieta e Nônô, Sábado e António Vieira, Dona, Natália e marido, Dina, Sábado e Giro Gomes, Daniel e Mámá. João Baptista, Tasso Dju, Rafael Barbosa e Pinto Marques foram incansáveis em compartilhar comigo o seu vasto conhecimento de Bandim e Bissau. João Arriaga e Domingos Nanque foram os meus fiéis assistentes e bons amigos. Albino Biai e Elsa Gomes também foram assistentes dedicados no inquérito ás famílias. Ainda em Bissau, gostaria de agradecer aos colegas no Instituto Nacional de Estudos e Pesquisa pelo seu apoio, conselhos e inspiração. Desejo mencionar Carlos Rui Ribeiro, Faustino Imbali, Mamadu Jao, Uco Monteiro and Raul Fernandes e ainda Julieta Barbosa and Nina Aimé. Finalmente, estou grata à minha família em Portugal pelo seu apoio através dos anos. A todos, os meus sinceros agradecimentos.

Sollentuna, April 2002

Ilda Lourenço-Lindell

For Leonard

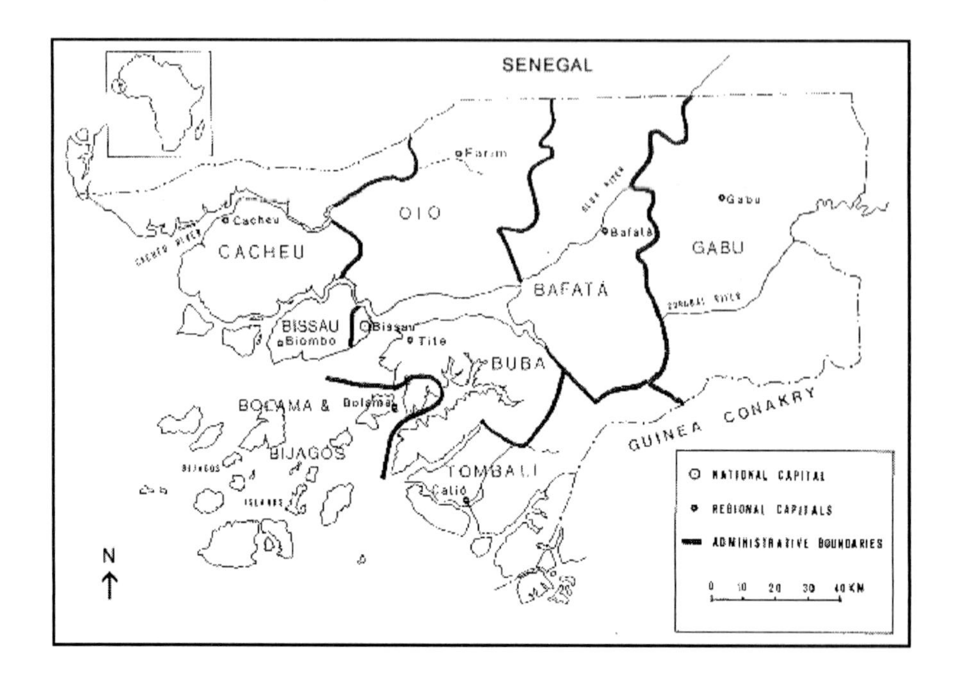

Map of Guinea-Bissau: administrative regions

Source: Dávila (1987)

1 The research problem, theory and method

1.1 Introduction

African cities: crisis and reinvention

People living in African cities today face great challenges. The deterioration of basic services, housing and environment, the falling access to secure jobs and sufficient incomes, and the virtual absence of state welfare provision, interpreted by many as symptoms of an "urban crisis", have been well documented (White, 1989; Halfani, 1997:14-6; Tostensen, Vaa and Tvedten 2001:9-11). Governments have often been unable or unwilling to respond to the needs and demands of urban citizens or have been obsessed with unrealistic modernising ideals for their cities (Stren, 1989:58, 63-4; Swilling 1997:6; Halfani 1997:20, 1994:148). The measures for economic stabilisation advocated by international financial institutions since the mid-1980s have had a heavy toll on the standard of living of most urban dwellers, with their effects on retrenchment, rising costs of living and falling real wages. Policies of deregulation of the economy and of labour conditions have produced deeper social inequalities and polarisation (Potter & Lloyd-Evans 98:162) at a time when media images of affluence are increasingly accessible to urbanites everywhere. The economic benefits of globalisation have largely bypassed Sub-Saharan Africa and its cities as these cities have become increasingly side-lined from the prosperous sectors of the new global economy[1]. This has further worsened urban employment problems. The contemporary situation in most African cities has been described as characterised by a shrinking, "aborted" or "truncated" formal economy resting uneasily on a large informal economy (Bangura, 1994: :811; Rakodi, 1997a:61; Rogerson 1997).

To be sure, urban popular groups have not passively watched their conditions deteriorate. They devise alternative ways of gaining access to land, housing, water and other basic services (Stren, 1989:61; Swilling 1997:10, Halfani, 1997:16). They create their own income sources and diversify them

[1] Rakodi (1997a:43-5; 1997b:555); Simon (1992:83; 1997:81-3); Halfani (1997:18-9); Rogerson (1997:340-2).

often through a variety of petty activities, build spontaneous market places and cultivate idle land in the city (Potts, 1997; Rogersson, 1997). They reinvent traditional socio-cultural practices in order to deal with the challenges of contemporary urban life and combine different social positions and multiple identities to access a wider range of opportunities in the diverse socio-economic environments of the city (Bangura 1994:821; Simone 1999:72, 80-3; Hecht and Simone, 1994:14-5, 36, 148-150). So as to meet a variety of needs, they create a variety of collaborative efforts. The current growth of associational initiatives in African cities is well documented (Aina 1997; Halfani, 1997:23, 32, Tostensen et al, 2001), even if some of these initiatives are induced and driven by external agents. Less visible forms of collaboration, albeit less documented, are of no lesser importance for survival in the city. These refer to networks of personal ties that people construct for mutual support, for accessing resources and for exchanging goods and services (Lourenço-Lindell, 2001; Hecht and Simone, 1994:15-6). Most of the above have been interpreted as representing an increase in informal social and economic activity. In fact, there is a consensus that contemporary African cities are experiencing an extensive informalization and that informality now constitutes a pervasive feature in most of them[2].

The urban scene is now characterised by an array of new actors involved in urban development, a multiplication of loci of power and governance, the revival of traditional practices and parochial groups, the increased ambiguity of social positions and identities, the diversification of livelihood strategies and the unplanned growth of the city. In their dazzling diversity and complexity, African cities challenge most existing models and theories of urbanization. Some have interpreted some of these developments as African cities reinventing themselves away from the Western project and its universalistic views of the world (Hecht and Simone, 1994:14-5, 19)[3] and as a "deconstruction of colonial cities (…) make(ing) way for a restructuring of urban life and conditions based on African mores and value systems" (Mabogunje, 1994:22). Many Governments, seemingly obsessed with the modernization project, are said to have distanced themselves from "the everyday cultural and social practices of the vast majority" (Bangura, 1994:810). Today, formal mechanisms are reported to regulate but a small part of urban relations and dynamics[4].

As they go about their daily lives, urbanites create "their own urban systems" with little care for law or public policy (Swilling, 1997:10). They build their own social institutions and norms to regulate a variety of exchang-

[2] Simon (1992:80); Onibokun (1994:264); Stren (1992); Kharoufi (1994:94); Bangura and Gibbon (1992:19); Rogerson (1997:345-351); Potter & Lloyd-Evans (1998:162); Halfani (1997:16); De Herdt and Marysse (1996); Nabuguzi (1994).

[3] On the inadequacy of identifying urbanity in Africa with progressive modernization, see also Swilling (1997:11); and Ferguson (1999:24-37, 86-93)

[4] See Stren (1989:61); Swilling (1994:345, 1997:9); Rakodi (1997b:569). See Bangura (1994:809) on a general erosion of formal regulatory mechanisms in Africa.

es, lending daily life in the city a degree of predictability and security. It is these creations, rather than the written law of the state, that govern urban social and economic life (Onibokun, 1994:264). And indeed, in the current urban governance debate, though much of the attention is placed on well-organised non-state actors, some writers refer to the existence of such less visible informal kinds of governance. Hecht and Simone (1994:13) speak of an "invisible governance (…) that maintains competing agendas and aspirations in some kind of functional and parallel existence". Halfani (1997a:155) argues for capitalising on "informal regimes of governance" that, in his view, give people access to basic urban resources [5]. These interpretations point to the necessity of anchoring urban formal management in popular practices.

But the recognition that informality is a major way by which urbanites handle the current economic and urban crisis is only a beginning. There is a need for critical assessments of how well informal ways of coping are withstanding the general deterioration of living conditions. There is also a need for a greater understanding of the inner workings of this vast urban informal field and of the social struggles unravelling within it, rather than assuming that this is an all virtuous sphere. Research outside the African context also calls for looking at informality in new ways.

Globalizing informality

The above could give the impression of African cities as being intrinsically different and increasingly distant from cities in the Western world. Indeed, there is a widespread notion that African cities have become increasingly marginal to processes of economic globalisation, as that they have been unable to compete in the growth sectors of the global economy (Rakodi, 1997a:43-5, 1997b:555; Simon, 1992:83, 1997:81-3; Rogerson 97:340-2; Halfani, 1997: :18-9). Surely, in many ways, African cities seem to be on divergent paths from those of better-positioned cities in global networks. In some important respects, however, African cities have become more like cities in core regions of the global economy and their futures seem increasingly interconnected rather than 'de-linked'.

In advanced industrial countries, the shift towards "flexible production" in combination with the dismantling of the welfare state has contributed to a worsening of conditions for the working class and a weakening of its bargaining power. Social exclusion, poverty and economic polarisation have all reportedly intensified, particularly in large cities (Castells, 1998; Sassen-Koob, 1989:61; Sassen, 2000:136, 142; Burbach et al, 1997:102-3). World cities today accommodate both large concentrations of capital and large

[5] See also Piermay (1997); Nsarhaza (1997); Mabogunje (1994:30, 31); McCarney, Halfani and Rodriguez (1995:121).

numbers of marginalised people (Potter and Lloyd-Evans, 1998:164; Sassen-Koob 1989:74; Sassen 2000:142-4; Short and Kim, 1999:53-7). The latter include many international migrants, including many from African countries, working in conditions that do not differ much from those in their home countries (Simone, 1999:84). Indeed, a "periphery" has been discovered within "core regions" and their major cities, giving rise to a "new geography of marginality" (Sassen, 2000:5, 140, chapters six and seven; Castells, 1998:129-147). It has been argued that global capitalism is producing a global underclass (Burbach et al, 1997:153-5, chapter two; Potter and Lloyd-Evans, 1998:180). At the same time, a globalised consciousness is also emerging (Appadurai 2000:8). A sizeable part of this growing army of the discontented is to be found in cities, which some writers have referred to as a "global urban upheaval" shaking cities in various continents[6]. In particular, disillusioned youths with few stakes in global capitalism are making themselves heard in cities everywhere, reflecting the shared predicament of youths in different parts of the world[7]. In these respects, the condition of the majority of urban Africans is therefore neither exclusive unique nor necessarily dead-ended.

There is another dimension to a shared experience between cities in Africa and post-industrial cities in the North. Major cities in core regions of the global economy have emerged as sites of informalization, as manifested in an increase in self-employment and in the casualization of labour[8]. There, informality has been reported to exist side by side with corporate culture (Sassen, 1998:154-5, 2000:123). Indeed, informal modes of operation now present themselves where they were least expected, i.e. in societies where high levels of state regulation were formerly attained and in world cities, the nerve centres of global capitalism. This, Castells and Portes (1989:13) argue, lends a new significance to informal modes of operation, as "old forms of production become (…) new ones" (p. 30). This informalization has been interpreted in different ways as will shortly be seen - for example as large firms going underground namely by using and benefiting from a large pool of vulnerable, exploited labour in the unregulated economy (Castells and Portes, 1989; Portes and Schauffler, 1993; Potter and Lloyd-Evans, 1998:180-1), or as resulting from grassroots initiatives with potential for future empowerment (Burbach et al, 1997). But the general picture is one of a global trend towards informalization of employment, linked in some way to the contemporary restructuring of domestic and international economies and to global deregulation. This realisation has inspired suggestive new labels for economic

---

[6] See Burbach et al (1997:28-32) for a reflection on the similar structural causes underlying riots in Latin American cities since the 1980's and the Los Angeles riot in 1992.

[7] Castells (1998:142) and O'Brian (1996:58), writing on the youth of the American city ghetto and Dakar respectively, both give a sense of an indefinitely postponed "adulthood" for male youth, as they are being denied the basic material conditions for assuming the responsibilities of adult life.

[8] Castells and Portes (1989); Sassen-Koob (1989); Sassen (1998:chapter 8, 2000:117-137); Burbach, Núñez and Kagarlitsky (1997:155), Castells (1998:72, 141). See also Gaughan and Ferman (1987).

informal activity, such as "post-industrial alternatives" (Gaughan and Ferman, 1987:24) and "post-modern economies" (Burbach et al., 1997:5).

In this respect too, we could speak of "a new geography of informality". This realignment renders obsolete spatial and temporal orderings of the world that have considered informality to be an exclusive feature of developing countries or the manifestation of remnant traditional relations and of an incomplete transition from a pre-capitalist to a capitalist mode of production, destined to disappear as incorporation into the international economy deepened and modernization took hold. This is not to say that informality in Africa is similar to that emerging in post-industrial societies. In African cities it both has a long history and assumes specific forms deriving from the interplay between external forces and indigenous structures (see below). But global trends of informalization may be providing a new impetus and a new twist to informal relations in Africa. In addition, this contemporary shared experience means that processes of informalization in cities in core and peripheral regions may inform each other. In this sense, the position of African cities is not merely one of "structural irrelevance", expressed in relation to the interests of global capital (Castells, 1998:162), but also one of conceptual relevance.

Research issues

This study is about processes of informalization in a particular city in West Africa, Bissau, the capital of Guinea-Bissau. These processes are analysed in a historical perspective, in order to uncover the forces that have been at work and the historical imprint on today's forms of informality[9]. Then I focus on what the contemporary widespread informalization, looming large in Africa and the wider world, has meant for the daily lives of disadvantaged groups in this particular city. I go about this task by studying the informal livelihoods of these groups. On the one hand, I will look at informal income-generating activities, particularly food trade, given its importance in the study area. On the other hand, I will address the social networks that urbanites engage in to sustain both income activities and consumption. A major aim is to assess how these different components of informal livelihoods are faring in the context of wider contemporary changes influencing urban conditions. Are people coping with wider changes through informal income activities and the use of social networks or are there groups that are becoming marginalised from networks of assistance and from activities that provide sufficient incomes? The social

[9] The term "informal" pertains to activities that fail to conform to at least one aspect of the written law of the modern state or that are regulated by other kinds of "laws". For a discussion of the definition, see section "Delimiting the informal" in this chapter.

relations pervading access to support and livelihood resources as well as the informal rules governing such access will be in focus.

The general picture that will emerge is that of an urban existence that could be compared to walking a tight rope. This idea is inspired by the local Creole expression "cai na balanso", i.e. falling off balance, that is frequently used by local small-scale traders to refer to the loss of one's working capital. Indeed, daily survival seems dependent on being able to keep one's business afloat as well as the ability to balance a tiny domestic budget. But it is also about being able to balance rights and obligations in assistance, responsibilities towards different people and different affiliations. This is because there is little room for mistakes in the current context of crisis. When survival hangs on a thread, having a safety net is of crucial importance.

The above research issues will be expanded upon in the rest of this chapter. The theoretical section below presents both the theoretical frame for the study and the research questions. I will begin with positioning the study within the main existing perspectives on growing informality and what this study hopes to contribute to these debates. I then discuss the importance of a historical approach to the study of contemporary informality, followed by a clarification of what is meant by "informal" in this study. I proceed with a discussion of discourses of relevance for approaching relations within the informal realm, including a reformulated social network approach to relations of assistance. This is followed by a section delimiting the scope of the study and presenting the structure of the book. The last part of this chapter deals with the research methods used in the study.

1.2 Theoretical frame and research questions

Perspectives on expanding informality

Two broad interpretations have been advanced to explain the origins of the pervasive informality described above. One perspective generally places the roots of informalization in the malpractices of the national state[10]. The state is portrayed either as oppressive or as a poor performer and obstructive of the entrepreneurial efforts among popular groups. This, some have argued, has resulted in a societal "disengagement" from the state, by which people devise activities that circumvent unfavourable public regulations and policies, sometimes reportedly with far reaching consequences for the credibility and outreach of the state. These alternative or informal activities are praised for the dynamism, flexibility, creativity and the solidarity they supposedly contain.

---

[10] Azarya and Chazan (1987); Azarya (1988); MacGaffey (1988) and Lemarchand (1988); Hyden (1990); de Soto (1989) for Lima. See also Galli and Jones (1987) for a similar argument for Guinea-Bissau.

They are celebrated as being both more congruent with indigenous institutions and values and inherently libertarian and democratic in their content. A boom in informal economic activity in this view represents nothing less than increased autonomy from state power and a major step towards a more democratic order. In spite of much criticism[11], this perspective has both inspired a large number of studies on informality in urban Africa (for example, Tripp, 1997, 1989; Dhemba, 1999) and come to inform the neo-liberal agendas of international institutions since the late 1980s onward.

International development and financial institutions now place the "informal sector" (usually meaning small enterprises) high on their priorities for Africa and its cities[12]. On the one hand, the sector has been depicted as a "seedbed of entrepreneurship" (World Bank, 1989:23), "a solid foundation for economic growth" and as representing a more sustainable form of growth (United Nations, 1996:1, 5). The sector is attributed a key position in economic recovery of both the continent and its urban areas. Since the late 1980s an increasing emphasis is being placed on issues of urban economic development and productivity and on the role of cities as "engines of growth" (rather than seeing them as being parasitic) in their national contexts. On the other hand, a renewed emphasis is being placed on the informal sector as a major element in strategies for poverty alleviation, not least in urban areas. At the same time, a shift away from public sector interventions and social projects is being advised. In these agendas an expanding informal sector is expected to provide sufficient incomes, basic services and social welfare to the urban poor. Policies of deregulation of markets and the rolling back of the state are said to provide an environment propitious to the blossoming of "indigenous" forms of economic and social activity. It is expected that small informal operators will benefit from a trickle down effect and that the grassroots will be "empowered" as the democratic potential supposedly contained within the informal sector is liberated (Gibbon 1993:17, 1995:18). Critics of the neo-liberal agenda argue that this discourse on the informal sector is intended to ward off the political threat posed by retrenched workers and to build an alternative popular legitimacy for adjustment programs while furthering their anti-state campaign of releasing the state from welfare and other responsibilities and transferring the burden onto the poor (and the informal sector)[13].

An alternative perspective, the "informalization approach", seeks to explain informality as an increasingly recurrent feature in late capitalism in

---

[11] See for example Gibbon and Bangura (1992); Gibbon (1995a); Roitman (1990). See also Sjögren (1998) for a review.

[12] On the general agenda for Africa, see for example World Bank (1989) and United Nations (1996). On the urban agenda, see World Bank (1991), World Bank (2000). For discussions of these agendas and the role of the informal sector in them, see Rakodi (1997a:58-61; 1997b:574-5); Jenkins (2000:137-140); Meagher and Yunusa (1996:1).

[13] Bangura (1994:794); Rakodi (1997a:61); Beckman (1992:90-93); Meagher and Yunusa (1996:1); Grey-Johnson (1992:79); Peattie (1987:856).

both developed and developing countries[14]. This approach is a development from Marxist structural approaches which, contrary to the neo-liberal discourse, have considered the role of the international and domestic political economy in shaping informal activities (see for example Portes, 1983; Moser, 1978). The informal sphere is seen as a *social process,* rather than a *sector*, to account for the political bargaining and the social struggles involved in the changes in the boundary between the formal and the informal (Castells and Portes, 1989: 12-3, 33; see also Sassen, 1998:157, and Meagher, 1995). The emphasis is on seeing current informalization as deriving to a great extent from strategies by capital to reduce costs, increase flexibility and protect its profits in the face of changing international conditions and of formerly attained high levels of state regulation and organised labour in industrialised countries (Castells and Portes, 1989:13, 26, 30; Sassen, 2000:118-125; Portes and Schauffler, 1993:49). Informal work is seen as an integral part of the global corporate economy and as providing a crucial infrastructure for the major growth sectors of the "new urban economy" in core regions (Sassen, 2000:123, 125, 142-4). In this perspective, expanding informal activities do not reflect a greater autonomy or represent the achievements of the unprivileged. Rather, they represent a disenfranchisement of the working class, a "downgrading of labour" and a worsening of working conditions (Castells and Portes, 1989:26, 27; Sassen-Koob, 1989:62; Sassen, 2000:124).

Informality as a facet of late capitalist accumulation is not necessarily irrelevant in the African context, in spite of the continent being increasingly peripheral to the interests of global capital. African cities continue to entertain a variety of exchanges with the rest of the world and to be arenas of accumulation, in spite of the widespread poverty that they contain (Rakodi, 1997a:52; Simon, 1997:86; Simon, 1992:77). Members of the domestic political and economic elites have been reported to be thriving on the deepening internationalisation of their countries' economies and on the policies of economic liberalisation and deregulation by engaging in global informal trade networks of such profitable goods as weapons, drugs and human beings[15]. These African international actors may be increasingly drawing on informal ways of operating in a way that is analogous to the informal strategies of flexible production employed by large firms in the North. If so, the seemingly "unregulated" city may be the fertile ground on which these actors are able to reap great profits (Halfani, 1994:148; Swilling, 1997:11).

This study finds considerable inspiration in the informalization approach, for its insights into informality as part of contemporary global processes and

---

[14] See Sassen-Koob (1989); Portes and Schauffler (1993) for Latin America; for Africa, see Meagher (1995), with Yunusa (1991, 1996); Lugalla (1997).

[15] Ghai (1990:15-6); Bangura (1994:800); Castells (1998:91); Burbach et al. (1997:8); Bayart (2000). See also Simone (1999, 2000) and Diouf (2000) on African actors in international and global networks.

for its concern with the consequences for the underprivileged. I share with this approach a scepticism towards the triumphalism found in the neo-liberal literature about informality.

> *Thus, in line with some of the concerns of the informalization approach, general goals in this study include understanding the dynamics of expanding informality in the study setting and assessing how the informal livelihoods of popular groups are faring in the current context of deepening internationalisation of the economy and a structural adjustment policy environment. How have the conditions of participation of these groups in the market changed? Are their survival networks being sustained or collapsing? In relation to neo-liberal assumptions, are the informal strategies of disadvantaged groups compensating for the withdrawal of the state and has this widespread informalization meant that popular groups have been freed from state encumbrance?*

In this effort, this research joins a new crop of studies on urban informality that have begun to document the changed conditions for small informal actors (see for example, Meagher and Yunusa, 1996:38-40; Lugalla, 1997:449).

But the informalization approach remains in my view insufficient to deal with the complexity exhibited by contemporary informality. To begin with, the informal sphere becomes too easily associated with victimisation and the downgrading of labour and the range of explanations for its dynamics tend to be narrowed to the imperatives of capital. One needs to consider the range of small scale activities that are not linked dynamically to the capitalist sector (as argued by Tokman, 1992:4 in the Latin American context) and to stay alert to eventual spaces of autonomy created by popular groups. Some elements of the early "disengagement" perspective may be of assistance in uncovering these spaces, albeit this requires dropping its assumptions of an all-virtuous, democratic and state-free informal sphere. In fact, while most analyses either focus on capital or on popular groups as the driving forces in processes of informalization, these processes seem to be too complex to be accommodated within any single of the existing perspectives.

> *This prompted me to explore the idea of an informalization process that involves multiple agents, a multifaceted process where both popular groups, capital and the state may have a role to play. This is what I will attempt to do in a longitudinal analysis of informalization in the study setting.*

Another major shortcoming that I see in the available perspectives on informality is their lack of consideration of social processes taking place *within* the informal realm, as they tend to focus solely on the vertical contradiction between small informal actors and capital or the state. Locating power and exploitation exclusively in capital or the state obscures other sources of domination and a variety of contradictions that are internal to the informal sphere[16]. The informal is usually portrayed as a black box, i.e. as an amorphous mass, moving uniformly in one and the same direction, in a way that lumps together a wide range of social relations and structural positions.

> *This study represents an effort to uncover the inner boundaries, the plurality of power relations within the informal realm and the myriad of social struggles that develop on a variety of fronts. These evolving social relations among informal actors, I will argue, are also part of the dynamics of informality and influence the conditions and well being of informal actors.*

At this level of the analysis the focus is on social relations pervading livelihood activities of the poor in the informal sphere, both in their income and social security components.

A spatially and historically informed informality

The contemporary expansion of informal activities in Africa cannot be reduced to a response to the state (as argued by Roitman, 1990) or to a novel feature in the age of late capitalism (as depicted for example by Burbach et al, 1997). The production of informality in African cities contains a historical depth that includes both various phases of capitalist penetration and evolved indigenous cultures and pre-capitalist forms of social and economic organisation (Mabogunje, 1990:134, 143; Roitman, 1990). Earlier specific forms of capitalist development in Africa entailed a partial formalisation of relations but they have never ceased to cohabit with these other indigenous forms of organisation, even in urban areas, supposedly the motors of modernization. In various instances, indigenous forms were reproduced and even reinforced, rather than eroded (Bernstein, 1991:30-49; Berry, 1985, 1989). Rather than a replication of Western forms of social and economic organisation, what has been found in African societies has been a syncretic articulation in a variety of fields[17]. In the process, both capitalist relations and pre-capitalist social formations have been transformed in ways that are locally specific. Thus change, rather than being a homogenising and unidirectional process along a predetermined path[18], has produced outcomes that are locally specific. These outcomes reflect the conditions of incorporation and participation of a parti-

---

[16] See for a similar argument among political scientists on state-civil society relations: Gibbon and Bangura (1992); Beckman (1997); Sjögren (1998). See also Roitman (1990) for an explicit call for analyses of power relations within the informal sphere.

[17] See, on syncretism: in the economic field, Mabogunje (1990); Simon (1992:100-2); in the cultural and political fields, Keesing (1981); Bayart (1993); Hecth and Simone (1994); Werbner (1996).

[18] For useful reviews and critiques on linear views of social-cultural change and urbanisation see, beside the references in the previous footnote: Gugler and Flanagan (1978:118.134); Basham (1978, chapter four); Ferguson (1999:24-37, 86-93). See also Halfani (1997:29-30); Simon (1992:82); Bangura (1994:812-3), on the plural logics determining the direction of urban change.

cular place in the international economic system and the ways in which local African societies respond. The same could be said of universalising perspectives on current processes of globalisation that tend to reduce spatial difference to a temporal sequence (Massey, 1999)[19]. A variety of local responses, ranging from resistance to Western hegemony to appropriation of external influences, make for highly spatially differentiated outcomes.

It is in this light that we should understand informality. The unique forms that informality takes in a particular place are the outcome of particular intersections between external forces and historically informed local responses. This can be analysed throughout a series of historical layers, each with its particular mix of formality and informality. Today's informal livelihoods and modes of operation have been shaped by locally specific historical processes that may go back to pre-colonial times[20]. Age-old frames of reference, practices and norms may inform modern practices of survival[21]. They may also help to explain some of the divisions, segmentations and power relations that we today find within the informal realm, where hegemonic actors may legitimise their power by appealing to a distant past.

In the context of the crisis, traditional socio-cultural practices have been said to have increased in importance in African cities as a means by which people endure economic deterioration[22]. In connection with this, issues of social change gain renewed relevance. A pursuit of these issues, however, requires a different approach from those that adhere to the universalistic notions of the modernization paradigm that inspired research on these issues decades ago.

In line with the above, I will try to discern how the informal realm has been shaped and reshaped through different historical periods in a particular place, entertaining a particular kind of relation with the world and containing specific historically evolved structures. This is my platform for understanding the configuration of informal relations today and to reflect upon how local structures with long historical roots are responding to contemporary wider processes.

[19] For example, see Simon (1992:100-2) and Giddens (1999) on how globalization supposedly undermines pre-capitalist practices and traditional family forms are predicted to enter extinction everywhere. For a critique of universalising views of globalization see also: Werbner (1996); Simon (1997:75-77); Hecht and Simone (1994:19, 35).

[20] See Roitman's (1990) call for addressing these deep historical dimensions of informality in Africa.

[21] On the continued importance and active role of traditional structures, practices and forms of interaction in African cities, see also Simon (1992:71-82, 100-2); Rakodi (1997b:566-7); Mabogunje (1990); Barnes (1986).

[22] Mabogunje (1990:41, 49); Rakodi (1997b:585); Hecht and Simone (1994:14-5, 150); Bangura (1994:821). One the proliferation of ethnic based unions among informal enterprise in African cities, see Lugalla (1997:447); Macharia (1996); Meagher and Yunusa (1996); Onibokun (1994:263).

Delimiting the informal

While the approaches presented above give very different pictures of processes leading to informality, there is an area of general consensus. The informal domain is usually seen as consisting of activities lying outside state regulation (see for example, Azarya and Chazan, 1987, Castells and Portes, 1989:12-3, Tokman, 1992:4). While many certainly do, this requires some substantial qualifications. Firstly, there are several dimensions to state regulation (such as registration, tax payment, abidance by labour laws) (Tokman, 1992:5), making it difficult to empirically draw the line between what is and is not regulated by the state. In fact, intermediate situations may dominate where agents comply with some regulations but evade others, as concluded by Tokman (1992) and his colleagues in the Latin American context.

Secondly, a narrow delimitation of the informal as consisting of that which is unregulated by the state carries the danger of essentialising the informal as non-state or against-state activities. Here, one stream within the civil society debate among political scientists provides a source of inspiration[23], in that it rejects a dichotomous view of state-civil society relations in which the latter is seen as having intrinsic characteristics such as being necessarily autonomous from and opposed to the state. Instead, we are advised to look into the dialectics of those relations, the interconnections between the two and their ambivalent positioning, as actors' strategies may range from competing for access to the state to opposing it. In this respect, the political behaviour of informal actors towards the state may be equally complex and unpredictable (Gibbon and Bangura, 1992:23). Indeed, some studies have focused on political networking as a major component of African informal economies (for example, Nabuguzi, 1994, Lemarchand, 1989 and Macharia, 1996). Recent developments in Africa render non-state views of the informal increasingly unrealistic. On the one hand, as complexity and social differentiation increase within informal economies, some informal actors have been found to benefit from positions in the state apparatus or from close links with the state. This points to a significant amount of straddling between the informal and the formal/state. On the other hand, pressures for state withdrawal and deregulation have not necessarily led to the absence of the state in supposedly "deregulated" spheres. In addition to some areas of regulation and provision having continued to be the official prerogative of the state, the state has also come to regulate many activities indirectly in various ways, among others through patronage relations (Kiondo, 1994). Given this complexity and diversity of the relations between state and informal actors, conceptualisations of the informal realm that are based on abstractions or that imbue it with essentialist or universalising characteristics, often aimed at furthering one

---

[23] For particularly useful discussions and reviews see: Gibbon and Bangura (1992); Beckman (1997); Sjögren (1998).

agenda or another, need to be replaced by a conceptualisation grounded on empirically based attributes.

Thirdly, focusing exclusively on the boundary between what is and is not regulated by the state leaves too much in the dark. Treating the informal as lacking regulation only contributes to the 'black box' syndrome mentioned above.

> *In this study I attempt to make visible informal types of regulation influencing the livelihoods of popular groups and to uncover the power relations that such informal kinds of regulation may involve and the micro struggles that develop around them. For informal regulation may be as subject to challenge and reformulation as state-based regulation*[24].

In this study, I have opted to generally consider as informal, those activities that evade at least one aspect of state legislated regulations (such as lacking a license, evading the payment of taxes and fees or not complying with labour laws) or that are entirely regulated by rules other than legal ones enforceable by state institutions. This is seen however, as a loosely delimited field of economic and social activity, whose boundaries are both blurred and permeable. Informal actors may oppose the state and its regulations as much as they may strive for access to the state. And state influence, in both its direct and indirect forms, may penetrate into segments of the informal realm. However, I am also interested in boundaries *within* the informal sphere and informal types of regulation by agents other than the state. As such, one could speak of an informal realm that, rather than being simply "unregulated", is in fact regulated in a variety of ways. This variety will surface throughout the book and will be returned to in the final chapter.

Inside the 'black box' of the informal sphere

Let me now turn to a consideration of the social relations *within* the informal sphere, the micro politics shaping its local dynamics and the conditions of the unprivileged. The focus here is on the social basis of informal livelihoods, both in their market and non-market components, i.e. the forms of social organisation and interaction that both sustain and constrain livelihoods. Survival in the city is accomplished through face-to-face interaction. Urbanites can seldom count on impartial overarching institutions to regulate relations and conflicts in urban society. It is also evident that the majority lack access to the modern technologies of communication that are said to neutralise distance

[24] In this sense, my motivation differs fundamentally from, on the one hand, discourses that do acknowledge the existence of "informal forms of governance" but assume that they constitute an all virtuous sphere, and on the other hand, from the anti-state agenda underlying the recent spur of interest in non-state forms of regulation in the discourse of international institutions, which assumes they are morally superior to state based regulation (World Bank, 2002).

in today's world. Indeed, most African urbanites are said to have been excluded from the "network society" found at the centre of contemporary "informational capitalism" (Castells, 1998:92-5). But they build another kind of "network society". Daily survival in the city builds extensively on networks of personal relationships through which the poor get access to living space, a plot to cultivate, credit, valuable price information as well as assistance on a bad day. The importance of personal relationships and social networks has probably intensified with the urban crisis, as that which can be expected from the state in terms of material assistance decreases and market based entitlements decline. In this difficult environment of constant insufficiency and uncertainty other kinds of entitlements need to be activated. In the process of establishing links with others to deal with the crisis, people generate expectations between one another, develop claims and create new rights and norms to govern relations and guide behaviour.

There are a number of discourses that may be of assistance in problematizing this vast realm of relations of assistance. These are the discourses on vulnerability and livelihoods, the old and new variants of debates on informal security systems, and the social network tradition. The first of these has grown out of a critique of conventional approaches to poverty for their excessive focus on cash income variables as well as for their undifferentiated and passive view of the poor. Firstly, the term *vulnerability* has been proposed as a conceptual tool to allow for a consideration of a wider range of dimensions of deprivation, including *social isolation* (Chambers, 1989, 1995, 1995a; Rakodi, 1995; Watts and Bohle, 1993). Differently from poverty, vulnerability means "not lack or want, but defencelessness, insecurity, and exposure to risks" (Chambers, 1989:1). As such, material poverty cannot be understood as the only source of vulnerability and neither can all of the poor necessarily be seen as equally vulnerable. Drawing inspiration from this, I would like to consider *social connectivity* (the antonym of *social isolation*) as a crucial dimension of well-being.

> *This study intends to address the obvious but often neglected idea that individuals and households are differently endowed in terms of the social resources they can rely upon for support. This is expected to make them differently vulnerable to the ups and downs of urban life.*

Secondly, a *livelihoods* framework has been developed to encompass the wide range of activities and ways in which people make a living. In this framework, livelihood components consist of people's capabilities (such as physical health and education), tangible assets (stores and material resources) and intangible assets (see Chambers, 1995a:23-9; Swift, 1989). One novelty of this perspective lies in its inclusion of "intangible assets" such as the *claims* that people can make on others for material or practical support[25]. These ideas suit my interest in the perceived *claims* or *informal rights* and norms of assistance that are created to sustain life in the city. I define these rights and claims as those not enforceable in a modern court of law but as being regulated through alternative systems of sanctions and rewards. However, this study does not strictly apply the livelihoods framework – i.e. it does not provide an exhaustive documentation of the vast range of household activities and resources – but focuses on some of the informal components of local livelihoods (particularly, food trade and inter-household redistribution) and the claims for support that have developed in these spheres. In fact, in the comprehensive enumeration exercise implied in the livelihoods framework, analyses often loose sight of the social relations involved in the claiming of support. Generally, how claims are established and exercised has remained poorly problematized[26].

> *This prompts me to probe the notion that people vary in their ability to exercise their perceived rights for support. I would like to uncover how claims are constructed, reconstructed and fought over, by addressing the power relations involved and the consequences for those who are not in a position to assert their rights.*

These issues can be further problematized by reference to parallel discourses. One can group these into two distinct perspectives which cut across disciplines and schools of thought and which continue to inform widespread assumptions concerning exchange of support and non-market interaction.

The first set of approaches emphasises shared norms for assistance. The early work by Mauss on the gift (1967) associated gift exchanges with enduring bonds between people and depicted reciprocity as a cultural imperative[27]. In its path, many have continued to look beyond "the depersonalised exchanges of neo-classical theory" and to search for the role of culture and sentiment in exchange relations (Rogers and Vertovec, 1995; Werbner, 1995; Cheal, 1988). The "moral economy" discourse stressed the social institutions and collective insurance mechanisms devised by (pre-capitalist) societies whose members were entitled to a minimum subsistence[28]. The "economy of affection" perspective (Hyden, 1983) depicted exchange in peasant African societies as governed by a social logic of reciprocity embedded in bonds of solidarity and moral or cultural precepts. Each of these schools has attracted their own share of criticism but some of it could apply to several

25 Rakodi (1999); Davies (1996); Downing (1990); Ellis (2000); Lourenço-Lindell (1996) are examples of work which considers such "intangible assets".

26 The hijacking of the term 'claims' by the 'social capital' discourse has hardly facilitated this task, as argued below. See for example Rakodi (1999), Ellis (2000) and Narayan (2000) where livelihood components are translated into a series of different kinds of 'capital'.

27 See Yan (1996) for a review of the anthropological debate on the gift.

28 A major proponent was Scott (1976). Other works that may be identified with that discourse are Gregory (1982); Watts (1984); Platteau (1991). See also Booth (1994) for a review.

of these discourses[29]. Among the most serious is that they have tended to ignore inequalities, antagonism and differentiation within "pre-capitalist" societies and to romanticise traditional norms. The latter are depicted as "moral", welfarist and non-conflictual. A variety of studies directly or indirectly inspired by this tradition often take for granted that social resources are equally available to everyone within a local community and consider exchange of support as essentially benign relations. By reducing the range of explanation to the "invisible hand of reciprocity", to borrow Lemarchand's (1989) fortunate expression, such perspectives preclude the possibility of conflict and politics in relations of assistance.

The most recent addition to this set of approaches, and the one that currently holds sway in the literature, comes under the label of "social capital". "Social capital" has been discovered as "the missing link" in development, and the solution to a variety of social ills ranging from "bad governance" to low incomes (World Bank, 1997:115; Narayan, 1997). This suits a wider agenda of placing the burden on extended family networks and other collective arrangements to provide a minimum of welfare, facilitate performance in the market and generally cushion against the hardships and gaps created by adjustment policies. The recent social capital discourse has not necessarily been an improvement in relation to earlier approaches[30]. The discourse bypasses the less virtuous side of this "social capital", for example how it may reproduce inequalities in society, and neglects its structural limitations. In addition, current uses of social capital that propose it as the property of "communities" rather than of individuals, mask internal differentiation and instances of exclusion (Harriss, 1997; Beall, 1997), an issue dear to this study.

A different perspective on informal support systems, albeit perhaps a less common one, is the political economy perspective. With its concerns with power, conflict and agency it seems to be a more fruitful point of entry into inequalities and change in support systems. Political economy approaches have, however, been said to display scepticism about collective efforts of insurance (Platteau, 1991; Lemarchand, 1989). This seems indeed to be too narrow a view to grasp the complexity of informal relations of assistance. I propose that a political economy approach to support systems be extended to incorporate instances of co-operation, so as to build a wider frame of interpretation from which to draw for empirical analyses of specific social realities. This can be done by rescuing some elements of the first set of discourses focusing on enduring social bonds, shared norms and collective efforts, while discarding their apolitical and non-dynamic components. This requires uncovering instances of "immorality", inequality, contradiction and instrument-

[29] For a critique see: Gore (1993); Booth (1994); Lemarchand (1989); Benda-Beckmann and Kirsch (1999).

[30] See for general critiques: Fine (1999); Portes (1998); Harriss (1997); Putzel (1997); Beall (1997); Levi (1996).

ality in "moral economies" and a perspective that does not regard cultural and moral norms as given or as being passively followed. Participants in these "moral economies" are actors who may engage in "unruly social practices" (Gore, 1993) and who may contest and reconstruct those norms. Conceiving of "moral economies" as fields of struggle and as a dynamic form of organisation that is capable of responding to wider pressures brings it closer to political economic concerns.

> *In line with the above, another task in this study is to go beyond one-sided views of informal relations of assistance and to illuminate informal support systems as being constituted by both relations of co-operation and relations of inequality and dependence, along a variety of axes.*

This implies that, in this study, the terms of 'support' and 'assistance' refer to both beneficial and pernicious ties, to egalitarian and unequal relations.

Another related cleavage in the literature refers to the rationality or the motivations underlying personalised forms of exchange. On the one hand, some writers emphasise altruistic relations, moral and cultural imperatives, as is generally the case with the first set of approaches. These views have been criticised for tending to draw a sharp distinction between market and non-market whereby these are rendered incompatible[31]. Others have a "rational choice" approach to support exchange which sees individuals as primarily self-interested agents driven by material calculations about returns and who act in such a way as to maximise them. This utilitarian view of social interaction, modelled upon market principles, has dominated in the political economic perspective but cuts across disciplines and debates and has become deeply entrenched in studies and statements about non-market exchange[32]. Again, either approach seems to be too narrow to grasp the range of possible motivations.

> *Thus, the study will attempt to illustrate how such apparently conflicting and opposing rationalities and motivations for interaction may coexist in relations of support, in and outside the market.*

One step in the direction of closing the above conceptual gap concerning rationalities is Sahlins' model of multiple forms of reciprocity (1984:193-6), which has been recovered by Lemarchand (1989) and Gaughan and Ferman (1987), but whose merits many recent analyses have been oblivious of. These authors envisage a continuum of a variety of forms of reciprocity or of

---

[31] For a critique see for example Booth (1994) and Lemarchand (1989). See also Appadurai (1995) for a critique of sharp conceptual distinctions between commodities and gifts.

[32] On this utilitarian view in the political economic perspective see Platteau (1991) and Lemarchand (1989); and Yan (1996) on such view in the gift discourse. See Swift (1989) for an example of an utilitarian notion of claims in the famine discourse, where he equates capacity to mobilise support in crisis with investments made earlier. See also studies in the social network tradition that emphasise competition in the mobilisation of support (Kapferer, 1969; Galaskiewicz, 1979).

modalities of exchange existing within informal economies, driven by different principles or motivations. One of the extremes is dominated by economic rationality and profit oriented activity governed by market rules. This is the realm of impersonal forms of exchange and instrumental exchange relations. The other extreme consists of a non-cash or social economy dominated by personal social ties, with loose expectations for return and with rewards and motivations beyond the exclusively economical. In between the two extremes there is a grey zone of a "cash-based extension of the social economy", rather than a clear-cut boundary between market and non-market. One could further think of the realm of personalised exchange – our concern here – as an overlapping of these various motivations and logics, rather than a field governed by a single rationality. This diversity of motivations may have relevance for how people value and prioritise their different relationships.

The social networks research tradition

This great diversity that I expected to find in relations of assistance prompted me to explore the social networks research tradition. The greatest attractiveness of network analysis lies in its ability to cross boundaries – social, geographical or conceptual – and in its potential for uncovering social processes cutting across them (Barnes, 1969). It enables us to represent reality in all its inconsistency, helping us to move beyond the dualisms that have opposed discourses on moral and political economy, market and non-market forms of exchange. Networks facilitate a disaggregated analysis of relations of support, instead of lumping them together under some label and assuming that all operate and respond to change in the same way. This seemed thus to be a promising tool with which to approach complex patterns of assistance and the variety of relations they entail.

Social networks emerged as an analytical tool in the mid-1950s and gained considerable renown through the works of students of the Manchester school and their concern for the structure of social relationships in urban areas of the Copperbelt in Africa[33]. Since then, social network analysis has been applied to a wide range of phenomena, particularly in urban contexts. According to Mitchell (1969), a social network may arise from a set of responsibilities and rights that are consciously recognised among a group of people. This links well with my concerns with *claims* for assistance on a variety of sources and sets of informal rights and responsibilities.

This early generation of network studies focused on the patterns of social interaction in the city by looking at a number of variables pertaining to the morphological characteristics of personal networks (such as size, the density

[33] See the collection of studies in Mitchell (1969).

of links, the frequency of interaction, the social and geographical range of networks) and their interactional characteristics (such as the purpose of the interaction and the balance in the flows)[34]. Some analyses explicitly related these network variables to people's capacity to mobilise support in situations of personal conflict, political competition and personal crisis. Persons having large, socially heterogeneous and dense networks (among other attributes) were often found to be in a better position than others to mobilise support and exert influence (Wheeldon, 1969; Mitchell, 1969). Some elements in this early tradition provide inspiration for how to go about uncovering variations in the social resources available to different urban people. Indeed, some of the variables are used in this study albeit in a simplified form, such as the size of networks and the direction of flows. However, developments in the network discourse took the direction of an increasingly complex quantification and statistical manipulation of network ties. As it grew in rigidity and obsession with rigor, the network method almost became an end in itself. In the process, "the individual as human being disappears in the network calculation" (Ottenberg, in Hannerz, 1980)[35]. Furthermore, many network analyses became ahistorical, portraying networks as static and detached from their social context[36].

There is now a renewed interest in the contemporary role of social networks in urban life. They appear among the priorities in various research agendas for urban Africa (Halfani, 1994:158; Rakodi, 1997b:563-7). But this interest is also clearly apparent in the agendas of international agencies and this has influenced the directions of a share of the research emerging on this subject. This latter research is linked to the broader discourse on social capital. In this discourse, networks are portrayed as filling at least two purposes. On the one hand, they are presented as playing a positive role in poverty alleviation, as they are viewed as one among several kinds of "civil institutions" in which the poor participate for improvement of incomes, services and welfare (for example Narayan, 1997, 2000). On the other hand, networks of personalised relationships are now seen as crucial components of market efficiency. Networks are said to improve the performance of enterprises, facilitate access to market information and the enforcement of business contracts, among other things, and are being advanced as alternatives to state regulation (see for example Barr, 1998, 2000; Fafchamps, 1996; Bigsten, 2000). In both cases, the analysis is usually premised on elaborate quantification of the descriptive, external attributes of social networks, continuing earlier trends in network

[34] For more thorough discussions of network variables, see Mitchell (1969), Barnes (1969), Bridge (1993), Lourenço-Lindell (2001).

[35] On the difficulties of applying the conventional network method and a more flexible and humanist view of network methods, see Hannerz (1980).

[36] Exceptions have been studies that relate social networks to class perceptions and identity consciousness, or to class responses to gentrification (Bridge, 1993; Hannerz, 1980). See also Anwar (1995) for a longitudinal study of changes in the networks of Pakistanis in the United Kingdom.

analysis. In this growing number of studies there is usually no serious consideration of either the wider structural constraints in which networks operate or the power relations contained in networks. Networks are in this way deprived of politics and, consequently, of change. These are the kinds of studies being used by the World Bank to legitimise its policies[37]. In the following discussion, I propose that we 'unpack' social networks in a different way, by focusing on the social relations they both contain and are inserted into, rather than merely looking at their external characteristics.

The politics of support mobilisation

The network notion is used here as a tool to map relations of assistance. By this I mean using networks to grasp the range and kinds of social resources available to individuals or households, by specifying the nature of their various social ties in terms of motivation, claims and power balance in the relationships. So conceived, networks should assist in the progress towards a major goal in this study.

> *This goal is to uncover the complex webs of relationships of assistance, the great variety and apparently disparate types of social relations, rationalities and motivations co-existing in assistance networks.*

Poor urbanites combine various kinds of relations and ties drawn from a variety of social settings in order to sustain their consumption and diversified informal livelihoods. But it can also be expected that people will vary in their ability to combine these ties.

> *So the study also intends to discern variations in these internal constellations of relations and probe whether these variations have consequences for people's vulnerability. That is, the particular constellation of social resources available to a poor individual or household will probably matter for its ability to get help in a crisis.*

I look upon networks as social fields where both co-operation and struggle take place. They contain internal divisions of rights and duties, imbalances in flows and power, with instances of dependence and marginality. Networks may be held together by rules or sets of informal rights which are enforced, defaulted upon, negotiated and contested. They conflate relationships built for different purposes, recruited in different social settings and underlined by various affiliations and identities. All of the above contribute to make networks fertile ground for contradictions that may give rise to action by discontented participants. This action may range from subtle manipulation of

---

[37] This is particularly notorious in World Bank (2000) and (2002), where considerable space is given to issues of social capital and to informal institutions in markets.

rules and positions to more confrontational forms, possibly against persons with powerful positions in networks. In this sense, networks could be thought of as containing in themselves both 'structure' and 'agency', as conceived in structuration theory in which these concepts entertain a dialectical relation[38]. On the one hand, divisions of power internal to networks may set limits to individual action. Relationships in particularly solidified networks may be difficult to discard, and deeply institutionalised rules may not be broken without consequences – and indeed, there may be instances where people are precluded from acting, or even from participating in networks altogether[39].

On the other hand, participants may try to influence rules to their advantage, to improve their position in the internal distribution of power and resources or to increase their leverage by investing in alternative relationships. I refer to this complex of possibility and constraint, of participation and marginalization, which networks of assistance represent as *the politics of support mobilisation*. This implies looking upon networks as fields of social process, i.e. they are constructed and reconstructed through the actions of participants who may have opposing interests. It also implies seeing networks in their wider context, as participants' positions in wider society constrain what can be achieved within and through networks. Such a dynamic view of networks should equip us to approach issues of change in networks of assistance, taking into consideration both their internal dynamics and wider processes in society.

From this point of view, pertinent sets of questions that will be pursued here include the following:

Firstly, issues of exclusion from and subordination in networks are addressed. Which groups are excluded from networks and what may account for this isolation? Who is unable to enforce their perceived rights? In what ways do people who are marginalised from and subordinated in networks struggle for their rights and circumvent the power of powerful persons in networks? Who is in a position to disconnect and who is stuck in assistance relations that they resent and what curtails their exit options?

A second set of questions pertains to how different types of relations or segments of networks interact or act upon each other (for example, old and new kinds of affiliations, market and non-market relations)? To what extent are they being kept in balance and to what extent are they giving rise to contradictions? Who is unable to combine different kinds of relations and to diversify their networks? What keeps people from freely moving between different kinds of affiliations and settings of interaction and from pursuing those kinds of relationships they most value?

Finally, how are networks of assistance changing in response to wider processes, such as deepening internationalisation of economy and culture,

[38] See Giddens (1999:17-24) on "the structuring qualities of rules".

[39] See Giddens (1999:14-5) on circumstances of social constraint.

economic liberalisation and changed living conditions in the city? And how are norms of assistance changing? Particularly, how are "traditional" or deeply institutionalised rules responding to the new conditions? If rules are indeed changing, what power relations are involved in their reformulation and what are the consequences of such change? Which groups are in a position to default on their duties? Are there groups loosing from the change, for example by bearing a greater burden or by becoming weakened in their rights?

In connection to this latter set of questions, let me specify a number of issues pertaining to changes in social networks as related particularly to declining urban living conditions.

Networks in the contemporary crisis

A central issue in the contemporary dynamics of social support networks pertains to how they are responding and evolving in the face of the current prolonged economic crisis. This has not been a subject of abundant research. But the existing literature presents divergent findings and interpretations of the role and potential of networks in a context of scarcity or economic hardship. Some studies generally emphasise the crucial and even renewed role of social networks in contexts of economic crisis, and how they are reactivated and intensified[40].

Some have gone one step further, however, and claimed that scarcity or poverty is in fact a precondition for the emergence of inter-household networks of assistance. These have recovered an old idea that "scarcity and not sufficiency makes people generous" (Evans-Pritchard in Sahlins, 1984:210) and take for granted that social networks are a resource that (all) the poor *do* have and that they *do* cope by using them[41]. The effects of material constraints or deepening poverty on such networks are left undiscussed. This over-enthusiasm about the potential of networks among the poor has gained new impetus in the social capital discourse. In the latter, social networks tend to be presented as the solution to poverty, as mentioned above, and tend to neglect the constraints placed on these networks by an adjustment-led development strategy [42].

---

[40] See for example: Dershem and Czirishvili (1998) on the role of social networks in the context of transition and crisis in Georgia, former Soviet Union; De Herdt and Marysse (1997), on the reactivation of exchanges of gifts and loans in Kinshasa; Loforte (2000) on how social ties beyond the extended family are being reactivated for a variety of productive and reproductive tasks in a neighbourhood of Maputo.

[41] See for example, Lomnitz (1977) in her influential book on social networks in Mexico City. See also Rocha's (1996) study of the role of social and economic resources of working-class households in the context of economic crisis in Guadalajara, Mexico.

[42] Worth mentioning, however, is the more nuanced stance forwarded by Moser (1996) in a comparative analysis of four urban communities, where she identifies elements of "social capital"

A few have forwarded the view that informal security systems are eroding as a result of a shrinkage in the availability of resources for redistribution or repeated shocks such as price hikes, while at the same time structural adjustment policies, such as retrenchment and "cost-sharing" schemes, increase dependence on such systems[43]. The famine discourse has also addressed social networks as part of a sequence of "coping strategies" in the context of crises of a sudden kind, such as a drought. The prevalent message in this discourse is that inter-household assistance breaks down in the face of crisis or, alternatively, increases under conditions of moderate scarcity but becomes exhausted with an intensification of the crisis[44]. These studies point to the limitation of networks in sustaining people through crises, an aspect which is neglected in many current analyses. But critical assessments of how social networks are coping in gradually deteriorating conditions in urban areas are still lacking. Furthermore, what in my view is missing is a disaggregated view of networks of assistance, which looks *into* networks, at how the different types of ties and social relations within them are responding. In the light of this, I would like to probe three issues:

> *Firstly, how are assistance networks among the poor faring in the face of the contemporary worsening of living conditions in urban areas? Are they cushioning the impact of economic hardship or are there groups falling off these informal safety nets and being left isolated? Secondly, how are different kinds of ties within networks responding to crisis? Which kinds of ties show greater resilience and which break down easily in crisis situations? Thirdly, how is economic hardship impinging upon social relations within networks (in terms for example of the power balance involved)?*

Scope and structure of the study

This study is about the dynamics and politics of informality in the West African city of Bissau. It addresses social processes impinging on informal livelihoods at two levels. At one level, I will describe overarching processes influencing the extent and nature of informality, at the city and national scales. These processes are discussed in chapters two and three, first in a historical perspective and then for the contemporary period. These chapters lay down the changing political economic environment in which informal livelihoods have developed in the city as well as the historically evolved indigenous structures

---

being strengthened while others are being weakened. Particularly in Chawama, a neighbourhood in Lusaka, some households are reported to have been pushed beyond being able to sustain reciprocity.

[43] See for example Devereux (1999) for urban and rural southern Malawi; and Benda-Beckmann and Kirsch (1999), based on reports from five countries at a regional seminar on informal security systems in Southern Africa.

[44] See Corbet (1987); Davis (1996); Adams (1993); Campbell (1990); Drèze and Sen (1989); Sahlins (1984).

and norms that continue to play a role today. This sets the stage for understanding contemporary configurations of informal relations described in later chapters, for assessing how the informal livelihoods of disadvantaged urbanites in their different components are faring in the present period and how institutionalised forms of assistance are changing. The two chapters also illustrate the multiplicity of agents involved in the production of the extensive informality we witness today, revealing a much more complex process than that portrayed by existing one-sided interpretations of expanding informality.

At another level, in the remaining chapters of the thesis, I analyse the social relations pervading the informal livelihoods of disadvantaged groups. The focus here is on the micro processes *within* the informal sphere. The general intention is to illustrate how these relations are part of the dynamics and the politics of the informal realm and influence the conditions of the disadvantaged. The analysis will uncover the complex webs and diversified nature of relations of assistance, ranging from egalitarian, altruistic and cooperative relations to self-interested, unequal and downright exploitative relations. Further, the analysis will explore how people are not equally positioned in these constellations of ties. They can be expected to vary in their access to assistance, in their ability to mix different kinds of support relations, in their ability to enforce informal rights, agreements and rules or to negotiate them to their advantage. The intention is to identify patterns of marginalization, dependence and subordination as well as the ways in which those who are disadvantaged act to improve their situation. Such an analysis should bring to light the multiplicity of contradictions and social struggles in which people get involved as they go about their informal livelihoods, including those struggles unravelling around informal kinds of regulation. This constitutes the multifaceted field of struggle which I have called *the politics of support mobilisation.* Finally, the ways networks of assistance are changing in the context of wider contemporary processes, including the deterioration of urban living conditions, will be addressed.

I go about this task by focusing on the general domain of food as my point of departure. Besides being a basic necessity, the procurement of which occupies a large share of the energies of many households, food trade in Bissau is both one of the most common sources of income for the poor and a sphere of accumulation for capital. In general, concentrating on food was a good way to learn about how the rich get rich and the poor get by in this city. Within this general domain, I focus on certain informal livelihood activities, particularly redistribution practices, food trade activities and, to some extent, food production. I look at social relations and sets of informal rules at work in these sub-sectors of the informal sphere.

I begin this second part of my study by introducing the study setting, in chapter four, where I present the most common livelihood activities. In chapter five I look closely into relations pervading cash income activities in the food market by focusing particularly on the sub-sectors of rice, fish and vegetables. In this chapter the changing conditions of small actors are highlighted, as influenced both by wider trends, government practices and evolving relations with other actors in the informal market. The sources of support for small-scale trade activities are discussed as well as relations involving inequality and exploitation, the ways that disadvantaged parties find to circumvent the latter and the spaces of relative autonomy that some small actors are able to create. Relations of assistance sustaining the food consumption of households are discussed at greater length in chapters six and seven. These relations include practices of redistribution and exchanges of food and money as well as relations pervading subsistence food production, notably rice being grown in the study area. The first of these two chapters deals with local variations in social networks of assistance and how the latter are affected by the crisis. Chapter seven focuses on kin-based relations of assistance and how they may be changing in the context of wider processes. The chapter also includes a discussion of assistance relations between urban and rural kin.

Thus, the study approaches informality from a livelihoods perspective, by looking at both cash income-generating activities, on which most "informal sector" research has focused, and at the social security role of informality. These two aspects have usually been analysed separately, conventionally understood as belonging to the distinct realms of the market and the non-market. While the chapters here differ in their focus in this respect, the analysis often crosses this division and views the two spheres as interconnected. The activities of the poor in both spheres are all about survival and making ends meet on a day-to-day basis, often by using the same means or contacts. In addition, it will become evident that the essential attributes usually associated with one sphere spill over to the other, thus further blurring the distinction.

Let me end this section with a few words about the spatial and temporal scope of the study. While the study sets informality in its historical context, the bulk of the thesis concerns the period after the mid-1980s when structural adjustment measures changed both living conditions and the scene for economic operation in the city. The upper time limit of the study is mid-1999. This coincides with the time of my last fieldwork and a period when political upheaval and armed conflict were causing changes in Bissauan society. The main study area in Bissau is the district of Bandim. With an estimated population of 40,000 inhabitants, Bandim is a large unplanned settlement with a very poor infrastructure. Bandim could be said to represent a number of other similar neighbourhoods in the city, but it is also distinct from others. During one of my periods of fieldwork, some work was carried out in another neighbourhood to gain a better idea of how Bandim fits into the wider city. Chapter four, as mentioned above, gives a closer presentation of the study area.

1.3 Research Methods

In this section, I will turn to the research methods that I used to approach the research questions outlined above. After a general description, I will go into a more detailed discussion of the main methodological components of the study.

My first encounter with Bissau was in late 1992, when I conducted fieldwork for a Masters degree. The general aim was to gain an idea about changes in urban food supply and consumption in connection with adjustment policies and how people went about meeting their food needs. I interviewed members of sixteen households in Bandim district about their food provisioning and their livelihoods. I selected them randomly but tried to diversify this small sample in terms of household food strategies and of the gender of the head of the household. Interviews included information about their cash income activities in general and food trade in particular, their engagement in a variety of food production activities and participation in inter-household food exchanges. As a complement, other individuals involved in food related activities were interviewed. Altogether, ten fishermen, fourteen agriculturists and eighteen rice and fish sellers were interviewed during the pilot fieldwork. I returned to Bissau in 1995 to deepen my knowledge of these issues, this time for my doctoral project. I carried out a household survey in order to get at the broad patterns of livelihoods in the study area. Semi-structured interviews were also carried out at that time with 38 small-scale food traders, with the general aim of learning more about the conditions and the social relations involved in these activities. The methods used in this fieldwork are elaborated below.

One last period of fieldwork was aimed at following up the survey findings through a deeper qualitative study of the networks of assistance of a number of households. However, events outside of my control forced me to delay my fieldwork plans and placed serious constraints on what could be accomplished when that phase of fieldwork did finally begin. I am referring to the armed conflict that erupted in the capital city and that lasted for a year. When I arrived in Bissau in May 1999, some two weeks after the war ended, I found a profoundly disrupted society. The war had caused a massive dislocation of population from the city towards the rural areas, and this was a moment when many were still returning from their refuge there. For many, livelihoods had entirely collapsed and they were completely dependent on humanitarian aid or on the charity of others. Others were slowly trying to patch their lives together from the few resources they had left. Several people reported that their buffer assets had been spent on necessities, their houses had been robbed and their small stock gone astray. On top of this, thousands of Bandim dwellers had very recently witnessed a massacre where many had lost loved ones. In short, this was a moment of trauma, anxiety and enormous struggle to stay alive. In the face of this reality, my considerable data needs seemed quite insignificant. I was forced to narrow down my research ambitions to what was feasible under the prevailing conditions. As a result of this situation my final phase of fieldwork was briefer than I had desired.

Throughout the duration of my fieldwork, apart from the major methodological components of the study discussed below – i.e., interviews with traders and households and the household survey – I deepened my knowledge in a variety of ways. Various local key informants were interviewed who were particularly knowledgeable about some aspect of relevance for the study. These included civil activists, some food traders, fishermen and elders. I learned a lot through spontaneous conversations, observations and considerable time spent at market places, supply sources, compound yards and private porches. During my stays in Bandim I had the privilege of establishing a rapport with women retailers and a number of families in the neighbourhood. One particular compound became my base of operations in the neighbourhood, my site of rest and leisure and a source of assistants.

Government officials or agents with a variety of relevant roles were interviewed. These included officials at the Department of Consumer Prices at the National Institute of Statistics and Census; at the Ministries of Commerce, Women Affairs, Planning. In the Municipal Government I interviewed officials of the Directorate of Markets, members of the Unit of Inspection of Markets and a municipal representative in charge of Bandim Market. In addition, international aid agencies and consultants involved in reformulation of policy were contacted. This group of interviews was valuable in providing information about changes in food supply, urban food markets and conditions of operation and about official attitudes towards informal actors and their practices. Finally, key persons from about ten civil organisations and associations were interviewed. Some of these were very important actors in the urban and national scene – such as the Guinean League for Human Rights, the National Movement of Civil Society and The Chamber of Commerce - and getting their perspectives on the changes occurring in Bissauan society was very productive. Smaller registered associations were also contacted, some of which were active in Bandim – such as the National Association of Christian Youth; Bandim Youth Association; and the Evangelical Church of Bandim. I also tried to gain knowledge of other unregistered local groups, such as rotating credit groups, groups of casual workers, and one local social club, the "Esperança de Bandim". A list of interviews can be found at the end of the book.

Finally, a variety of secondary sources were used, on which I will comment below. The duration of my fieldwork in Bissau totalled five and a half months.

The household survey

I adopted a combination of qualitative and quantitative methods, hoping to draw on the strengths of each. The household survey was intended to help me discern the representativity of certain phenomena that I discovered during my first fieldwork and to equip me with a good basis for further qualitative work.

After administering the survey in Bandim, I decided to run it in another neighbourhood called Cupilon. Given the shortage of information on the city, this was meant to provide me with a frame of comparison. The two neighbourhoods represent two different milieus in terms of the ethnic composition, household structures and provisioning strategies and moderate aggregate differences in living standards. They can be said to represent conditions and patterns in a number of other neighbourhoods in the city and to cover some of the internal diversity contained within the city (see chapter four).

The survey schedule was kept simple but touched on a wide range of issues pertaining to household livelihoods. These included the income generating activities of all household members and the corresponding work status; aspects of household food diets; sources of food for the household; the frequency and source of gifts received; and the sources of assistance in times of need. Households involved in some form of food production were asked for some basic information about the intensity and scale of operation in those activities, the use of eventual surpluses and the sources of the means of production. A number of simple questions were also recorded for food trade enterprises in the household. These questions concerned the type of food being sold, the source of merchandise, when the enterprise was started, selling site, main uses of earned incomes and whether traders had any savings. The sizeable share of households involved in food production and trade provided a broad idea of these activities in the two neighbourhoods.

The number of households covered in the survey was 335 in Bandim and 118 households in Cupilon. This corresponded to about 9 and 10 per cent of their respective populations. No list of households was then available from which to draw the sample and a conventional address system was non-existent. Thus sampling was drawn from residential units on a map, which required substantial work in updating existing maps of the area. Houses were systematically selected from the map and the households living in them were interviewed. The resulting sample may contain a somewhat higher proportion of households in the poor socio-economic strata and belonging to the ethnic group with ancestral roots in the area, than is the case for the total population. But later statistical analysis revealed that there was only a slight bias, with only a modest impact on the results.

The household unit was defined as the group of people who ate together. The preferred respondent was the person in the household supervising food preparation and purchasing, which usually meant a woman. The survey team consisted of myself and two assistants, one male and one female. They were high school graduates and experienced in this kind of work. We practised together and tested the questionnaire before starting. They were dedicated and added many personal notes to the questionnaires.

Encounters with traders

As mentioned above, in my first pilot study in 1992 I carried out a number of interviews with food traders. Interview schedules inquired about basic characteristics of those activities, such as scale of operation, sources of supply of inputs and merchandise, choice of selling site, refilling of stock, variations in prices and length of the working day. Traders were also asked about the main difficulties experienced by them, their relations with official institutions as well as the sources of initial capital and help for their trade activities. The household responsibilities of the trader and how the income earned was used were also discussed. In the household survey that I conducted in 1995, a number of simple questions were recorded for food trade activities of household members. A total of 527 such enterprises were recorded taking the two districts together. These questions concerned the type of food being sold, the source of merchandise, when the enterprise was started, selling site (which gave an crude indication of the type of selling conditions and demand they catered for), the main uses of earned incomes and whether the trader had any savings. This provided a broad idea of retailing activities in the neighbourhood. Other smaller quantitative procedures were also used during the fieldwork, such as a one-time inquiry about the sources of supply (of vegetables and fish) of all sellers present on a particular day in six market places in the city.

In 1995 I also carried out interviews with 38 new food traders – fourteen in vegetables, fifteen in fish, and nine in rice. Traders were selected from the household survey according to the product they sold and their availability and were interviewed in the privacy of their homes. Some were sought at the market place instead, in order to cover certain categories poorly represented in the survey. These included sellers commuting from rural areas or categories that were in a minority or virtually absent from the neighbourhood and the local market places but quite visible in the wider city, such as retailers of frozen fish. The interviews were guided by a checklist. Besides general information about the enterprise, the conversations covered personal working histories and assessments of the general viability of the enterprise and its evolution. Issues relating to the domestic context, such as uses of and control over income, the trader's responsibilities in the household, and the balance between household needs and business requirements were discussed. Traders were asked about issues of access to merchandise, working assets and selling sites and strategies used to improve that access. They were also asked about the nature of informal relations and agreements with suppliers and the various sources of assistance, including those who assisted when traders lost their working capital. In this way I recorded the networks sustaining the income activities of individual traders.

In 1999, a few more interviews were carried out with different categories of traders in an attempt to update myself on some of the changes and to address other knowledge gaps. Unfortunately, difficult fieldwork conditions did not facilitate a systematic follow-up on the bulk of data collected earlier – for example by seeking and talking to earlier respondents – which would have deepened the longitudinal dimension of the study. In total, a little over sixty commercial operators of different kinds were interviewed in the course of the periods of fieldwork. While most of the interviewees were retailers, five wholesalers and two large import-export firms were also interviewed.

This material was supplemented by interviews with a range of informants, including knowledgeable traders, government officials or representatives with roles pertaining to the management of market activities, and through time spent observing and conversing at the local market places and at supply sites.

Social networks as methodological tools

As mentioned in previous sections, a social network approach was adopted to investigate in a systematic manner the variety of social relations of assistance of households. The results of this systematic study are presented in chapters six and seven.

The aim was to record, for a number of households, what social connections they had with people not belonging to the household and with whom household members engaged in exchange of assistance. This included the social ties providing help in moments of crisis and sustaining household livelihood activities, as well as participation in groups that provided some kind of support[45]. But a particular effort was placed on understanding ties sustaining household food consumption. This mixture was necessary since these various spheres of assistance, [at least] among the poor, were found to be inseparable in practice. And yet, the data collected represent only part of the total network of a household – which would include for example social relationships used for securing access to housing, water or simply for leisure time.

I used the household survey carried out in 1995 for drawing my sample for the network study. Time constraints forced me to narrow down the range of complexity that could be included. First, since the fact that the inclusion of a wide cultural diversity would immensely complicate such a study, I decided to

[45] Networks were delimited as consisting of those social ties that actually responded to appeals for assistance, although I also asked about people that were not responsive but had the obligation of assisting.

leave out people belonging to the Eastern ethnic groups. These constitute a minority in Bandim and differ considerably from the groups comprising the majority of the population in the neighbourhood, for example in their Islamic religion and the structure of domestic groups. Secondly, while there is social differentiation in Bandim and a study of social networks among different socio-economic groups would have been of interest, my greatest concern was with the poorer strata. Therefore, I restricted the study to households that had emerged from my household survey as having a "poor" or "very poor" diet, based on simple indicators of food affordability (see chapter four for an elaboration of this classification). This naturally influenced the types of networks I could expect to find. Since the composition of personal networks reflects an individual's position in the wider society, focusing on the poor meant that I would be dealing primarily with networks of survival. Networks of accumulation certainly exist in the city and stretch into the neighbourhood, but these are only superficially addressed in chapter three.

I wanted to explore how households sharing a general condition of material deprivation differed in their vulnerability in terms of the social resources at their disposal. Based on the questions in the household survey dealing with the extent of their engagement in non-market transfers, I identified potential cases of weak and intensive participation in support networks. The survey data also facilitated the identification of considerable differences within compounds in the neighbourhood, with some households scarcely participating in transfers of food. This prompted me to select households from each of these groups, which proved to be a rewarding exercise. By these filtering procedures, I obtained a pool of households that seemed to fulfil the basic criteria from which I could pick cases for network analysis. In this final selection I tried to balance the sample in terms of gender of the head of the household, of whether households did or did not reside in a kin environment and in terms of types of livelihoods. Altogether there were thirty cases selected for a network analysis. In two thirds of the cases the respondent in the household was an adult woman (a wife or a head of household), while for the remaining cases the respondent was a male head of household . Given their reproductive responsibilities in the household, women seemed generally more aware of the day-to-day inter-household food exchanges. They could also identify the usual sources of help drawn on during times of hardship that lay outside of their own personal networks - although more detailed information about their partners' networks was more difficult to capture. Thus, in the face of time constraints, a sample of respondents with a large share of women seemed to be the best choice.

The conversations took the form of semi-structured interviews. A checklist was used to make sure that certain aspects were systematically pursued, mainly pertaining to the social ties enumerated. After the interviews, a chart was filled in for each household with a few characteristics about each tie (or set of ties) and information about which ties were the most valued and reliable.

The conversation often began by talking with respondents about their experience of the war - the priority subject for most people at that time. In spite of the difficult circumstances in which my respondents were at the time of fieldwork, they were often eager to talk about their war experience and the help they could get or not get from others, which made conversations gratifying for both parties. At some point of the interview, I updated the information about the livelihoods of the household by comparing the situation that had been registered in 1995 with that prior to the war and the current situation. Then information on assistance networks was collected for the period immediately before the war, or the "normal" situation, given the great disruption that the war had caused to people's networks. Regretfully, the difficult fieldwork conditions hindered me from capitalising on the time gap between periods of fieldwork and from building a truly longitudinal analysis of the studied networks. However, respondents were requested to give their impressions of how their assistance networks had changed in the last ten to fifteen years.

Specifically about the support that could be mobilised by the household, people were asked whether they felt secure that they would always be able to get help from someone and what it would mean for them if they lost those connections. Questions about the social heterogeneity and geographical range of the network were also asked. The nature of respondents' social ties was explored by eliciting their perceptions about their various relationships. Respondents were asked about perceived motivations and expectations concerning the reciprocation of gifts and favours and the consequences of being unable to reciprocate help. Their impressions about the balance of power in their relationships was elicited, that is whether this was an exchange between social equals or if the respondent perceived him/herself to be in a position of dependence, or conversely felt exploited or burdened by some of the ties. I asked whom they thought had the obligation to assist them in case of need, i.e. whose assistance they felt they were entitled to and if they could count on that source of assistance. They were asked to evaluate their position in networks and kin groups and whether it was an advantageous or disadvantageous one. Respondents were encouraged to say whether they had felt neglected or unfairly treated and to what means they resorted to assert their perceived rights.

Respondents often had sharp perceptions about these matters and were surprisingly vocal about their appreciation of, or dissatisfaction with, some of their relationships, considering that they were in several cases entrusting these feelings to a stranger. My ambition was not to elicit supposedly objective accounts for later quantitative manipulation. It was the respondents' subjective view of the social relations they were involved in and their own judgement of the nature of those ties that interested me. Because, ultimately, it is the subjects' own perceptions that guide their practices and their own senses of fairness and unfairness that eventually compels them to act. The meanings that people attribute to their different ties inform their choices about which ties to nurture and preserve at all costs and those which they will get rid of at the first opportunity.

Finally, a few words about the reliability of the network data. In some of the cases, I had established a relationship with the respondents during earlier phases of fieldwork. This is likely to have leant the resulting information a higher degree of reliability than in the cases where I had had no contact prior to the interview. Data that was collected within compounds consisted often of interviews with more than one household in the same compound as well as with the head of the compound, allowing for the cross-checking of information. On the whole, this variety of data – composed of interviews with compound households (a total of eight), heads of compounds (three), other members of the local nobility such as the chief and various key informants – account for a considerable reliability of my findings on the institutionalised norms and relations of assistance amongst this group in Bandim. My impressions were also shaped by the considerable time I spent in compounds during my various periods of fieldwork. I had good relations in at least two of the compounds since former years and during my final fieldwork I lived in one of them.

For the remaining respondents, I had to rely on individual interviews conducted during one or two encounters, given the fieldwork circumstances. I am however, deeply grateful for the time these respondents did give me. It could have been useful to interview other members of someone's network and to collect the views of several members of the household, as I realised from one case where I did have the opportunity to do this. For example, women and men move in different social settings, are involved in different activities and thus have different contributions to make to such a study. But the compromise made here was that the one respondent interviewed in the household would be asked to report, to the extent that was possible, on his/her activities and social connections as well as those of the other adult members, even though these were often vague ideas. This was partly compensated by selecting respondents from both sexes, which gave a general idea of the way networks are gendered.

In spite of the above constraints, the set of data collected has allowed me to identify some general patterns, processes and points of tension, based on multiple references to similar phenomena and recurrent themes in the interviews.

The names of participants referred to in the book have been changed to protect their identity.

Secondary sources

The study also makes use of a variety of secondary sources. Sources with a historical character were useful for my longitudinal analysis in chapter two. Documents from the colonial period were gathered at archives in Lisbon. These include city laws, descriptions of, and plans for the city, as well as ethnographic studies conducted under the auspices of the colonial authorities. I have also made use of more recent and comprehensive historical analyses of the country, based on a variety of historical records – for example Pelissier (1997), Mendy (1994), Galli and Jones (1987), Bigman (1993) and Rodney (1970). Longitudinal analyses of the city are almost non-existent – except for Silveira's article (1989). The history of the neighbourhood under study, Bandim, has remained undocumented as the area was a bastion of resistance to colonialism and was probably considered unwelcoming by colonial researchers. Here, the historical information that I gathered from elders and other key persons in the neighbourhood proved very useful.

In the post-independence period, an externally financed Health Project operating in the neighbourhood has conducted surveys in Bandim. These have dealt mainly with health conditions. Particularly the more recent surveys conducted by the Project, covering the entire population of Bandim, were valuable in providing some basic parameters for planning my own data collection. In the post-independence period the amount of studies and data for the city as a whole are slim. A few studies of survival strategies in the city and of other neighbourhoods have been written in Dutch and German, inaccessible languages to me. There is, however, a series of studies on the socio-economic impacts of structural adjustment conducted by researchers at Instituto Nacional de Estudos e Pesquisa (INEP) in Bissau. Some of these address conditions in the city. They are often based on qualitative methods but usually give scant attention to methodological details. They have, however, been invaluable in making visible points of consensus among local researchers and in providing a general picture of the changes in conditions in the city and of the political economic environment in which these changes have taken place. The latter was also facilitated by an analysis of new legislation and policy documents that I gathered from government institutions and international aid agencies, as well as of internal documents collected from civil organisations and associations, and supplemented with interviews.

A few studies have dealt more specifically with informal economic activities, although some of these are inspired by a neo-liberal perspective. Among these, there is Crowley's (1993) comprehensive study of the informal economy in Guinea-Bissau, based on a mixture of qualitative and quantitative methods of data collection at four locations in the country, including Bissau. Together with a couple of other smaller reports, it helped place my data in a national perspective. At the city level, a couple of studies provided a basis of comparison with my own findings. These consist of a survey based study of market women in Bissau by Delgado et al (1989) and of a study edited by Monteiro (2001) of the largest market place in the city, based on both interviews and a broad survey in that market. This group of studies has been helpful in complementing my own efforts in understanding contemporary processes of informalization in Guinean society.

2 A history of informality in Guinea-Bissau

This study looks upon informality as a process. And as a process, informality changes in its contents and boundaries, through time and in ways that are locally specific. In Africa, this process has deep historical roots, which are of relevance to an understanding of the contemporary configurations of informality, as proposed in chapter one. This and the next chapter address the historical overarching processes shaping informality in Guinea-Bissau and its capital city. Chapter three will deal with contemporary trends in the period starting with the adoption of structural adjustment programmes in the mid-1980s. The present chapter describes processes before that turning point and reaching back to pre-colonial times. Together, these chapters depict how informal relations in a particular place have been shaped and reshaped through a series of historical layers, as a result of the evolving interplay between external forces and local responses. The unique forms that informal livelihoods assume today in a particular place, in this case Bissau, are the result of these locally specific historical processes. Part of the segmentation, differentiation and power relations contained within the informal realm today have also evolved from this past.

In this chapter, and for each of the three historical periods considered – the pre-colonial, the colonial and early post-independence periods – I will attempt to describe the particular mixes of formality and informality[46]. This will be analysed in relation to the particular forces at work and the conditions of participation in the international economy at that moment in time as well as the changing local conditions for social reproduction. Related to this, I will consider which agents have been involved in the social production of informality in each phase. A major issue pursued is how pre-capitalist forms of social and economic organisation have been reproduced and changed through time to continue to inform practices of survival in modern times. In general, I try to lift up the specific structures and processes that have given informal relations in Bissau their specificity. For each period, I begin with

[46] Throughout the chapter, my use of the term "informal" is consistent with the definition I advanced in chapter one, i.e. as pertaining to activities that falter in at least one aspect of the written law of the modern state or that are regulated by other kinds of "laws". This does not preclude the state from being an agent (directly or indirectly) in shaping informal relations. Naturally, this definition applies with certain difficulty to the analysis of the pre-colonial period, before the process of formalisation took hold.

processes at the national level and then narrow down the scope to specific changes in the city, occasionally glancing at my study area in the city, Bandim.

The reflections presented here are based to a great extent on secondary sources (see chapter one for a discussion of these). Longitudinal analyses of the city are almost non-existent and the studied neighbourhood is no exception, in spite of its rich history of pre-colonial forms of organisation and resistance to colonialism. In trying to construct a history of informality in the city and the neighbourhood, I make use of different kinds of documents produced during the colonial period, such as descriptions of Bissau, urban plans and city laws. From this period, there are also a few relevant ethnographic studies and historical analyses based on the accounts of early European travellers, though most authors writing during this period were involved with the colonial establishment. Obvious exceptions are the texts of Amilcar Cabral, the leader of the Guinean independence movement. There are other independent, more recent and serious historical analyses based on a variety of historical records, which have been invaluable to the writing of this chapter – for example Rodney (1970), Pelissier (1997), Mendy (1994), Galli and Jones (1987), Bigman (1993). My own interviews with elders and other key persons about historical trends in the studied neighbourhood, Bandim, helped in building a longitudinal view of the area. Based on this mixture sources, I will present one possible narrative of historical developments in Guinea. This is naturally constrained by the gaps and eventual biases present in the literature being used and by the narrow range of sources on which this account is based. A good part of the general descriptions offered here rests however on a consensus among several observers.

2.1 Adapting (im)moral economies (- 1915)

In this first section I will briefly present social, political and economic structures existing prior to effective colonial occupation, as described by a variety of writers. Indeed, some dimensions of contemporary informal livelihoods derive from this early history. I will refer to both their "moral" and "immoral" elements, because some of these internal divisions continue to pervade some informal relations in the study area today[47].

When the Europeans arrived at the coasts of Guinea sometime around the 1440s they found a conglomerate of different groups with their own political and economic structures. On the one hand, there were a variety of coastal peoples - such as the Pepel, the Manjaco, the Mancanha and the Balanta – which I will refer to as "the coastal groups". On the other hand, there were

[47] See chapter one for a presentation of the term "moral economy".

"the Eastern groups", that is, the peoples inhabiting what is today the eastern part of Guinea-Bissau such as the Mandinga, that was later joined by the Fula as a consequence of the northwards expansion of the state of Futa Jalon in the 18th century. These groups differed in their internal social and political organisation, which ranged between horizontal structures, such as those of the Balanta, through the hierarchical structures of kingdoms and chiefdoms among the Pepel, Manjaco and Mancanha, to the complex structure of classes and castes among the Eastern groups.

Let me briefly describe the pre-colonial structure of hierarchical coastal groups as depicted by a variety of authors, as the largest share of residents in the studied neighbourhood identify themselves as belonging to these groups[48]. The spirits of the ancestors were the highest authority, followed by the king with religious and judicial authority over a number of chiefdoms. Beneath him, there were a council of elders and chiefs governing the life of villages. Within the latter, the heads of familial groups held authority over members, held control over the land of the compound and the labour of women and youth. There were noble lineages such as the "Djagra" among the Pepel, from which kings and chiefs could be recruited. This political-spatial hierarchy was connected to a parallel hierarchy of religious figures, so that political and social institutions were sanctioned by religious ideologies. An important part of these hierarchies are still identifiable today in the studied neighbourhood, Bandim, impinging upon rights and obligations in provisioning (see chapter seven).

Several authors refer to what may have been elements of a "moral economy" in these early societies. There are references to mutual assistance between compounds and age groups in rice production among the Pepel (Ribeiro and Cardoso, 1987:9, 11), to the impossibility of kings and chiefs disposing of land to outsiders (Rodney, 1970:35; Mota, 1954:312) and to Councils of Elders as a welfare institution (Quintino, 1969:913)[49]. However, and although these texts say little about struggles around divisions of rights and responsibilities in these early times, it is also clear that the above hierarchies of power were reflected in a differentiation in terms of control over labour and land, with kings, chiefs and religious figures being at a great advantage in these respects (Mota, 1954:312; Rodney, 1970:34; Viegas, 1936:136). These are said to have controlled the necessary power and the resources to mobilise the extensive labour required for clearing new rice fields, with the workers having virtually no rights to them (Bigman, 1993:16).

[48] For a description of these structures see: Rodney (1970:29-31); Cissoko (1987:23); Mota (1954:311-2); Viegas (1936:143); Quintino (1969:897-9, 877, 903-5, 913); Carreira (1967:59); and Ribeiro and Cardoso (1987:11), for the Pepel of Biombo.

[49] See also Bigman's (1993:2) historical analysis of the food economy in Guinea and Cape Verde, where she emphasises the moral elements of production systems in these and other pre-capitalist African societies.

According to Quintino (1969:913), members of this privileged class could accumulate wealth through the control of women and youth, a position that was facilitated by them being the performers of important ceremonies. This differentiation may have implied that nobles and commoners had differing capacities to feed themselves[50]. These moral and immoral elements of precolonial coastal societies partly continue to inform practices among some groups in my study area today, as I will discuss in chapter seven.

Coastal societies were not isolated or turned in on themselves but were part of wider economic and political systems. The territories of the Pepel, Manjaco and Mancanha were unified into a political federation of chiefdoms until the late 19th century and exhibited a well organised system of periodic rotating markets, drawing on a large attendance of women and children[51]. Such markets, locally known as *lumo*, declined under the pressures of the modern state but have been revived in the lastest years, and are now part of the strategies employed by a number of urban traders today (see chapter five). But Guinean peoples were integrated into much larger political and commercial networks. They were at the Western end of Senegambia, an area crossed by Trans-Saharan trade routes and, from the 13th century, they came to pay tribute to the Mandinga kingdom of Kaabu[52], which was part of the empire of Mali (Rodney, 1970:26-7; Galli and Jones, 1987:11; Barry, 1990:9).

In the fifteenth century Portuguese traders of Cape Verdean origin, known as *lançados*, started trading with local peoples along the Guinean rivers, assisted by the *grumetes*, African boat hands. They traded in European products, local gold, ivory and particularly slaves from the 16th century, which they gathered from local rulers and traders. The slave trade in Senegambia has been said to have fostered despotism and centralisation of power among indigenous ruling elites who were able to access this new source of wealth (Barry, 1990::12; Bigman, 1993:23). Social contradictions between rulers and commoners are said to have been accentuated – as the "immoral" elements of local societies also probably did. In this period, the kingdom of Kaabu achieved its height in connection with the slave trade (Lopes, 1990:22) and a specialised commercial group, the Dyula, emerged among the Mandinga and thrived on their itinerant trade activities connecting the Atlantic and the interior. The Dyula are reported to have survived the fall of the Kaabu kingdom (Lobban, 1979:43; Lopes, 1990:21) and were later joined by the Fula in trading activities. These traders from the Eastern groups of Guinea, today known as *djilas*, have lately regained great visibility in both the urban and the national

---

50 See Rodney (1970:37) for such an argument on Sierra Leone, based on late 18th century descriptions.

51 Rodney (1970:30-32); Carreira (1967:49-50); Mota (1954:312-3); Bigman (1993:17); Quintino (1969:874).

52 This kingdom occupied what is today the eastern part of Guinea-Bissau, The Gambia and Casamance.

economic scenes, after many years of antagonism with the modern state (see chapter three). In fact, the early ethnic-gender specialisation in trade that is apparent in this period, consisting of males from the Eastern groups and women from coastal groups (see above), continue to structure participation in trade activities in Bissau today.

Bissau: the power of the unwritten rule

Let me now turn to parallel developments in the area that would become known as Bissau, to see how indigenous local elites saw their power reinforced and how they remained the true "regulators" in the emerging settlement for centuries.

With the rise of the Atlantic trade a settlement of *lançados* and *grumetes* emerged in the estuary of the Geba river, on the so-called "Island of Bissau"[53] in the 16th century (Rodney 1970:142; Santos, 1971:483; Martins in Faro, 1958:211). This settlement would become known as Bissau[54]. By the seventeenth century, the small group of huts had grown into a typical trading post (Governo da Colonia, 1948:357-8; Mota, 1954:74). Bissau received the title of captaincy, subordinated to the administration in Cape Verde, and the first figure of Portuguese authority settled in, together with a small garrison. Portuguese authority in the area would, however, continue to be challenged and circumscribed by the local rulers for centuries. According to various descriptions, there were three kingdoms within just a couple of kilometres of the trading post, namely Bandim, Antula and Intim, with the latter ranking highest (Map 2.1).

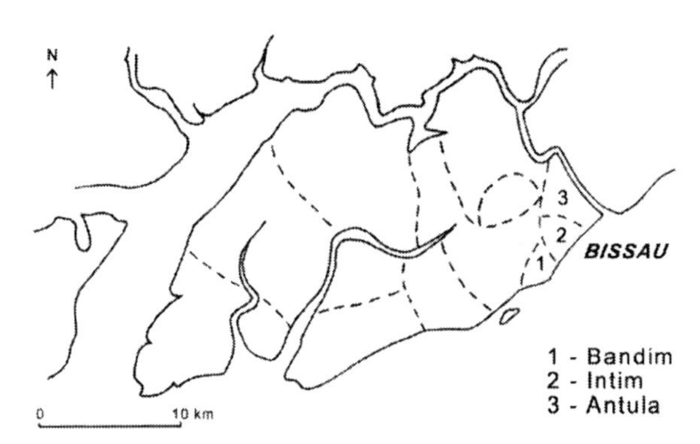

Map 2.1 Pepel kingdoms on the "Island of Bissau". *Source: Carreira (1960:280).*

[53] "Island of Bissau" is the territory that Pepels claimed to be their ancestral lands.

[54] This name has its origin in the collective name of the original occupants of the island, the "Boçao". They would later become known as the Pepel (paper, in Portuguese), a name derived from the procedures of tax payment by the Portuguese to Pepel kings, according to local oral history.

With the advent of the Atlantic trade, the local Pepel developed exchange relations with the trading post and traded directly with European ships. Pepel kings in Bissau engaged in the flourishing slave trade of Bissau which became a very important source of wealth for them (Rodney, 1970:106,117, 146; Bigman, 1993:20). Rulers reportedly used the slave trade for handling internal rivalries and in this way were able to reinforce their power position in local societies, probably increasing internal tensions and deepening unequal relations[55].

Not surprisingly, Pepel rulers vigorously defended their enhanced position vis-à-vis Portuguese interests, through various strategies that ranged from open war whenever the Portuguese tried to tamper with their privileges, to sporadic alliances and peace accords often aimed at resuming international trade. Indeed, the Pepel of Bissau offered European domination remarkable resistance, which would only finally be put down in 1915[56]. Pepel-Portuguese relations were in a permanent state of tension for centuries. Pepel kings often put the trading post under siege, cutting off the water supply and ordering the closing down of the local fair where the local population came to sell their goods. At times the Pepel gathered warriors by the thousands from their several kingdoms (and beyond) and inflicted terrible defeats on Portuguese troops. At issue were some recurrent areas of disagreement. On the one hand, the Pepel seemed reluctant to give up their autonomy and sovereignty over their territory, as evidenced in the difficulties of raising a fort and the impossibility of imposing taxes. In fact, several commentators state that before military conquest it was the Portuguese Crown who was paying taxes to local kings (Cissoko, 1987:24; Mendy, 1994:139, 142, 204; Cardoso and Ribeiro, 1987:8).

But the Pepel of Bissau were far from averse to the opportunities created by international trade. Indeed, they repeatedly frustrated Portuguese attempts to monopolise such trade. Not only did the Pepel ignore Portuguese trade regulations and conduct "contraband" trade, particularly in the village of Bandim, but they were also unyielding about their rights to trade freely with ships from different nations which called at their ports[57]. This impossibility of upholding a monopoly and of simply "resisting the gentiles" (as one captain-major put it) resulted in the temporary extinction of the captaincy of Bissau in

---

[55] See Pelissier (1997:266) on intra-Pepel wars during these early times. See Mendy, 1994:130; and Martins in Faro, 1958 on unequal relations in these ancient Pepel societies.

[56] This is well documented. See: Santos (1971:484-9); Governo da Colonia (1948:360); Rodney (1970:147-151); Martins in Faro (1958:208-9); Mendy (1994:130, 132, 141, 190, 221).

[57] In the late 17th century one particularly insistent captain-major José Pinheiro ended up being imprisoned and then beaten to death by the Pepel king, Incinha Té, after asking the former whether he thought he was the Lord of the land. Té also sent a letter to Lisbon explaining his commercial policy to the Portuguese king. Free trade resumed. Concerning these trade related conflicts, see: Pelissier (1997:77); Rodney (1970:147-151); Governo da Colonia (1948); Santos (1971:484-5); Mendy (1994:123-6).

the early eighteenth century (Santos, 1971:487; Rodney, 1970:151; Mendy, 1994:126-7). The captaincy would be re-established fifty years later. But the hegemony of Portuguese power in the area was to remain impracticable for a long time after that and Pepel power remained unshaken. Honório P. Barreto, a representative of the Portuguese authority in Bissau, writing in the mid-19th century, stated himself that the Pepel king of Intim was the true governor of Bissau: he made law in the trading post, imposed fines on its inhabitants and arbitrated over their disputes (according to Mendy, 1994:139, 142, 177, 190, 241; Pelissier, 1997:77). Settlers who ventured outside the walled trading post did so at great risk[58].

This permanent threat held Bissau under the strong hold of the Pepel. Accounts from the mid-nineteenth century portray the Portuguese settlement as having been squeezed between the moat, the muddy shore and the big wall, and as suffering from poor ventilation and filthiness (Governo da Colónia, 1948). Its 570 inhabitants lived in crowded and unhealthy conditions and were hindered from owning even an inch of land on the Pepel island outside of the walled settlement. The physical expansion of Bissau would only begin after 1913/15 when the big wall was demolished and the military campaigns of Teixeira Pinto "pacified" the last group of "insurgents". This long history of resistance is part of the collective memory of the Pepel, the group with ancestral roots in the urban district studied here. The local Pepel still recall Bandim as having been a haven for dissidents and impenetrable to the Portuguese prior to "pacification". Their tradition of resistance would be reawakened with the rise of nationalist movements only some forty years later. This resistance to colonialism may partly explain the persistence of traditional structures in Bandim through time.

Summing up this period before effective colonial occupation took place, the picture that emerges is that pre-colonial forms of political and economic organisation adapted to the new opportunities opened by the early phase of incorporation into a world economic system and local hegemonies of indigenous traders and nobilities were reproduced rather than erased throughout this period. This was also the case in Bissau. Here, the singularly intense and prolonged resistance shown by the local Pepel to colonial attempts at domination – combined with the peripherality of this colony in relation to the wider interests of the Portuguese Crown – seems to have perpetuated the hegemony of the unwritten rule in Bissau into the 20th century. The relevance of this resilience of ancient structures in the face of external pressures is that they continue to provide points of reference for contemporary informal ways of provisioning and distribution of resources and food in the study setting today.

[58] Description by Martins in 1831, in Faro (1958:209).

2.2 Colonial rule and informality (1915-1974)

After the bloody military campaigns of Teixeira Pinto, Portugal was finally in a position to consolidate its authority and to embark on a more effective economic exploitation of what had become "Portuguese Guinea". Portuguese authorities established modern structures of administration and began to enforce earlier laws and create news ones – such as those pertaining to the hut tax, forced labour, cash crop cultivation, land tenure, and those defining the civil and political rights of natives (Mendy, 1994:278, 284-296; Espinosa, 1994:19). They also determined which structures should be "modernised" and brought under the direct control of the modern state and be regulated by its modern laws, and which should be governed by local custom and thus remain informal. The vast majority of Guineans were assigned a "native" status, i.e. one in which their rights were limited to those regulated by customary law. This freed the colonial government from responsibilities towards them and in many cases made them vulnerable to abuses by their chiefs. In this way, the colonial government contributed to the permanence of certain traditional institutions, although their content would not remain unchanged. In this section I will discuss these changes as well as the altered conditions for most of the population in the colony and their engagement in activities which escaped the control of the colonial state, activities which one may call informal.

The racist content of colonial ideology was disguised by a discourse of cultural assimilation and political integration. It disavowed any sweeping elimination of indigenous institutions and customs and instead recommended a long-term integration of African populations into Portuguese culture and institutions[59]. Indigenous kings and village heads became recognised by law as native authorities, but with the new role of agents of the colonial government. At the local level, daily life was governed by these transformed traditional institutions. The new native policy partly formalised these indigenous institutions by regulating their duties and rights, and even their appointment and deposition. In a strategy similar to that of indirect rule in British colonies, indigenous authorities were used as intermediaries between colonialists and African communities. They were, for example, expected to participate in tax collection, force upon their populations the cultivation of export crops, and guarantee a supply of labour to colonial authorities. Compliant chiefs were then granted certain benefits. In this position, chiefs could accuse and deliver their own subjects to the administrator for punishment. It is likely that they used this as a means of maintaining their powerful position and their abuses of power towards their own people are said to often have gone unpunished. This possibly fostered a deepening of immoral elements, i.e. inequality and contradictions, in some of the local societies.

[59] See, among others, Mendy (1994: 285, 294-6) and Cardoso (1992:32-5) for a discussion.

The above situation led some authors to see chiefs in Guinea as entertaining an alliance with the colonial power and of being able to retain most of their privileges from pre-colonial times[60]. But the extent of this political symbiosis between colonial and traditional authorities seems to have varied between groups, with hierarchical coastal groups such as the Pepel, usually being considered as particularly non-cooperative[61].

In the sphere of production, Bigman (1993:33) describes how wealthy Fula political and religious figures used customary mutual aid groups to cultivate groundnuts for them, transforming those groups into "more or less permanent wage labour". As such, groundnuts for export were being produced with traditional methods, through (adapted) customary relations and on customary land (Mendy, 1994:29). Even market production on land concessions, which were initially meant to encourage a large-scale modern commercial agriculture, turned out to be based instead on peasant production, though in the form of share-cropping (Espinosa 1994:3, 24-5; Bigman, 1993:35-7; Galli and Jones, 1987:28). Against a background of exploitative sharecropping contracts, coercive groundnut cultivation and the practices of colonial and native authorities, conditions in the countryside worsened. When drought hit the region in 1942, the conditions were set for a widespread famine in Guinea (Ribeiro, 1989)[62], the severity of which affected even the indigenous quarters of Bissau - as described to me by elderly residents of Bandim. The colonial economy remained largely an economy of extraction, with minimal investments in the development of the productive base. As in other parts of West Africa, capitalist interests were met without significant changes being made in the relations of production[63]. This usually meant that work conditions were regulated by rules other than the written law of the state, although the state's absence from these realms was certainly a conscious one.

A modern capitalist sector would, however, emerge in the sphere of circulation. The period of the "New State" regime in Lisbon (1926-1974) saw a firmer subordination of Guinea to Portugal and Guinea was turned into a market for Portuguese products and a supplier of raw materials to the metropole (Galli and Jones, 1987:25-6; Mendy, 1990:29-30). External and internal trade became concentrated in the hands of a large Portuguese company, Casa Gouveia, and by establishing a network of trading centres to which producers were forced to deliver their cash crops. Legislation was created to out-law the

[60] See for example Mendy (1994) and Fernandes (1993).

[61] Cardoso and Ribeiro (1987:13-15) and Ribeiro (1989) for example argue that colonial rule saw the "de-structuration" of the Pepel political and socio-economic system. Their account however seems to be too extreme, ignoring how the local structure of authority partly adapted to the changes brought by colonialism.

[62] See Comité information Sahel (1974) on similar consequences of intensive groundnut production in neighbouring countries.

[63] See Cardoso (1992) on Guinea-Bissau. See Bernstein (1991) on how capitalist penetration reproduced "petty commodity" relations in West Africa.

activities of small independent traders, but *djilas* continued trading across the borders illegally as they had done since pre-colonial times, as well as in the villages and urban suburbs (Mendy, 1990; Castro, 1980: 350-1, 357; Galli and Jones, 1987:33, 38; Crónica da Colónia in Bigman 1993:42). As the system of weights, credit and prices practised at trading centres was reportedly corrupt, exploitative and disadvantageous in comparison to those of neighbouring countries, producers began to reduce production, migrated or smuggled their crops across borders instead of selling them to the state (Galli and Jones, 1987:41; Bigman 1993:42-3; Castro, 1980:355-6).

As a consequence, official export volumes began to stagnate. Castro (1970:347) estimates that in the 1950s the colonial authorities were able to acquire only about one fifth or one fourth of total production. According to Galli and Jones (1987:38-41, 51-2), market shortages of grain ensued. These responses by producers and *djilas* were antagonistic to colonial interests and could possibly be said to have represented a conscious strategy by these popular groups to circumvent the exploitative practices of the state and the formal sector, as proposed in the disengagement perspective (see chapter one). But this is insufficient to explain the spectrum of informal relations existing and being reproduced in Guinea under colonial rule. As mentioned above, the capitalist sector also relied on informal relations of production to ensure the supply of export crops.

The above account can be summed up as follows: informal relations continued to occupy an important position throughout this period in both the spheres of production and subsistence. Firstly, capitalist accumulation relied upon relations that were not governed by the written law of the modern state, such as those that prevailed in the production of export crops. Secondly, in the process of articulation between capitalist and customary relations, indigenous elites among some ethnic groups were able to strengthen their economic position at the expense of ordinary people. These powerful groups continued to be major regulators, though under new conditions, in the daily lives of ordinary people. Thirdly, the colonial state created laws to regulate some parts of the Guinean economy and society and left other parts to be governed by traditional rules, as these were functional to colonial interests. In this way, the state itself consciously helped to maintain certain traditional sets of rules in place. Fourthly, worsened conditions of social reproduction in the colony fostered economic activities that evaded the control of the colonial state, and which worked against its interests. These parallel or informal activities, judging from available accounts, would never be extinguished, as will be seen in the next section. But let us look at developments in Bissau during the colonial period.

Colonial Bissau: a city divided

Military subjugation of the Pepel marked the beginning of a new era for Bissau. The physical expansion of the settlement took off[64]. From the late 1930s the pace of change accelerated. As the principle area for groundnut production moved from the South to the Northeast of the colony, Bissau became the natural channel for exports and the privileged place of exchanges with the international market. Connected to this, the seat of government of Guinea was transferred from Bolama to Bissau in 1941, resulting in a concentration of both commercial and administrative functions there. Trade warehouses, government buildings and residences multiplied and the city gradually gained a European appearance and layout. The once insalubrious historical centre became a modern commercial district where the latest European fashion was displayed. Major basic infrastructure was developed to serve the colonial centre, along with the construction of health, educational and recreational infrastructure and a port for international trade. The European centre became the visible expression of the prosperity of mercantile capital and of the modern colonial state.

Analyses of Bissau in the colonial period are scarce. The following discussion relies to a considerable extent on documents produced by the colonial government and descriptions written under its auspices, such as those by Mota (1954) and Carreira (1960). Independent analyses that are referenced here include those by Amilcar Cabral (1974, 1980), Silveira (1989), Castro (1980) and Cardoso (1992).

Spatial segregation and dual systems of rights

In order to safeguard the European image of the colonial centre and ensure that African elements were kept under control, the development of the white city was carefully regulated and monitored. Plans for urban development were issued to direct the life and expansion of the city. One of these plans created a physical boundary, the "urban perimeter", to separate the colonial centre from the African quarters (Colónia da Guiné, 1948:21; Governo da Colónia, 1948: :379-80; Silveira, 1989:84, 97) (Map 2.2.). In the area within the perimeter, all land held under customary rule by the local population was expropriated by the City Council. Development within that area became the sole jurisdiction of the Council. The traditional contructions were cleared and the people living in the African quarters that had once surrounded the fortified settlement were pushed out to the periphery. The urban plan of 1948 clearly states that "the native quarters are to be located outside the urban perimeter" (Colónia da Guiné, 1948:20). This institutionalised the spatial and social segregation of the

[64] For descriptions of the expansion of colonial Bissau, see: Silveira (1989:84); Governo da Colónia (1946:233, 1948:376-383); Colónia da Guiné (1948; Mota, 1954:76-7).

city that separated the colonisers from the colonised. In the quarters lying outside the perimeter the colonial authorities rejected any responsibility for the provision of social and physical infrastructure. Most schools were located within the urban perimeter and asphalt, electricity and piped water did not reach beyond this area (Silveira, 1989:94). According to Mota's (1954) discussion of urban development in Guinea, this sharp separation between the white and the African city and the conditions in African quarters were typical of other Guinean urban centres: the indigenous town at the periphery of the white settlement lacked "urban" characteristics. He depicts it as "a large village or conglomerate of villages (...) an immense shelter for the indigenous population that works or idly wanders in the white city" (p. 73).

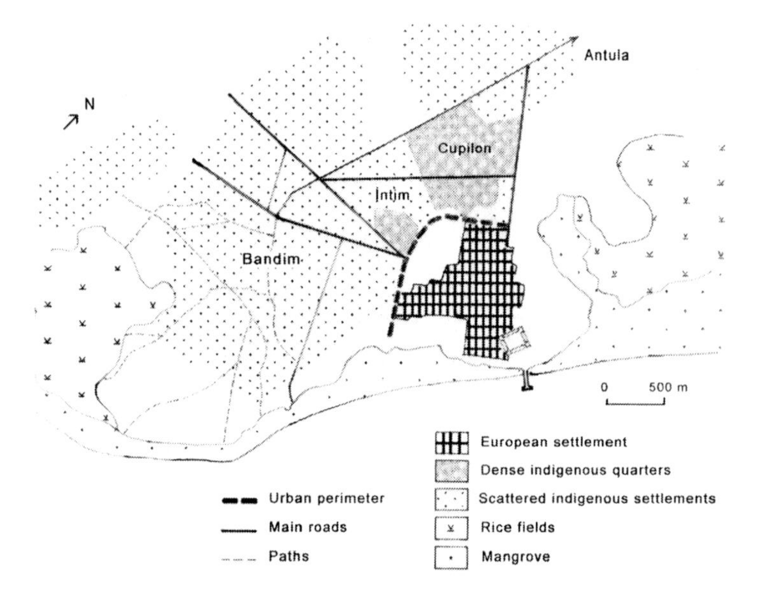

Map 2.2 Spatial segregation in Bissau in the mid-1950s

Based on: (a) Map of Portuguese Guinea, 1:50,000, sheet Bissau, Junta das Missões Geográficas, Ministério do Ultramar, 1952; (b) Map of Bissau, 1:20,000, Boletim Cultural da Guiné Portuguesa, (1947, 2:7); (c) drawings by Silveira (1989:82).

This then, was the kind of environment in which rural migrants settled. The influx of the indigenous population to the city increased, leading to the expansion and increasing density of the African quarters and, in some areas, to crowding and increased health risks. The indigenous periphery of Bissau became ethnically heterogeneous. It included the host communities of the Pepel of Bissau, the old group of *grumetes* pushed away from the urban centre, Pepel migrants from the rest of the island and migrants of various ethnic origins. Presumably based on the 1950 census, Mota (1954:78) refers to a total indigenous population in Bissau of about 13,000[65]. Of this number, approximately 45 per cent were Pepel, followed by members of other coastal groups, and with groups from Eastern Guinea forming the minority. The modest presence of members of the Eastern groups, the majority of which profess the Islamic religion, led Mota to see indigenous Bissau at that time as "essentially an animist city" (p. 78), a situation which has now changed. Some quarters became ethnic clusters – such as those of Cupilon and Gambiafada where the Eastern groups tended to concentrate (Mota, 1954:78). Many migrants also settled in the areas corresponding to the old kingdoms of Bandim, Intim and part of Antula. Together, according to the 1950 census, these three areas housed more than 12,500 (in Carreira, 1960:281-3). According to data from that same census, the area of Intim was the most ethnically heterogeneous among the three, and was also the most populated and fastest growing. By contrast, Bandim, with its 1,213 residents, had a much lower population density and about 80 per cent of its residents were Pepel.

Among the migrants, Mota (1954:73) refers to a significant share coming and going between town and village. An important stream of migrants was, according to Carreira (1960:285-6), composed of youth, possibly eager to attend school, earn money or simply to escape the authority of the elders. However, he states that large numbers of youngsters tried unsuccessfully to enrol in schools in town and job opportunities were not sufficient to absorb this large influx. Both Mota and Carreira comment on youngsters roaming in town or engaging in criminal activities.

Living outside the urban perimeter did not only entail living in a difficult environment but also acted to influence the claims one could make on the colonial authorities and one's rights in the white city. From the outset of effective occupation, the colonial authorities created a legal distinction between civilised and natives, corresponding to two different sets of rights. A special political and civil status was created for natives, known as the "native code" (Mendy, 1994:285-7; Cardoso, 1992:36-8), and according to which, people living in indigenous settlements, leading indigenous ways of life and who could not read or write Portuguese were considered "natives" and excluded from the full rights of Portuguese citizenship. Their political rights were restricted to indigenous political institutions and could not be exerted in relation to European institutions. 'Natives' civil rights - such as those in the spheres of property, inheritance, family and obligations - were to be governed by customary law. This also applied to the population of Bissau. The urban perimeter dividing the European from the native city reflected and reinforced the distinction between "civilised" and "natives". The vast majority of those living outside of the urban perimeter held the legal status of "natives" which kept them from exercising any rights through modern institutions and left

[65] This may be an underestimation as censuses went hand in hand with the payment of the head tax and people had thus good reason to avoid enumeration.

them without alternatives to traditional institutions. Of relevance is the fact that a significant amount of land lying outside the perimeter continued to be governed by customary rules. This meant that traditional rights of access to rice fields continued to apply among local Pepel and to be an important basis of subsistence.

The native code was revoked in the 1960s. But a third legal category was created, the "assimilated", to describe those Africans who had attained Portuguese standards of culture and literacy and who were thus eligible for integration into modern structures (Cardoso, 1992:50; Lobban, 1979:20). The share of the urban African population that attained the full rights of Portuguese citizenship would, however, remain a minority. According to the census of 1950, Bissau contained almost half of the "civilised" population in Guinea. Nonetheless the "non-civilised" population of Bissau was 13,463 of a total of 17,255, i.e. almost 80 per cent (Mota, 1954:67). Mota argues that in spite of the growing number of migrants settling in the city, the number of Africans attaining a civilised status did not increase. The "assimilated" category, i.e. the group of supposedly detribalised Africans, would remain rather small until independence. The significance of this large-scale exclusion from the ability to exercise the formal rights of modern society lay in the necessity for a continued reliance on informal rights for survival, customary or otherwise. It is in this light that we need to see the conditions of participation of the African population in the wider city's economy. For while they were segregated to the urban periphery, this growing "non-civilised" or "non-assimilated" population was an integral part of the daily life of the colonial centre, especially so as it supplied the necessary labour and produce to its residents.

Working in the white city

The above-mentioned distinct legal categories of urban dwellers participated differently in the urban economy. The 1950 census showed that, for the whole colony, the "civilised" population was mainly employed in the "modern sector" – loosely and insufficiently defined as jobs in commerce and public administration, including the military and health personnel. By contrast, it employed only three per cent of the "non-civilised" population. This very limited access of Guineans to secure employment meant that the majority were left to their own economic initiative. Amilcar Cabral, who was to become the leader of the independence struggle in Guinea, offered an analysis of the contours of the social structure in towns in the 1960s. Particularly useful was his disaggregation of Africans (Cape Verdeans included) based on their different material conditions in the city. Below those occupying high and middle official positions and liberal professions came "petty officials" and employees in commerce who held work contracts. These two groups enjoyed an assured living and a secure monthly pay. Next on the social ladder were workers without a contract and thus with an insecure work situation, which Cabral considered the embryo of a working class, or "our little proletariat" (Cabral, 1974:54, 57). Among these were dock-workers, boat hands, domestic servants, workers in repair shops and small workshops, construction workers, porters working in shops as well as petty traders, i.e. the male *djilas* traders and women marketers, whom he does not mention (see Carreira, 1960:284-5). On the lowest rung were found beggars and prostitutes, as well as recent young migrants that lacked steady employment (Cabral, 1974:51; 1980:33, 36). These groups in Bissauan society working in unprotected conditions would qualify as informal workers, according to my understanding of "informal" (see chapter one). So let us look at the work conditions of some of these groups.

While Africans' existence on the urban periphery *per se* saw little direct interference from the colonial authorities (aside from tax collection), and were left to fend for themselves, their activities in the colonial centre were strictly controlled. Legal ordinances were promulgated to regulate and give clear instructions about what could and could not be done within the "urban perimeter". They also specified the sanctions for cases where such regulations were contravened. Such ordinances can be conceptualised in terms of a "formalisation" of urban life. But this formalisation would remain partial, principally because the rights of the mass of "non-civilised" suppliers of labour and goods remained only loosely regulated, seemingly with the aim of freeing employers and the state from the responsibility of protecting them. Retirement schemes for example were, according to Cardoso (1992:47), restricted to workers in the public sector, which was dominated by those with a civilised or assimilated status. Let me illustrate with the examples of two types of work - trade activities and casual work - both of which have been historically important in the city and are today among the most common sources of income for its residents. I will analyse their contemporary forms in later chapters.

Trade activities within the urban perimeter became heavily regulated through municipal law. One example concerned the legal dispositions (Governo da Guiné, 1968: 9-10, 16-7) which regulated itinerant trade and activities in the municipal market place, the latter of which women engaged in. It regulated, for example, what could be sold, licensing and fees, quality controls, how to behave and required from sellers a high level of attendance. The same legal document gave an extraordinary amount of power to municipal agents in the market place and stipulated that any vendor showing disrespect towards these agents could be suspended from trading for a period of up to 90 days or be permanently excluded in case of repeated offence. Scope for pressing for changes in such conditions was thus limited. Although their trading activities were being taxed, marketers had no rights to pensions, sick leave or other welfare benefits. In chapter five I will argue that the practices of municipal agents today are no less despotic than those employed by agents in these early days.

Dockworkers and other workers lacking formal contracts were often paid by the day or worked under short-term agreements (Silveira, 1989:83). This category came to be known locally by the name of *surni* or "contract workers". My older respondents who had done this kind of work during the colonial era, explained that under such agreements, as soon as the task was terminated and payment had been made, the employer had no further obligations towards the workers. The latter could not claim for compensation from either employers or the state for work-related accidents or for periods when there was no work. For these workers, who were periodically recruited and then made redundant from the modern economy (possibly following the cycle of the groundnut economy), it meant that they could not rely exclusively on these activities for their survival (even should they wish to). With this in mind, it is worth noting that during that time the majority of *surni* workers at the docks were Pepel. This was the ethnic group with the greatest potential of keeping a foot in a traditional subsistence economy. According to my informants, men of the host Pepel group in Bandim, holding rice fields around the city, would take a few days work at the docks, after which they would go back to rice cultivation and other activities organised according to customary rules. Pepel migrants came from the proximate hinterland of the city and could also return for the agricultural season if they so desired (see chapter seven on the rural ties that many of these migrants still maintain today). Others joined groups of single men living in the town, in which accommodation, food and occasional income were shared as a way of surviving the irregularity and insufficiency of *surni* opportunities.

Salary levels were generally low. Castro (1980:353-4) affirms that the salaries of domestic, semi-skilled and non-skilled workers in Guinea in the 1950s were half those paid in neighbouring countries. Non-skilled African workers such as dockworkers earned one third of the salaries being paid to Europeans (See also Cabral, 1980:36). Castro argues that, in relation to food prices, real wages, particularly for non-skilled workers, were miserable. He describes how they were ruthlessly exploited as well as their bad and often risky working conditions (p. 366-7). He also mentions the strikes made by workers within this group against a large Portuguese trading company. After one strike carried out in 1956, employers made concessions. However, a dockworkers strike in 1959 – which one my interviewees, Rafael Barbosa, helped organise - ended in the massacre of fifty workers and the wounding of many more at the hands of the colonial police (Sarrazin, 1978:35-37). This event served as a trigger for the armed struggle in Guinea. Not surprisingly, given their conditions in the city, dockworkers became one of the main urban groups who engaged in the liberation movement (Fernandes, 1993:40). I will discuss the contemporary conditions of casual workers in later chapters, as this is an informal economic activity upon which many urban men rely.

More than a decade of colonial war fostered important changes in the city. It caused an unprecedented flow of refugees from the rural areas to the security of the city resulting in a rapid population growth in the capital. Another change was that the city became increasingly isolated from the rural areas and its international dependence accentuated (Silveira, 1989:95; Davila, 1987:46). This was reflected in an increasing dependence on financial transfers from Lisbon and on consumer goods imported from the metropole.

Persisting traditional structures

The subordinated fashion in which most Africans participated in the modern urban economy and the meagre conditions of reproduction to which they were subjected contributed towards the continued promotion of other sources of provisioning and types of allegiance, namely those available in the African quarters. Their exclusion from the full rights of citizenship in the modern urban society certainly added to the need to keep indigenous systems of rights and obligations alive. Unfortunately, this "world" was not seen as sufficiently interesting for the researchers of the time to explore. Here, the historical reminiscences I was entrusted with by Pepel seniors in Bandim and my interviews with key informants are particularly useful. Among the latter, there are two people who have played key roles in the urban and national scenes, both residing in Bandim. These are, Mr. Mr. Rafael Barbosa, co-founder of the PAIGC; and Mr. Pinto Marques, presently vice-president of the Guinean League for Human Rights, former vice-president of the City Council and former president of the PAIGC neighbourhood committee.

Let me begin with the traditional political and social hierarchy in Bandim. Military subjugation of the Pepel kings of Bissau in 1915 did not eradicate their power or level out Pepel society. Engaging the collaboration of Pepel chiefs (as was the strategy of colonial authorities) seems to have been difficult, according to both Barbosa and Marques, and relations between them and colonial authorities were usually less than friendly – though this did vary from one chief to another and chiefs reportedly "collaborated" in the collection of taxes. What is clear is that Pepel chiefs in Bandim (and apparently in the wider city) did not benefit much materially from colonialism - at least not to the extent that chiefs seem to have done. Their material base remained essentially the traditional one – such as the "crown's assets" and tributes from their subjects. Also, chiefs of Bissau did not usually move easily within the colonial bureaucracy. So, in this instance, we cannot speak of an indigenous elite thriving on the political and material opportunities facilitated by colonialism, as is reported to have been the case among other groups in Guinea and as well as in other African colonies[66].

For decades after "pacification", chiefs in Bandim maintained a strong position among their subjects and remained the main authority outside the urban perimeter. For example Oburri, who ruled for twenty years in Bandim (1947-67), is still recalled as a powerful man who instilled fear in the local population with his mystical powers[67]. But my interviewees also agree that Pepel chiefs came to experience a certain decline in the extension of their powers. Several of them suggested that this decline started in the mid-1950s (although one suggested the 1970s) and that it was related to reductions in the amount of land held by chiefs (due not only to sales but also to expropriation by the state), to their loss of economic power, to the swelling numbers of migrant residents as well as the opportunities and alternative worldviews that the urban environment had to offer. Today, the chief of Bandim and his entourage continue to hold religious power and some influence over the "sons of the land". At lower levels of the hierarchy, the Pepel host group continues to be arranged into domestic groups organised around common descent, which gather into collective work groups for the subsistence production of rice on land ruled by customary law and inherited according to matrilineal law. All these cultural practices are alive in Bandim today and structure access to important livelihood resources as well as redistribution flows, as will be discussed in chapter seven.

To summarise, colonial Bissau became a deeply divided city along racial lines. This division was reflected in a sharp spatial segregation and an institutionalised duality of rights. Africans' lives in the city were formally state regulated only in so far as this facilitated monitoring their presence in the colonial centre and also to uphold its European image. But this was a partial formalisation of their livelihoods. Policy was such that the burden of reproduction fell on the shoulders of African workers, and their existence in the African quarters was intentionally left to be regulated by indigenous rules. Activities pursued in these neighbourhoods, governed by rules other than the written law, may have been both a necessity in the face of a subordinate participation in the modern segment of the urban economy and a form of resistance to complete incorporation into it. For resistance to colonial domination, though less overt than before, did not end with the military campaigns of Teixeira Pinto. In this respect, it is pertinent to note that Bandim neighbourhood in particular became a major base of operations for militants of the liberation party doing clandestine mobilisation work in the city, according to one of my key informants, Mr. Rafael Barbosa, and the accounts of residents.

---

[66] See for example: Bryceson (1990) on Tanzania; and Berry (1985) on Nigeria.

[67] Chronology of chiefs in Bandim, 1947-1999, based on interviews: Oburri (1947-67), Mbacanhan (1967-??), Malam (19??-84), Quinté (1984-95), Mpote Cá (1995-98), Lefa Nanque (1998-).

2.3 The Party-state: engagement and disengagement (1974-1983)

Guinea-Bissau gained independence in 1974 after more than a decade of war with the colonial power. Popular political participation was high at independence. The liberation party PAIGC (Partido Africano da Independencia da Guiné e Cabo Verde) succeeded in mobilising large sections of the Guinean population and uniting a great variety of groups and positions into a high degree of political cohesion. Ideologically oriented towards the aspirations of the masses, the single Party state was anchored in a wide popular base through an elected National Popular Assembly and elected local councils - village committees or neighbourhood committees in urban areas after independence (Chabal, 1984:139-149; Rudebeck, 1988:63). Mass organisations were created for women, the youth and workers.

In the Party's discourse of national unity, ethnic identities and traditional political structures were to be discouraged. The latter, seen as formerly strategic to colonial domination, were shaken by the popularity and modern ideology of the PAIGC[68]. Some of its powers (for example justice functions) were removed from traditional instances and transferred to the local structures of the modern state. These changes also took place in the Pepel chiefdoms of Bissau, judging from information given by elders in Bandim and other key informants[69]. In Bandim, for example, the handling of land conflicts passed partly from traditional hands to the neighbourhood committee. This suppression of traditional authority in this early post-independence period was, however, tempered by a fear of the mystical powers of traditional power figures, apparently one of the weapons at their disposal until today, as I repeatedly heard in both interviews and informal conversations. In the opinion of Koudawo (1996) traditional forms of organisation survived through this period as a frame for alternative ways of life and a refuge for activities autonomous from the authoritarian state, as they had done during colonial rule.

The Party proclaimed itself as the leading force in society and declared a socialist orientation towards development, with a discursive emphasis on social goals[70]. The state assumed a leading role in the economy[71]. Among other things, it largely monopolised external trade and established a network of some 230 commercial outlets, the People's Stores, throughout the country, with the function of collecting cash crops from peasants and supplying con-

[68] For a discussion of the role of traditional structures in national politics in Guinea, see: Koudawo (1996); and Fernandes (1993).

[69] For example, Mr. Pinto Marques, who was a member of the neighbourhood committee in Bandim in this period.

[70] See for example Monteiro and Martins (1996: 158, 182-5) on the revolutionary goals of educational and social policy of PAIGC prior to structural adjustment..

[71] See Galli and Jones (1987), Embaló (1993) for descriptions of the Guinean economy during this period.

sumer and producer goods at prices fixed by the state. Private trade outside this state-controlled network was declared illegal.

Only a few years after independence, disappointment began mounting[72]. The state became increasingly centralised, repressive and insulated from popular influence. Local formal political structures began falling apart. Mass organisations were strictly controlled by the Party and did not allow for participation in top-level decision making. The political coalition on which the state rested (between the intellectual leadership of Cape Verdean origins and the military leadership of peasant origins) weakened in favour of a stronger "bureaucratic bourgeoisie". The government distanced itself from initial social goals and failed to improve the conditions of the population. In the countryside, producers experienced deterioration in terms of trade. The People's stores were insufficient in their coverage of the territory and functioned inefficiently and irregularly. The Party rapidly lost its political and economic credibility.

The responses of Guineans to this lack of effective means of political participation and of minimum opportunities for economic improvement are well documented[73]. In brief, some producers migrated to neighbouring countries to grow cash crops there instead, or sold their goods at higher prices through clandestine networks, resulting in a sharp decline in sales of both food and export crops to official outlets. *Djilas* offered an alternative to the unattractive prices and sporadic supply offered by official channels and, as a result, the smuggling of rice and cash crops across borders reportedly intensified. Smuggling seemingly deprived the government of taxes but also of export products and thus also of foreign exchange. State dependence on external assistance for importing food and covering the budget deficit increased. The external debt grew rapidly and shortages in basic items became frequent.

Similar processes of an expanding parallel or informal economy were reported for post-independence Ghana and Guinea (Conakry) by Azarya and Chazan (1987) who interpret these processes as representing a disengagement of popular groups from the state. In Guinea-Bissau, judging from the available accounts – some of which are clearly inspired by the disengagement perspective[74] – the above responses may have possibly contained elements of a conscious disengagement. But the story is more complicated than this, as will become clear as we turn to what was happening in Bissau at this time.

[72] For a discussion of this aspect see: Rudebeck (1988); Chabal (1984); Galli and Jones (1987:98); Galli (1990).

[73] Handem (1987); Galli (1990); Galli and Jones (1987), chapters five and six; Bigman (1993), chapter seven.

[74] Galli and Jones' work (1987) in particular, building on a "disengagement" interpretation, lead to the conclusion that freedom from state intervention is the solution for a dynamic rural economy. This could be interpreted as legitimizing adjustment policies of economic liberalisation. They were criticised and the issue was readdressed by Galli (1990), in her article "Liberalisation is not enough".

Bissau: "rice coup" and informalization

As stated above, Bissau's population had started to grow at a rapid pace during the colonial war. Estimated at 25,000 in the mid-1960s, it grew to some 70,000 in 1970 (Davila, 1987:29). This rapid growth continued after independence. The 1979 census reported a population of 109,214 while the last census in 1991 counted 197,610 (RGPH, 1991). The population is currently estimated at around 300,000.

The available literature dealing with this period, with few exceptions, focuses on conditions in the countryside. Bissau is mainly addressed in its national context, and is portrayed as a consumer of a large share of the national resources, the beneficiary of state policies, and as an enclave increasingly distanced from the rural masses (see for example Augel, 1996). And indeed, investments were concentrated in Bissau, particularly in a few large industrial projects whose record of success turned out to be only modest. The urban-based public sector expanded with the nationalisation of all industrial and commercial enterprises. But the extreme concern of authors with the "urban bias" distracted them from looking into conditions within the city and into how different groups were faring during this period. Firstly, a share of the population consisted largely of low skilled migrants who had difficulty in finding a niche in the formal wage sector. Secondly, several authors report severe food shortages and chronically empty state stores in the city. This was seen as a result of the non-collaboration of rural producers, the heavy reliance on imports and aid for the supply of food coupled with a trade deficit and the lack of foreign exchange (Bigman, 1993:110; Funk, 1993:206-8; PCGB, 1991:120; Chabal, 1984:155, 8). Ration coupons were required for the purchase of imported goods in state stores and a large amount of time was spent queuing to acquire them. A parallel market in goods and exchange currency began to grow in the city (Tvedten, 1991:69). These developments in their general features were not exclusive to Bissau but have been reported for other countries in the region that followed the same orientation in the early post-independence period[75].

Different groups in the city were, however, affected differently by these trends and were positioned differently to cope with the scarcities. Some are even reported to have benefited from them[76]. For example, government employees are said to have had priority access to food rations. Having a public job or contacts with the Party and Party organisations thus facilitated access to basic items. Particularly high-ranking state officials who controlled the flow of imports and the employees in state stores are reported to have benefited from chronic food scarcities. They are said to have used nepotism and corruption and to have taken part in large-scale smuggling and hoarding of goods with the

---

[75] See for example O'Laughlin (1996) on urban Mozambique.

[76] See Funk (1993:209), Fernandes (1994), Bigman (1993:115) and Galli and Jones (1987:69).

goal of charging exorbitant prices in the informal market. Fernandes (1994) argues that basic goods, rarely to be found in official stores, circulated through "clientist networks" which sprang from the state and nationalised enterprises. As he puts it, "informal circulation laid the foundation for a private accumulation by the state bureaucracy" (p. 34). This group thus derived great power from their manipulation of the interface between official and parallel distribution systems.

The majority of the population in the city had no protection against these practices. According to Bigman (1993:115) large numbers were recent migrants lacking both access to public employment and state contacts. This large group had to find ways to survive outside the wage and state marketing systems (see Funk, 1993:209 and Handem, 1987). Informal trade in the city also grew as a response by this group, seemingly outside state control. The state's attitude to this increasing informal activity which escaped its control was negative. It fought the *djilas* as they were powerful competitors and directly inflicted losses on the state's coffers. Making strategic use of a socialist morality, the state denounced *djilas* as being immoral elements in society. Galli and Jones report that the *djilas* were, at times, imprisoned for long periods without trial, and accused of hoarding and speculation. The government also antagonised other groups that were trying to make a living from petty trade. According to Bigman (1993:114) women who travelled to rural areas to buy produce to sell in the city had to pass intra-national checkpoints set up by the government to control contraband. In Bissau, the police regularly harassed sellers in the market places and confiscated their produce, as I heard from several of my interviewees with long trading careers in the city. Funk (1993:208) states that even petty traders were accused of hoarding goods and became the scapegoats for the food shortages.

Contradictions grew out of the progressive centralisation of power and popular discontent with food shortages (Funk, 1993; Fernandes, 1994; Galli and Jones, 1987:93-4). When a faction split turned into a military coup in 1980, conditions were ripe for the widespread popular support for the new regime led by President Bernardino Vieira. The coup became known as "the rice coup", triggered by food shortages but reflecting deeper contradictions[77]. The coup changed the balance of power in favour of the military faction of the PAIGC. It also brought about a change in political discourse towards the reaffirmation of ethnic identities and traditional powers, which grew into an alliance between the latter and the President, eventually leading to a reinforcement of those powers[78]. Concerning the involvement of officials in informal economic practices, some were exposed and purged. But the change in regime did not put an end to these practices nor did it bring much change in the material conditions of the masses or, indeed, to the level of repression.

---

[77] For a discussion of the coup see Chabal (1984:158); Lopes (1987, 1988).

[78] See Fernandes (1993) and Koudawo (1996).

Informal systems of distribution were, on the other hand, gradually taking more and more space (as reported by Embaló, 1993:56-7)[79]. Bigman (1993: :114) states that in spite of harassment the *djilas* prospered. Petty traders resisted and increased in numbers, beyond the control of the government. Their creation of spaces of economic activity outside of, and in antagonism to, the state, could possibly contain elements of a disengagement from the state. Indeed, similar processes of expanding informality in other African urban areas have sometimes been interpreted in this way[80]. But the growth of informal activities seem not to be attributable solely to an autonomous move away from the state on the part of popular groups, judging from the above accounts of the involvement of state officials themselves. In addition, nothing has been written on the relations between those informal state agents and small informal actors, which is crucial in judging the degree of autonomy the latter enjoyed.

In any case, the above trends set in motion a process of informalization of livelihoods in the city, which, over time, were to attain the overwhelming dimensions that we witness today.

2.4 Conclusion

In this chapter I have tried to trace historical processes with a bearing on contemporary configurations of informality in Bissauan society, and the forces shaping informality in different political economic contexts. I began by high-lighting pre-colonial forms of political and economic organisation with relevance to the present. On the one hand, the early contours of a speciali-sation in trade activities along ethnic-gender lines emerged in this period and are still visible today in the city. On the other hand, I described some of the pre-colonial political and economic structures, hinting at both their moral and immoral elements in an attempt to avoid the common trap of romanticising history or the nature of African traditions as necessarily imbued with moral attributes. Elements of a pre-capitalist differentiation within local societies may assist our understanding of contemporary hierarchies and power relations among some groups in the study setting, as will become clear in chapter seven. Pre-capitalist structures, or at least their ruling groups, were reinforced, rather than weakened during this early phase of incorporation into a world economic system. In Bissau, the remarkable resistance that indigenous groups raised against alien interests that clashed with interests of their own delayed the entrenchment of colonial authority, the enforcement of modern law and

[79] The fact that the government forced journalists to lie about the date of arrival of the next shipment of rice, as reported by Galli and Jones (1987:98), indicates its vulnerability in the face of alternative economic agents.

[80] See for example Tripp (1987) on Dar-es-Salaam.

perpetuated the power of the unwritten rule into the 20th century in Bissau. The resilience that these ancient structures would show throughout history is relevant in that they continue to inform contemporary informal practices and to provide frames of reference for structuring obligations and exchanges in the supposedly unregulated realm of the informal, as will be seen in later chapters.

The period of effective colonial rule saw a formalization of some sets of relations by subjecting them to the written law of the state. But this was accompanied by a convenient relegation of other sets of relations to customary kinds of regulation. In this division of labour in regulation, indigenous elites often did not loose their grip over local populations, as traditional sets of rights were the only option available to many Guineans. This legal institutionalisation of a dual system of rights helped perpetuate informal sets of rights and modes of livelihood in both countryside and city. Capitalist accumulation itself relied to a considerable extent on informal relations, as exemplified by adapted customary relations in cash crop production and by the casual workers without contracts that trade firms hired in the city. These informal practices would persist into present times and possibly even expanded, as will be seen in the next chapter. While the above sets of informal relations may have been functional to colonial capitalism, there were other kinds of informal activities that seemed to work to the disadvantage of the colonial system. Here I am referring to the ways in which small scale traders and producers avoided state backed commercial channels.

The newly independent state set out to repress forms of social and economic organisation that evaded its reach. Small private traders and traditional elites became unpopular in official discourse. But as the state failed to back its modernising ideals with improved material and political conditions, these repressed groups with long historical traditions began to regain space. Economic activities reported as being autonomous from and antagonistic to the state increased, giving continuity to practices during the colonial time and to precolonial patterns of exchange in the sub-region. But the growth of these parallel or informal activities cannot be explained simply on the basis of the strategies of popular groups, as suggested by the disengagement perspective (see chapter one), given that other actors seem to have been involved in the drive for informalization. Developments in the early post-independence period highlight how this growing informality was partly predicated upon a degree of engagement or complicity with the state.

Indeed, in this history of social processes of production of informality a variety of agents have emerged. Indigenous elites have generally retained an important role in regulating activities at the local level. The modern state has varied in its attitude and policy towards traditional structures and activities lying outside its direct supervision. In some periods however, it has shaped these fields, directly or indirectly, in the ways mentioned above. Capital itself relied on a variety of informal relations for accumulation. Subordinate groups in Guinean society have through history made use of informal alternatives when formal and state policies worked to their disadvantage. This multiplicity of agents of informalization will also surface in the next chapter which deals with the contemporary period and will be returned to in the final chapter.

Informality has taken specific configurations in this particular place, as a result of the historical processes described here. Portuguese Guinea occupied a very marginal position in the Portuguese colonial empire and was kept in a state of extreme underdevelopment. The colony remained to a large extent an economy of extraction and on the eve of independence there was virtually no industry. After independence Guineans did not experience any significant improvement to their material conditions. In this context, informal relations have always occupied an important role in both production (for example in the production of cash crops) and social reproduction. Traditional structures and practices have survived into the contemporary period with considerable resilience. These specific forms of informality as they appear in Bissau differ from those in other parts of Africa where, for example, informal income activities have more recent origins (see Mhone, 1996 on Southern Africa), where a considerable proletarianization has taken place, and where land has been expropriated or commercialised. In several of the above respects, however, the Guinean experience relates to the West African context in which it is inserted.

3 Informality in contemporary Guinea-Bissau

This chapter addresses the contemporary process of deepening informalization in the context of various changes including the introduction of structural adjustment programs. While informalization was already under way prior to these changes, it has changed in scale and content. This chapter fills a double purpose. On the one hand, it describes the new political economic environment in which this extensive informalization has been taking place, thus providing the backdrop that will facilitate an understanding of the changing conditions and the efforts of the urban vulnerable as described in later chapters. On the other hand, it discusses the social processes of informalization since the mid-1980s and the contending but converging forces involved in the production of this extensive informal realm, in the light of theoretical perspectives laid down in chapter one. While some of these processes loom large in international space, they take particular forms at the local level. This chapter deals with these overarching aspects of the politics of informalization, while later chapters will address particular sets of social relations operating in concrete sub-sectors of the informal sphere.

The chapter will display the eventful decades of the 1980s and 1990s. During this period structural adjustment programs were implemented, the structure of exports changed with far reaching consequences for the urban economy, the first multiparty elections took place in 1994, a civil society emerged on the urban scene, and an armed conflict erupted with a major impact on the urban population.

The discussion relies on a mixture of sources, although this will not always have solved the dearth of city-wide data and the gaps and thinness of information on the wide societal issues addressed. Interviews with government officials and agents, persons involved in the process of policy reformulation and legislation for the informal sector, combined with the collection of policy documents and new legislation helped me build an idea of the interests at stake and the groups involved in that process. Key persons of at least ten civil organisations and associations were interviewed, which assisted in grasping the broad changes in the political environment in which informalization has taken place. Concerning the informalization of economic activities, particularly trade which is one of the most important in the city, beside some quantitative data from the survey, interviews were conducted throughout my fieldwork with more than sixty persons involved in trade. Most of these were small-scale operators but one tenth were wholesale and import-export firms. Several of these wholesalers became valuable key informants. The understanding that I gained through these methods is complemented by other studies, such as a comprehensive study of the largest market place in the city by Monteiro (2001) and others, Fernandes and Delgado's (1988) survey of women traders in the city, Crowley's (1993) study of the national informal economy for USAID and La Mettrie's (1992) study for FAO.

My assessment of how living conditions are changing in the city is based on a combination of my own data, such as the results of my household survey in two neighbourhoods of Bissau, Bandim and Cupilon[81], as well as other studies. Most of these are part of a series of studies on the socio-economic impacts of structural adjustment conducted by researchers at Instituto Nacional de Estudos e Pesquisa (INEP), few of which have an urban focus. These studies are often scarce on methodological details, but together they provide a more or less consensual view of changes in the city among this group of resident researchers. Finally, there is a series of yearly reports of the evolution of the macroeconomic performance of the country by Aguilar with others. It is based on this mixture of sources that I will try to depict contemporary processes of informalization in Bissauan society.

3.1 Structural adjustments and informalization of livelihoods

In 1983-84 an externally funded Economic Recovery Program and a Plan for Economic Stabilisation introduced some "liberalising measures" to Guinea-Bissau. These were succeeded by a more comprehensive adjustment strategy from 1986 (World Bank, 1987:2-9; Aguilar and Stenman, 1997:25-6). This was followed by a history of ups and downs in macroeconomic indicators, "government indiscipline" and suspended disbursements, as described by Aguilar and his co-authors, until the mid-1990s when "performance" is considered to have improved. At the time of writing, the country is continuing to implement adjustment programs, now under the label of "Poverty Reduction Strategy".

The adoption of adjustment measures marked a turning point towards a neo-liberal strategy of development under the "encouragement" of the donor community[82]. The "policy mix" proposed for Guinea-Bissau was similar to

---

[81] As stated earlier, Bandim and Cupilon represent two different milieus in terms of the ethnic composition, household structures and provisioning strategies and moderate aggregate differences in living standards. They can be said to represent conditions and patterns in a number of other neighbourhoods in the city and to cover some of the internal diversity contained within the city.

[82] This becomes clear from a review of their documents, studies and priorities for assistance (see for example ALC, 1994; Sobral, 1994; SSP, 1990; La Mettrie, 1992). They tended to reward "good performance" with financial assistance and to withdraw it when international financial institutions

that implemented in other countries undergoing adjustment (World Bank, 1987; Aguilar and Stenman, 1996; Costa et al., 1994). Market forces and private sector investment were to play the leading role in the generation of economic growth and the provision of services and the role of the government was to change from direct intervention in the economy and direct public investment towards facilitating private sector expansion. A rationalisation of the state was considered necessary in order to reduce the deficit of the public sector. In this logic, public enterprises ought to be privatised, phased-out and cost-recovery should be introduced. The size of the public investment program was to be reduced, with the social sectors occupying a secondary place. Down-sizing staff and freezing salaries in the public sector were also part of this expenditure-reducing strategy.

Changed urban living conditions

The high costs of adjustment measures for urban populations have been widely documented[83]. In Bissau, adjustment policies were to lead to successive waves of retrenchment in the public sector, long delays in salary payments (Aguilar and Stenman, 1996:28; 1997:33; Aguilar 1998:16) as well as to the withdrawal of subsidies on rice for public workers (interview F Reis 1995). More generally, the liberalisation of prices – including those of the staple food, rice, formerly protected by price controls – the gradual increase of import taxes on rice, repeated currency devaluations, a high average yearly inflation and repeated inflationary surges[84], have all been said to have contributed to an increase in the urban consumer prices for rice[85].

A study of the evolution of poverty lines in Bissau largely based on different surveys of household expenditure was conducted in 1986, 1991 and 1993 (Costa et al., 1994). The study concluded that living standards in Bissau improved slightly between 1983 and 1991 and declined between 1991 and 1993. The improvement reported for the first years is difficult to justify, given the changes mentioned above, some of which the authors also acknowledge. In addition, in spite of careful methodological considerations, the different methodologies and sample sizes of the different surveys on which the analysis

---

withheld disbursements, risking ruptures in the import of basic goods (Galli 1990:61; Aguilar and Stenman, 1997:26, 30; Aguilar and Zejan, 1992:27, 37; Aguilar and Stenman, 1993:17).

[83] For an early and influential work on the social costs of adjustment see Cornia et al (1987); for a recent review, see Zack-Williams (2000).

[84] Among the several causes for these inflationary surges identified by Aguilar and his co-authors was the great vulnerability of the country to external shocks such as the one that occurred in 1995 with a sharp increase in world prices for rice, when domestic consumer prices for this staple went up 41% (Aguilar and Stenman, 1996:11, 1997:60).

[85] Interviews with S Mané 1995, Quintas, 1995; Aguilar and Zejan (1992:33-4); World Bank (1987:14, 39); La Mettrie (1992:60).

is based (not to mention the omission of the size of the samples and of how they were selected in each case) awake some doubts about the validity of the longitudinal comparison. Among other researchers there seems to be a consensus that, while different groups were affected differently, a large share of the population of Bissau has been experiencing a persistent impoverishment since the beginning of the adjustment programs. They often illustrate this by referring to the increasing gap between monthly salaries among low rank public workers and the consumer price for a 50-kilo bag of imported rice[86]. And indeed, imported rice, the main staple food consumed in the city, has been reported to be particularly vulnerable to speculation (Aguilar and Zejan, 1992:33).

The ability of Bissauans to buy enough food seems to be below desirable levels. A survey on cereal consumption in urban areas published in 1991 and based on a sample of 439 households selected sytematically from different areas in Bissau found out that 55 per cent ate 1.5 meals or less per day (ICMU, 1991). From my own survey in 1995 covering some ten per cent of the population in two neighbourhoods (see chapter one for methods), two thirds of households in Bandim and slightly over half in Cupilon were eating one meal a day - "the 24-hour-shot". Almeida and Drame (1993:238-40), in their discussion of the effects of adjustment policies in the health sector, also report signs of worsening undernutrition, with a worrying situation in Bissau with 34 per cent of children under five suffering from severe or moderate undernutrition, based on a study carried out in 1991 by the Ministry of Education and with a comparison to earlier data from the mid-1980s[87]. They comment on women's increased burden with income earning activities particularly in the city and on their lack of time for attending to the needs of their children. Indeed, some commentators report on the appearance of street children in the city (Cardoso and Imbali, 1996:229; Pehrsson, 1991:50). Thus, while adjustment in Guinea-Bissau has been characterised as "one of the more positive experiences in Africa" (Aguilar and Stenman, 1997:32) – in terms of for example increases in gross domestic product (p. 25-34) – a considerable share of Bissauans have apparently seen their conditions worsen[88].

[86] For example, in the first half of the 1980's low rank public sector wages lied between 3,000 and 5,000 PG and a 50-kilo sack of rice cost 900 PG (personal communication by Jonina Einarsdottir, resident researcher at that time). It has been reported that in 1989, a bag of rice would absorb 91 per cent of those wages and in 1994 the minimum monthly salary was insufficient to purchase a bag of rice (Almeida and Drame, 1993:239; Paulo and Jao, 1996:264). See also Cardoso and Imbali (1996:224-6) and others in the INEP series on the effects of adjustment.

[87] See also PCGB (1991:120) on the nutritional problems among the children of urban wageworkers in Bissau.

[88] See for example Zack-Williams (2000:61) on persistent widespread poverty in Ghana, considered to be another "successful adjuster".

Revived informal and traditional forms of provisioning

Compounding worsening conditions on the income side, urban families have been facing a further decline in access to social services. This has often been the case in other countries undergoing adjustment, where cost-recovery programs, commercialisation and privatisation of urban services have been encouraged by international institutions (Aina 1997:425-6; Gibbon, 1996:779-80; Zack-Williams 2000:62). Some of the INEP studies on the effects of adjustment deal with the social sector, with data collection not being restricted to Bissau but usually concentrated there. They generally report a similar ideological shift in social policy. This has been reflected in the health sector in the adoption of the Bamako initiative. In the education sector in the mid-1980s the government accentuated selection mechanisms for example by setting age limits as part of its strategy of rationalisation of costs, forcing a large number of young people to give up their school careers (Monteiro and Martins, 1996::160, Monteiro e Silva, 1993:170-2, 216; Almeida and Drame, 1993:243). Together with impoverishment, this has been reported to have contributed to falling levels of attendance at secondary schools. These trends have placed Guinean youth at the crossroads of struggling for a place in the informal economy or becoming delinquent - the appearance of organised robbery gangs assaulting well-off residences and persons asserts that a share has chosen the latter option. Access by poor urban families to health and education has been particularly hurt by these measures and by the privatisation of services (largely unregulated in the case of health). These services are reported to have become unaffordable to the majority of the urban population (Almeida and Drame, 1993:252-3; Paulo and Jao, 1996:264, Monteiro and Martins, 1996:179, 181).

In the above context of changing conditions for social reproduction in the city and the country, there has been a turn to informal and traditional forms of service provision. This is not simply a matter of popular preference, as traditional healers have become part of national health policy since 1987, probably as part of a strategy of cutting public expenditure (Paulo and Jao, 1996:243-4; Almeida and Drame 1993:246-50). Others report a re-emergence of traditional forms of socialisation and education institutions such as Koranic schools while official schools in some areas have closed down[89]. This is to be seen in the context of a more general revival of traditional institutions and ethnic identities in the country. After the coup d'etat of 1980 the political discourse changed towards a valorisation of indigenous Guinean cultures and traditional powers in Guinea-Bissau, a trend that has been accentuated by the turn to

[89] See Monteiro and Martins (1996:181, 206) and Dias (1992). I also found this in some villages in the North and East of the country while conducting fieldwork for a study on girls' participation in official primary education.

multipartyism in the 1990s[90]. This is the local expression of wider contemporary trends of resurgence of indigenous cultures and forms of (social) organisation, religious and traditional practices and increasing social fragmentation along neo-traditionalist lines, with religious and ethnic movements becoming increasingly visible in the social stage in Africa (Bangura, 1994:821-2; Zack-Williams, 2000). Neo-traditional powers may have stakes in the new order of political legitimacy that international financial institutions have tried to orchestrate (Bangura and Gibbon, 1992:22).

Considering these trends, and as Bissauans can count with less and less assistance from the state, among other things in what concerns social security, one may expect reliance on traditional and other informal kinds of provisioning and assistance to be increasing. These alternative forms of provision and assistance are the central theme in later chapters where I discuss their social content and viability in the context of an adjustment-led development strategy.

Parallel to a heightened role for informal and traditional forms of social provision, some form of informal work has become the main way of earning a living in Bissau. It is to this informalization of income activities that I turn to now.

Changed "informal sector" policy

Policies of economic liberalisation have changed the conditions for making a living in the city. The liberalisation of the economy was set in motion through several revisions of legislation that introduced increasing degrees of liberalisation of domestic and external trade, of prices and decreasing institutional and legal barriers to private sector expansion. They were also intended to facilitate and simplify licensing of commercial establishments and legal procedures for access to commercial activity[91]. The number of registered private traders operating in the domestic market has increased (Gomes, 1993:137) but the expansion of unregistered enterprises has been dramatic in both the country and the city. The policies that were to be adopted towards this expanding informal economy are not made explicit in the strategy papers of the international financial institutions but in the documents of other donors to Guinea-Bissau[92]. These documents point to the important and expanding role

[90] See Fernandes (1993) and Achtinger (1993). See also Koudawo (1996) for a discussion of the revival of *manjuandades*, a traditional kind of social club, and their role in contemporary Guinean politics.

[91] See for example Decrees 22/86, 23/86, 28/88, 29/88; and Garcia, 1993; ALC, 1994 and Sobral, 1994 on the process of new revision of legislation and for the resulting laws see decrees 29/94, 30/94 and Texto final, 1995. Domestic groups participating in the latter revision were able to preserve for government the possibility of intervening in prices occasionally, to the disappointment of the foreign consultants, as becomes clear in Sobral (1994:10-11).

[92] See for example SSP (1990); La Mettrie (1992) for FAO; Sobral (1994) for USAID.

of small informal operators in the national economy and propose that support is given to them and that they be considered in national development. That support has yet to come.

In 1994 the USAID sponsored work meetings with participants from the government and the private sector to analyse and propose changes in commercial laws. It was decided that the 'informal sector' should not be repressed but supported (ALC, 1994). Interestingly, the Chamber of Commerce that represented the interests of large traders was a driving actor. The issue of *who* participates in processes of policy formulation is an important aspect to be considered (Mohan, 2000:84). This revision resulted in the enactment of new laws that aimed to simplify procedures for registration and to determine that hawkers and other small traders were to register their enterprises for a fee. One can suspect that behind this attempt at formalising such economic activities lay an ambition on the part of the state to tap this potential source of revenue - although marketers were already being charged a daily fee by municipal collectors. The large unregistered economy has been perceived as representing a hinder to the broadening of the very narrow domestic tax base of the Guinean state and it has therefore been explicitly targeted in adjustment fiscal policy (see Aguilar and Stenman, 1996:34). The simplification of the procedures was expected to encourage "informal" practitioners to register. Monteiro (2001:71) refer to a certain "tendency for formalisation" in Bandim market "as businesses flourish". However, the prohibitive size of the fee - of 300,000 Guinean Pesos[93] - has rendered this option impossible for all those who are living hand to mouth and those whose businesses have regressed rather than flourished (see chapter five). In addition, the benefits of registering are most probably perceived as limited by this group, given the small returns that municipal fees have had in the past (see chapter five). Not surprisingly, the majority of small traders seem to have remained unlicensed, judging from information from about sixty traders that I interviewed, most of them in this category – thus I will refer to them as 'informal' (see chapter one for a definition).

Thus, as has been often the case in other African countries (Gibbon, 1993::14), the main positive difference that structural adjustment policies have meant for informal operators has been the removal of restrictions on their operations. A change in official discourse has taken place, away from the condemnation of small traders in earlier years (see chapter two). However, it should be added that behind this discourse adopted under the pressure of donors, there is considerable deviation in practices. This aspect will be returned to and discussed in chapter five. In connection to this change in policy the conditions for survival in the city have been altered. Indeed, some form of informal work has become the main way of earning a living in Bissau.

[93] Decree 30/94, Boletim Oficial da República da Guiné-Bissau.

As I have discussed in chapter one, this pervasive informality has come to characterise the economies of most cities on the continent.

Informalization of income activities

In my household survey conducted in 1995 in the two neighbourhoods of Bandim and Cupilon I collected information pertaining to the nature of household income activities (type of employer, size of enterprise, contract, social benefits etc). More than half the households in both neighbourhoods depended mainly on income activities that one could label as ”informal” – these were activities where participants lacked a written work contract and social benefits such as paid sick leave and which offered irregular incomes. Almost one third of the respondents relied on a mixture of informal and formal work (where 'formal' is characterised by features opposed to the above). This broad category included working for other households or individuals as well as casual work for firms. But the greatest share made a living from self-employment, particularly in trade activities, which constituted over half of all income activities registered in my household survey (see chapter four for greater detail).

Indeed, given the historical dominance of commerce in the urban economy and the undeveloped nature of the industrial sector, trade is the economic sector that has probably suffered the greatest expansion in the context of policies of liberalisation (Embalo, 1993) – other expanding sectors being transport, construction and workshops (such as furniture, repair-shops). This is the sector from which both capital derives its accumulation and the less advantaged derive their incomes[94]. Cardoso and Imbali (1996:213) encapsulate this well in the expression: from the bottom to the top ”we are all *djilas*”, meaning that what matters today in Bissau is no longer having a waged employment or a school diploma, but knowing how to play the market game[95]. A variety of groups have come to use the informal economy as a way of dealing with the changes, albeit in different ways and for different purposes.

Among the studies carried out at INEP, Cardoso and Imbali (1996) and Duarte and Gomes (1996)[96] have in particular studied the impact of adjustment on urban families and on the 'informal sector' respectively. According to these studies, low ranking public workers, faced with a drastic decline in living standards had to find ways of supplementing their meagre public wages and

[94] Concerning the trade activities of the latter group, those reported by the surveyed households consisted overwhelmingly of tiny enterprises of one-person, operating at the survival level (see chapter four).

[95] See also Monteiro and Silva (1993:206) on the decreased importance of education in the social mobility of individuals.

[96] Cardoso and Imbali (1996) study is based on a study of 50 families in Bissau; Duarte and Gomes (1996) are not clear about the size of their sample.

retrenched workers had to devise new forms of earning a living, often by developing informal income activities in trade, transportation and workshops[97]. Some had the means and the contacts obtained in the public sector to facilitate a successful operation of informal activities. The rest of the urban population however, has had less access to those resources and the majority seems to have flocked into petty activities where both investments and returns are small or to sell their labour in the informal market (as discussed later in this chapter). These interpretations by Guinean researchers are in line with what has been observed in other crisis and adjustment situations in Africa[98]. The contraction of formal sector employment has usually fostered the engagement of large numbers of wageworkers and the middle-upper income classes in informal activities. While a restricted number have been able to set up flourishing enterprises often employing informal labour, the traditional occupants of the 'informal sector' have been reported to loose out in the increasing competition posed by new entrants. The result has been an increasing differentiation and polarisation within urban informal economies.

Participation in the informal economy has been structured not only by (former) occupational status but also along gender, ethnic and age lines. Two groups have regained visibility in small-scale trade activities in the country, both of them having historical skills in trade (see chapter two). These are the locally designated *djilas*, i.e. male itinerant traders usually belonging to Eastern ethnic groups (Fula, Mandinga, etc), and *bideiras*, referring to female traders, a large share of whom belong to coastal ethnic groups (Pepel, Mancanha, Manjaco, etc). They are part of a marketing system, described by Crowley (1993:14) and la Mettrie (1992:67-8), in which traders are linked by shifting and flexible ties into a decentralised and unbounded network that connects markets located in different areas. These include *lumos*, i.e. weekly rotating markets and cross-border trade. Traders keep a diversified portfolio of products that they carry in small quantities, allowing for a rapid turnover and for rapidly changing routes, markets and products. A share of these traders may hold trade licenses, but the relatively small size, the shifting nature and geographical looseness of their enterprises mean that they easily escape various taxes and fees as well as registration. Their numbers have been said to have expanded greatly with the liberalisation of the economy as official restrictions and many internal customs were lifted and transport opportunities improved[99].

---

[97] See also a study of small enterprises in Bissau by Ribeiro et al. (1990).

[98] See Nabuguzi, 1994:16 for Uganda; Lugalla (1997:437-443) for Dar-Es-Salaam; Meagher and Yunusa, 1991, 1996 for Zaria; (Zack-Williams 2000:67-8, Gibbon, 1993:14-5 and Bangura 94:802 for general reviews.

[99] Interestingly, itinerant actors have been considered a nuisance for merchant capital, as it transpires from a document by the Chamber of Commerce (Parecer, 1995). On this issue, see also: La Mettrie (1992:67-8) and Crowley (1993:22-8).

Small-scale trade in the city shows signs of this gender-ethnic specialisation found at the national level - although women of Eastern groups and the younger male generation of coastal groups also participate[100]. From the second half of the 1980s onwards, young men have migrated in large numbers from the Eastern province and have become numerous in trade activities in the city, principally in the sale of imported foodstuffs and rice. Some have built successful trade careers often by engaging in vertical business networks headed by import-export firms[101]. The participation of women in general in market activities has been reported to have intensified under structural adjustment in studies of informal activities in Bissau (Gomes and Duarte, 1996:98, 100; Delgado, 1989:15). This echoes trends in other cities undergoing adjustment, usually related to women's increased responsibility of compensating for declining incomes in the household as well as social services (Lugalla, 1997:443; Sparr, 1994; Daines and Seddon, 1991; Manuh, 1994; Dennis, 1991; Brand. et al, 1995). Among women from coastal groups who are more frequently engaged in the sale of local produce, I found few flourishing businesses[102] – on the contrary, many operate at a survivalist level and others have seen their conditions deteriorate, as I will discuss in chapter five. The ethnic segmentation, and possibly differentiation, that is visible in the market in Bissau can be seen as the local version of trends in Africa towards new or increasing inequalities between ethnic groups in the context of adjustment[103].

The numbers of informal operators in the city has also been swelled by the youth that face poor prospects of securing a wage job in the formal sector upon completion of their studies. This has been compounded by the introduction of selective measures in the education sector and by the economic hardships imposed by adjustment (Cardoso and Imbali, 1996:235; Duarte e Gomes, 1996:98-100; Monteiro e Silva, 1993:216, 172). Even children are increasingly required to earn an income. This has not been studied for Bissau but is very visible in the city. It is also part of a more general trend under conditions of adjustment and crisis (Zack-Williams, 2000; Bangura, 1994). To summarise this section, it can be stated that a variety of groups have used the informal

[100] This is a popular perception but has also surfaced in surveys of urban traders by Monteiro (2001) and Delgado (1989:9). The proportions of different groups vary however for different market places, with different positions in the hierarchy of market places in the city.

[101] This was the case of a couple of the wholesalers whose trade histories I collected. See also Monteiro (2001:28-30) and Crowley (1993:31).

[102] See the survey based studies by Delgado (1989:15), Delgado et al (1989:2) and Monteiro (2001:32-3, 51) on the low literacy skills of women traders comparing to male ones.

[103] See for example Macharia (1997) for Harare and Nairobi and Meagher and Yunusa (1996) for Zaria. See also Bangura (1994) and Zack-Williams (2000). In the Guinean context, ethnic based differentiation may be perceived as "new" divisions, given the facts and myths concerning the national unity, probably related to the long armed struggle against the colonial power, the insistence of Amilcar Cabral, its leader, on a Guinean identity rather than ethnic ones and later the political discourse subsuming ethnic divisions to the contradiction between Creoles with Capeverdean origin and "genuine" Guineans.

economy to adapt to deteriorating urban conditions. From this, a differentiation among informal actors can be expected, given the different skills, resources and social position that different groups had on their departure to explore the informal sphere.

Informal actors remap the city

In the context of the above trends, market places in Bissau have experienced a great expansion with economic liberalisation. According to my interviews with various officials, formerly existing markets have grown and many new markets have appeared. Most of them are spontaneous markets, i.e. they are unplanned and the traders themselves have built their structures, often of a temporary nature. Of the approximately twenty market places existing in Bissau in the first half of the 1990s, most of them were of this kind and had never benefited from any construction or provision of basic services by the municipal authorities, according to officials who had an overview of the market places in the city. These suburban markets – as is the case of Caracol market in the studied neighbourhood presented in chapter four - sell mainly basic goods such as food, and particularly low cost food, i.e. the cheapest types of fresh fish and vegetables. Imported food stuffs are only sold in small quantities with higher value foods such as meat, eggs and fruit present in only negligible amounts (Lourenço-Lindell, 1993:63).

Modern food outlets in the city centre such as super- and mini-markets and other licensed shops sell mainly imported and thus expensive goods. Several of them were forced to closed down because of the impoverishment of a large share of the urban population which has reduced demand for their products. However, one should add that, by selling right outside their doors, small informal operators pose competition to formal outlets and challenge both shop owners and municipal regulations. Informal market places, particularly of the spontaneous variety, are the ones offering the low quality, cheap and portioned goods that are in greatest demand. In fact, while spontaneous markets and commercial activity mushroom in the suburbs, the historical commercial centre near the port, once the heart of the city, has decayed. The locus of commercial activity in the city has shifted to the periphery of the city. The few remaining formal shops in the centre cater for a minority of the urban population, as does the oldest market place in the city, Central Market, located in the centre. This market, where the whole population of Bissau once came to shop on a daily basis, has now become known as "the cooperants' market". It sells for example handicraft goods, high quality fish and expensive fruits. It is interesting to note that in contrast to the crowded Bandim market, Central Market had in 1995 vacant selling places, according to a municipal official.

In addition, the suburban population (which in Bissau means residents beyond one kilometre from the historical centre) has less and less motivation to travel to the city centre: not only are the goods being sold there unaffordable, but they also have little use for the services that formal institutions have to offer. These include the banks that offer much reduced services to the general public, the governmental and municipal institutions in which normal citizens have little confidence for solving their problems and the decaying and unaffordable health services. Apart from the occasional activity at the port when a ship arrives and groups of men gather in the hope of getting work for the day, compared to the liveliness of the suburbs, the city centre appears to languish along with the waters of the Geba River.

One can say that the informalization of the urban economy has drastically changed the landscape of the city. Small informal actors have been actively engaged in this process. With their mobility they create new agglomerations of traders and build new markets where loci of demand emerge. These markets are the result of tens of thousands of unprivileged urbanites taking matters into their own hands and in this way coming out of invisibility in the city. But this remapped urban landscape is as much a reflection of their agency and creativity as it is of their marginalization from more profitable scales of business. These spaces of informality contain both instances of relative autonomy as well as deepening subordination. This is because the "enabling environment" created by adjustment policies enabled new sources of exploitation and new forms of exclusion to arise or intensify. Indeed, other powerful actors have inscribed their imprint on the informalization process, namely the state and capital.

3.2 State and capital adjust[104]

There is a consensus among observers of Guinean adjustment that a minority group, composed mainly of large merchants and high ranking state officials, has greatly benefited from changes in the political economic environment[105]. I will briefly discuss the ways that state and capital have responded to new

[104] The 'state' in Guinea - referring here to its attributes as prior to the 1999 change of regime - is a highly centralised institution. Multi-ethnic in discourse, the state has sought part of its legitimacy with neo-traditional power holders and, after economic liberalisation, with private capital. The first multi-party elections took place in 1994. To the present, elections for local government have not occurred. In what concerns 'capital' in Guinea-Bissau, it has been composed of both private and public enterprises during the adjustment period. For its largest share it consists of merchant capital, deriving accumulation from the sphere of trade in international commodities. It has been historically organised as a hierarchical marketing system, which continues to characterise to some extent large-scale trade in specific import-export products, particularly cashew nuts and imported rice (see La Mettrie, 1992 and Crowley, 1993 for a description of these firms).

[105] See particularly Galli (1990), Imbali and Cardoso (1996), Cardoso (1994), Gomes (1993), Cardoso and Imbali (1993), Handem (1987), Fernandes (1994), La Mettrie (1992).

challenges and opportunities derived from adjustment policies and changes in international demand. This is of relevance in explaining the conditions of disadvantaged urbanites and their informal livelihoods.

One of the changes mentioned above pertains to the rise of the cashew economy. In the early 1980s, responding to a continuous fall in world prices for groundnuts, a new cash crop, cashew nuts, began to be exported by the state trade enterprise which was later joined by private operators. Export volumes increased rapidly (Bigman, 1993:115; Aguilar 1998:34). The major part of the cash crop is supplied by small producers (Galli, 1990:64, Aguilar and Zejan, 1994:99, A/Z92:30-1) who exchange it with traders for imported rice or money. These traders are connected to import-export firms who import rice from Asian countries to be bartered at the farm gate and export the cashew nuts to countries such as India for processing[106]. These firms benefit greatly from the substantial differences in the value of the two products on international markets.

Although these growing exports may have impacted positively on macroeconomic indicators (Aguilar, 1998:34), the cashew-rice economy has discouraged rice production in the country (Gomes, 1993:143) and has acted to accentuate dependency for food imports[107]. The close connection between the two commodities has led to a disinterest in importing rice outside of the cashew season[108]. The urban population, which is particularly dependent on rice imports, has had to put up with sharp fluctuations in the availability of rice and with speculation of rice prices. In addition, a very significant share of urban dwellers has become dependent for their incomes on informal activities that are related to the cashew-rice nexus. They have, however, been drawn into such activities in a subordinate manner, as will be discussed below. At the same time, a few mostly urban-based merchants and government officials have enriched themselves in this business. Thus Bissau, through which these international commodities are channelled, has come to harbour visible and sharp contradictions.

According to several researchers, new financial resources that became available with adjustment such as credits intended for export agriculture and for the import of basic goods, were seized by the same small group, i.e. private importers, including high rank officials, and the (partly privatised) state

[106] See Crowley (1993) for a detailed study of marketing systems in Guinea-Bissau, including that of cashew. Monetary exchanges seem however to be becoming more common nowadays, according to my key informants in Bissau as well as to personal communication by R. Aguilar in 2000.

[107] Rice surpluses are still being produced in the southern regions. Indeed, during the colonial period the country used to export rice.

[108] Volumes of rice imports reflect more the size of the cashew harvest on a single year than the domestic estimated needs. Cross-border re-exportation of imported rice to the neighbouring countries also contributed to the unreasonably high quantities of rice imported.

marketing agency, Armazéns do Povo[109]. This group prospered from unpaid loans (and the related cashew-rice trade) while small-scale informal activities were excluded from these credits. The same researchers agree that the influence of the state over the economy has not waned[110]. Rather, according to Fernandes (1994), formerly clandestine private accumulation by bureaucrats (of the sort mentioned in chapter two) simply continued. The state and state actors continued to participate in external trade in strategic products such as rice and cashew (la Mettrie, 1992:59) and continued to exert a degree of control over private trade, both domestic and external[111]. Several commentators argue that some of this influence was exerted through an alliance that developed between private actors and public officials, enterprises and institutions[112]. This alliance would grant selected private firms access to trade licenses, foreign currency and adjustment credits, as well as impunity upon their default on repayments[113]. It also encouraged the state to turn a blind eye to their avoidance of fiscal obligations, side-stepping of legal procedures and circumvention of customs controls, as has been reported by Crowley (1993:1) and Dias (1993:217)[114]. The state withdrew from protecting urban consumers from speculation in prices of imported rice by not enforcing its orders to merchants and by gradually ceasing to make use of its legal prerogative to occasionally set a price ceiling[115]. The state has also showed little concern for the exploitative conditions which capital imposes on several groups of urban dwellers, as I will discuss in the next section. The stage was set for deepening

---

[109] See on this issue: Galli (1990), Imbali and Cardoso (1996), Cardoso (1994), Gomes (1993), Cardoso and Imbali (1993), Handem (1987), Fernandes (1994), La Mettrie (1992). La Mettrie (1992:62) describes a highly concentrated distribution of these credits, based on data supplied by the National Bank of Credit, with 40 per cent of the funds being allocated to only three beneficiaries, 75 per cent to 23 while the remaining 1271 received 25 per cent.

[110] This has also been found in other adjusting countries in Africa: Gibbon (1993:12); Mohan (2000:90); Nabuguzi (1994:10); Bangura and Gibbon (1992:16-7, 22, 25).

[111] At the domestic level, internal customs persisted here and there for many years, as I myself witnessed in 1995.

[112] Galli (1990:58-60), Cardoso (1994), Gomes (1993:137) and Cardoso and Imbali (1993:35); La Mettrie (1992:59); SSP (1990:11). See also Monteiro (2001), who refer to businesses in Bandim market place owned by "invisible owners", whom they believe are persons working at the central and local governments who have found partners to be the façade of their businesses. This corresponds to popular perceptions.

[113] For example, a middle-rank official of the Ministry of Commerce in 1995 declared to me that import authorisations and credit were given for importing rice with no later inspection of whether the corresponding rice did was imported.

[114] Similar trends have been reported for West and other parts of Africa, where import firms, defaulting on legal obligations and loans but enjoying the political protection of the state, have been in a good position to benefit from the opportunities created by trade liberalisation (Gibbon, 1996: 767-9, 776-7, 781; 1993: 23; Nabuguzi, 1994:15-20; Dias, 222-3; Hashim and Meagher, 1999:107; McGaffey and Bazenguissa-Ganga, 1999:179, 187).

[115] Based on interviews with: F. Sanhá, Consumer Association, 1999; F. Reis, Ministry of Commerce, 1995; R. Dias, Chamber of Commerce, 1995; Braulio Lima, director board of the partly state owned trade enterprise Armazéns do Povo, 1995; key informant interviews in 1995 and 1999.

contradictions in the Guinean society, a skewed distribution of economic opportunities and increasing social polarisation between those who benefited from the reforms and the rest of the population that did not.

Thus merchant capital seems to have been in a good position to benefit from opportunities opened by economic liberalisation. Indeed, while Guinea-Bissau has been unable to attract investments by global capital[116], a problem it shares with most African countries in this global age, the country and its capital city seem to have become more deeply integrated into business networks in the sub region[117]. This is manifest in the increasingly visible presence in Bissau of merchants and traders originating from the neighbouring countries[118]. These cross border networks are said to have revived and to have become important in strategies of accumulation in the sub region in the wake of economic liberalisation. Often linked to global markets, these networks also make use of ancient trade routes and religious solidarities such as Islam (see chapter two on these historical patterns)[119]. The firms involved have been reported to often evade fiscal duties and other legal precepts (Gibbon, 1996: :776-7; McGaffey and B-Ganga, 1999:179, 187), which means they may be classified as "informal" (see my definition in chapter one).

Indeed, while large trade enterprises operating in Guinea are usually referred to as belonging to the "formal sector" since they involve a degree of licensing, tax payment and contacts with the bureaucracy, a share of their operations is run informally. Two of my interviewees – one, a representative of the Chamber of Commerce and the other a member of the private-public enterprise Armazéns do Povo, complained that the costs of formality – referring to taxes, customs, expensive bank credit, overvalued official exchange rate and bribes – were just too high and the advantages too small. In addition, in one of the documents of the Chamber (Parecer, 1995) it is evident that Guinean capital is facing competition from both foreign merchants and itinerant traders. It is in this context that merchant capital seems to be making increasing use of informal strategies for accumulation in order to deal with the new challenges and opportunities posed by economic liberalisation. I will dwell for a moment on these strategies, particularly those that have implications for the conditions of disadvantaged groups in the city.

---

[116] On the various causes of this, for the Guinean case, see: SSP (1990:26); Dias (1992:4); la Mettrie (1992:60); Aguilar and Stenman (1996:37).

[117] This was probably facilitated by Guinea-Bissau becoming a member of the UMOA (Union Monetaire de l'Ouest d'Afrique) in 1997. See Dias (1993), for one of the rare analyses of dynamics in the sub region from a Guinean perspective. See also La Mettrie (1992:66).

[118] Monteiro (2001) for example report the high number of foreign traders and merchants in Bandim market and describe briefly the networks that facilitate this immigration.

[119] On trends of intensified cross border trade in West and other parts of Africa, see: Gibbon (1996:768-75); Mbembe (2000:283); MacGaffey and Bazenguissa-Ganga (1999:180-1); Hashim and Meagher (1999:99-100).

Informalization as accumulation strategy

Based on what I learned from a small number of interviews with members of merchant firms - two import-export firms and six rice wholesalers – as well as on a couple of studies of the Guinean trade sector (Crowley, 1993 and La Mettrie, 1992), informal contracts and relations of clientelism pervade the hierarchical networks linking import-export firms, middlemen and wholesalers. Such personal contracts often entailed access to capital and merchandise but also subordination to the patron[120]. These vertical networks dominating the growth sector of the Guinean economy seem to be quite exclusionist, often along kinship, ethnic and religious lines, with Islamized groups being particularly well represented[121]. I repeatedly heard frustrated remarks about the great difficulties of penetrating these networks. "I want to get into the rice business, Y and X also want to. But *who* is going to help us?", one said. This may be creating an ethnic (and gender) differentiation in the urban commodity market and one that has probably evolved from age-old ethnic-gender specialisations in trade (see chapter two).

Other informal relations being used by merchant capital relate to a wide infrastructure of informal workers and operators that facilitates accumulation by large firms. On the production side, advancing credit to small producers in the form of consumer goods in exchange for cash crops, at exploitative rates, has been a historical feature of capitalist accumulation in the country (Crowley, 1993:14). In addition, and with the growth of the cashew economy, large numbers of urban women leave for the rural areas during the cashew season to work on the farms of relatives or non-relatives[122]. They work under a variety of agreements but based on the understanding I gained through conversations with many women engaging in these activities, they work under conditions that seem to be largely unregulated by the state. The consequence of this is to perpetuate or intensify petty commodity relations in the countryside, which has been historically important in the country and other parts of West Africa (Bernstein, 1991).

Informal outlets have become important channel through which merchant capital markets its products[123]. Gomes (1993:141) refers to merchants who imported goods with adjustment loans and then resold them on the "parallel

[120] A group of importers enjoying privileged access to formal financial institutions and government bureaucracy has been said to dominate the informal financial market in Bissau, making most other entrepreneurs dependent on them for credit (Monteiro, 2001).

[121] For reflections on similar contemporary trends in African cities and societies, see Simone (1999:81, 86) and Bangura (1994:804).

[122] My survey in Bandim in 1995 revealed that in almost 40 per cent of the households this was practised.

[123] By 'informal' outlets I mean those outlets where activities do not comply fully with state legislation. For example, small market traders in Bissau, while paying their fees to municipal collectors, often lack a license which is required by law. Therefore, I will treat market places generally as 'informal outlets'.

market". According to Crowley (1993:22), since liberalisation merchants have used *djilas* to penetrate the more remote areas of the country. Similarly, in the city, large trading firms have opened warehouses in the unplanned market places that emerged around the city in the context of liberalisation and in this way have become the suppliers of a myriad number of small informal retailers (dealing particularly in rice). This constitutes perhaps a more recent informal strategy by capital, in that in former periods only stores could legally retail rice in the city. The nature of the informal relations that have developed between suppliers and small retailers will be explored in chapter five. There I will also discuss the conditions of these small retailers, as these conditions are part of a driving question in the study, i.e., how informal livelihoods are faring in the context of economic liberalisation and adjustment.

Merchant capital in Guinea-Bissau seems to increasingly make use of informal labour. This has been facilitated by the limited concern of the state in protecting workers and the priority given to creating an "enabling environment" for private business. This echoes trends on the continent and beyond of a casualisation of the workforce, abandonment of labour legislation and informalization of work relations among some private industries in a context of adjustment, heightened competition and changing relations of international dependency (Bangura, 1994; Nabuguzi, 1994; Gibbon, 1995; Meagher and Yunusa, 1991). In Bissau, trade firms employ permanent workers at their warehouses and shops although, as some have affirmed, waged permanent labour is used to a limited extent and is often recruited on the basis of kin and friendship ties[124].

A larger category of labour being used by trading firms consists of day labourers that work under conditions that are unprotected by the law. This is a labour category that has had a historical presence in the city, judging from Amilcar Cabral's (1974) description of workers without contracts in the colonial period (see chapter two). During my fieldwork I came across a large number of men who depended on this kind of work and discussed with some of them (and with an employer) the conditions of casual workers. Today, firms contract unskilled workers for a short period to perform tasks such as loading and unloading of ships and trucks. Day workers are often organised into groups with a headman who cultivates contacts with employers and negotiates with them the terms of the collective work agreement. These are often unwritten agreements that simply stipulate how much payment workers may expect, often by the day or by the task. According to my interviewees, these agreements do not involve any conditions concerning taxes or social security. As such, these workers cannot expect any compensation either from their employers or the state for periods without work or for accidents occurring on the job. When the task is terminated and payment has been made, no further

[124] See Monteiro (2001), Ribeiro et al (1993), Cardoso and Imbali, (1996:219).

obligations exist between the parties. The advantages for employers are obvious. Casual workers are hired only when and if they are needed and periods of slack trade in international commodities are bound to affect them negatively. In this way, the costs of seasonality and uncertainty in the economy, and possibly of heightened competition among firms, are passed on to workers and their families[125].

Though historically important, the extent and the conditions of day workers seem to be changing. Although hard data is lacking, it would seem that the importance of this form of labour has increased in Bissau in the last decade or so. This can be deduced from the expansion of the cashew-rice trade, the increased number of import-export firms following economic liberalisation and the increasing numbers of people that have been forced into dependence on casual work by retrenchment policies but also by a large influx of migrants in a context of formal sector contraction[126]. The expanding number of casual workers has most probably increased competition among them for casual jobs with implications for the irregularity and size of their incomes (see chapter six). In addition, this group seems to be particularly exposed to ruthless exploitation because their informal work relations with capital differ greatly from those that are rooted in long-standing kinship or other affinities and that are regulated by shared cultural codes, particularly considering the absence of enforced universal work codes[127]. In this light, social networks linking casual workers with their headmen and large enterprises could be interpreted as playing a role in securing a large supply of workers for firms[128]. But casual workers have also developed horizontal networks of assistance among themselves for buffering against difficult work conditions. These latter networks will be described in chapter six, as well as how they are faring in the current context.

In sum, merchant capital operating in Guinea-Bissau seems to have intensified its use of informal strategies in the context of economic liberalisation. This has actively contributed to a deepening informalization of the urban economy by drawing increasing numbers of urban dwellers into informal labour relations and international commodity circuits. Capital has been assisted in its ascension by protection from the state and by its privileged position to manipulate and straddle the formal-informal interface. These trends are

[125] Within families, these costs tend to be further passed on to women, as I suggest in chapter seven.

[126] See Zack-Williams (2000:60) on how daily-wage work is where a share of the victims of adjustment policies are often found, referring to those who have been "structured out of employment".

[127] It is interesting however to note how official local judicial institutions, the called Courts for Small Causes created in 1994, have gone "informal" to a certain extent, to meet the requirements of increasingly informalised labour contracts: they consider oral contracts as legally binding, as long as one witness was present (interview with judge Filomeno T. P. Veiga, 1999).

[128] See Meagher (1995) on the role of social networks in the control of labour.

an important component of the contemporary politics of informalization of livelihoods in the study setting and beyond.

3.3 Deepening contradictions and growing associational life

In this section I will briefly consider the political context in which the informalization of livelihoods has taken place, as this is part and parcel of the evolving material entitlements of popular classes and the viability of their livelihoods. In particular I will present some of the political and organisational responses of Bissauans to the challenges of declining living conditions. I rely on the accounts of other observers of the democratisation process in Guinea-Bissau as well as on my own interviews in 1999 with representatives of about ten associations, a couple of them holding important positions in civil society and having a general view over the aggregate of registered groups[129].

The above discussion has revealed the increasing inequalities and contradictions in Bissauan society. Merchant capital and state actors have benefited greatly in the political economic environment of adjustment while a large share of the urban population is said to have seen their material conditions deteriorate. In addition, Guinean social scientists have argued that the liberalisation of the economy under the conditions described above have only led to heightened corruption and nepotism on the part of the Guinean state and a centralisation of power in the person of the president (Fernandes, 1994; Cardoso, 1994). In spite of the first multiparty elections in 1994 and other changes towards democratisation, government attempts at repressing protest and autonomous initiatives did not cease[130]. The interpretations of the above writers run against views that see adjustment policies as conducive to democracy (see Iheduru, 1999 for a recent example) and join a broader critique exposing how adjustment programs have often enhanced political repression and attempts at delegitimizing popular resistance, namely by a manipulation of terms such as "civil society", "empowerment" and "governance" (Bangura, 1992:68-79; Beckman, 1992:94-105; Mohan, 2000; Brown, 2000).

These developments have led to growing opposition and dissent, even within the leading Party, PAIGC. The adjustment period has witnessed an abundant record of political crises, including several accusations of attempted coups, the execution of dissident high officials in 1986, and the imprisonment

[129] The groups/persons contacted included, among others: Mr. Pinto Marques, vice-president of the Guinean League for Human Rights; Mr. Fernando Saldanha, president of the Forum of Non-Governmental Organisations and vice-president of the National Movement of Civil Society; representatives of the Association of Consumers, of Projects of the Evangelical Church of Guinea-Bissau, of the National Association of Christian Youth, and of the Association of Youth of Bandim. For more detail, see List of Interviews.

[130] Based on my own interviews with leaders of civil organisations in 1999. On the process of democratisation in Guinea-Bissau, see Cardoso (1994) and Rudebeck (1997 and 2001).

and murder of politically influential persons (Aguilar and Stenman, 1993:1; Aguilar and Stenman, 1997:2; Aguilar, 1998:1). The biggest crisis turned into an armed conflict in 1998, triggered by mutual accusations between the ex-President and a high-ranking military official about illegal trade in weapons with the separatist movement in Casamance, Southern Senegal. The conflict put Bissau under siege for a year until the rebel troops finally took over the city in May 1999 with the widespread support of the urban population who were hungry for change[131]. In the aftermath of the war there was intense political activity and those that had enriched themselves during liberalisation became targets of criticism by the transitory government. Large merchants were threatened to pay back their immense adjustment loans or their assets would be confiscated. The president of the Chamber of Commerce, an organisation representing the interests of this group, resigned. A price ceiling for rice was announced and enforced for the first time in several years. Although popular expectations were high at that time, the state of high political insecurity was far from over as indeed would soon become apparent[132].

But the period of adjustment has also witnessed a series of popular responses to threatened political rights and material conditions. As in other cities undergoing adjustment, organised protests by students, teachers and other public workers became frequent from 1991 onwards. Trade unions, both new and old, now autonomous from the tutelage of the PAIGC, became active in organising such large-scale protests, while the mass organisations of the Party went into decline[133]. In fact since the 1990s there has been an upsurge of organisations and associations in civil society that lacks precedent in the local history and that resonates similar trends in much of urban African[134]. The number of non-governmental organisations (NGOs), foreign and domestic, has increased rapidly (interview with F Saldanha, 1999) as available funding has increased. Mr. Saldanha who holds a key position in the NGO environment, called these organisations "*Contra*-Governmental Organisations" to emphasise the "extremely hostile" relations between them and the government[135].

A number of organisations have been engaged in resistance to state policies and repression. A major actor in this field has been the Guinean League for Human Rights that was formed in 1991. According to Mr. Pinto Marques, one of its vice-presidents who I interviewed in 1999, the League pressed the

---

[131] See Gomes (1998) and Rudebeck (2001) for a thorough account of the conflict.

[132] These post-war events are based on my observations in Bissau, where I arrived some two weeks after the end of the conflict. See Rudebeck (2001) for later political developments.

[133] Based on my own interviews and on the reports by Aguilar and Stenman (1993:1), Aguilar and Stenman (1997:2) and Aguilar (1998:1).

[134] On these broad trends, see Aina (1997) and Tostensen, Tvedten and Vaa (2001). See Koudawo (1996) and Rudebeck (2001) on a discussion of the emergence of a civil society in Guinea-Bissau.

[135] On these antagonistic relations in Guinea-Bissau, see Koudawo (1996), though he shows concerns about these NGOs being new sites of accumulation. For a more extreme scepticism on the motives behind NGOs in Africa, see Chabal and Daloz (1999).

government for transparency and respect of civil rights, while its leaders were targets of political violence. Other smaller pressure groups have emerged such as the Association of Consumers of Goods and Services. According to its president and internal documents, concerns include the low level of purchasing power of the population and the association tries to press for governmental control of prices of basic items (ACOBES, 1997; interview with Mr. Sanhá, 1999).

During the war crisis of 1998-9 when popular antagonism towards the regime reached new heights, a broad national organisation was formed – the National Movement of the Civil Society for Peace, Democracy and Development – which aimed to congregate the dispersed smaller groups. The Movement grew rapidly and played a key role in organising public marches and pressing for reconciliation[136]. It gathered a wide range of groups with a variety of concerns – such as human rights, environmental issues, economic development, the interests of professional groups – with a varying geographical anchorage – ranging from those with international links to those restricted to home areas and urban neighbourhoods. The Movement included a considerable number of youth groups and a few women's organisations and encompassed groups from across the religious spectrum. This gathering of very disparate and particularistic purposes is interesting at a time when resistance has been seen as generally tending to retreat into "localisms" (Mohan, 2000: :94; Bangura, 1994). It may generate the kinds of linkages that some have considered indispensable in the articulation of an alternative to hegemonic national and international forces determining local conditions (Brown, 2000: :182; Beckman, 1992:99).

Surely, as usually is the case, not all groups in this emerging "civil society" will necessarily be oriented towards the pursuit of social justice, democracy and the protection of unprivileged groups. Take for example the Chamber of Commerce, Industry and Agriculture – an organisation that existed under another designation during the colonial period, was suppressed after independence and recreated in 1986-7[137]. This organisation represents the interests of a dominant group in society, namely those of merchant capital, which developed a relation of complicity with the state in the context of adjustment and was a major beneficiary of market reforms. It was also a privileged partner of dialogue with the donors and the government in the process of reformulation of economic policy, as mentioned earlier in the chapter. Not surprisingly, this type of organisation tends to rank high in the neoliberal conception of "civil society" and its attempt at creating a pro-adjustment political environment

---

[136] Based on my own interviews with Mr. P Marques and Mr. F Saldanha in 1999 and the Movement's internal document (MNSC, 1998). See also Rudebeck, 2001:31.

[137] My judgements about this organisation are based on one of its internal documents (Parecer, 1995), other documents referring to it as well as interviews with one of its representatives, Mr R Dias, 1995, and with a few merchants.

(Beckman, 1992:101). The group represented by the Chamber, with obvious stakes in the (pre-armed conflict) political-economic order has interests potentially antagonistic to those of groups resisting that same order.

The list of collective efforts by Bissauans does not end here. Beyond the above more formalised segment of ”civil society” (i.e. registered groups) there is a universe of less visible, more informal kinds of arrangements linking individuals together, which seem be more common among women and the poor. These deserve particular attention in environments where there is little popular engagement in formal associations. Small informal operators in general have had a reputation of usually being poorly organised collectively (Sanyal, 1991), which is partly confirmed by the low participation of such actors in registered associations in Bissau (Monteiro, 2001). This however, does not necessarily mean a realm of atomised actors, as will become clear in later chapters. In certain neighbourhoods as Bandim, seemingly poorly endowed with associational life in a formal sense, organised social activity of a more informal kind provides the framework for daily interactions. The rest of the thesis focuses on these informal collective efforts, which will surface throughout the book in their various guises. In the study setting these consist of, among others, rotating savings groups, income redistribution groups, neighbourhood religious congregations, and loose-knit social networks (based on primordial ties, friendship or business interests).

They facilitate physical existence in the city by providing urban dwellers with a degree of welfare and access to livelihood resources. While their political potential is less obvious than that of highly visible and politicised forms of organisation, some have argued that they are not necessarily without political consequences and may embody everyday forms of resistance to unfavourable impositions from the top, which should not be attributed a lesser status than open protest as a form of struggle, and may at times grow into organised forms of action (Daines and Seddon, 1991). But as with the more formal components of ”civil society”, this is not a universe to be imputed with inherent virtuous attributes of politically progressive, democratic, harmonious, as will unravel throughout this thesis.

3.4 Conclusion

This chapter has described processes of informalization in the context of structural adjustment policies. On the one hand, a shift in official policy towards the “informal sector” took place under the ”guidance” of international institutions and donors and gave further impetus to trends that were already under way prior to adjustment. The groups of small traders that resisted the restrictive policies of the colonial and early post-independence state expanded greatly with the liberalisation of the economy. On the other hand, the hardships imposed by adjustment and the contraction of the public sector would swell the numbers of urbanites dependent on informal activities to earn a living. The degradation of conditions in the social sector would intensify popular dependence on informal ways of provision of services and of guaranteeing at least a modicum of social security.

Apart from these groups, merchant capital has also utilised informal relations, including poorly regulated labour and outlets as a means to deal with the challenges of economic liberalisation, increasing competition and perceived high costs of formality. In this process, increasing numbers of urban dwellers - seasonal cashew pickers, casual workers and rice retailers - have been drawn into informal arrangements linked to global commodity circuits and have come to work under conditions that are not of their own making – see chapters five and six. These groups constitute an infrastructure facilitating accumulation in vertical networks that stretch into international space and that are oiled by state connections, kinship and religious affinities. Such informal modes of operation could be interpreted as the local variant of the strategies of flexible accumulation, including subcontracting and informalization, being used by trans-national corporations and firms in the industrialised countries. The state, besides assisting merchants in their ascension, has openly or covertly continued to participate in the economy. More precisely, one can speak of a selective absence whereby the state seems to have deliberately withdrawn from certain spheres such as the provision of basic services to all and the protection of vulnerable groups.

The informal realm has attracted a wide range of groups that use it for varying purposes that range from survival to accumulation. Indeed, a variety of forces seem to have converged in the contemporary historical moment to produce a pervasive informality of Bissauan society. This variety points to the insufficiency of existing single-stranded understandings of expanding informality that I discussed in chapter one. The reported resilience and expansion of the informal activities of popular groups prior to adjustment show similarities to trends emphasised by the disengagement approach. But in the face of the informal strategies of powerful groups in Guinean society it seems unrealistic to consider contemporary informalization as a major step towards autonomy from the state and the formal sphere. In fact, instances of both disengagement from and engagement with the state seem to have been at work. Much like others have argued in a parallel debate on the relations between state and civil society, the relation between the state and the informal sphere seems to be an ambivalent one comprising both complicity and antagonism (see chapter one). Although the political behaviour of informal actors may be too complex to predict, the Guinean case points to the need of looking at the varying motivations and opportunities that different groups may have to engage and disengage and at their differing structural positions vis-à-vis the state. It suggests a selective permeability between the formal and the informal in which those few in a position to manipulate the formal-informal interface seem to have fared better than others in the context of adjustment.

In the last two chapters I have tried to depict how informal relations have evolved in this particular place to inform how informality appears today. To begin with, in Guinea-Bissau, the realm of formality has always been restricted as has the extent of proletarianisation and unionisation, and capital has always relied to some extent on informal relations in order to accumulate (see chapter two). Today, Bissau occupies an extremely peripheral position internationally, by most criteria[138]. This is manifest not least in the considerable number of international co-operation organisations that have closed their offices in Bissau during the last decade and moved elsewhere. Bissau has also remained invisible to the interests of global capital – being incapable of rendering basic financial services through formal channels or even a regular supply of energy. This small capital city is, nevertheless, a stage of accumulation where a small group of African firms have developed their own particular forms of informal capitalism informed by a deep historical past. A share of informal activities for income generation and for provisioning exhibits the same imprint of history, as reflected in the vigour of old categories of small-scale traders and pre-colonial social hierarchies of provisioning today. In this respect, Bissau is to be situated in the context of wider West Africa where traditional forms have shown particular resilience.

[138]See Simon (1997) on the position of Bissau in an international hierarchy of capitals, according to a number of indicators.

4 The study area: setting, living standards and livelihoods

This chapter is a presentation of Bandim, the studied neighbourhood, its conditions, inhabitants and their livelihoods. It also situates the neighbourhood in the context of the wider city. I begin with a description of the groups living there and of the pace of population growth and the infrastructure conditions in the district. I then move to a discussion of local livelihoods, economic activities as well as the food strategies of households in Bandim, including food transfers and food production activities. Finally, I address local levels of well being, focusing particularly on levels of food consumption.

In this description I make extensive use of the results of my household survey from 1995. The survey was carried out both in Bandim and another neighbourhood, Cupilon, in order to contextualise my findings in Bandim, given the dearth of data on the city. Another valuable source of data used here derives from health related studies and full censuses that an externally financed organisation, "Health Project", has been doing in the area, some dating back to 1978. In later years they have also collected data on the neighbouring district of Belém, thus allowing for comparisons with Bandim. Their data were very useful in complementing my own and for comparing results pertaining to basic information on the neighbourhood[139]. The analysis by Acioly (1993) and Dávila (1987, 1991) of housing conditions and policy in Bissau helped set Bandim in the wider context of the city.

In earlier chapters aspects of the history of Bandim have been highlighted. Preceding the founding of the colonial settlement, groups of people from the Pepel ethnic group with ancestral rights to the land lived in villages under the authority of the king of Bandim. After centuries of resistance to European domination the colonial settlement finally began its expansion in the 1910s. Indigenous quarters and settlements around the colonial centre, like Bandim, were defined as not being part of the modern city thus relieving the colonial authorities of the responsibility of providing basic infrastructure and social services there. In these quarters, dwellers were faced with very limited opportunities for social mobility, enjoyed few modern rights and were left to fend

[139] The reports of the Health Project that I use here are Frej et al. (1984), Health Project (1994) and Scholte et al (1997). Colleagues at the Project kindly supplied me with some basic data while they were still processing the results of their latest census. This assisted me to plan the sample for my own survey.

for themselves. The rights they could exercise were mainly those of a customary kind. Since independence, Bandim residents have experienced limited improvements in living standards and in the provision of services.

Today, elements of pre-colonial political and social organisation are evident among the "host group", i.e. a group with ancestral roots in the area who call themselves the "Pepel of Bandim" and who are part of the wider Pepel ethnic group. They have survived ninety years of urbanization and a variety of modern political regimes. The hierarchical political structure that evolved from pre-colonial times is still present (see chapter two). Bandim continues to be the seat of a Pepel kingdom or chiefdom – and a much coveted one (according to the chief himself, interviewed in 1999), with appointment following customary rules. The chief enjoys the advice and allegiance of an entourage of *ministros* (ministers) as well as elders in the chiefdom who in turn are the heads of *tabancas* (villages) and compounds. The lineage has remained important among this host group which is reflected in the unabated importance of funeral ceremonies, a lineage ritual. Lineage is also a central means of organising inheritance of rice land around the neighbourhood as well as the organisation of rice production. Members of the host group continue to live in residential and corporate groups based on lineage membership, what I will refer to as compounds (see map 4.2). Within these domestic groups the traditional social hierarchy has largely been retained. Heads of compounds control the distribution of rice fields, holding the largest ones themselves and are key redistributors of rice within the compound (see chapter seven). They continue to have religious power over members of compounds derived from their privileged relation to ancestors. These privileges continue to give persons ranking high in these respects authority over their subordinates.

The larger share of Bandim's population consists of migrants. They began to settle in Bandim and other "indigenous quarters" during the colonial period (see chapter two). According to interviews with elders and residents, migrants initially settled in the compounds of the host group but increasingly built their own houses on land that they bought from traditional holders. While land sales have been illegal, settlers simultaneously acquired permission for construction from the municipal government. According to Health Project (1994:30), 66 per cent of the houses are occupied by their owners, who sometimes lend or rent out some of the rooms. Upon arrival, many migrants tend to search for their "relatives" in town, i.e. people with who they have affinities of kinship, lineage and village of origin, and in this way may build extended families or clusters of households. More than 40 per cent of the households interviewed in 1995 stated that they had kin relations with other households co-habiting in the same house. A large share of settlers are first generation migrants. According to my survey about two thirds of the heads of the households surveyed were not born in Bissau, but 55 per cent had moved to Bissau before independence in 1974. The majority have today no explicit obligations towards the Pepel nobility of Bandim but many instead owe allegiance and deference to seniors and relatives in their home villages.

The largest ethnic group in the neighbourhood is the Pepel, accounting for about half of the heads of households according to my survey (or 43 per cent in 1993/94 according to Scholte et al, 1997:21). This high per centage is to be seen in the context of the wider city where different ethnic groups tend to cluster in different neighbourhoods. However, and although the neighbourhood was ethnically less heterogeneous than other areas in the city in the 1950s (chapter two), Bandim has come to contain considerable diversity. The Balanta, Manjaco and Mancanha ethnic groups are numerically important, the latter two being considered as culturally proximate to the Pepel. From the 1980s the Fula and Mandinga from the eastern parts of the country have increased in number and become more visible in the neighbourhood. They have come to form small residential clusters in the district and account for about seven per cent of the heads of households in my survey in 1995 (or about 11 per cent of the total population according to Scholte et al, 1997:21). These groups are predominant in other neighbourhoods such as Cupilon and Gambiafada. They can be considered as culturally distant from the former groups in their Islamic religion, structure of domestic groups and economic traditions. These broad ethnic divisions also have significance for differentiation in the neighbourhood in terms of some social indicators (see below).

4.1 Population growth and infrastructure

The larger part of the district is contained in an area that is delimited by three tarred roads, which also delimit my study area, though the neighbourhood has grown beyond these roads (map 4.2). The large administrative area of Bandim is divided into two sub districts, Bandim I and II.

Bandim houses some ten per cent of the population of the total population of Bissau, now estimated to be over 300,000 (INEC, 1991:17). The population in the area has experienced a rapid growth during the last few decades. The number of inhabitants was reported to be 1,213 in 1950, 6,217 in 1979, 17,602 in 1987/89, 19,358 in 1991, and 26,148 in 1993/94[140]. Considering a population growth of seven per cent per annum as registered in the 1990s (Scholte et al, 1997:1), today's population in Bandim may have surpassed 40,000. One can describe this growth as a process of 'densification', based on interviews with elders and key informants and on existing maps. According to their descriptions, in the 1940s Bandim still consisted mainly of scattered groups of

[140] Sources of data: a) for 1950, Carreira (1960:281-3). b) for 1979, Frej et al (1984:8). c) for 1991, national census data, INEC (1991:17). d) for 1993/4, district census by Health Project of Bandim, Scholte et al (1997:1, 14). Figures may be underestimated, except for the Health Project data, because of the close relation between censuses and collection of head taxes until a few years ago.

huts. By the 1970s a line of houses with an improved appearance had begun to appear along the main roads delimiting the district. Parallel to this, the density of buildings was increasing within the neighbourhood as increasing numbers of migrants settled there. My informants reported a marked acceleration in house construction from the 1960s onwards, coinciding with an increase in the pace of growth of Bissau triggered by the independence war in the rural areas (Acioly, 1993:40).

Bandim is one of many unplanned settlements that occupy most of the built-up area that surrounds the old colonial centre[141]. In several respects, Bandim could be said to be representative of many of these other settlements. Crowding in houses in Bandim has been reported to be high, and to have risen from a mean of 10.9 persons per house in 1978 to 16.4 persons per house in 1993/94 (Health Project, 1994:20). Each house usually contains several household units. The average size of households was around 5 persons in 1993/94 according to Health Project (1994:19) and seven persons according to my own survey in 1995, and the number has reportedly increased through time (Scholte et al, 1997:20). A high number of persons per house has been reported as being a characteristic of most popular neighbourhoods in Bissau, pointing to a "housing crisis" in Bissau (Dávila, 1991; Acioly, 1993:41-2, 53).

Photo 4.1 One of the main streets in Bandim

In their appearance, houses in Bandim do not differ much from those in the surrounding rural settlements, except in the density of construction. As in most other neighbourhoods of Bissau (Dávila, 1991:105; Acioly, 1993:41), houses are single storey and are mainly built of sun-dried mud bricks. Roofs consist of corrugated iron or, to a lesser extent, of straw. According to the Health Project (1994:22-5), some thirty per cent of the households have access to

[141] See Acioly (1993:36-45) on the evolution of unplanned settlements in Bissau.

electricity (though voltage is too low and supply is highly irregular) and a mere 3.2 per cent have access to a private water tap. The most common source of water for household consumption is from open wells, the easy contamination of which is a cause of concern (Health Project, 1994:22-5). To a lesser extent households also use public standpipes, which I estimate to be about five or six for the whole neighbourhood. At these pipes, water is sometimes only available at night, forcing women (those usually responsible for fetching water) to queue at the standpipes late at night, depriving them of rest and risking their safety. As Bandim lacks a sewerage system people mainly use pit latrines. The sanitation conditions in Bandim have been considered among the worst in Bissau by the writers of the above report (p. 6), who refer to three cholera epidemics in the area. The level of provision of such basic services has however been reported as being extremely low for most of the city (Dávila, 1991:107; Acioly, 1993:40).

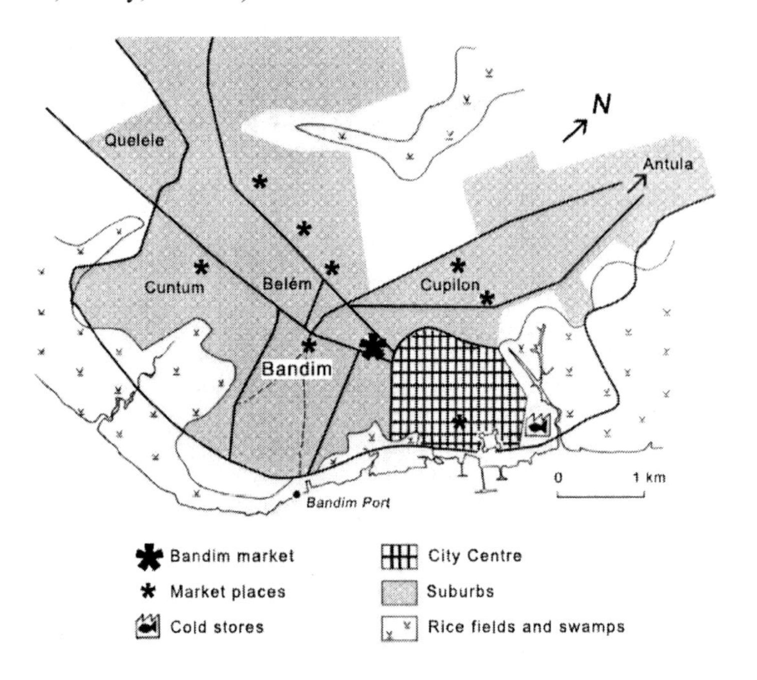

Map 4.1 Bissau

Based on: (a) Map "Bissau and suburbs", 1/10,000, sheet Antula, Comissariado de Estado das Obras Públicas, Construção e Urbanismo, 1991. (b) Drawings in Scholte et al (1997:5) and Crowley (1993:7).

Public lighting is virtually absent within the neighbourhood adding to a sense of insecurity at night. As solid waste is not being collected by the Municipal Council it is burned in households' yards or dumped in the open. At the local food market place, Caracol, there is usually a high pile of garbage that presents a health risk to sellers and consumers alike. Within the quarter, accesses are not tarred but consist of pathways many of which become drainage channels during the rainy season.

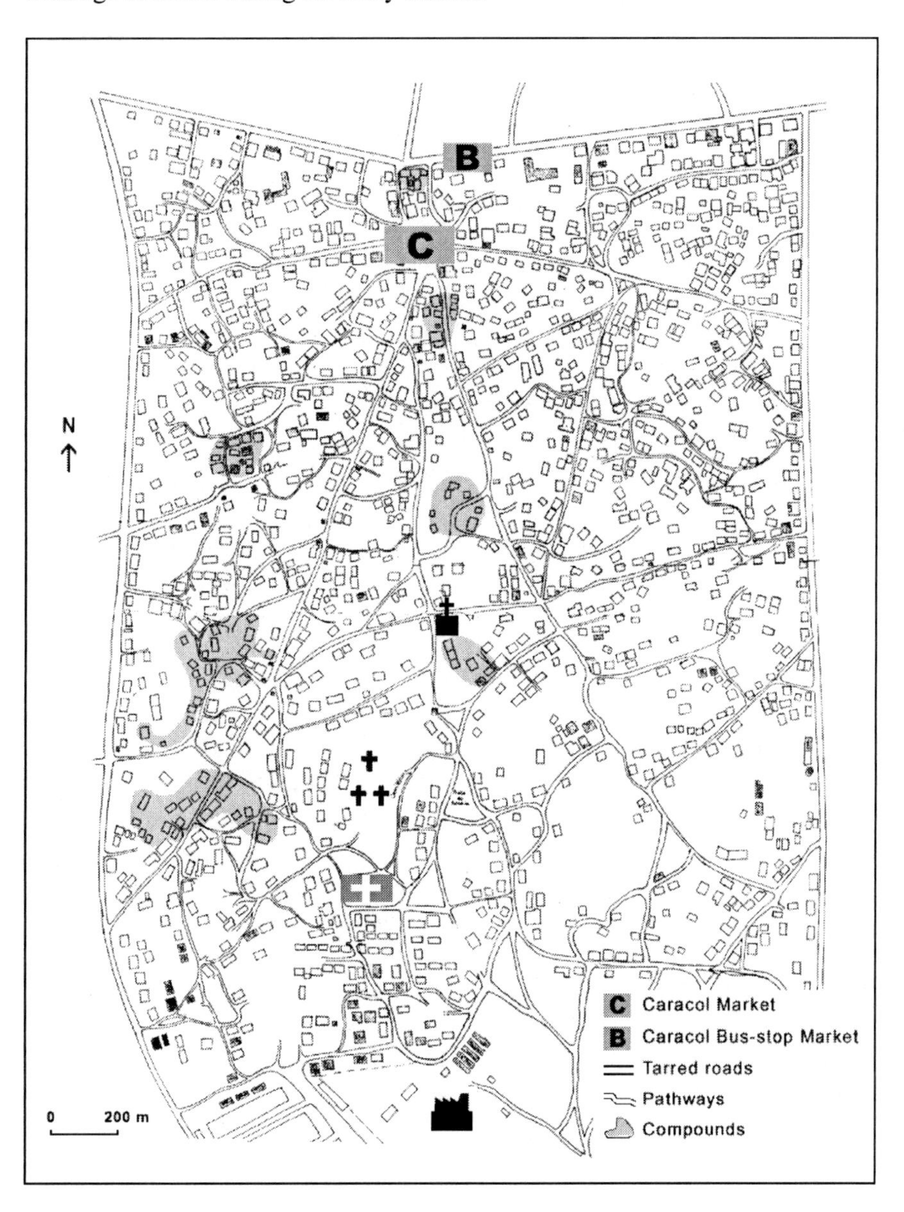

Map 4.2 The neighbourhood of Bandim, 1995

Based on own fieldwork.

As far as social infrastructure is concerned, the main asset of Bandim is a health centre – "Hospital de Bandim" – opened in 1993 with foreign assistance and later co-financed by the Ministry of Health and the Health Project, which also does preventive health work in the neighbourhood. Cuts in financing, particularly on the Ministry's side, have led to reductions in the services available to the population, as reported by the director of the centre, Doctor Rosa Mendes who I interviewed in 1999. The other source of health care in the neighbourhood is traditional medicine. Regarding educational infrastructure, there are a couple of schools located on the edges of the neighbourhood but these do not necessarily serve primarily Bandim's population. The most visible form of education within the neighbourhood consists of a large number of so-called "under-the-tree-schools" which literally function under a tree or on a private veranda where gatherings of children sit on the pavement. In the heart of Bandim there is also one legalised private school with capacity for 1,300 students. I interviewed the director, Mr. Martinho Nanque, in 1999 and he mentioned that a large share of the students come from outside Bandim. The school was built without any foreign assistance but with the help of parents and students as well as loans (including one from a parliament deputy). According to him it is partly a 'communitarian school' as 30 per cent of its students could not afford to pay any fees. However, in his account, "the government is not pleased with private schools" and had thus tried to block the advancement of the school in a number of ways, in spite of its legal status.

The number of other local initiatives in the provision of services for the neighbourhood is modest. Brigades of voluntary men have at some point patrolled the neighbourhood at night, given the lack of security experienced by residents at night and the fact that the local police station has been reported to be understaffed (according to judge Filomeno Veiga at the local court, interviewed in 1999). There were also a couple of youth associations whose representatives I interviewed in 1999 and that relied exclusively on fees from their members. One had just been formed and had the ambition of bringing about improvements in the neighbourhood (interview with Sátiro Almeida, 1999). The other group was part of a national evangelical youth organisation whose members participated in recreational activities and occasionally co-operated with the local government in cleaning the streets in the city centre and the main market in the city (interview with Moreira Indi, 1999). The neighbourhood itself, however, had not benefited from any such initiative.

Another important local grouping is the local evangelical church that is attended by a few hundred people. There are also social clubs, *manjuandades*, which are recreational and also welfare groups which have historical roots in Bissau. One of them has become renowned throughout the country for its performances, sometimes in support of political figures or parties[142]. Less

[142] See Koudawo (1996) for a discussion of the political role of *manjuandades* in Guinean politics. I also interviewed the leadership of such a group in Bandim in 1999 just after the fall of the Vieira

visible although fairly common groupings also exist, such as welfare groups among casual workers and rotating savings groups. Such groups are not novel in the city. Both are discussed in greater detail in chapter six.

Official structures of government have waned in the neighbourhood. Since the transition to multiparty politics, the single party's neighbourhood committees ("*comités de bairro*") have ceased to function and the local branch of its former youth organisation has closed down. What still remains of official structures is the local official court ("Tribunais de sector"), created in 1994 and located in the neighbouring district of Belém. It is meant to serve the population of Bandim in solving minor conflicts (interview with judge Filomeno Veiga, 1999). I do not know how widespread the use of this court is but traditional ways of administering justice are frequently used. These include turning to respected seniors or the chief to solve a conflict or, as I myself witnessed a couple of times, using existing traditional courts or appealing to mystical powers to correct perceived injustices.

Some of the above features and trends are far from specific to the study setting. But in the case of Bandim one can hardly speak of a boom in externally funded non-governmental organisations or community-based organisations as has been the case in many neighbourhoods across urban Africa (Aina, 1997; Tostensen, Tvedten, and Vaa, 2001). Apart from the Health Project, Bandim's residents are still very much left to fend for themselves.

4.2 Livelihoods

Let me turn to the livelihood strategies of residents/households in Bandim. Here, the data from my household survey in 1995 are of use in providing a general picture as well as the background for more qualitative analyses in later chapters. I will begin with cash income generating activities. Respondents were asked to enumerate the activities of all members of the household (i.e. the group of people eating together) for the preceding twelve month period starting with the activity, who in their estimation, was most important in terms of income generation. For each activity, questions were asked pertaining to whether incomes were fixed or variable, whether a contract had been signed and if the worker enjoyed paid sick leave, as well as for whom the household member worked for and the size of the enterprise. Up to five activities per household were processed statistically and these are summarised in table 4.1. Trade clearly dominates as the most common household cash income activity. This is most often pursued by women, as trade is considered to be a female

regime. Our encounter was surrounded by tensions as the victorious military Junta was pressuring them about their political allegiance, given their earlier open support to ex-President Vieira - of which the only resulting material benefit, I was told, were six wrist-watches bearing the picture of the President.

activity among coastal ethnic groups such as the Pepel, Mancanha and Manjaco, whom constitute the majority of the population in Bandim. But there are also male traders, usually from the Eastern groups, though these are a minority among residents in the neighbourhood. As such there is a gender and ethnic based specialisation in trade activities that has deep historical roots, as described in earlier chapters.

Table 4.1 Income-generating activities in Bandim

Type of income activity	(a) 1st household activity	%	(b) Sum of income activities	%
Food retail trade	125	39.1	490	61.6
Food wholesale trade	2	0.6	4	0.5
Non-food retail trade	17	5.3	33	4.2
Construction work	23	7.2	36	4.5
Needlework, weaving	6	1.9	16	2.0
Repairs, incl. Car mechanics	14	4.4	16	2.0
Woodwork, furniture	9	2.8	11	1.4
Other manufactures	11	3.4	13	1.6
Taxi, chauffeur	20	6.3	26	3.3
Laundering, cleaning, domestic work	9	2.8	22	2.8
Shipping work at the port	12	3.8	14	1.8
Secretarial work	7	2.2	13	1.6
Working at restaurants, bars	7	2.2	9	1.1
Watchman, guard	4	1.3	6	0.8
Work in government administration	8	2.5	9	1.1
Military and police	6	1.9	17	2.1
Education and health services	9	2.8	19	2.4
Culture, recreation and religion	7	2.2	7	0.9
Development organisations	4	1.3	6	0.8
Collective transport (road, air, sea)	8	2.5	11	0.6
Other	6	1.9	8	1.0
Agriculture and fisheries	6	1.9	9	1.1
Total	320	100	795	100

(a) Refers to the first income activity enumerated by each household, loosely corresponding to the main income activity of the household. (b) Refers to all income activities (up to five activities per household and adding up to a total of 795), disaggregated by type of activity.

Within trade, retail trade of food items (including drinks and charcoal) are particularly important. In 40 per cent of the households food trade was the first activity named by respondents, giving a rough indication of its importance as the main source of income for a large share of households. Its importance further increases when considering the wider universe of income activities of households: of a total of 795 activities that were processed statistically, 66 per cent consisted of trade, with food-retail alone accounting for 62 per cent.

All other income activities that were reported are much less common in the neighbourhood but some are worth mentioning. After trade, activities related to house construction such as making bricks are the most common sources of income, particularly for men. There is considerable construction activity in the neighbourhood and the city – this includes not only the high pace of construction of shelter for migrants but also to the building of high standard and luxurious villas such as the "Ministers' Quarter" on the outskirts of Bandim. House construction is followed by running a taxi or being a chauffeur (also a male activity) as well as cleaning and doing domestic work for others, usually performed by women. These are followed by dressmaking and weaving, repairs including car mechanics, and carpentry, activities which are all usually male driven and account for the presence of several workshops in the neighbourhood. About as common were income activities related to positions in the military and the police and those related to education and health services. A further activity worth mentioning is loading work at the port, historically important for men in the city.

The modest position that agriculture and fisheries as income generating activities occupy is due to the fact that people engaging in those activities marketed their produce themselves and were therefore classified as "traders". From a total of 490 food trade activities, 44 pertained to the retail of agricultural and fisheries goods produced by the household itself (see below for more detail). A further 159 were associated to processing activities carried out by the seller, particularly the production of cashew wine and the roasting of groundnuts but also the making of ice-cream, cooked foods and fried pastries.

Food trade activities

Here I present some of the broader characteristics of food trade, as this is the most common source of income for households in Bandim and one of the livelihood components that I will discuss in detail in chapter five. One particular section of the household survey focused on the food trade activities of members of the interviewed households. Information was collected for up to three household trade enterprises, which added up to a total of 527 enterprises,

398 in Bandim and 129 in Cupilon[143]. Food trade is an economic activity where women are most numerous, with the exception of imported foodstuffs and meat. There certainly is a differentiation among food trade enterprises in terms of scale of operation as will become evident in later chapters. But the survey data reveals that the vast majority are small (usually one-person) and low-income enterprises. Over 70 per cent of the interviewed sellers declared that they did not manage to keep any savings. In addition, 38 per cent of the sellers estimated that they spent all or virtually all of their income on food and a further 22 per cent more than half. This suggests the importance of these activities for the food security of the households involved.

Enterprises dealing in vegetables and fruits and locally produced alcoholic drinks were the most common in Bandim (23 and 22 per cent of enterprises respectively). The latter consist mainly of cashew wine, which constitutes a major source of income in the neighbourhood during the cashew season. Almost 40 per cent of the surveyed households in Bandim engaged in seasonal picking of cashew and production of cashew wine for sale. Large numbers of women leave the neighbourhood for cashew farms in the rural areas where they harvest the cashews, deliver the nuts to the owner of the trees and press the juice for sale in Bissau as wine. Some women perform these activities in the cashew areas surrounding Bandim that are usually held by members of the Pepel host group. After vegetables and alcoholic drinks, the largest category of traded foodstuffs in Bandim was groundnuts. Women usually buy groundnuts, roast them and then re-sell them. Fish selling was the fourth largest category. The remainder of the enterprises were spread among the other categories of food. These include trade in fish, which traders catch themselves or acquire at Bandim's artisanal port or at the industrial cold stores located in the eastern end of the city (Map 4.1). Many local products are seasonal so that sellers are often compelled to resort to other types of goods or income activities when these are out of season.

The source of merchandise varied between own production (38 per cent), from other retailers or producers (42 per cent), and a smaller share from wholesalers (22 per cent) who are present in the local market places as well. Virtually all enterprises were retail enterprises. One fourth sold just outside their homes, a popular site for selling cashew wine in the evenings but also other petty goods. Almost one fifth sold on the streets. The largest share of food sellers however, operated in the local market places. Some seven per cent sold at Bandim market which is located just outside of Bandim quarter (map

[143] Within the household, enterprises were identified as distinct from each other when they operated independently from each other or different types of foodstuffs were being traded. Foodstuffs were classified into the following different types: local rice, imported rice, other imported foods, fish and seafood, palm oil, vegetables and fruits, groundnuts, meat, non-alcoholic beverages, cashew and palm wine, other alcoholic drinks, bread, cooked food, wheat cakes, ice and ice-cream, spices and seasoning items, and others.

4.1). Built during the colonial period, Bandim market has expanded greatly with economic liberalisation. This market place has been described as the largest centre of commercial activity in the country. According to Monteiro (2001) and his colleagues in their detailed study of this market in the late 1990s, Bandim market gathered about 3,000 traders, had a large estimated volume of business and informal financial flows were said to exceed by far those of commercial banks. And indeed, the market and its adjacent area is where import-export firms have preferably located their large warehouses. The market offers a variety of high value goods. Small traders also endeavour to find a place there, as reflected in the large numbers selling from wooden tables or the pavement. But access to a selling space there is not easily attainable (Lourenço-Lindell, 1993). Many petty traders operate instead at lower rank market places, such as Caracol market or Caracol bus-stop market, located in Bandim district (map 4.2).

Some 35 per cent of the recorded enterprises operated at Caracol market. This is one of the many spontaneous market places that have multiplied in the city with economic liberalisation. The market began around 1988-89 as a gathering of sellers and by the early 1990s had grown to about 400 retailers, as I myself counted. The market has not benefited from any improvements or basic services on the part of the municipal authorities. Conditions are very elementary, with virtually no sanitation and with big piles of waste. Caracol consists of some three or four wholesale stores selling imported rice, a dozen or so tiny permanent and semi-permanent shops tended by men selling mainly petty imported foodstuffs and a large number of women sellers using wooden tables or simply displaying their goods on the ground. The latter sell mainly fresh fish, local vegetables and rice. The market offers mainly basic goods such as food, and particularly low cost food, i.e. the cheapest types of fresh fish and vegetables as well as as few imported foods in small portions.

Combinations of sources of income and food

Returning to income generating activities in general, the information collected gives a broad idea about the conditions of job and income security. Activities varied in terms of whether they included written contracts and paid sick leave, whether income was fixed or varied and the size and type of enterprise. On the one hand, there were income activities which could count on written contracts, paid sick leave and a fixed monthly wage – what one would usually refer to as "formal wage work". On the other hand, other income activities lacked written contracts, sick leave benefits, and a regular income – the usual attributes of "informal work". The latter activities often took the form of self-employment[144].

[144] On the predominance of self-employment in the informal sector in urban West Africa, see for example Trager (1987).

But in this category one should also include situations of apprenticeship and casual work for firms, common for example in shipping work at the port and in construction work, although these rather common work situations were not easily discernible from the data. Households were then classified according to their particular mixes of income activities in these respects (table 4.2). The largest share of them were dependent for their incomes on "informal" kinds of work. A minority relied exclusively on "formal wage work". Another sizeable group depended on a mixture of the above two sorts of work situation for cash income. Finally, 28 per cent of the households declared to have additional non-work sources of income, such as rents, pensions and regular remittances. In sum, about 90 per cent of the households relied to varying extents on informal income generating activities to meet their needs.

Table 4.2 Type of work situation prevailing in household income generating activities

(a) Households depending on "informal work"	191 (45*)	57
(b) Households depending on "formal wage work"	31 (7*)	9
(c) Households depending on a mixture of (a) and (b)	103 (32*)	31
Households depending excl. on non-work income	8	2
Total	333	100

(*) Number of households who, in addition to income generating activities, also had non-work income.

Given the insecurity of work and irregularity of cash incomes to which so many households are subjected, it is important to highlight other components of local livelihoods. This may be approached by looking at the various sources of food for the household. Indeed, this was a major focus in my survey. The survey data made it possible to get a general view of the most important sources of food for households in the neighbourhood and to roughly classify households according to how they combined those sources. Reliance on gifts and engagement in food production activities were important sources of food and a smaller share also received transfers from employers (table 4.3). Indeed, only a minority of the households were exclusively dependent on purchased food. The majority combined different sources of food to meet household needs. The most common combinations in Bandim were, (a) purchased food, gifts and own production and (b) purchased food and own production (table

4.4)[145]. So let me dwell for a moment on non-purchased food sources in Bandim.

Table 4.3 Sources of food for households

		Own production			
Purchased	Employer	Farming	Fishing	Stock raising	Highly reliant on gifts
11 %	20 %	38 % (126)	10 % (33)	51 % (51)	55 %

Table 4.4 Household combinations of sources of food

Dependent exclusively on purchased food	11
Purchased food and gifts	10
Purchased food and own production	26
Purchased food, own production and gifts	33
Other combinations of different sources	20
Total	100

To begin with, one fifth of the households could count on transfers of food, particularly rice, from an employer as a part of the wage. In half of the cases this involved work under a written contract, possibly in situations where employers have easy access to imported rice. This has long been a practice among large employers in the city[146]. More common were other types of food transfers, namely food gifts. Respondents were asked whether and how frequently the household had been given food, meals or money by non-household members (i.e. people not eating regularly with the household) during the preceding year. Around 70 per cent of the households responded affirmatively. More than half declared to receive such gifts very frequently, that is, several times a week or a month or could count on regular transfers.

[145] These calculations include households participating in cashew picking. Those who had this as their only "food" production activity numbered 38 households, i.e. some 11 per cent of the sample.

[146] Although payments for services in the form of food can also be found in more traditional production spheres as is the case with rice production where the owners of fields in Bandim "pay" occasionally recruited labour totally or partly in food and wine.

These households I came to consider as "highly reliant on gifts"[147]. Respondents were further asked where their relief came from when they were out of food or money to buy it[148]. The majority (82 per cent) of those that admitted to sometimes finding themselves in this situation could count on help from someone, usually neighbours and relatives. The remainder declared this not to be the case for them and reported that they instead simply did not eat or resorted to begging. Thus, while gifts seem to be an important component of provisioning for many households in Bandim, one should not ignore the share of those who are potentially isolated and disadvantaged in this respect. This is an issue that will be pursued in greater depth in chapters six and seven.

Some 63 per cent of the interviewed households in Bandim were involved in some form of food production[149]. One particular section of the survey was directed towards these activities. Let me begin with agricultural activities, in which 38 per cent of the households had engaged during the preceding twelve months[150]. Vegetable gardens can be seen inside the neighbourhood where house density permits and also on its fringes. In addition, rice fields surround the neighbourhood where staple food is produced on lineage land (map 4.1). But the surveyed households had access to farming plots in a variety of geographical locations: 66 per cent of the plots registered lay in the vicinity of the neighbourhood while the remaining share were located in other parts of the urban fringe as well as in the rural areas of origin. Only seven per cent of the plots had been bought, with the larger part having been accessed through distribution by an elder, inheritance and through borrowing. Finally, in the case of almost half of the plots, households had started cultivating them during the preceding ten years. This would suggest a possible intensification of this activity among households in Bandim. Similar trends of increased involvement in food production by urban dwellers have been reported for some other urban areas in Africa and the developing world (see Rogersson, 1993, 1997; Drakakis-Smith, 1991, 1993; United Nations, 1996a).

Agricultural activities included production for both subsistence and for the market. In the latter case, they were counted in the above analysis as being part of food trade activities. The former is notoriously the case of rice production in the swamp land that surrounds Bandim and the city (map 4.1). Rice is cultivated mainly by the Pepel who have ancestral rights to tracts of land in the

---

[147] On the importance of gifts and loans in other African urban areas, see: Vaa, Findley and Diallo (1989) on Bamako; Devereux (1999) on ; and De Herdt and Marysse (1997).

[148] Only about half of the households admitted to sometimes reaching this situation, which seems too optimistic a picture when compared to the other indicators of consumption for the neighbourhood – see below.

[149] The figures go up to 74 per cent if one includes cashew picking. These results could have been slightly inflated by sampling procedures, as members of the Pepel, with priviledged access to farming land in the neighbourhood, turned out to be slightly over represented in the sample.

[150] This corresponds to 126 farming households. In addition, a total of 152 farming plots were registered and some information was collected for each of these.

area. Access to rice land and the organisation of rice production activities are structured along gender and generational division in which women and junior men are at a disadvantage (see chapter seven for greater detail). Market oriented production is more common among horticultural producers, invariably women. Almost half of those recorded (a total of 49) sold their produce. Taking the group of farming households as a whole, among those who sold part of their harvest (42 households), 70 per cent used most of the resulting income for purchasing other food items for the household and the remaining used it for other basic expenses of the household. This indicates the importance of agricultural activities by urban households in providing both food and incomes, resembling findings elsewhere (Drakakis-Smith, 1991, 1993; United Nations, 1996a).

About one tenth of the households had male or female members engaged in fishing. Most of these caught a few kilos of small size fish in the mangrove area and adjacent rice fields that surround Bandim. The fish was mainly used for household consumption but one fourth of them also sold their catches. A few households, usually their male members, also practised more market oriented fishing off shore, using canoes. Commercial fisheries, in spite of their modest presence in the sample, are part of an intense economic activity in Bandim. They land their catches at Bandim port which is the city's artisanal port that lies on the outskirts of Bandim (map 4.1). This is the main supply point of fresh fish for the city and gathers fishermen and women fish sellers from all over the city. With its proximity to the residential area of Bandim, the artisanal port provides an important income opportunity for large numbers of women sellers who reside in the neighbourhood. Finally, half of the households raised small stock and fowl. In 80 per cent of the cases animals are raised for own consumption. Among those who did sell at least some of their animals and fowl, half declared that they spent most of the income on food for the household. In fact, from a number of conversations I learned that raising a pig could be a strategy for buffering against future consumption crises in the family or for investing in a small business.

In sum, households in Bandim generally rely upon a mixture of types of income generating activities – though with a clear predominance of informal kinds of work – and a variety of food sources ranging from purchase in the market to gifts and own production. This picture fits well with the notion of "multiple modes of livelihood", introduced by Mustapha (1992) to characterise income strategies in conditions of crisis and adjustment. Others have referred to a diversification of livelihood strategies in the context of adjustment (Bangura 1994; Zack-Williams, 1993).

Within the neighbourhood, aside from these general patterns, there is variation in the livelihoods and food strategies of households reflecting the skills and the resources at their disposal. These differences become also evident between neighbourhoods. The survey findings for the neighbourhood of Cupilon provide a base for comparison. The main difference concerning income and food strategies lies in the level of involvement in food production, which is much lower than in Bandim: some 37 per cent of the households in Cupilon engaged in any type of food production, with 11 of the households farming, 25 per cent raising stock and none doing any fishing. As in Bandim, trade is the most common income activity but there are differences in the types of trade pursued. For example, the processing and sale of cashew wine, so important in Bandim, was practised by only four households in Cupilon. This is related to the large Muslim majority living in this neighbourhood. Preference for trading in the proximity of the home rather than at market places was also higher here, though this is structured by gender. Differentiation within and between neighbourhoods can also be seen in levels of well-being, to which I now turn.

4.3 Living standards

Let me present some data that give some idea of the level of social development and well-being of Bandim's residents. Regarding the level of education, my survey data revealed that 37 per cent of the heads of households surveyed had never attended school (an average of 41 per cent in 1993-94 according to the Health Project, 1997:22). Another 40 per cent had not gone beyond primary education. Within Bandim, the Project found considerable variations between age groups and between adult men and women, with half of the women being illiterate compared to 28 per cent of the men. Across neighbourhoods, Bandim is worse off in this respect compared to neighbouring Belém (Health Project, 1997:22) and Cupilon (my survey).

The rate of infant mortality is high in Bandim[151] and improvements have been only modest[152]. By following a large cohort of children between 1990 and 1995, the Health Project calculates the infant mortality rate in Bandim at 110 - 124 per thousand (1997:33). Again, figures are clearly worse than in the neighbourhood of Belém where the rate is 84 per thousand. The Project also found variations between zones within the neighbourhood and marked differences between ethnic groups, namely with Pepel children being in far greater risk than Fula and Mandinga children (p. 35). Physician Rosa Mendes, director of Bandim Health Centre whom I interviewed in 1999, was of the opinion that nutrition problems are more acute among the Pepel. In particular, she ex-

[151] Infant mortality rate refers to "the number of infants that die before reaching 1 year of age, expressed per 1,000 live births" in a given period of time (World Bank, 2001:278). The rate in Bandim is well above the 91 per thousand average for Sub-Saharan Africa (World Bank 2001:243).

[152] Scholte et al (1997:34) report a mortality rate for Bandim children up to three years of age that lies between 129 and 244 per thousand. Frej et al (1984:66) report for 1978/1980 that 25 per cent of all children below five years of age died in Bandim.

plained, the migration of mothers towards cashew production areas for prolonged periods – something that has increased during the last one and a half decades with the growth of the cashew economy - has had a serious impact on the health of children in the neighbourhood. To this gloomy picture we still have to add HIV which, according to her, is on the increase in the area.

Other aspects of the level of well-being in the neighbourhood can be revealed by looking at food related indicators. In my survey I tried to make an assessment of households' level of food consumption and purchasing power by using proximate indicators. Respondents were asked about the number of meals that adults in the household usually ate per day. The survey included the recording of the frequency of consumption of a few basic food items of varying cost (rice, meat, fish and vegetables), both during the two days preceding the interview and how often in a week such items were usually consumed. Another question was directed to the amount of staple that households purchased at a time. This was based upon the assumption that people bought in bulk if they could afford to since this is cheaper than buying smaller amounts. In addition, respondents were also asked to estimate the share of household income spent on food and how often they found themselves without food or money to buy it[153].

The results of the above sets of questions provide a consistent picture of general consumption levels in Bandim (table 4.5). Two thirds of the surveyed households in Bandim ate only one meal a day, i.e. they did not usually eat in the morning and the evening, something that has become so common that there is a popular expression for it – "the 24-hour-shot". Concerning the cost of their diets, an almost as large a share of the respondents (60 per cent) could not afford meat and consumed fish (usually of a very small and cheap variety) most days of the week. A further 14 per cent could not even afford to eat fish three or more days a week and, among these, there was a group that frequently ate "clean rice", i.e. boiled rice without any sauce of meat, fish or vegetables. The households who usually bought rice by the kilo were more numerous than those who could afford to buy it bulk, i.e. by the 50-kilo bag. Finally, of the 255 that were able to answer the question, 70 per cent declared to spend all or

[153] The question on the share of income spent on food is a classical one in more conventional household consumption surveys, relying on detailed registers of all income or expenditure of a household. Given the numerous methodological problems this implies, respondents were instead asked to give their own estimates, pre-coded into five categories, i.e. whether less than half, about half, more than half, all or virtually all or more than the total household income was spent on food. This is only a very rough estimate since women are usually kept uninformed of their husbands' incomes and women often hide the true size of their profits from them. While this makes it nearly impossible to get reliable figures pertaining to aggregate household income, the results are suggestive in that they represent the perceptions of the respondents (who was preferably the person responsible for food purchases in the household) of the general economic condition of the household and of the manoeuvring space available for meeting household needs. The question on how frequently households were without food or money, though still showing a high level of frequency, turned out to give a generally too optimistic picture.

virtually all of their income on food, with some even claiming to spend more than their income[154].

Based on some of the above questions, it was possible to build an aggregate consumption indicator and a classification of households in Bandim into four levels of consumption: “extremely poor”, “poor”, “less poor” and “non-poor”[155]. A minority of the households were found in the “non-poor” level, that is they typically ate three meals a day and included meat in their weekly diet. Another fifth were classified as having a “less poor” consumption. The majority (70 per cent) turned out to be in the “poor” and “very poor” levels of food consumption, that is, they ate one meal a day, did not consume meat and frequently found themselves without food or money to buy it.

Table 4.5 Food consumption indicators

Number of meals per day			Staple purchases			Aggregate consumption indicator			
One	Two	Three	Retail	Bulk	Both	Very poor	Poor	Less poor	Non-poor
68 %	22 %	10 %	59 %	38 %	3 %	14 %	56 %	22 %	8 %

Thus, while the general picture is not encouraging, one should note the existing differentiation in the neighbourhood in terms of these indicators. In search of some of the axes of this differentiation, I cross tabulated the above food related indicators with other variables, such as certain attributes of the head of the household (table 4.6). First, the level of consumption clearly improves with the level of education of the household head. Secondly, the ethnic belonging of household heads also has significance. Heads of households that stated to belong to the Eastern groups (mainly Fula and Mandinga) are clearly better off in terms of food consumption than those of other groups. Members of the Eastern groups constitute a modest share in the sample in

[154] This set of data could potentially be affected by the slight bias present in the sample towards the poor strata, as acknowledged in chapter one. However, when I later statistically manipulated the sample so to remove that bias, results differed minimally from the original ones – for example the percentage of households that ate only one meal a day differed only in two per cent. This prompted me to use the original results.

[155] The differences between households lying in adjacent categories are not always great. But a consistent criterion was applied so that households reporting similar situations in what concerns the above questions would be placed in the same category. Households eating one meal a day, with a diet that was poor in animal proteins (that is, do not eat meat and eat fish four or less times a week) and that could never afford to buy rice in bulk were coded as “extremely poor”. All other households eating only once a day were considered as having “poor consumption” (except if they had a weekly diet that was rich in meat). The “less poor” category consisted of all households eating two meals a day (except if they had a weekly diet that either was very poor or rich in meat). The “non-poor” typically ate three times a day and included meat in their weekly diet.

Bandim, i.e. 24 households in a total of 335. But the results for Cupilon, where these groups constitute the majority of residents, seem to confirm this differentiation in consumption indicators along broad ethnic lines. Thirdly, female headed households were twice as probable to be found in the "very poor" consumption category as male headed ones. This resembles findings elsewhere that women are both suffering the worst effects of adjustment policies and assuming increasing responsibility for their families[156].

But female headed households also had a larger share in the "non-poor" consumption category, which suggests some differentiation in this respect among this group of households. These findings require some qualification: a share of these women heads of households may be wives in polygamous marriages because in the city poligamic wives often live in separate houses. Directing the survey to household units (i.e. food consumption units) acted to conceal some gender aspects. But the gender dimensions of the food economy and assistance are brought to light in later chapters.

I also cross tabulated food indicators with the kinds of sources of income and food for the household. Those who relied on "informal work" are more represented in the "poor" and "very poor" consumption categories than households relying on "formal wage work" or a mixture of the two. Households relying exclusively on purchased food are clearly better off, while households involved in food production and reporting a high reliance on gifts showed a tendency to be more represented in the poorer categories of food consumption.

Table 4.6 Cross tabulation of level of food consumption with attributes of heads of households, in absolute figures.

		Aggregate consumption indicator				
		Non-poor	Less poor	Poor	Very poor	Total
Education	Never attended school	7	22	73	23	125
	Attended/finished primary school	9	29	83	14	135
	Attended secondary school or higher	12	23	30	10	75
Gender	Female	12	19	55	23	109
	Male	16	54	131	24	225
Ethnic group	Coastal groups	9	56	169	43	277
	Eastern groups	5	11	8	0	24
	Other	14	7	9	4	34

In terms of general levels of food consumption, Bandim seems to be worse off than other parts of the city. Firstly, the various food related indicators I used in my survey consistently showed a better situation in Cupilon than in Bandim. For example, a smaller share ate one meal a day (55 per cent) and a larger share were able to eat three meals a day (20 per cent). Secondly, the studies

[156] For general discussions, see: Sparr (1994); Daines and Seddon (1991); Zack-Williams (2000). See Manuh (1994) on women in Ghana, and Dennis (1991) on women in Nigeria.

and censuses carried out by the Health Project reveal consistently worse social indicators for Bandim as compared to neighbouring Belem (Health Project, 1997:1). Finally, an official survey on urban cereal consumption covering 439 households systematically selected from a variety of neighbourhoods in Bissau concluded that 55 per cent of households in the city ate on average 1,5 or fewer meals per day (ICMU, 1991). As shown above, my survey in 1995 indicated that some 68 per cent of households ate only one meal a day. This potentially locates Bandim below the average for the city, though the time gap needs to be considered.

In my description of Bandim, I have pointed to differences from other areas in the city, particularly Cupilon – a neighbourhood that I chose precisely because it differed from Bandim in a number of ways. The kind of data discussed here is missing for other areas of the city. But on the basis of the superficial impressions that I developed of the rest of the city during my fieldwork, Bandim seems to be representative of some other neighbourhoods in the city, such as Cuntum, Quelélé, Belém and Antula. These areas are similar to Bandim in that they too have (or had) an identifiable Pepel political hierarchy and have a similar ethnic composition, with probable implications for the predominant income and food strategies pursued. Where people from coastal ethnic groups are most numerous, women tend to engage primarily in trade and where clusters of local Pepel exist, part of the staple food will be provided through rice cultivation in their paddy fields around the city. Cupilon, on the other hand, is representative of other neighbourhoods where there is a concentration of people from Eastern groups, such as Gambiafada. Among these groups, as we have seen, men engage preferably in trade. However, it is difficult to assert whether the differences in food consumption and social indicators along ethnic lines that both my survey and the surveys by the Health Project suggest are generalisable to other neighbourhoods. Bigger differences can, however, be expected between any of these areas and some clearly high-income areas in the city. Conditions in Bandim certainly contrast with the affluent appearance of the Ministers' Quarters (Bairro de Ministros) located in its vicinity or of sections of the city centre where diplomats, expatriates and high-ranking public officials live.

Compared with other African urban areas, Bandim and the city in which it is located may seem quite unique. The "pre-capitalist" structures among the host group in Bandim show considerable resilience. The old Pepel political hierarchy is the only available form of authority at work in Bandim today. New neighbourhoods in urban Africa often consist of communities of strangers and may lack a clear local structure of power (Simone, 1998). Also, the corporate groups and residential arrangements based on lineage membership that exist in Bandim seem to have become the exception rather than the rule in African cities. While in Bissau urban growth has gradually engulfed these traditional clusters, it has not seriously shaken the lineage structure nor caused the power of elders to collapse. Several factors have intervened in their preservation, including a good deal of resistance and a very peripheral and specific form of capitalist penetration, as discussed in earlier chapters. But in addition, the fact that the market came to them means that members of the host group were not removed by migration from their ancestral lands, the economic base for lineage cohesion. A good share of these lands were not expropriated but remained under customary law, allowing for important production activities to continue on these lands under the control of elders. When considering the West African context, however, these features are less unique[157]. Looking upon ancient forms of organisation in Bandim as not being necessarily encapsulated in tradition or impermeable to change opens possibilities for comparing how such forms in different places are changing in response to external pressures.

[157] On the persistence of the institutions of lineage and chieftaincy in other West African cities, see: Barnes (1986), Gugler and Flanagan (1978), Peil (1981).

5 Informal relations in food trade

In chapters two and three I discussed processes of informalization of the Guinean society and the city. At this point in the book I will turn to an analysis of those processes at the neighbourhood level, although frequently spilling over to the rest of the city and in constant dialogue with trends in the wider society. The spotlight is now turned particularly to disadvantaged groups and their struggles. This and the next chapters will deal with the multifaceted relations pervading informal livelihoods in Bandim. This chapter focuses on a livelihood component that is explicitly played out in the market, food trade.

As I discussed in chapter one, much contemporary work on expanding informality shares an over-enthusiasm about the potential of informal activities for emancipation and material security. This chapter is a critical assessment of whether this is in fact the case. In Bissau, as reported for other African cities, the informal economy is no longer the exclusive refuge of the poor but is a sphere where a variety of groups have developed strategies with varying purposes that range from survival to accumulation (see chapter three)[158]. In a context of increasing differentiation and competition, what can be expected is an intensification of social struggles within the informal realm. Those at the bottom have increasingly to struggle on a variety of fronts to preserve their right to subsistence.

The chapter addresses the variety of social relations influencing the conditions of small informal traders. On the one hand, I will discuss the 'vertical' relations with government agents and merchant capital, the exploitation and subordination that these relations impose on small traders, the struggles of the latter to circumvent them as well as the *modus vivendi* that may be reached. On the other hand, I will look at relations "at the bottom", i.e. those among small and medium scale actors *within* the informal realm. At this level, the focus is on the relations that sustain market activities. In relation to these, the collective efforts and solidarity among the disadvantaged are highlighted. But instances of marginalization and exploitation are also explored, including informal kinds of regulation that influence the conditions of operation of small operators. The questions that I address are as follows. Who is excluded from such agreements? Who qualifies and what are the trade-offs involved? What

[158] On similar trends in other parts of Africa, see: Meagher and Yunusa (1996; Lugalla (1997); Zack-Williams (2000); Nabuguzi (1994); Manuh (1994).

alternatives do the excluded find, how do they respond to their exclusion? How do traders circumvent or attempt to influence the practices of informal regulators? This approach differs substantially from the somewhat naïve but widespread views of networks supporting market activities as invariably driven by trust, as inherently benign, communitarian in their interests, egalitarian and equally accessible to all[159]. As will be seen, in the context of economic liberalisation new constellations of relations have developed along with new alliances as well as with new tensions and sources of exploitation.

My intent, on the one hand, is to expose the dynamics that are placing increasing burdens and constraints on those at the bottom and, on the other hand, to account for how those in a disadvantaged position struggle on various fronts, collaborate to increase their room of manoeuvre and even create spaces of relative autonomy. Social relations within the informal realm will emerge as being far more complex than is often assumed.

Some of the issues addressed are specific to certain sub-sectors of urban food trade, while others are more general and cut across the various sectors. This prompted me to structure the chapter accordingly. I begin by describing the conditions in which small informal traders operate. I then proceed to discuss the relations between the local government and small actors, followed by a presentation of the various sources of support and collaborations available to different extents to small traders. I then move into a sectoral analysis of three sub-sectors of urban food supply: rice, fish and fresh vegetables. These sub-sectors will illustrate slightly different points, but all unravel the complexity of relations of solidarity and domination permeating activities within them. This sectoral analysis will facilitate a detailed understanding of the changing conditions of and for small traders in relation to adjustment policies. It will evidence the changing social relations in specific sub-sectors, which include both new sources of exploitation and new spaces of resistance.

The variegated discussions contained in this chapter are based on a variety of sources of mainly primary material. To begin with, the household survey that I conducted in 1995 elicited basic information about the food production and food trade activities of household members. A total of 527 enterprises were recorded[160]. Other smaller quantitative procedures were also used during

[159] See for example Tripp (1997).

[160] From a total of 527 enterprises, 398 pertain to residents in Bandim and 129 in Cupilon. From the range of income activities pursued by the various household members during the twelve months preceding the survey, a maximum of three food enterprises per household were inquired. The criteria to distinguish different enterprises were based on who is responsible and the type of food being sold. This means that two members of a household selling the same product but operating independently and with separate budgets are classified as two different enterprises. Also, a person who trades different types of foodstuffs is registered as responsible for different enterprises, since the information collected varies greatly between different food products. Foodstuffs were classified into the following groups: local rice, imported rice, other imported foods, fish and seafood, palm oil, vegetables and fruits, peanuts, meat, non-alcoholic beverages, cashew and palm wine, other alcoholic drinks,

fieldwork, such as a one-off inquiry in several market places about the sources of supply (of vegetables and fish) of all sellers present. The analysis relies to a great extent on the interviews with producers and traders that I conducted throughout the duration of my fieldwork. Altogether around sixty rice, fish, and vegetable traders were interviewed. Several wholesalers and two importer firms were also interviewed in the course of the fieldwork. Though some traders were interviewed in 1999 in an attempt to update earlier material, difficult fieldwork conditions did not facilitate a systematic follow-up on the bulk of data collected earlier. Besides the groups mentioned above, I interviewed a variety of persons who were knowledgeable in the range of issues addressed here including persons engaged in trade. Government officials or representatives with roles pertaining to the management of market activities in the city were interviewed on these matters. Time spent on observation and informal conversations at the local market places and at supply sites were very instructive. Two other studies dealing with trade activities in the city, those by Delgado et al (1989) and the other by Monteiro (2001), provided important complements and sources of comparison with my own data. Given the dearth of secondary material, the above primary sources are the basis on which I build the analysis in this chapter. More detailed methodological explanations can be found in chapter one.

5.1 The Informalization of urban food supply

'Falling off balance'

Food trade is where a large share of the urban population has sought to find the means for survival. The liberalisation of the economy resulted in a true explosion of small-scale food traders in the city. They hawk in the streets and on the footpaths, they sell on the roadside, they have stalls in the market places and they sell outside their homes. Daily life seems to consist of selling and buying, in an incessant movement occupying all days of the week and most hours of the day. No sooner are the last candles blown out by the rows of petty traders selling late into the night along the main roads, than life starts pulsing again long before dawn in the direction of the fishing port or the bus terminal, from where many head off to some near or distant market place in search of new merchandise.

But how are small informal traders really faring? Does this liveliness represent an increasing emancipation, as some have interpreted it? While small traders have come out of invisibility and set in motion irreversible develop-

---

bread, cooked food and sandwiches, wheat cakes, ice and ice-cream, spices and seasoning items, and other (eggs, fermented milk, etc).

ments in the city, the same policies that gave them greater room for manoeuvre have also generated dynamics that are threatening the livelihoods of many. I would like to briefly address the precarious conditions in which many food traders find themselves.

The extensive informalization of livelihoods in the city, with many people seeking incomes in the sphere of trade, has implied an invasion of the market by a large number of sellers in the last one and a half decades. My 1995 survey of trade enterprises within households revealed that of the 527 enterprises recorded the overwhelming majority (about 90 per cent) had started during the ten years preceding the inquiry[161]. Two thirds had started during the preceding five years and about one fourth had started just in the preceding year. This could indicate an explosion in food trade enterprises in the city since around the mid-1980s, coinciding roughly with the introduction of adjustment policies. What can be expected is an intensification of competition among food traders, a problem that surfaced repeatedly during my lengthier interviews with traders.

In the face of increasing competition, retailers frequently change type of merchandise, supply source and selling site. This fluidity of market activities could be interpreted as standing for considerable experimentation, the trial-and error strategies of small actors or their own kind of 'flexible production strategies'. For a share of retailers, however, this attests more to the permanent chase for consumers, in an attempt to keep their share of market demand. Flexibility and mobility appear to be crucial for survival at the bottom. In this process, market locations seem to be continuously on the move. A good example of this is Caracol market within the studied neighbourhood. Between two periods of fieldwork, the original location had been completely abandoned and sellers had moved their businesses to an adjacent area. Other "ghost markets" can be found in the city.

The survey data suggests that a large proportion of these entrepreneurs concentrate at the lower end of the informal trade economy, i.e. in small and low-income activities. As described in chapter four, the overwhelming majority are one-person enterprises. Moreover, the majority of the interviewed sellers did not manage to keep any savings and a large share spent most of the resulting incomes on food. This suggests poor prospects for the majority to develop their enterprises, a situation contrary to neoliberal expectations that economic liberalisation would automatically set informal enterprises on the path to growth. Instead, a large share seemed literally to live hand to mouth. For this group, as I came to realise in the course of my fieldwork, daily survival was about managing a tiny capital and a tight household budget, with virtually no room for unforeseen changes. It sufficed one day of slack demand

[161] This number of enterprises includes those recorded in both Bandim and Cupilon neighbourhoods. When differences between the two neighbourhoods are significant, they appear disaggregated in the text. On the sampling procedures for the survey, see chapter one.

or one household member getting sick to cause the loss of one's working capital. This common condition is captured in the abundantly used local expression 'falling off balance' (in Creole, *cai na balanso*). It has also inspired the allegorical title of this book, which compares the situation of many to that of the circus artist, in a constant effort to maintain balance and permanently on the verge of falling.

The difficult conditions for many traders are naturally not only related to the rapid increase in their numbers - which itself is probably a result of deteriorating incomes pushing more household members into the market place. Increased costs of production in some sub-sectors, particularly businesses dependent on imported inputs, have probably increased difficulties to start up in business and certainly made it difficult or impossible to continue in business. For example, the sale of fried pastries that had seemed quite popular during my earlier fieldwork, had, on my subsequent visits become less common with several people telling me that they had abandoned it due to the increasing prices of cooking oil, sugar and flour, all of which are imported. Fresh fish, as shall be seen in the sectoral analysis, is another such branch where increased production costs have caused difficulties to fishermen and fish traders alike. These difficulties are compounded by a decline in urban purchasing power (see chapter three).

In these circumstances, it is not surprising that I found many cases of "involution" among food traders. In my conversations with traders I tried to elicit their own assessments of how their conditions of operation had changed compared to earlier years. Their answers do not have statistical significance because the aim was not to get a sample that was representative of their respective groups in the city. But the frequency with which certain aspects were mentioned is worth mentioning because they signal conditions and trends experienced in a similar way by many traders. There were frequent references about decreased scales of operation, longer working hours and increasing frequency of 'falling off balance'. This is also the understanding that some municipal officials had of the general conditions for small traders (interviews with A. Camará, 1995 and S. Mané, 1995). These changes will be discussed later in the contexts of specific food sub-sectors. But the emerging picture is one of a share of the urban population being increasingly marginalized from the general economic growth that has been said to have been taking place in the country - one of the fastest in the sub region prior to the 1998-9 war, according to Aguilar and Stenman (1997:v). This is in line with findings in studies in other African cities that have documented intensifying marginalization within the informal economy and increasing competition at its lower end under conditions of adjustment[162]. This study intends to concur with this mounting evidence that challenges neoliberal assumptions that informal work

[162] See Meagher and Yunusa (1991, 1996); Lugalla (1997); Manuh (1994); Brand et al (1995); Nabuguzi (1994); Zack-Williams (2000).

in an "enabling environment" will provide basic levels of income and well being for the working poor.

To be sure, the magnitude of marginalization varies between sub-sectors and groups with some seemingly more affected than others by the above trends and with some even enjoying a degree of relative autonomy, as will be seen below. There is also considerable differentiation within the informal economy, as will become clear in the sectoral analysis. Some groups have been in a position to gain an advantage from economic liberalisation and informalization, and for some, these have meant renewed opportunities to accumulate. But in general, for poor informal actors, prospects for emancipation and an enjoyable standard of living seem merely to have been moved further away. The differentiation and multiplication of actors in the informal economy has been accompanied by an intensification of old or an emergence of new forms of exploitation and oppression. For poor actors, liberalisation has meant that they now have to struggle on a wider range of fronts – including against the practices of local government, as discussed below. Throughout the chapter, the strategies of small traders to circumvent these various holders of power, the compromises they make and the collaborations they build will gradually emerge. I will begin by discussing their relations with this long established and persistent actor in the urban food market, the local government.

5.2 The relations with local government

In chapter three I discussed how the state played a role, directly or indirectly, in the informalization of the economy. Here, I would like to discuss the relations between the local government and informal food traders. Interviewed traders told me that prior to economic liberalisation, they operated under the constant threat of the confiscation of their produce by municipal agents and were forced to sell covertly. The persistent increase in the number of traders and the shift in policy under the pressure of international organisations rendered such hostile practices by the local government impracticable. But the local authorities have continued to be an important actor and to have an influence over the conditions of small operators. In spite of the official policy of "facilitation", the authorities continue to have hostile and discriminative attitudes towards them. This section deals with this persistent contradiction, the ambivalent attitude of local government to informal operators and the resistance strategies used by the latter. The discussion is based on interviews with traders and government officials as well as on my own observations at the market places.

How do government officials perceive this growing army of private small entrepreneurs and spontaneous markets? The opinions of individual officials seem to be very disparate. In an article, B. Cardoso, Minister of Planning in 1989, praised the great potential of "popular production" in Guinea (Cardoso, 1989). In 1995, a municipal official in charge of the management of the urban market places told me that he considered informal trade to be "what gives life to Guinea" and what supplies the population. He was of the opinion that "it should be protected and facilitated" (interview with Sérgio Mané, 1995). On the other hand, a medium-rank official at the Ministry of Commerce whom I interviewed in 1995 predicted the future extinction of spontaneous market places through law enforcement[163]. At the Municipal Council, others expressed similar unrealistic modernising ideals. In 1992, an official involved with the administration of markets expressed to me his disapproval of such markets and the desirability of their eradication. To confirm this latter set of perceptions, the news agency Lusa recently reported that the government had levelled about 800 stalls at Bandim market, by using bulldozers and tear gas[164]. So let me discuss this persistent contradiction between Municipal Council and small traders.

Before going into local government practices, a few words on the status and nature of this institution should be mentioned. Local government in Guinea-Bissau is not as yet a directly elected body. Local elections have been in discussion for several years and in 1995 new laws were approved regulating the powers of local government, but the government seems to have delayed the process (Rudebeck, 1997:46) and elections have yet to take place. Autonomy from the tutelage of central government (and the PAIGC) has been limited[165]. This politicisation of local administration influences decisions concerning urban management.

The municipal government is responsible for the management of market places and some other commercial activity in the city. This "management", in most cases, seems to be reduced to the daily collection of fees at market places. In 1994 the Council created the Department for Inspection of Markets - whose members I interviewed in 1995 – in order to check daily fee tickets, shop licenses and eventual debts owed to the Council. Its scope was, however, limited to the Central and Bandim markets "due to lack of financial resources", I was told. In the remaining markets, the only representatives of the Council were fee collectors. Indeed, market places constitute one of the biggest sources of revenue for the Municipal Council, according to its budget presented by Costa and Silva (1996). Given its feeble economic situation, the Council is particularly diligent in that task. Fees are charged even in spon-

---

[163] Professor Renato Aguilar, advisor to the World Bank on macro-economic policy for Guinea-Bissau, also informed me that, in his repeated contacts with government officials through the years, he has perceived a general dislike for small informal actors.

[164] http://www.lusa.pt/noticiaslusa/notocia.asp?id=843715 (16 January 2002).

[165] See Costa and Silva (1996:89) for a discussion. Cardoso (1994:14) also exposes the overlapping of the post of President of the Municipal Council with functions in the central government and the PAIGC.

taneous markets, without the Council ever providing any infrastructure or services. To further illustrate this extreme diligence, during the armed conflict of 1998-99 that struck the city, during periods of relative calm urban refugees would return to the city and timidly begin rebuilding their small businesses. Even under such conditions of extreme adversity, sellers told me, municipal collectors were charging them fees - as they also did immediately after the end of the war as I myself witnessed. One of the municipal officials involved with the management of market places declared not to have any control or knowledge of how the resulting revenues were used. What is obvious is that they have not been used to upgrade the elementary conditions of most market places in the city.

Two types of fees are charged, monthly fees for those having permanent structures in the market place, and daily fees for all the others with only makeshift or no structures in the market. The former is a fixed amount per square meter, the latter is arbitrary and based on an estimation of the volume of goods being sold[166]. Small retailers are invariably found in the latter category. Here, arbitrariness reigns. Firstly, variations in fee levels from one market to another resulted in situations in which retailers operating on a larger scale and in a higher ranking market place such as Bandim would pay less compared to smaller retailers in a poorer market like Caracol, as I detected among my interviewees. Secondly, no scales were used to determine fee amounts and the daily fees being charged were far higher than those stipulated on the official table, which I acquired only with great pains from the Council - no wonder then that sellers had no knowledge of this official table. Thus traders in this category are particularly vulnerable to the arbitrariness of collectors' behaviour. When business is slow the small retailers often have to pay repeated fees for the same merchandise. This is typically the case of small rice retailers, among whom I found many widows and young girls[167]. This seriously depletes the meagre incomes of many. It became evident that small pavement traders could, by the end of the month, actually end up paying more to the Council than shop owners who were paying a fixed monthly fee. The difference in terms of per cent of income spent in fees would probably be even more striking as the latter usually handle higher value goods. This indicates the discriminatory practices of the Council and their bias against the weaker traders.

---

[166] In former times, the products would be weighed and five per cent of their value paid to the Council (interview S Mané 1995).

[167] A small rice retailer in 1995 would frequently take three days to sell one 50-kilo bag of imported rice. Retailer earnings for such a bag were around 25,000 PG then. After paying a daily fee of 8,000 PG three times for the same bag, the retailer would be left with only 1,000 PG. The motivation to continue selling was the share of the merchandise consumed by the retailer her/himself. In any case this scale of rice retailing consists of one of the lowest forms of retail trade in Bissau, in which only those without other options will engage.

Council collectors hold considerable power in the market places. This is compounded by the fact that collectors do not rotate between markets but are based in one market place, turning it into what someone called "their own earldom". As such, this is a position that does not differ much from that of colonial municipal agents (see chapter two). In most market places, there are no checks whatsoever on their actions[168]. This helps them to establish a hold over the sellers and fosters irregular practices and allows for considerable arbitrariness on their part. Collectors may charge lower fees to their acquaintances and can decide whether or not to exonerate a seller from paying the fee. Alternatively, they may propose to the retailer the payment of a lower fee in exchange for relinquishing the fee ticket. Another seller told me that she sometimes paid the fee in goods, also in this case giving up the fee ticket. One cannot avoid getting the impression that municipal collectors use their position to earn an extra income, to supplement their meagre salaries from the Council.

Given the arbitrariness and despotic behaviour of Council collectors, relations between sellers and collectors are often strained. I did not witness any open conflict myself but there are a variety of hidden forms of resistance. Since the quantity and value of goods influenced the size of the fee, a common practice was to hide part of the merchandise or to cover more valuable goods with less valuable ones in order to reduce the size of the fee. This in turn resulted in fee collectors sometimes charging the same fee for differing amounts of the same product, to the detriment to those selling smaller amounts. Many considered the fees to be expensive and some said that if they were to pay the whole fee they would inevitably 'fall off balance', i.e. they would loose their working capital. In a couple of cases traders sold other petty goods on the side of their main merchandise as a way of raising the money to pay for the market fee. Other traders avoided collectors' fees altogether by only turning up at the market outside of collecting hours, usually during the morning, which is also the period of greatest demand. One of the interviewees asked permission from an elderly man to sell from his porch, located just outside the Caracol market, where collectors had no authority to charge fees. Yet others completely moved their businesses to places where collectors did not operate or to marketplaces where the fees being charged were lower. More generally, and as mentioned in chapter three, most small traders have refused to register their enterprises thus ignoring the new legislation. These forms of non-compliance by small traders deprive the government of a share of its revenues and challenge policy directives concerning the 'informal sector'.

Crowley (1993:33-9), reporting on a variety of market places in the country, points to similar contradictions and avoidance strategies. She also tells how these tensions triggered a strike among retailers in a market place in Olossato.

---

[168] With the possible exception of Bandim market where there is an official co-ordinator and where the Department for Inspection was active, although this does not necessarily mean that these agents had the power or the will do restrain collectors' irregular practices.

Monteiro (2001) also describes the relations between local government in general and trader associations in Bandim market as being conflict-ridden: traders complain about the oppressiveness and arbitrariness of public agents as well as their lack of accountability. Here, it should be mentioned that there is a poor level of collective organisation at the lower end of the informal trade spectrum - with the exception of the widespread rotating credit groups (discussed later on in the chapter) which are not oriented to interaction with the government. As discussed in chapter three, the one trader organisation that has enjoyed a privileged relation with the government at least until recently and participated in the process of revision of legislation is the Chamber of Commerce, representing the interests of merchants and importers-exporters.

The relations between the municipal government and the informal actors are not exclusively discordant. It should be recalled that both central and local government members have been reported to have found their way into the market place, the "veiled faces" of Bandim market, as suggested by Monteiro (2001) (see chapter three). This implies collaboration with a segment of the informal market. If so, this means a 'selective permeability' at work, in which some informal operators feel insecure and oppressed by municipal agents, while others enjoy co-operation and even business partnerships with them. This is the same kind of partiality of behaviour and ambivalence that characterised central government institutions described in chapter three.

In sum, while spontaneous market places appear and grow beyond the control of the local government, this has not meant its retreat as an actor. Local government has stakes in the informal activity taking place within these markets and its agents are in a position to influence the conditions of small actors. It benefits directly from the proliferation of market places through an expanded source of revenue but possibly in less visible ways too. Its practices tend to be arbitrary, discriminatory and biased against small-scale trade, where the poor of the city eke out a living. The free hand that the local government gives to fee collectors in the market places only worsens its oppression and exploitation of the poor. Thus, whatever the official discourses, changes in legislation and donor pressure for a positive attitude towards informal actors, this contradiction has not disappeared. This challenges interpretations that see the expansion of informal activities as an autonomous move away from the state (see chapter one). Indeed, other writers have reported a similar resilience in the hostility of attitudes held by local governments in other African cities in the adjustment period[169]. This casts a gloomy shadow over certain expectations that decentralisation in public administration is necessarily a positive fillip for informal sector development (Sanyal, 1991:54) if it is not accompanied by more accountable and participatory methods of governance than at present. But struggles from the oppressed in this area are not to be neglected.

---

[169] See for example Lugalla (1997) for urban Tanzania.

5.3 Relations supporting market activities

As stated in the introduction to this chapter, small informal traders are embedded in a myriad of personal relations and networks that help them keep a foot in the market. These relations range between partnerships between two persons and more collective arrangements, between family based and market grounded relationships and between egalitarian and unequal relations. Later in this chapter, in the sectoral analyses, I will address the unequal and exploitative relations that develop in the market. In this section I focus on those structures of support that small food traders in general use to keep their businesses afloat - forms specific to particular sub-sectors are discussed in the sectoral analyses. Firstly, there are those originating in the family. Secondly, there are a variety of co-operative efforts among sellers in the market that are aligned along various axes of affinity. Individual sellers are placed differently in this constellation of possibilities and this position is not without consequences for the fortunes of their businesses and their own well-being. These issues of access are often glossed over by analysts of the informal economy.

The family embeddedness of small traders

Relatives emerged as an important source of support for small-scale trade activities in the study setting. This support takes a variety of forms. To begin with, a good share of the retailers interviewed had gained access to their selling sites either through friends or a more senior female relative. Access to a good selling site – that is, one where there is demand for one's products – is not to be taken for granted, even in seemingly unstructured agglomerations of traders, with length of career and frequency of operation apparently playing a role. Similarly, a senior relative with long experience was in several cases the source for learning marketing skills. Arrangements between "tutor" and novice varied, from cases where the latter was paid a sum of money daily to cases where only occasional compensation was received. This closely resembled apprenticeship situations in other economic sectors.

Even the smallest businesses will usually require some investment. Equipment is kept to a minimum by the majority and often comprises only a wooden table or just a bucket and something to display the goods on - except for those who produce and process their own merchandise. Getting access to merchandise normally requires some cash or start up capital - except when the retailer had managed to reach a credit agreement with the supplier right from the beginning. Traders were asked how they had got their start up capital and what sources of credit they used when they 'fell off balance', which for some was a frequent occurrence. Formal sources were never mentioned. A number of them had started up with cash raised in other trades. But by far the most common source of credit was from close relatives - i.e. often siblings, parents, the husband and his close relatives, with husbands alone accounting for about one third of all the respondents. Interest was usually not charged. However, some traders said that repayment periods for loans were short, and that they were sometimes denied credit. This is not surprising given the generally harsh material conditions experienced by most people. The family also assists the businesses in other ways. A husband, son or brother may do the preparatory work for commercial gardening or build a market table or a shade for the female trader. Cooking and caring for the trader's children while she was away was most often carried out by one of the older children, usually a daughter. This might mean that most adult women are themselves busy earning an income and that an increasing burden is being laid on children. In a few cases the trader may be assisted in selling by a child of her own (or another young relative). But the overwhelming picture that emerges from both my survey and my interviews is of self-employed traders with no capacity to employ labour.

This extensive reliance on family support to keep one's business running could be seen as part of a wider trend towards an intensified "familiarisation" of businesses and affiliations in the market. This has provoked concerns that such a trend may reinforce traditional axes of subordination and the position of dominant figures in the family while eventually constraining independent action or at least open confrontation[170]. The importance of the family embeddedness of women's businesses in particular has been noted before in other contexts (Dennis, 1991; Ndiaye, 1998; Sow, 1993). How women's trade activities interact with social relations in the domestic realm in the current context of adjustment will be discussed in chapter seven, after having presented relations in the domestic field. At this point, I would like to make three comments. Firstly, this considerable dependence on the family, and particularly on male relatives in the study setting, suggests the need for caution in interpreting women's intensified involvement in the market as being automatically liberating from domestic structures. Secondly, kin may be seen as both an asset and a constraint for small traders, although individual traders vary in their positioning in this equation. As the findings show, it is a major source of support for their businesses. Illustratively, when I asked sellers what they considered to be the biggest difficulties they faced in their trade, one of them answered, "lack of a husband". In several cases husbands were both an important source of credit and major contributors to household food expenses. In other cases, women traders carried the main burden for provisioning other

[170] See Sanyal (1991:48) for a general argument about axes of commonality and discord in mobilisation among informal sector workers. Meagher and Yunusa (1996:40) refer to the proliferation of ethnic and religious associations rather than trade-based unions in Zaria. Macharia (1997) stresses the importance of ethnic based networks for informal enterprises in Nairobi and Harare.

household members. This included situations where adult males were either absent or could not be counted on because they were "out of work" or for receiving small or irregular salaries (see chapter seven).

Indeed, the domestic context of women's businesses revealed itself as a key factor in the frequency of 'falling off balance', i.e. loosing one's working capital. The two main reasons for this to occur, as perceived by respondents, were slow turnover of merchandise and being forced to spend their capital on food for the household. They reported that they not only spent a greater share of their earnings on food than in former times, but a good number of them were convinced that they also shouldered a greater share of household food costs than their husbands did. Not surprisingly, several complained that they now 'fell off balance' more frequently. And indeed, from my interviews I could identify a general connection between the extent to which this occurred, i.e. the precariousness of women's businesses, and the absence or presence of adult male members in the household who were willing or able to contribute towards household expenses - although, naturally, this is not the only factor at play, as will become evident.

Finally, the persisting connections with the wider family in the context of increased participation in the market involve a cycle of reciprocities: part of the merchandise is often used as gifts to relatives (sometimes including lineage members), possibly as recognition for past assistance or as an anticipation of future help. This affects immediate incomes but, as one respondent chose to put it, "I cannot disappoint them because one day I might need them". In addition, as will be seen in chapter seven, women are increasingly shouldering the responsibility for assistance to family members in vulnerable situations.

Thus, the interconnections between family and market are less straightforward than some analysts would make us believe. Even within the same study setting, variations on this theme can be expected to be great. The domestic circumstances in which women traders are inserted vary widely. Similarly, the range of available kin in town often varies, as does the extent of its responsiveness and the extent of its material resources. In addition, in the multicultural environment of the city, the relation between women's market activities and their condition in the domestic realm will vary for different subcultures. Here, a large share of the sample consists of women from coastal ethnic groups (Pepel, Mancanha, Manjaco), who account for the greater share of women food traders in Bissau. So these findings are not generalizeable to women belonging, for example, to the Islamized Eastern groups who have become a visible group in the market but who are a minority in my sample and in Bandim. Their situation generally differs from the former in terms of the domestic structures in which they are inserted and in their gender roles. Women of the coastal groups share a long trade tradition dating back to the pre-colonial era, as was discussed in chapter two. Thus their market activities and their mobility in pursuing them are quite accepted. As women in other societies in West Africa where they have long trade traditions, most of my respondents keep their own money separately from their husbands' and decide upon the use of their own incomes. Many did not show their incomes to their husbands while at least as many did. In general, these women seem to enjoy a degree of economic autonomy. Gender roles of provisioning seem however to be changing, as will be discussed in chapter seven. Thus far, the findings discussed here suggest that the family embeddedness of women's businesses varies considerably. This pertains both to the extent of support provided by the family and to the constraints it may impose on individual traders, which points to the need to consider instances of both co-operation and conflict in the domestic realm.

Co-operation between sellers

Market activities give traders the opportunity to develop relationships beyond the family. I would like to turn now to forms of co-operation among traders *in the market* that are not primarily kin based but draw on a variety of affinities and motivations. These are the moral economy elements in the market, to which some have attributed communitarian as well as emancipatory characteristics. And indeed, some of these revealed themselves to be of vital importance for the sustenance of market based livelihoods, and for some, they seem to have replaced kin-based forms of welfare. But, I will argue, these need to be nuanced by issues of access.

No formal associations of assistance were available to traders residing in the neighbourhood. So I will be referring to informal kinds of co-operation. Among these, some forms of support are more organised and thus "visible" while others are more fluid or more difficult to isolate. Let me begin with the latter types.

To begin with, there are informal channels of exchange of crucial information for daily business decisions, concerning for example the supply situation and the prices at different supply sources as well as about demand conditions for a certain product. A good example are the information strategies used by fish traders: decisions over which supply source to choose and what behaviour to adopt towards suppliers on a particular day was conditional upon the information that one got from other sellers early in the day. This could have a collective effect as these exchanges of information occasionally even grew into co-ordinated action to influence the prices of suppliers (see section 5.5). Informal trade in Bissau seems to rely to a considerable extent on the exchange of such information. This seems not to be restricted to the city area but to extend to a wider geographical scale of operation, as a share of urban traders supply themselves at rotating markets that are dispersed in the rural areas - two of which I had the opportunity to attend. These market places, which have deep historical roots (see chapter two), continue to link producers, traders and consumers in different locations in the country[171]. Among my respondents I found instances where urban traders co-operated by each travelling to a different rotating market so as to draw on the advantageous prices that different markets offer for different products.

There were also a number of other collaborative practices. Firstly, once at the market, traders selling the same type of product tend to agree on a single price "in order to avoid problems", as one explained to me. Indeed, prices for the same product within one market varied very little. Judging from the statements of a couple of elderly vendors, this is an old practice that was already in place during the colonial era. But there were also cases, particularly those selling their own produce, in which vendors sold larger bundles for the same price causing dissatisfaction among other retailers - see section 5.6. Secondly, retailers at the market may help each other in selling their produce. For example, when one seller has sold her merchandise she may help to sell the merchandise of a colleague so that she could leave the market earlier. When a seller has to leave her selling spot momentarily, she may leave her merchandise in the care of a trusted colleague. Sellers may also help each other to pay for the market fee when one is short of money. Some may even get a loan from a colleague when business is going badly. Not all traders could count with this mutual help, however.

In my interviews I tried to discern what kind of affinities facilitated mutual help at the market. Naturally, and as is evidenced in the literature, these affinities will vary from one place to another[172]. As mentioned earlier, in Bissau there is a certain division of labour in the market place along ethnic and gender lines, with men from the Eastern groups dominating in the supply of meat and some imported foods, while women, particularly those from the coastal groups, predominating in the trade of fresh foods. A certain ethnic-gender clustering in the market around certain products (as well as in the neighbourhoods) may to some extent facilitate gender or ethnic solidarity. Concerning lineage, some respondents considered that this too facilitated co-operation between market traders while at least as many considered that it did not make any difference. However this does not prevent it from being important for other purposes. Members of the local evangelical church, on the other hand, tended to give preferential treatment to each other in the market place.

There are, however, at least as many opportunities for interaction *across* these axes in the market place, where the different subcultures and genders meet. These crosscutting interactions may be egalitarian - such as when Mancanha women share their agricultural skills with women from other ethnic

---

[171] See Crowley (1993) on the revival of this kind of markets in the country.

[172] For example, Macharia (1997) reports on the pervasiveness of ethnicity structuring market relations in Nairobi; and Ndiaye (1998) refers to the importance of brotherhoods in supporting informal traders in Dakar.

groups - or unequal, as with certain types of informal agreements that sometimes link suppliers with retailers. In the latter case, there are clear instances where gender, ethnic and class differences overlap and eventually reinforce each other - as seems to be the case of relations between suppliers and retailers of imported rice discussed in section 5.4.

A much more generalised basis for mutual help between interviewed traders was friendship. This cuts across a variety of affinities and senses of belonging but the interviewees indicated that the main basis for such help pertained to acquaintances between women selling in the same area of a market place. Many of these relationships may be temporary, given the fluidity of market activities themselves in the form of frequent changes in selling sites and type of merchandise. But many long-term relationships also develop in the market place, countering certain assumptions that collaborative efforts in the 'informal sector' tend to be short lived. Among these, I often encountered pairs of women traders that co-operated closely. These kinds of partnerships have been noticed among women informal traders in other African cities (Tripp, 1989 for urban Tanzania; Brand et al, 1995 for Harare). They may be relatives, neighbours or friends and usually deal in the same kind of product. They may have separate funds but accompany each other throughout all the steps of the work day, helping each other in the purchase of merchandise, in carrying it, selling it etc. They also help sustain each other's businesses through the frequent setbacks. These were usually women of similar material situation, and as such, we can conceive of their relation as one of solidarity between social equals. While their partnership lends them some security and moral support, their often precarious condition and the fact that they are exposed to the same market shocks as they trade in the same product, put limits on what that solidarity can achieve.

The above forms of co-operation among sellers are of a rather loose kind. I turn now to a particularly institutionalised form of co-operation in the market.

Rotating savings groups

The occurrence of rotating savings groups among women informal traders in Africa is well known in the literature. They are the "true banks of Africa", to borrow someone's description of the importance of these informal means of banking in the absence of formal sources of credit. Even in the current general context of positive policies towards the informal sector, credit facilities have tended not to reach small operators but have mainly benefited large-scale operators or people with good connections in formal institutions. Unfortunately, most descriptions of these groups tend to focus exclusively on their positive features and to gloss over issues of differential access and their sustainability in times of crisis. Some praise them as genuine popular responses and imbue them with potential for emancipation from formal institutions and oppressive domestic structures[173]. What follows is a brief description of such groups in the study setting, based on respondents' accounts of their participation in them. I attempt to emphasise both their crucial role in lending a degree of security to traders but also the structures of access involved.

Abota (*abotas,* plural), as rotating saving groups are locally known, is one of the most institutionalised forms of informal co-operation in Bissau, with a well established set of rules and dating back at least several decades, as reported by elderly traders. This form of saving is so widespread in Bissau that it attracts people from all layers of society, from small retailers to academics. As such, it cannot be viewed exclusively as an emancipatory strategy of the poor. These groups vary extensively in various respects. Firstly, they vary greatly in terms of the amount being paid. Secondly, they may join people sharing the same type of business and working location or people operating different kinds of businesses and in different locations. But usually they gather people with similar similar material condition and scales of business, i.e. their ability to pay an agreed amount of money. Thirdly, they differ in the types of affiliation on the basis of which they recruit their members. *Abota* groups may emerge around old lines of affiliation such as people from the same compound or lineage, probably because chances of holding people accountable are perceived as higher. But other *abotas* join together people of different backgrounds, based for example on acquaintances created at the market place, and may bridge over different ethnic groups and genders. In my interviews there were references to all of these variations.

But what are they and what are their functions? *Abota* consists of a group of people who each agrees to regularly contribute an agreed amount of money into a common pool. Members then take turns in collecting the gathered sum. Honesty is the major requisite for an *abota* to function well. Members need to believe that the person entrusted with the group's savings will return it to the group and that the other members have the capacity to make their regular contributions. Where these had failed, as reported by many, the group had dissolved and many were discouraged from participating again. Respondents declared that they joined in an *abota* in order to help them save for more occasional expenses such as clothes, medicines and burial ceremonies. In fact, the amount of money collected by each member does not differ from the amount invested and the basic aim is, as one phrased it, "not to eat up" all of one's earnings. *Abota* has another crucial function. When one member is on the verge of 'falling off balance' or facing unexpected expenses in the household, turns may be altered to assist that person, as several respondents

---

[173] For uncritical assessments see for example, Lugalla (1997:447); Sow (1993:112); Brand et al (1995). For optimistic appraisals of the political potential of informal credit groups see: Tripp (1989); Daines and Seddon (1991). An exception is Rosander (1997:17) who calls attention to feelings of mistrust in such associations, with individual interests overshadowing internal solidarity.

reported. Someone also declared that participation in the *abota* had helped her to increase the scale of her trade. In this way, *abota* plays a crucial role in keeping members in business and provides a safety valve for the trader and his or her dependants. In fact, I came to realise from my study of the social networks of households in 1999 (see chapter seven) that some people that could not count on a supportive kin network in times of hardship relied extensively on such market based security mechanisms such as *abota*. This raises the possibility that *abotas* may constitute one alternative to kin based support systems and one which may eventually have emancipatory potential for women. Unfortunately, this is not a resource available to everyone.

Indeed, *abotas* have their own barriers of access. They are inherently selective, since an *abota* group usually gathers people with capacity to pay an agreed sum and requires that contributions be made regularly, even when one has been hindered from selling or when business has failed and earnings are minimal. Thus I found considerable variations in this respect. The size of savings being rotated varied greatly. Moreover, while some were able to participate in several *abotas* simultaneously, others did not participate at all. Among the latter, some expressed that they did not trust others in the market, often referring to earlier disappointments. Others were hindered from engaging even in the cheapest *abota*, as they were forced to spend all of their earnings on food, could not generate sufficient earnings or incomes regular enough to participate and 'fell off balance' frequently. For example, among fish sellers usually only those handling sizeable amounts of fish (40 kilos or more) had the capacity to engage in *abota*. Ill health in the household was a compounding problem referred to by several, creating difficulties in fulfilling the compromise with the *abota* group - two interviewees had in fact ceased to participate due to this very reason. Thus one gets the impression that *abotas* contribute to accentuate differentiation among traders. On the one hand, *abota* participants enjoy a degree of security and some may even slightly expand their operations when their turn to collect comes - although the latter is strongly limited by the general conditions of heightened competition and shrinking demand. On the other hand, those with the most precarious incomes and health, and thus in the greatest need of such a safety net, are excluded, which perpetuates their marginalized position in the market. In fact, since paying capacity and trustworthy relations in the market are conditions for participation, *abotas* seem to have become a good indicator of both how prosperous a business is or how well integrated a seller is socially in the market place.

An issue deserving further research is the effect of adjustment policies on savings groups such as these. The available interpretations in the literature can take completely opposite directions, as is illustrated by two texts analysing changes in the informal sector in the context of structural adjustment: Lugalla (1997:447) refers to informal credit schemes in urban Tanzania as working very well; while Meagher and Yunusa (1996:ch5) give a dreary picture of credit groups collapsing under increasing household pressures and declining real incomes. The long tradition of *abotas* in Bissau would make the study of their evolution a worthwhile effort. In particular, it would be interesting to see whether they were formerly accessible to virtually anyone interested and whether they have become increasingly selective. It is most likely that increasing numbers of traders are unable to participate, given the increasing precariousness of their livelihoods.

Let me summarise the key findings in this section on the sources of support available to small traders in the study setting. A large proportion of the respondents (mostly females) were dependent on the help of relatives, including husbands and their kin. This questions the real possibilities for these women to use their trade to emancipate themselves from patriarchal kin structures should they wish to do so, as family support may be anchored in power differentials within the household and the extended family. Having a supportive husband seemed to make a considerable difference to the stability of women's businesses - this is at least so among groups where women's market activities have a long history and are generally accepted. One-sided views in the literature are inadequate to capture the complexity and variations in this interplay between women's conditions in the market and the family. This issue will be discussed at greater length in chapter seven, but I am suggesting in this section that a more nuanced perspective is advisable, one that is sensitive to the fact that the family may act as both an asset and a constraint. I also discussed forms of co-operation more specifically located in the market that seem to lend some resilience to informal enterprises and in some cases provide one possible alternative to kin-based support. However, the relatively egalitarian forms of support among traders discussed here are not necessarily accessible to all. The more organised collective efforts such as rotating savings groups marginalize the poorest, further contributing to differentiation among traders in the market. This makes a case against over-enthusiastic views of the emancipatory potential of collaborative efforts and social networks in the market to allow 'disengagement' from state, capital or patriarchy at home.

In sum, food traders appear to be differently placed in these various networks. Differential access to informal support in market activities, often glossed over in the literature, ought to be considered when looking at differentiation in the informal market. In this study setting, factors that seemed to be of importance were size of earnings, having a supportive kin, and being socially well integrated in the market, for example having colleagues that you can trust to leave your goods or savings with.

I will now turn to the analysis of relations that are specific to sub-sectors of the urban food economy. These sub-sectors consist of rice, fish and vegetables. This sectoral analysis deals with kinds of processes and struggles about which it is difficult to generalise. It illustrates the great diversity of relations at work, the particular forms of informal regulation, the specific tensions and contradictions that emerge in particular sub-sectors and the kinds of the struggles they give rise to. The section addresses the changing social relations in the context of economic liberalisation, with both new sources of exploitation and new spaces of resistance. It brings to light processes and axes of differentiation among informal operators and the conditions of small traders in particular sub-sectors.

5.4 The rice sub-sector: fighting merchant capital

Rice is the sub-sector where contrasts are the sharpest. I discussed in chapter three how a small group has thrived on rice imports, the main staple food consumed in the city, in close connection to the export of cashew nuts. The signs of the affluence of this group are there to be seen in Bissau. They range from the continual building of new and luxurious houses to the large warehouses with endless piles of sacks of rice. Side by side with this prosperity, sometimes literally seated on its doorsteps (often the case of rice retailers), are those bearing the costs of that same prosperity. Ironically, rice trade has become both a major sphere of capital accumulation and of income strategies for survival for a share of the urban poor. Indeed, this sub-sector of the urban economy, where the penetration of capital has been deepest, encapsulates and makes extremely visible the widening social inequality in the city.

I discussed in chapter three how merchant capital in the context of economic liberalisation is making extensive use of informal strategies. Among these strategies is the use of informal outlets for the marketing of this international commodity, which had in former periods, been sold in licensed stores. Merchant capital could not remain indifferent to the great expansion of market places and informal trade in the city. Importers opened warehouses in and around Bandim market, now the main business centre of the city, where they are close to the other agents in the rice marketing chain, both merchants and small retailers, licensed and unlicensed. Wholesalers in their turn also opened their stores in more peripheral spontaneous market places in the city, such as Caracol market. In this process, capital has engaged and subordinated a large number of small rice retailers. I will discuss the contradiction that has emerged, illuminate the conditions in which rice retailers operate, as well as the alternatives they seek. The analysis is based on interviews conducted between 1992 and 1995, with two rice importers, six wholesalers and owners of rice stores, some of which became key informants, and sixteen retailers operating both in Caracol and Bandim markets.

Rice retailers in general in the city face difficult constraints. For one thing, they are many. In addition, their profit margins are generally narrow, squeezed as they are between the high (and variable) prices of their suppliers and a low urban purchasing power. Several of the retailers interviewed reported a deterioration of their businesses compared to earlier years when a 50-kilo bag of rice cost less and sold faster. In their accounts, their real incomes were higher then and 'falling off balance' was less frequent. Different scales of operation could however be identified among rice retailers.

Some retailers were able to purchase several 50-kilo bags of rice from their suppliers at one time, often of various types, and sold several bags in one day. These were often young men. For another category, the scale of operation and the size of earnings were so small that their small enterprises seemed to be constantly on the verge of collapse. This group was only able to buy one bag at a time and it could take them up to three days to sell. After paying repeated daily market fees for the same stock, whatever meagre incomes these sellers had made were frequently swallowed up by municipal collectors. This scale of rice retailing seems to attract those whose options were severely curtailed. For some it constituted a last resort activity to which they turned when earlier businesses had failed and they were left without capital to pursue more profitable options or when parallel businesses were suffering from occasional disruptions. For others, it was something they did in order "not to be idle", not to be completely without any income or "not to steal", as some expressed it to explain that it was barely worthwhile. Many elderly women engage in this kind of trade and I talked to at least four who operated in such precarious conditions. Their old age and physical limitations restrained their range of income opportunities, namely by inhibiting their mobility within the city and beyond. Thus differentiation among rice retailers seems to be structured to some extent by gender and age, although uncovering all the factors involved would require further research. Credit agreements between retailers and suppliers also seem to play a role[174]. I will now turn to the social relations between retailers and their suppliers.

In the city, imported rice is channelled down a hierarchical chain from an importer through wholesalers to the retailers. Rice retailers buy one or more 50-kilo bags of rice and then sell it in quantities of one kilo or less. Some of the interviewed retailers had reached an agreement with one particular supplier who compelled them to always buy from him. At the same time, the contract enabled them to buy their merchandise on credit and eventually to have access to some rice when supplies in the store were low (or being hoarded). On the basis of my interviews with both retailers and wholesalers, one could say that being a relative or an acquaintance of the supplier often qualified for this preferential treatment. From another angle, it is also obvious that these informal agreements between supplier and retailer placed the latter under a firmer grip of merchant capital. These retailers become part of the hierarchical

[174] In addition, the roots of the conditions of the poorest retailers are not to be sought exclusively in the market, but also in the familial context of retailers - for example, the elderly women selling rice often had a large number of dependents including grandchildren making claims on their small incomes. This is an issue I will return to later.

dependence relations and of the vertical chain of credit originating from importers. As one wholesaler explained to me, it is only after the storeowner has recovered the rice loans that he advanced to a dozen or so retailers that he can repay the importer at prices decided by the latter. In their turn, retailers who get their merchandise on credit will also pay back after having sold it and taken a share of the profits. In this light, retailers could be said to be sellers by commission, with wholesale prices decided above them and margins of profit largely beyond their control given the low demand elasticity for this staple food[175]. At the bottom end of the hierarchy, dependence can be such that some of the sellers seemed not to be able to do without this credit, in some cases on a long-term basis. The latter indicates their persistent inability to accumulate any savings, while accumulation at the top proceeds.

Other interviewed rice retailers rotated between several suppliers, buying from the one offering the most favourable price, which usually meant no credit. This may indicate that some may lack the necessary contacts and acquaintances for reaching an agreement with a supplier. In a couple of cases interviewees expressed dislike for borrowing from a single supplier and refused to do so.

Rice retailers face structural constraints posed by capital in yet other ways. The price of a 50-kilo bag of rice at most of the storehouses investigated, with one exception, was the same for consumers and retailers. This means that the retailers will only be approached by consumers who cannot afford to buy in bulk from the store, which is cheaper. Fortunately or unfortunately, this is the situation for many consumers. To complicate things further, at least three of the stores did not only sell in bulk but also by the kilo and usually at the same price as that of retailers. Thus retailers are not only competing among themselves but also with store owners and their close associates working for these owners.

Considerable seasonal variations in the supply of rice also have serious consequences for small rice retailers. When the market is flooded with imported rice the retailers may have difficulty in selling and therefore incur losses. After the cashew season is over, towards the end of the rainy season (August to December), rice shortages become common. On the one hand, importers then have lower motivation to import rice. On the other hand, hoarding of rice to sell at higher prices during the rainy season is also common among storeowners. One wholesaler told me that during the cashew harvest season he used to have 30 to 50 bags of rice in store, in the rainy season however, the amount could reach 200 to 400 bags. Small retailers complained that the more they paid for a bag of rice the lower were their earnings as these were pressed by the low purchasing power of consumers. When rice prices

---

[175] Meagher and Yunusa (1996:4.1) also refer to how some better equipped enterprises in Zaria expanded their operations through increasing subcontracting to small informal operators, such as hawkers, for distribution services.

were hiked, one explained, 'falling off balance' was unavoidable. Thus, the costs of sudden price hikes are disproportionately laid on the shoulders of retailers. And here it is reasonable to assume that whatever networks of support small retailers may have to assist each other through the crises and absorb the shocks, may be in fact oiling the machinery of accumulation at the top – though they may also be subversive, as exemplified below.

In sum, at the top, merchant capital benefits greatly from the activities of thousands of small-scale retailers, a large share of whom barely make a profit. Informalization at the bottom in the case of imported rice can be said to facilitate accumulation by merchant capital. But small retailers do not passively accept either the high prices imposed on them or the variations in rice availability, whether real or artificial. To reduce their dependence on and vulnerability to merchants' practices, many diversify the range of products they sell and their sources of income. For example, one of the retailers also sold cigarettes from the same market spot. Others made soap or roasted peanuts. Yet others sold a variety of grains and dry vegetables. Among these, one group that is of particular interest is that of the retailers who combined the sale of imported rice with that of domestic rice - six of the interviewees were of this category.

The southern regions of Guinea-Bissau produce an abundance of rice. Surpluses have had difficulty in reaching the capital due in part to poor infrastructure and the limited interest of large merchants for this cereal. However, domestic rice seems to have become more visible in the urban market places during the last number of years. I met rural producers at Caracol market who had travelled from the south to sell their surpluses in Bissau. But urban-based retailers have also engaged in the trade of this cereal. Some of the interviewees travelled to the south in search of rice - and those who did so had relatives there. Others travelled to *lumos* - the rural rotating markets located in different parts of the country - where rice producers came to sell their surpluses. The revival of this type of market place with ancient traditions (see chapter two) has facilitated the intensification of the flows of domestic rice brought into the city by small traders - particularly during the months following the harvest, i.e. December to February. Retailers selling domestic rice consistently reported that, even with increased transportation costs, their returns were often higher than those from selling imported rice. One retailer explained that while suppliers' prices for imported rice varied a great deal, the producers' prices of rice in the south did not vary much. Here, urban traders seemed to have ascended to a position in which they were able to buy cheaply from farmers and sell dearly in Bissau, apparently provoking responses by local producers[176]. In

[176] According to one trader, farmers in Catió in 1994 had suddenly stopped selling their rice to traders for that reason and others had recently increased their prices. In addition, urban-based traders had come to face the competition from rice producers from the south selling themselves their products in Bissau.

relation to this, it would be worth pursuing the issue of whether the relative autonomy gained by urban traders from merchant capital in this way is creating other kinds of contradictions, namely among small actors.

The decision of these retailers to search for an alternative cereal to imported rice seems to be an intentional strategy to circumvent high wholesale prices and variability in supply. In spite of the modest amounts of Guinean rice in the city, this increased flow was not necessarily without consequences for the imported rice business. Some of the retailers said that domestic rice sells more rapidly than imported rice and that when there is Guinean rice in the market imported rice takes longer to sell – although one respondent disagreed with this opinion. Domestic rice was reported to be in greater demand and some could even sell it at a higher price than that of imported rice. It is doubtful whether the still modest amount of domestic rice in the city markets has generated any major concerns among merchants and their patrons. But these are interesting signs of consumer and retailer resistance against a policy of rice imports and the interests of capital attached to it. Significantly, however, this domestic rice option that gives rice retailers a margin of manoeuvrability is not open to everyone. As was mentioned above, the smallest scale of rice retailing consists of those whose options are severely curtailed, including by age. Young girls and elderly women are limited in their mobility and are probably more dependent on suppliers of imported rice in the proximity of their selling sites.

The above analysis of the evolving social relations between actors in rice distribution in the city in the context of structural adjustment clearly shows that economic liberalisation has not lead to the liberation of small informal actors. Rather, it facilitated the penetration of merchant capital into spontaneous urban market places and its domination of the supply of the main food staple consumed in the city. In the process, small retailers were drawn into close relations with capital and into international commodity circuits. New dependencies were fostered between wholesalers and small retailers, turning the latter into the lowest link of a patronage network facilitating accumulation at the top. The emerging picture is one of an informalization that favours rice importers, leaving a large share of retailers on the threshold of survival. Indeed, the rice sector exhibits great polarisation. Those at the bottom handle this deepening contradiction in different ways. Some enter into tacit agreements with wholesalers. But others have made efforts to circumvent the exploitative practices of suppliers of imported rice, namely by diversifying suppliers and by seeking more favourable terms elsewhere, namely with rice farmers and at rotating markets.

5.5 The fish sub-sector: informal regulation and differentiation

The fish sub-sector encompasses a greater variety of contradictions and relations. After hinting at the "vertical" contradiction between industrial and artisanal fisheries, I move onto the relations between suppliers and retailers to uncover the kinds of antagonisms, alliances and struggles that unravel at these nodes of distribution. In particular the section illuminates the importance of informal regulation, with its own structures of access and discrimination, for the conditions of those trying to make a living in this sphere. The means devised to influence the practices and circumvent the power of these informal regulators are also discussed. The discussion is based on a variety of sources. Observations and conversations at supply sites were very instructive. Knowledgeable informants such as people with a good grasp of what was happening with artisanal fisheries and market supply were important sources. Finally, I interviewed ten fishermen and at least twenty-four fish sellers of different categories.

Sources of fish supply

The supply of fish to the urban market emanates from a number of sources. Firstly, large-scale cold stores located in the eastern outskirts of the city are the source of frozen fish (see map 4.1 in chapter four). In these stores, foreign industrial fisheries have deposited a share of their catches as part of their fishing agreements with the Guinean government. At the stores, retailers must buy their supplies from a restricted number of intermediaries holding official licenses that allow them to buy fish directly from the stores. Secondly, traders travel weekly to the Bijagós Islands to supply themselves with fish caught by fishermen and then sell to retailers at the Pidgiguiti port in Bissau[177]. Thirdly, there is an artisanal port in the city, Bandim port, where fishermen land their catches and sell them to both intermediaries and retailers. The scale of operation of fishermen at this port varies widely[178]. The largest enterprises operate large motor canoes and catch up to one ton of fish. Such enterprises are often headed by foreign fishermen settled in Bissau (the so-called *Nhomincas*) who have a long tradition in commercial fisheries.

---

[177] This is based on my observations and conversations at the ports of Bubaque and Pidgiguiti as well as with interviews with one of these middlemen and retailers using this supply source. A fuller account of this business can be found in article by Gomes and Duarte (1996).

[178] At one of its edges, the port harbours smaller-scale fishermen operating with small dug-out canoes, whose activities I have documented in Lourenço-Lindell, 1993. We leave them aside here, as their importance to supply the urban fish market is limited.

Commercial artisanal fisheries in Bissau initially expanded considerably with economic liberalisation but this expansion proved hard to sustain [179]. On the one hand, the prices of fuel, oil, ice and nets increased considerably and this was compounded by recurrent shortages which encouraged speculation and increase prices. On the other hand, in the face of declining urban purchasing power, fishermen complained that it became increasingly difficult to sell their catches and that they were sometimes forced to lower prices to unreasonably low levels, given the lack of appropriate refrigeration facilities. The fishermen interviewed reported that profits from catches were insufficient to allow investment and expansion of their enterprises. Some said that they were fishing less frequently than a few years earlier and some had abandoned fishing altogether. Besides suffering from the direct and indirect effects of structural adjustment policies, fishermen were also competing on unequal terms with industrial catches in the cold stores owned by the state or private ventures. While artisanal fishermen had high and fluctuating costs of operation, fish at the cold stores were being sold at much cheaper prices[180]. Some fisherman perceived the state as being the main obstacle to the development of artisanal fisheries, expressing a contradiction between artisanal and industrial supply in Bissau.

I will now turn to the social relations in the marketing chain, beginning with those between retailers and artisanal fishermen, in order to discover other contradictions as well as forms of co-operation and resistance. These relations have an important gender dimension, as retailers are invariably women.

Informal regulation at the artisanal port

The artisanal port of Bandim, located on the shore of Bandim district, is the main source of fresh fish for the city markets. This once calm creek has become a locus of intense activity that is difficult to capture in text. Upon the arrival of the fishing canoes people climb into them and fill up boxes with fish while hundreds of women wait at a distance with empty boxes and buckets. Men drag themselves through the mud between the shore and the canoes carrying boxes of fish on their heads. On the shore, small stalls serve cooked food and women sell a variety of foodstuffs. Pick-up lorries wait to drive sellers and their merchandise to the various market places. What goes on at Bandim port is not merely the landing and wholesaling of fish but a plethora

[179] Based on interviews with fishermen and key informants, namely: Agostinho Silva, head of the Department of Consumer Prices at INEC, with extensive knowledge of food marketing in Bissau; Idrissa Djaló, owner of an artisanal fishing fleet and a local expert on fisheries. See Tvedten (1991).

[180] For example, in 1995, one kilo of first quality fish was being sold by the fishermen at 7,000 PG and by the cold stores at 5,000 PG, and a box of 40 kilos cost up to 1,000,000 PG at the artisanal port while a 20-kilo box cost 150,000/180,000 PG at the cold stores.

of income activities for a wide cross-section of people. In fact, by the time of my last fieldwork, the port had developed into a market place in its own right. Furthermore, the port encapsulates a variety of social relations whose complexity defies any simplistic assumptions. Conversations at the port and interviews with fish sellers (fifteen of which bought fish regularly at the port) helped me to discern the organising threads of this perplexing activity, the informal rules at work, and the instances of exclusion, dependence and co-operation.

Photo 5.1 Fish sales at the port of Bandim

The higher costs of artisanal fisheries naturally affect actors down the distribution chain of fresh fish, including consumers. Squeezed between the high prices of fishermen and the declining purchasing power of urban consumers, many fresh fish retailing enterprises face difficulties. The great increase in the number of women entering the fish trade business since economic liberalisation seems to have contributed to a certain saturation of the fish market and to increasing competition between fish retailers.

Varying scales of activity can be identified among fish traders at the port. Among interviewees, the purchases ranged from five to 120 kilos, reflecting significant differentiation among these traders. Market conditions for fish traders in general have become tougher - these differences are very visible at the port as some retailers carry large boxes while others have only buckets. Interviewed retailers consistently complained (except for one case) that fish had sold more rapidly in former years and that they now had to stay at the market longer working hours to sell all of their fish. Many affirmed that their real incomes had declined. Several reported that they had been forced to reduce their scale of operation. Two cases were particularly illustrative of this "involution". Formerly able to buy a 40-kilo box of fish, both retailers had to begin associating with one or two others to buy that same amount and one of them had even been impelled to go down in scale and purchase by the bucket. While a variety of personal circumstances (such as childbirth or the decease of a family member) often causes downswings such as these, more structural factors are also at work. Indeed, a substantial number of the studied enterprises were in a precarious shape. A greater part of the interviewees declared that they had no savings and that they often did not recover their working capital by the end of the day, i.e. they frequently 'fell off balance'. Even some of the women with long fish trade careers were managing extremely fragile businesses.

These difficulties faced by fish traders were aggravated by uncertainty related to a considerable variation in fish prices at the port. This variation reflected above mentioned fluctuations in the supply and prices of basic means of production, the supply of frozen fish in the market and the seasonality of artisanal catches, with generally lesser amounts of fish being landed at the port during the rainy season, from June to November. During this season the fishermen would also raise their prices to a level which was not affordable to many retailers, as reported by several interviewees. Some retailers expressed the idea that they were being exploited by the prices set by fishermen during conditions of limited supply. One could say that traders' access to merchandise is not only dependent on the vagaries of nature and market supply of the means of production but is also related to the price setting practices of fishermen. Indeed, the swelling number of fish traders in the city following economic liberalisation seems to have given the fishermen the upper hand in the supply chain of fresh fish. Their dominant position however, is not unlimited especially considering both the external constraints on their businesses (see above) and sellers' responses to their prices. Let me elaborate on the latter.

When the supply of fish is scarce many retailers delay their purchase either because they lack the money or because they anticipate that demand will be low for such expensive fish. Retailers can hang out at the port for hours waiting for the fishermen to lower their prices. Constrained by limited refrigeration possibilities, fishermen are often forced to do so in order not to risk wasting a part of their catches. When there is an abundance of fish at the port sellers may refuse to buy at all or will buy a smaller quantity than usual, in the fear of not being able to sell all of their fish - this is relevant for this perishable product, particularly for the majority of traders who do not own freezer boxes. This is yet another factor that forces the fishermen to lower their prices. Retailers also use more organised ways to influence fishermen's prices. When they anticipate that fish will be scarce and expensive on a certain day, groups of retailers who usually purchase by the box (i.e., sizeable customers) agree to show up with small buckets instead of their large boxes. This collective bluff, I was told, was meant to make the fishermen anxious and induce them to lower their prices. Finally, among those buying by the box, many have enlarged the carrying capacity of the standard 40-kilo boxes by widening their edges by heating them. Otherwise, as one explained, retailers would be unable to recover what they had paid for the box.

Traders' access to merchandise is regulated not only by prices but also by informal rules and contracts. Here, fishermen often have a dominating role and are in a position to regulate competition among retailers to their own advantage. Normally, the fisherman responsible for each canoe makes a list of the retailers interested in his fish and later, when he decides to begin the sale, he calls them according to the order of their arrival. Those allowed to register are usually larger scale purchasers carrying 40-kilo boxes. Small-scale vendors, those purchasing by the bucket, could not register and instead were kept waiting until those with large boxes had been served. Yet another category did not need to register. I am referring to traders - usually among larger scale ones buying by the box - having an informal contract with one of the fishermen. Basically this type of contract gives the trader the right to a share of that fisherman's catch, sometimes given on credit, as well as the obligation to purchase from him even when the quality and price of his fish are less favourable than those of other fishermen on the shore. This agreement assures the trader that she will be a priority customer and gives the fisherman the security that a part of his catch will always be sold. These mutual security arrangements seem to be important in the face of significant variations in supply conditions.

However, these agreements are not necessarily egalitarian or equally accessible to all fish traders. I came to realise that many did not participate in them, either because they were excluded or because they refused to engage in what they perceived as unequal partnerships. This was most often the case of small-scale retailers but even those operating at a larger scale sometimes had no fix supplier. Reaching an informal contract with a fisherman made a large difference in the conditions of operation of sellers and appeared to be one factor of differentiation among them. In fact, such agreements seemed to work against those who were excluded. On the one hand, those without such a contract had to walk to the port in the middle of the night – under the fear of being assaulted on the way - in order to rank high on the fishermen's list. Even then there was no guarantee that they would get any fish when their turn came around, either because the fish had run out or had been promised to other customers. On the other hand, those with a contract can spare themselves these discomforts as they are assured that their merchandise will be waiting for them. In addition, given their lower chances of getting fish directly from the fishermen, particularly when catches are scarce, sellers lacking contracts often become dependent upon those having contracts. The latter have risen to a position where they can act as intermediaries and make a profit without even needing to go to the market place. Hindered from direct access to the fishermen's produce by such discriminatory informal regulation, traders without a contract become subjected to the price setting practices of intermediaries. At this level, informal agreements sometimes also developed between a retailer and a particular intermediary. Such agreements may or may not involve short-term credit, with some intermediaries establishing their own group of steady customers.

Secure access to merchandise through informal contracts with fishermen seems to be most common in three main circumstances. First, wives, relatives or close acquaintances to the fishermen often get preferential treatment by the latter. Second, some women sellers have enough capital to be in a position to help the fisherman when his business is suffering a setback. This usually takes the form of lending him money to buy fuel and other production inputs. As was explained above, such setbacks have become frequent for many artisanal fishermen. Third, most of the (female) retailers that I interviewed mentioned contracts based on sexual favours and some were convinced that this was the main strategy used to get a contract. In the opinion of an elderly fish seller, flirting with the fishermen to get contracts was something that had developed recently.

Sexually 'sealed' contracts constitute the darker and possibly newer side of these agreements. Given the significance of an informal contract with a fisherman for securing access to merchandise, and indeed for influencing the fortune of their businesses, many sellers missing the capital and the close family or friendship ties with the fishermen may be induced to make use of the last asset at their disposal, sex. Even this asset is not equally available to every one, with younger women being at an advantage. Elderly traders, besides often lacking the considerable physical strength that this business requires, may also be constrained in the use of sexual strategies. Indeed, some of the older women, in spite of their long fishing careers, were managing extremely fragile businesses. Sometimes a certain contempt or resentment towards women with such loose behaviour could be identified in the accounts of those that either failed or refused to engage in sexual-business relationships with their suppliers.

Informal arrangements also pervade fish supply at the cold stores, in spite of the nominally formal nature of this supply source. There, retailers have access to frozen fish through a restricted number of middlemen who hold licenses to collect fish in bulk from the stores and then resell it just outside the cold stores to sellers without licenses. The relations that store employees entertain with these middlemen involve informal (if not illegal) components such as the sharing of the profits from the sales outside the store. Also, when fish is scarce in the cold stores, two retailers reported that bribes are paid to store employees in order to release some of the stored fish. As at the port, some retailers had a contract with one of the licensed middlemen thus making them priority customers. This allowed them to arrive later to the stores and gave them the possibility to buy fish on credit. Others reported not to have such a contract and simply bought the fish from the middlemen offering the best prices (retailers in both categories were interviewed). As stated earlier, prices at the stores varied little - at least in 1995, varying only slightly between the different stores - but middlemen varied their prices according to the general supply of fish in the market and retailers complained about their speculative practices. Those without contracts and credit arrangements probably suffered more from these variations in prices and risked not getting fish when supplies at the stores were low.

At variance from conditions at the port, holding a license was considered an important factor in climbing up the frozen fish marketing chain. However, and not surprisingly, there were barriers to acquiring such a license. Some retailers told me they did not even know how to get such a license. One of them had tried to get one at the Ministry of Fisheries for years but was always turned down, pointing out that she lacked the contacts. This discrimination at the level of formal institutions certainly compelled some retailers to enter informal agreements with suppliers in order to secure a position in this distribution chain. As at the port, there were references to sexual strategies, where partners of different sexes were involved.

Thus retailers without contracts at both the artisanal port and the cold stores seemed to share a disadvantageous and less secure position. In the face of this, how did they respond? Two of the retailers had switched supply sites, from a cold store to the Bandim port, not only because of perceived advantages in terms of costs and profits but also because of their exclusion from agreements with suppliers. They reported that many others had done the same recently and that while some of them had already reached a contract with a fisherman, others had not. But besides those that actively pursued a personal agreement with one supplier, by whatever means, there were others that refused to engage in contracts that they felt were exploitative, particularly those of a sexual nature. A couple of my interviewees consciously diversified their suppliers at a particular supply location, and four of them even regularly toured between the various supply sites in the city in order to avoid sexual harassment or exploitation by a fixed supplier. Traders bound by a personal agreement with a supplier seemed not to rotate between supply locations as easily, as they usually lacked a contract in the other sites and would in fact jeopardise the one that they had, as was clearly the situation of one of my interviewees. Avoidance of suppliers that were perceived as exploitative was also evident concerning middlemen transporting fish from the islands. Retailers were aware of the great difference in the prices these middlemen paid to fishermen and the prices they charged in Bissau and some perceived this as unfair and bought fish from them only as a last resort[181].

[181] Judging from the costs reported by one such middleman I interviewed and the prices paid by retailers in Bissau, the profits that were being made by the former were indeed very high (between 1,500,000 and 2,000,000 PG in 1995).

The relative autonomy that these retailers may have attained from exploitative personal relations with suppliers seemed often to be at the sacrifice of a more stable and eventually successful business. To counter their unfavourable position in the supply chain, women lacking contracts use more egalitarian ties to improve their access to fish. In a couple of cases small retailers pooled their money so that they could then buy in bulk and get a better deal than if they bought separately by the bucket. Among friends, when one had not succeeded in getting fish on a particular day, another shared her merchandise with her colleague without making any profit on that fish - as one interviewee put it, "tomorrow may be my turn". Retailers also keep each other informed about changes in supply and prices of fish and, as described above, occasionally co-ordinate their actions to get better deals with suppliers.

There is one category of small-scale fish sellers that stand in stark contrast with the gloomy prospects of other small retailers. These are people not dependent on a supplier but who sell fish caught by themselves or their close relatives. They sell modest amounts of fish mainly of small size and value, particularly the locally called *bentaninha*, which are caught with snares in the mangrove or with hand-nets in the flooded paddy fields and rivers. The women selling this type of fish are usually either relatives of rice farmers in Bissau or travel from the proximate hinterland of the city. Particularly the latter have increased drastically in number with the improvement of communications and economic liberalisation. Perhaps because they are largely unaffected by the rising prices of imported or expensive inputs or by variations in producer or middlemen prices[182], they actually seem to thrive in a context of shrinking urban purchasing power. The very cheap fish they offer sells much more rapidly than superior varieties of fish, as it is the only kind of fish that a large share of urban consumers can afford. Meagher and Yunusa (1991:4.1) have commented on the emergence of similar pockets of rising demand among the low-income market in the context of adjustment as a result of shifts in demand and diets towards cheaper and lower quality foods in Zaria.

Indeed, with their low operation costs *bentaninha* sellers are able to lower their prices to levels that no one else in the market can compete with. At Caracol market, where they are in large number, they arrive early, display their fish on the pavement on the edges of the market and three to four hours later they have already left. This can be compared with the average twelve hours that the other interviewed fish retailers spent at the market place. They represent tough competition to other sellers in the fish market. Several of the other fish retailers - and even the head of a large artisanal fishing enterprise - complained about this. They said they had difficulty in selling their fish whenever *bentaninha* sellers were in the market place. One other respondent partly blamed them for the reduction in scale of her business. Yet another told

[182] Their costs are restricted to the imported nylon thread that they use to construct the nets and transportation costs for those coming from outside Bissau.

me how she had abandoned the selling spot that she had earlier managed to get inside the market and moved her business outside to where *bentaninha* sellers were and thus where customers flocked. This particular type of small sellers thus seems to enjoy considerable autonomy, although this is hardly a reason for celebration as the relative advantage that they have in the market reflects negative trends in urban purchasing power and dietary changes.

Photo 5.2 *Bentaninha* sellers at Caracol market

From the above discussion it becomes obvious that a great differentiation has emerged in the context of market liberalisation among women fish sellers. At the upper end, one finds women operating stocks of up to 400 kilos. These usually handle frozen fish of high value, often enjoy a relatively secure access to merchandise and own expensive equipment such as freezer boxes - these make a big difference in these enterprises that deal with such a perishable product as they facilitate large purchases and reduce the risk of spoiled left-overs, and thus of 'falling off balance'. At the bottom, where a much larger number can be found, are very small retailers that own little more than a bucket, handle only small quantities of fish, frequently 'fall off balance' and lack agreements with suppliers. This latter group is particularly vulnerable to variations in fish supply and prices, given the current structure of informal relations of supply – with the exception of the resilient *bentaninha* traders mentioned above. Some of the factors playing a role in this differentiation have been mentioned, such as age, access to capital or having a personal relationship with suppliers, sometimes of a sexual kind[183]. This differentiation

[183] In addition, based on both my observations and Monteiro (2001), there seems to exist a certain ethnic clustering with women from the Eastern groups becoming particularly visible in frozen fish supply and women from coastal groups, particularly the Pepel, engaging more often in the distribution of fresh fish as well as in the fishing of *bentaninha*.

in fish trade also has a certain relation with different selling conditions and the type of market place being used by these different categories of traders. From a rapid one time survey in the fish sections of Bandim and Caracol markets I could see that in the former, large scale retailers selling high quality fish from industrial fisheries were numerous[184], while in the latter market place fresh fish from artisanal fisheries dominated. This reflects the different structure of demand at these markets that are placed differently in a hierarchy of market places in Bissau.

In sum, this section illustrates various useful points. The fish sub-sector contains a variety of contradictions and alliances. The first contradiction addressed here was that existing between industrial and artisanal fisheries, which had consequences for all of the agents along the distribution chain. The cold stores, the outlet of industrial fisheries - in which the state in some cases still held a share in the mid-1990s - are seemingly the most formal segment of the fish sub-sector with access supposedly regulated by state institutions. However they benefit from informality to a great extent in that they reach the public through a range of unlicensed retailers and are the arena for a variety of informal (if not illegal) agreements between store employees and middlemen, blurring the formal-informal boundary. Regarding the privileged position of these latter agents, there are barriers to formalisation such as those hindering traders from acquiring a middleman's license, in spite of the official policy of facilitation.

Informal contracts are also of crucial importance at the more informal end of fish supply, i.e. artisanal fisheries, where regulation is completely of an informal kind. Also here there are barriers involved in getting an informal contract, as many lack the capital, the kin ties or the sexual assets that facilitate entering one. Here, the contradiction lies mainly between medium and small-scale actors, with fishermen in a dominant position as regulators of prices and competition among traders. The relevance of informal agreements for the fortunes of fish trade enterprises also mean that retailers choose and switch supply sources not just in response to differences in price and potential profit, as a behaviour exclusively guided by market rules would imply, but also in search of a personal relationship with a supplier that will give their businesses a more stable existence and potentially an upswing. However, some women traders opted for alternatives to subordinate relationships with fishermen, such as egalitarian types of partnerships, and found ways of influencing their practices. In addition, spaces of autonomy could definitely be found in the fish business, as illustrated by *bentaninha* sellers. Finally, fish trade illustrates the considerable differentiation that may exist in a realm numerically dominated by women, challenging simplistic assumptions that women are invariably trapped in petty activities. It supports evidence from elsewhere

[184] There is one area in Bandim market with lined up freezer boxes where these large-scale retailers store their frozen fish.

of a growing differentiation among women in the context of adjustment and liberalisation, albeit with a majority of women operating at survival levels (see introduction to this chapter).

5.6 The vegetable sub-sector: intricate forms of diversification

Urban market places have apparently become much better supplied with fresh vegetables since the liberalisation of commerce. Women dominate the production and sale of vegetables, especially those of coastal ethnic groups, and among these the Mancanha are prominent in their horticultural skills. Although not new, small-scale commercial horticulture in and around Bissau has experienced a revival in the last one and a half decades according to interviewed officials and experts. But there is also an increase in the number of rural women commuting to the city to sell their produce there, as well as of urban residents supplying themselves at rural rotating markets dispersed in the country. The result has been a rapid increase in the number of people engaging in the production and sale of vegetables in the urban market places.

These trends may be partly interpreted as part of a more general "greening of cities" recorded for other urban areas in Africa and the developing world in the context of deteriorating economic conditions for urban dwellers (United Nations, 1996a; Rogersson, 1993, 1997). While some have expressed concern that urban agriculture may be as yet another realm of oppression of the poor (Sanyal, 1987), a large share of studies have adopted celebratory tones, lauding it as the solution to the problems of the poor. This section does not aim to present a comprehensive account of urban agriculture activities and their potential or limitations. Rather, it attempts to make a critical assessment of the conditions and relations pervading small-scale production and sale of horticultural products as a sub-sector of the urban informal economy[185]. Firstly, I will try to illuminate the changing conditions of operation for the participants and the changed relations of distribution in the context of adjustment (in a sub-sector totally dominated by women). Secondly, a great variety of social relations will emerge, including relations of solidarity and of subordination, as well as spaces of relative autonomy. Since analysing all of these relations in depth would require a study of its own, this complexity is only briefly sketched here. The discussion is based on interviews with 13 vegetable sellers, horticulturists, some quantitative data from my household survey[186] and interviews with knowledgeable persons, such as an agronomist of the Ministry of Rural Development and officials at an earlier urban agri-

[185] Another important farming activity in the study setting, that of subsistence rice production and its attendant social relations, are discussed in chapter seven.

[186] 49 households had members engaged in horticulture and almost half of these sold more than half of their production during season.

culture project in Bissau, the "Green Belt Project". One study connected with that project, conducted by Moustier (1993), is also a valuable source.

The complexity of the supply of green vegetables to the urban market almost defies description. One way of beginning to disentangle this complexity is by giving an overview of the various supply sources of fresh vegetables to urban market places. In April 1995 I let one assistant conduct a rapid survey on the origins of foodstuffs in six market places in Bissau – Santa Luzia, Pefiné, Kirintim, Caracol, Caracol bus-stop market and Bandim, with the latter two having wholesale functions (see table 5.1 and map 4.1 in the last chapter). A total of 372 vegetable retailers were approached. The largest share of vegetable traders in most of the markets (except for the two wholesale markets) consists of traders who grew vegetables themselves in Bissau. Another important category concerned traders that cultivated in rural areas, where they were probably resident. A share of traders did not grow the vegetables themselves. Instead they bought them from producers who either cultivated in plots around the city or in rural areas. These producers gather at wholesale markets such as Caracol bus-stop market[187]. Yet other retailers travelled to *lumos*, i.e. rotating markets in the rural areas, to buy their merchandise.

Table 5.1 Sources of fresh vegetables for all traders in six market places (in percentage of the total number of vegetables traders)

	Caracol	Caracol bus-stop	Bandim	Kirintim	Sta Luzia	Pefiné	Total
Produced by trader in Bissau	44 (23)	33 (20)	35 (27)	38 (25)	59 (13)	51 (48)	156
Produced by trader outside Bissau	19 (10)	63 (38)	44 (34)	33 (22)	0 (0)	0 (0)	104
Bought from producers in Bissau	19 (10)	0 (0)	15 (12)	29 (19)	14 (3)	43 (40)	84
Bought from producers outside Bissau	17 (9)	3 (2)	6 (5)	0 (0)	27 (6)	6 (5)	27
Total no. traders	100 (52)	100 (60)	100 (78)	100 (66)	100 (22)	100 (94)	372

[187] A similar one-time inquiry on the geographical origins of fresh vegetables conducted by Moustier (1993) in nine markets in 1992, using a sample of 166 sellers, corroborates my results. The average percentage of retailers selling produce grown in Bissau (68 per cent) is also the largest category. The results differ in that this survey also captured cases in which vegetables had been brought from Senegal, and in a modest 19 per cent of retailers selling produce originating from other areas of the country, which is certainly related to the exclusion of an important wholesale market, Caracol-bus stop, from the sample.

Access to land

A crucial issue for sellers growing their own horticultural products in the city is access to land. They may gain access to land in three main ways. Firstly, women may get agricultural concessions from the municipal government, which has legal control over urban and peri-urban land[188]. Secondly, some respondents had got access to land made available through an earlier externally financed project, the Green Belt Project. Indeed, according to project officials, in 1992 the project supported 1095 cultivators spread throughout the city. Participants in the project complained however, that they risked loosing those plots because of the high rents being charged. Thirdly, a share of the respondents grew vegetables on customary land. There is a dual system of land tenure in which the state is the owner of all land and may grant concessions and traditional systems of land allocation have also been maintained. This duality of land tenure with persisting customary or informal components is not exclusive to Bissau, as documented by Piermay (1997) for Kinshasa, Attahi (1997) for other cities in Francophone Africa, and Gough and Yankson (2000) on Accra.

Production on customary land is dependent upon the consent of Pepel elders. This includes cultivation in parts of the paddy fields after the rice has been harvested. Two groups of women grow vegetables there. The first group consists of women living in compounds of the group with ancestral rights to that land. These women have no inheritance rights to this land and are dependent on males and seniors in the compound for gaining access to a plot. Most of these women have to give priority to rice production activities during labour demanding periods, according to the sexual division of labour in the compound[189]. The other group consists of women belonging to the Mancanha ethnic group who are renowned for their horticultural skills. They "borrow" land from the local Pepel in exchange for a (symbolic) rent. These women usually have horticultural production as their main livelihood for most of the year. They may hold different plots that they cultivate either simultaneously or in different seasons. But as living costs climb and competition between sellers increases in the market, local Pepel women have begun to claim customary land that their male relatives used to rent out to Mancanha women, in order to grow vegetables themselves on that land.

This short description of a complex issue suffices to disclose the importance of informal land tenure systems and the attendant power relations for commercial horticulture in the city. It also hints at the multiple ways in which land used for commercial horticulture in the city has been regulated, ranging

[188] On urban land policy in Bissau, see: Acioly (1993:59-67) and Dávila (1987:68, 1991:103).

[189] From April to June many of these women will also engage in the picking of cashew nuts in the plantations of their male kin. For this group, cash income activities are to be conceived partly as a strategy of the extended family, providing for both the cash needs of the family and expenditure with rice production.

from customary rules to those of an official institution such as the Green Belt Project. Some interviewed women cultivated different plots under different tenure regimes and were thus subjected to different relations of allocation simultaneously. Their ways and possibilities of influencing these relations in the different systems most probably also varied. While, according to one of the participants in the Green Belt Project, women were organising collectively in 1995 for lower plot rents, changing the rules of land allocation in the compound probably require more subtle strategies.

Concerning other inputs into commercial horticulture enterprises, there is considerable mutual giving and borrowing of seeds and tools among horticulturists, particularly those who are relatives, neighbours and friends. Indeed, several complained that imported inputs are out of their reach as they are too expensive. Skills are also transferred in this way, even across ethnic groups, with the Mancanha being considered as valuable advisers. Men may be hired shortly for the tasks of digging wells, fencing and preparing the land, otherwise male relatives may perform those tasks for free and in one compound collective work had been used to fence the horticulture plots for all the women in the compound.

Trade in vegetables

We can now turn to the sale activities in the city. One could broadly divide them into three categories that participate in the vegetable market in different ways, although a certain overlapping of roles occurs. These are firstly, those horticulturists that wholesale their produce, I call these *producer-wholesalers*; secondly, those who retail their produce, these are the *producer-retailers*; and thirdly, those vegetable retailers who have to purchase their merchandise, i.e. simply *retailers*.

Vegetable producers with a sufficient harvest may operate at the wholesale level. Some may sell at the large and multi-functional Bandim market where access to selling space seems to be largely restricted to sellers with a regular attendance and long careers. Another wholesale market place for vegetables appeared in the early nineties by the side of the road which forms the northern border of Bandim (see map 4.2)[190]. It grew up next to a bus stop and is therefore well connected to both the hinterland and other parts of the city. That which I refer to here as the 'Caracol bus-stop market' is the meeting point for vegetable growers and traders from a wide range of places (see table 5.1 above). Horticulturists cultivating in the green spaces in different parts of the city come here to sell their produce. Others come by bus from the rural areas (from Biombo, Safim, Prábis, located on the island of Bissau but also from as

[190] About half of the interviewees either sold or bought vegetables at this market. I also spent some time at this market, talking to sellers.

far as Bula and Bissorã, some 40 and 75 kilometres away, respectively) and return the same day or stay overnight in town in the homes of relatives, to sell eventual remaining produce the next morning. Some traders who procure merchandise at rotating markets in different parts of the country also come to sell vegetables here. Retailers from all parts of the city gather at Caracol bus-stop market to purchase vegetables that they sell at the different market places the following morning. "This is where business is" one seller told me when explaining why she came all the way to Caracol-bus stop instead of selling at one of the market places closer to her residence.

Caracol bus-stop market hardly qualifies for even the most liberal understanding of the term 'market'. It consists of a brief gathering of people who crowd into the small space between the road and the houses bordering it. Goods are displayed on the ground, no tables or shades are there to be seen. The gathering begins around mid-afternoon, attendants do their business and three to four hours later all are gone, and the place swept clean. Little trace is left of the intense exchange activity that took place there earlier - one effect of this short-duration being that these sellers do not need to pay market fee collectors as these operate mainly in the morning. And yet, in spite of its ephemeral nature, this market constitutes a major point of distribution of vegetables for the entire city. A similar fleetingness can be seen in the rotating markets around the country, as well as in the apparent ease with which participants combine or shift between roles - as producers, wholesalers and retailers in the vegetable sub-sector - from one season to another or even during the same day. This transient character of many informal market activities does not necessarily divest them from established routines, personalistic agreements and structured relations. In fact, the emergence of new nodes in the vegetable supply chain, as represented by Caracol bus-stop market, has been accompanied by evolving ways of connecting to and relating with different agents in that chain, by new collaborations as well as tensions. Let me briefly illustrate some of these, as they revealed themselves to me by the interviewees operating in the various nearby markets.

Producer-wholesalers come with their produce to the Caracol bus-stop market regularly. This allows a share of them to establish fixed retailer customers, which is advantageous given the perishable nature of the merchandise. Retailers may also try to build a personal contact with a wholesaler, which may or not lead to sales on credit. Retailers generally did not voice complaints about exploitative practices on the part of wholesalers and competition between the two categories seemed not to be an issue of concern. Wholesalers charge lower prices than retailers, or more accurately, make larger bundles of vegetables, but they sell mainly during the afternoon, while retailers operate mainly in the morning as is the case with other food retailers. This is the time of the day when people are shopping for the main, often the only, cooked meal of the day.

Photo 5.3 Vegetable traders in Caracol market

Competition did seem to be an issue between the *producer–retailers* and *retailers*. *Producer–retailers* seemed to have a different schedule of operations from *producer–wholesalers*: they worked on their plots in the afternoon and sold their produce in the market places during the morning, i.e. at the same time as retailers. The latter complained that they had difficulty selling their products when the former were at the market place and had to stay longer hours at the market, because *producer–retailers* were able to make larger bundles for the same price. A certain distrust and uneasy feelings towards this group of cultivators could be detected at this level. In addition, there seemed to be a difference in the stability and precariousness of business between these two categories: besides earning less than those selling their own produce, *retailers* clearly 'fell off balance' more easily because they needed to recover their capital on a daily basis in order to be able to buy more the next day, while for the other group the costs of the enterprise were spread over time and new supplies were not dependent on having capital on a particular day. This particular resilience and competitiveness of the *producer–retailer* category in horticulture seems analogous to that of *bentaninha* fisher-retailers mentioned in the fish section. They represent spaces of relative autonomy in the informal economy.

Although some categories within the sector seemed to be doing slightly better than others, there were signs of market saturation. The increase in the number of sellers and the declining purchasing power in the city led to a saturation of the market in certain products and to heightened competition among sellers. Many of the interviewees complained about increasing difficulties in selling all of their produce in comparison to former years and about a decline in their real earnings from vegetable sales. This perhaps provides a sobering example of the fact that the agricultural activities of urbanites may not provide sustainable incomes to the poor, contrary to what has often been assumed.

The interviewees dealt with these tougher market conditions in a variety of ways. Some diversified their sources of income by conducting different types of businesses simultaneously or at different times of the year, in order to fill in seasonal gaps in supply or idle periods in agricultural work. This was the case with about half of the interviewees, who besides selling vegetables engaged in the processing and sale of cashew wine, in small-scale fish retail, in the sale of beer and in the sale of fried pastries. Some were in a position to combine roles within the vegetable sub-sector, by selling both their own produce and that of other horticulturists, in different seasons of the year or simultaneously. In this way they diversified the range of vegetables they sold, compensated for a small harvest or improved the stability of their businesses. Some sought to diversify or to get better prices by combining a range of sources and locations of supply, stretching well beyond the city into the rotating markets in the countryside and across the national borders[191]. In the process, new or intensified connections between places and between people have emerged or revived.

To summarise this section, the period of structural adjustment has presented producers and traders of fresh vegetables in the city with both opportunities and constraints. Commercial horticulture has expanded and the increased supply of fresh vegetables to the city has implied intensified exchanges between city and countryside. On the production side, regulation of access to basic means of production take a variety of forms, including informal means of accessing customary land and non-market exchange of working materials. Here, elements of both solidarity and subordination seem to play a role. On the distribution side, liberalisation of the economy has fostered new nodes in the vegetable supply chain as well as the emergence of new relations between the different groups of participants. Here, I could find for example informal agreements between producers and retailers. Although some tensions seemed to be emerging in an environment of heightened competition among vegetable

[191] Only one of the interviewed vegetable sellers used to travel to Senegal to buy her vegetables, but Moustier (1993) captured several such cases. Traveling to neighbouring countries is common among urban-based traders, in search for a variety of goods.

sellers, relations of a clearly exploitative kind between suppliers and retailers, common in the rice and fish sub-sectors, could not be identified on the basis of my empirical data. Compared to other sub-sectors of the urban food economy, vegetable supply to the city seems to generally constitute a space of relative autonomy for many women. Generally, this section highlights the intricate combination that these small actors make of economic activities, sources of merchandise, land tenure systems and locations.

5.7 Conclusion

Adjustment policies of liberalisation and deregulation of economic activity have presented Bissauans with both opportunities and constraints. Decreased risks of confiscation of goods and the gradual lifting of internal customs for example were probably welcome by groups of small traders who had for years tried to make a living illegally. And indeed many seem to have made creative use of these newly gained liberties and mobility, by combining different locations, exploring new niches, creating new market places and nodes of interaction. But interpreting these changes as the ultimate victory of the poor would be out of place. In fact, their struggle has just begun. Let me summarise the case made here.

Firstly, the local government continues to be a crucial actor in the urban economy. Its practices are at great variance with the official discourse about the informal sector. The local government has benefited from the exponential growth of food markets in the city, as these are the main source of its revenues, while delivering little in return. Moreover, besides using a fee system that is discriminative of the smallest traders in the market, it turns a blind eye to the irregular practices of its fee collectors. Secondly, private merchant capital has penetrated the growing spontaneous markets in the suburbs and subordinated the small retailers it supplies. This was particularly the case with imported rice. Although there was a degree of differentiation among retailers, for many this was one of the least profitable businesses and one of last resort. Not surprisingly, this is the option most accessible to elderly women and young girls. In these conditions, networks of support at the bottom, by keeping rice retail businesses floating, may ultimately be subservient to the accumulation interests of merchants. That is, it is probable that networks of accumulation are thriving at the cost of networks of survival. But I also showed examples where the networks constructed by retailers were subversive of those interests.

Thirdly, in the three sub-sectors analysed there were signs of saturation at the lower end of the market, though to different degrees. This was perceived to have been the result of the invasion of the market by large numbers of sellers, a decline in the purchasing power of consumers and increases in the prices of merchandise. All of these can be related, directly or indirectly, to adjustment policies.

Given the above pressures, not surprisingly, many respondents claimed to be spending an increasing number of hours at the market place in an attempt to sustain income levels and smaller retailers frequently 'fell off balance', i.e. lost their working capital. Some had been forced to decrease the scale of their operations and others had abandoned certain market niches. These findings converge with other studies of changes in conditions in the lower layers of the informal economy in a context of adjustment, i.e. a trend towards intensified marginalization as well as exploitation, as returns for low income activities are pressed down and the use of informal labour is intensified[192]. For the majority of those depending on trade-based livelihoods, their vulnerability seems to have increased.

I have tried to present a view of the struggles of those experiencing these threats "from above" - the deeper penetration of merchant capital, a persistently hostile local government and the burdens related to adjustment policies. But these are not the only constraints against which small actors have had to resist. Liberalisation has allowed for a wide range of relations to develop *within* the informal market, which influence the conditions of operation of small actors. The social relations pervading food supply have certainly attained new levels of complexity. These are manifest in a multiplicity of agents in distribution chains, a variety of modes of operation and types of social relations, including customary regulation of access to resources - this was notably the case of access to land by horticulturists. In exploring new opportunities and coping with new strains in the market, informal actors develop a variety of personalistic ties, co-operative arrangements and informal agreements with market colleagues, suppliers, employers, friends and relatives. And here, I have argued, lies a whole new range of possibilities and constraints, and indeed a whole new front of struggles to discover.

I have attempted to illustrate the wide variation in the nature and content of the relations involved, a variation so often ignored in the literature, not least in the "social capital" literature. I discussed issues of solidarity, co-operation and companionship in the market, as exemplified in this chapter by instances of partnership between women and rotating savings groups. But I also attempted to avoid romanticised and reductionist views of informal relations at the bottom and ventured into the politics of support *within* the informal realm. Indeed, these relations can be as much a source of relief and success as they can be of subordination and marginalization. For example, rotating savings groups tend to exclude the poorest. Other relations are of an extremely subordinating nature, as was the case with some of the relations operating at the artisanal port. Among these evolving constellations of informal relations in the

---

[192] Meagher and Yunusa (1991, 1996); Lugalla (1997); Brand et al (1995); Manuh (1994); Zack-Williams (2000); Nabuguzi (1994).

market, in the context of liberalisation various regulatory agents have emerged or become more visible within the informal economy. While they themselves may be subordinated to wider constraints, they have ascended to a position from which they could influence the fate of other informal operators. Examples of these were artisanal fishermen regulating prices and competition at Bandim port and customary holders of land used by horticulturists. In the first case, these less visible forms of governance had created their own forms of discrimination and unaccountability. This should throw serious doubts on neoliberal assumptions that these types of informal agreements and rules are necessarily suitable substitutes for or inherently more democratic than state regulation.

The chapter has shown how individual actors are differently positioned in these informal networks of both benign and pernicious ties. Those living hand to mouth, lacking the physical strength or, in some cases, the sexual assets, often found themselves excluded and marginalized. Many traders revealed an acute awareness of these inequalities and of the vital importance of such ties for the survival of their businesses. Not surprisingly, traders often purposefully chose a course of action within the range of options available to them. Some struggled for inclusion and even chose to engage in unequal partnerships with suppliers in their pursuit of enhanced retail careers. Others opted for a disengaged position from such partnerships. Instead, they sought ways of circumventing informal power bases in the market and pursued more egalitarian alternatives, eventually at a material cost. These choices are illustrated particularly in the fish sub-sector but these different courses of action also surfaced in the relations between small actors and more powerful actors in the food market, such as rice wholesalers and municipal fee collectors.

In sum, small informal actors find themselves struggling on a variety of fronts, and with varying degrees of success. Processes of exploitation and marginalization seem to have deepened in the informal realm under conditions of adjustment, lending strength to other recent studies[193]. But the magnitude of these processes varies between and within sub-sectors of the urban informal economy, as do the types of relations at work. In some cases spaces of relative autonomy have emerged, as was the case of *bentaninha* sellers - albeit their competitive position in the market is no reason for celebration as it signals an impoverishment of the urban population. This confirms the indeterminacy of social struggles and the need to look at concrete empirical situations.

The same caution is advisable when addressing the conditions of women informal operators, major protagonists in this chapter and the object of widely divergent interpretations in the literature. There is considerable differentiation among women traders in Bissau, which echoes findings elsewhere, in a context of adjustment (Brand et al., 1995; Ndiaye, 1998; Lugalla, 1997). But for a

[193] See Lugalla (1997); Nabuguzi (1994); Meagher and Yunusa (1991); Manuh (1994); Brand et al (1995).

large share, one can hardly speak of an empowerment through their increased engagement in the market. The dependence of women traders on support from relatives, particularly male ones, is significant. Patriarchy in the market and official institutions also continue to discriminate against women. The majority of them continue to operate at survival levels or have seen their conditions deteriorate. This is in line with other studies that have found women overwhelmingly concentrated in the least profitable activities and that have reported a worsening of their conditions in the informal economy (Meagher and Yunusa, 1996; Brand et al., 1995; Lugalla, 1997). In the face of this, over-enthusiastic accounts of women's achievements in the market, automatically spilling over to the domestic domain, in the contemporary context of crisis and adjustment seem unrealistic[194]. In spite of the overwhelming burdens being placed upon them, however, the co-operative efforts of small women traders help, to some extent, attenuate the harsh conditions in which they work, provide them and their dependants with a measure of material security and occasionally with an opportunity to circumvent the power of those influencing their conditions.

[194] See for example, Tripp (1989) and Sow (1993).

6 Social networks sustaining household consumption

The last chapters have dealt primarily with informal relations pervading small-scale trade activities, the most common source of income for residents in Bandim. This and the next chapter will focus on relations of assistance that sustain households' consumption. In chapter seven I will concentrate on kin-based support and how it is changing. In this chapter I address a wider variety of sources of support. I will begin by presenting groups that have some welfare functions in the neighbourhood. Then I will proceed with an overview of social networks, their most common configurations, the various sources of assistance and how people combine them.

The discussion sets out to highlight how relations supporting consumption are faring in the face of prolonged economic crisis and worsening urban living conditions. There is currently an over-enthusiasm in the mainstream literature, particularly in the social capital discourse, about the potential of social networks to provide welfare to the poor. This is founded on an assumption that social resources are something that the poor *do* have and *do* cope through. This chapter is an assessment of the effects of material poverty and the hardships imposed by adjustment policies on social networks of assistance. How viable are the collaborative initiatives of the poor in the context of an adjustment-led development strategy? Are they really protecting the poor or are there groups 'falling off' these informal safety nets? Related to these questions, issues of differential access to assistance will be explored to show that the poor are differentiated in terms of their ability to mobilise support.

A second aim in the chapter is to highlight the multiple nature that social relations of assistance can take and the variety of motivations and rationalities that social networks may contain. This is intended to move the analysis beyond one-sided interpretations that see informal support systems as either driven by self-interested motives or as the result of moral and cultural imperatives. In connection to this aim, I attempt to make a disaggregated analysis of the various social relations of assistance existing within networks in order to probe into whether variations in the constellation of these relations have consequences for people's ability to mobilise support in situations of crisis. Such a disaggregated analysis will show how different kinds of relations vary in their levels of resilience in the face of crisis.

I used social networks as a methodological device to explore issues of marginalization from networks of assistance, the complex webs of relationships of assistance, and the apparently disparate types of social relations and rationales pervading them. 'Networks' were used to systematically collect data on the range of social resources available to households and the nature of their various social ties in terms of motivation, claims and power balance in such relationships. The resulting data are necessarily subjective as it relies on respondents' own judgements about the social relations they were involved in. The interviews touched upon social ties facilitating access to important livelihood resources and then focused on relationships sustaining consumption and generally assisting the household in times of need. The social networks of 30 households were studied, the household being understood here as a consumption unit, i.e. the group of people who eat together. Data were collected mainly during my final phase of fieldwork in 1999 and under difficult conditions as it immediately followed the 1998-99 armed conflict. Methodological details of the network study are presented in chapter one.

6.1 Local configurations of assistance

Let me begin by introducing the main sources of assistance available to Bandim dwellers, particularly those sustaining their consumption. I will divide them into groups within which support is exchanged and looser social networks of assistance. I will begin with the former, while the latter will occupy the rest of the chapter.

Solidarity groups

In the neighbourhood there are several kinds of groups within which exchange of material support often occur. Firstly, rotating savings groups are popular in the market place and beyond (these are discussed in chapter five). Secondly, there are *manjuandades*, a kind of social club with a long history in Bissau, which serve recreational and economic assistance functions for its members. This source of assistance is not easily accessible to everyone because membership quotas and the ritual of entrance imply costs that are prohibitive to many[195]. There are two other kinds of groups that have significance in the study setting and which seem to be more accessible to the local poor. These are redistribution groups among casual workers and the local evangelical

[195] This is based on an interview with the leaders of one of these local groups, the locally renown "Esperança de Bandim" in 1999 as well as on my interviews with sellers who were asked whether this kind of affiliation mattered for their relations of assistance in the market.

church. I will now consider their virtues and shortcomings under the contemporary conditions.

Redistribution groups of casual workers

Throughout my fieldwork I encountered many men in Bandim who were dependent on casual work (*surni*, in Creole). I had the opportunity to discuss with a handful of my interviewees their casual work activities. The local term of *surni* refers to short-term work tasks that lack written contracts and that have deep historical roots in the city (see chapters two and three). It is a general term comprising a great variety of activities, ranging from digging wells for small-scale horticulturists to loading work for import-export firms. It is performed either individually or in groups and encompasses both skilled and unskilled workers. Many of those *surni* workers that I met were redundant workers. Casual work has most probably increased in the city, as it has elsewhere in the developing world and beyond (see chapter one)[196]. This may be interpreted as a result of both retrenchment and the extensive use that capital is making of it in the context of economic liberalisation and the booming cashew economy (see chapter three).

There are organised groups among casual workers within which members inform each other about casual jobs and are hired as a group to perform labour intensive tasks, often relying on a headman who cultivates contacts with potential employers and negotiates with them the terms of the collective work agreement. These groups often develop welfare functions. For example, should only some members of the group get day work, the other members who do not can often count on receiving a share of the incomes. Members also assist each other in need. "If I get *surni*", one explained, "I separate a share and give to the first two members that I encounter". When he himself was out of *surni*, he "circulated" in certain places until he met one of the others. When he and his family were out of food, he sought help from another member of the group and if the latter had something to give or lend, he could not refuse. This particular group had existed for more than ten years. Willingness to work and honesty were considered indispensable for such a group to hold together. The men that I interviewed on these matters often expressed that they felt secure that they would always be able to get help from a *surni* friend when in need of assistance.

The viability of these support groups among *surni* workers needs, however, to be considered. Firstly, *surni* workers consistently complained that gaining *surni* work was now much more problematical than had previously been the

[196] On the changed conditions of workers in the context of neo-liberal policies, see for example, Potter and Lloyd-Evans (1998:186) on cities of the developing world, Bangura (1994:797) on Africa and Gibbon (1995:19-21) on Zimbabwe.

case. They gather daily at the port and other sites where day workers are usually hired. Their increasing numbers seems to be stiffening the competition. I repeatedly heard how *surni* men went without work for long periods of time. Secondly, not surprisingly, the size of incomes earned and then redistributed among workers is reportedly low[197]. Thirdly, *surni* workers, who today originate from a variety of groups, can probably rely to a lesser extent on the types of subsistence production that would have sustained casual workers in earlier times during slack periods (see chapter two). Day workers have been found elsewhere to be one segment of urban labour that has been seriously hit by the hardships that adjustment has imposed on them (Zack-Williams, 2000:60).

These welfare groups among casual workers are interesting in two ways. Firstly, they illustrate an instance in which networks for survival are clearly functional to capital that utilises this kind of labour[198]. They sustain a large reserve of casual workers, in many cases clearly below survival levels. These workers correspond loosely to a category of labour (port workers, shippers, loaders etc) that has historically been a locus of resistance in Bissau in relation to import-export firms (see chapter two). It remains to be seen whether their horizontal networks of assistance will gain a political content so as to contest their exclusion from the vertical networks of accumulation that they partly subsidise and to demand a larger share of the profits that the latter command. These aspects are too part of a 'politics of support mobilisation', as outlined in chapter one.

Secondly, these groups are an example of the unexpected forms that collaboration can take. They were often referred to as being composed of men from a wide variety of ethnic groups and residing in different parts of the city. In this sense, they differ considerably from the exclusive vertical networks mentioned in chapter three and from inward-looking kinds of support exchange in the city (see chapter seven), possibly counteracting the social fragmentation and the "localisms" that are visible in Bissau as well as in other African cities (Bangura, 1994; Simone, 1998). Networks of casual workers are connecting different social settings, neighbourhoods and bridging diverse ethnic affiliations. These widely spread networks require of participants that they bear flexible and diverse identities. One could say that they integrate the city both spatially and socially. Furthermore, these are precisely the kinds of linkages at the bottom that may grow into a broad base of action against hegemonic actors (Brown, 2000:182; Burbach et al, 1997:163). How these

---

[197] One interviewee described to me the situation of her husband, who used to take day work at a car repair workshop after he was discharged from the state public transport enterprise. She once observed when her husband shared the meagre cash he had earned on a certain day with four other surni mates; what he kept was not even enough to buy a days portion of rice, she said.

[198] See Meagher (1995) on the role of social networks in securing a supply of labour.

rather cross-cultural networks relate to traditional kin sources of support will be considered in chapter seven.

Religious groups

Religious associations of various kinds are a major feature of contemporary urban life in Africa[199]. In Bandim, one third of my network respondents regularly attended catholic churches or the local evangelical church. The latter, with a few hundred members, is the religious group I became most acquainted with. This is a congregation that is not exclusive of different groups in that anyone can become a member overnight. The constraint to the church as a locus of solidarity lies in its being generally poor and largely cut off from external sources of material resources, as I realised from my interaction with its members and conversations with its leaders[200]. Within the church, I was told, only three persons were in a position to help others materially. Since the resources of the church are scarce and a large share of the members are poor, the help it may provide to its members is necessarily very restricted. For example, one member told me she got help from the church when she lay sick in the hospital, "because nothing is free in the hospital anymore". Some women heads of households also received a little money from the church occasionally. But I met others in a similar condition who either did not or had ceased to receive any help - "there is much poverty in the church", one explained.

In spite of its limited material basis, the church provides a field of intense interaction of various kinds between the members. Besides providing an alternative realm for leisure and recreation, church going seems to introduce a level of solidarity and trust among its members that facilitate material exchanges. Firstly, several of my acquaintances in the church received occasional relief or help in starting businesses from those few members in a better off position – sometimes these represented their only source of security and they preferred to call on their help than that of close kin, other compound members or seniors. Secondly, Christian sellers informed me that, at the market place, credit was more easily given to customers and by suppliers if they were also Christian. In a couple of cases, church affiliation had helped in securing permanent employment.

The congregation also worked as a platform for women and youth to organise themselves into groups linked to organisations operating at larger scales - as was the case with the Organisation of Christian Women of Guinea-Bissau and the Evangelical Youth of Guinea-Bissau, whose members I

---

[199] See Gifford (1998); Simone (1998); Mohan (2000); Oruwari (2001); Sundberg (1999). For other empirical studies touching upon this, see: Loforte (2000), Espling (1999).

[200] In this sense, this church differs substantially from other Christian churches in Africa with important international connections (Gifford, 1998).

interviewed. These initiatives emerged autonomously from the former state mass organisations for women and youth – of these mass organisations, at least the latter operated in the neighbourhood[201]. The church has also been a platform for individual members to link up with external Christian entities - such as the evangelical mission located in Bandim and the internationally financed Evangelical Project whose local representative I interviewed in 1999 – or even to migrate abroad.

The danger remains that the social networks that take shape among members of the church will be insulated from those of others who follow different religions.

Overview of social networks

I turn now to networks of personal ties with which participants exchange assistance. This section introduces the broad patterns of variation in social networks in the study setting, the different kinds of social settings that people draw upon to construct their networks and their varying ability to diversify their networks in this way.

The data from my household survey provided a first glance at patterns of exchange in the neighbourhood, particularly concerning inter-household transfers of food and money. More than two thirds of the households had been given food, meals or money by outsiders during the preceding twelve months. Such transfers came mainly from relatives and neighbours living in the same house or compound as the respondent household but 17 per cent also received gifts from residents in other urban districts and 10 per cent from the countryside. More than half of the households received gifts several times a month or received regular transfers (table 6.1). I considered these households as "highly reliant on gifts". By cross-tabulating this with other variables, I realised that households who had a "very poor" level of food consumption, had women as heads of household, cohabited with other households related by kin (particularly those living in compounds) and had diversified sources of income and food tended to be somewhat more represented in this category of "highly reliant on gifts". Conversely, "low reliance on gifts", reported by slightly over one third of the sample, was more common among households that depended on a narrow range of sources of food and income, i.e. depended mainly on

[201] These initiatives have included voluntary cleaning in the city centre and collective efforts for income generation activities, although in the latter case their representatives complained about limitations in economic resources and capacity of implementation (interviews with a group of women participating in the Organisation of Christian Women and the with a member of the board of the Evangelical Youth of Guinea-Bissau). See Sundberg (1999) on how new religious movements may provide opportunities for women to organise politically and improve their status. See Gifford (1998) on the importance of relations between chirches and the state.

wage work and purchased food, and had "non-poor" levels of consumption[202]. This is not to say that the poor are necessarily well endowed with networks of assistance, as is visible in table 6.2 and as the more qualitative analysis will show.

Table 6.1 Degree of household reliance on gifts

Degree of reliance	No. of households	Per cent
(a) High	184	55
(b) Moderate	27	8
(c) Low	123	37
Total	334	100

(a) Reported to receive gifts several times a month or regular money remittances.
(b) Reported to receive gifts several times a year.
(c) Reported to receive gifts once a year or less.

Table 6.2 Cross-tabulation of degree of reliance on gifts with level of food consumption and gender of the head of the household

		Degree of reliance on gifts			
		High	Moderate	Low	Total
Gender of head of household	Female	62	6	32	100 (109)
	Male	52	9	40	100 (225)
Food Consumption indicator	Non-poor	39	4	57	100 (28)
	Less poor	60	14	27	100 (74)
	Poor	53	7	40	100 (186)
	Very poor	64	9	28	100 (47)

In connection to food production activities questions were also asked about out-flows of gifts. Households involved in such activities, such as farming and fishing, often shared their produce with others. In the majority of cases they shared with neighbouring households but also with relatives living in other parts of Bissau and in the countryside. A more general question was posed about whether food was given to people in need, even when the remaining food would not be enough to meet the household's needs. The vast majority answered affirmatively. This is related to a general morality of sharing whatever one has with those in need, although one tenth – those who answered negatively - did not apparently share this morality.

---

[202] For an explanation of these various categories of consumption, see chapter four.

It was the above variations in participation in food transfers that prompted me to pursue these issues through qualitative work. The results of the household survey also became the basis for selection of 30 cases for my in-depth study of social networks of assistance. I will begin my description of the general features of these networks by saying a few words about the composition of the sample of the studied network cases[203]. To begin with, the sample was exclusively oriented towards households that emerged in the household survey as having a "poor" or "very poor" level of food consumption. I am thus dealing with the networks of the poor. In an attempt to narrow the wide cultural diversity in the neighbourhood, the Eastern ethnic groups, a minority in Bandim, were left out. Half of the households had a mixture of wage jobs and non-wage work such as trade. Wage work pertained mainly to the situation prior to the war, with the armed conflict forcing most employees to join the ranks of the casual workers. About two thirds of the households were at the time partly dependent on casual work. Trade, particularly of the petty sort, was present in virtually all households and in five of them - all headed by women - was the only source of income. About one third of the households were involved in farming. Two thirds had relatives as neighbours and half of the cases were households headed by women. In two thirds of the cases women were the respondents. Given the time constraints, priority was given to the housewife when selecting a household respondent. Although it was not possible to collect detailed information on the personal networks of each household member, women were in a good position to describe usual sources of help for the household in times of hardship, as they are the most engaged in matters of daily food provisioning in the household.

The first set of differences that become visible when looking at the group of cases is the variation in the size of networks, i.e. the number of personal ties on which one can rely for assistance. Almost half of the cases appeared to have relatively small networks, with few people to turn to, while one third had visibly large networks. This is important in that those with narrow networks usually expressed feelings of insecurity about chances that they would get some help from somebody in a moment of crisis.

Some general remarks can be made about the balance of flows between partners and the range of economic status contained in social networks, based on people's perceptions of these. In one third of the cases the direction of flows varied for different ties within the same network. A minority declared to be giving more to their various exchange partners than they received. Almost half the sample, however, portrayed themselves as receivers, i.e. they were unable to return assistance to the same extent to most of their exchange partners. This is maybe not very surprising given the fact that I was aiming at "the poor", but the seemingly dependent position of this group is not irrelevant.

[203] On how the sample was planned, see chapter one.

Concerning differences in economic status, about one third of the respondents perceived their exchange partners as being in a material condition similar to their own and another third considered some of their partners as being in a better economic or work situation than they themselves were[204]. These dimensions of networks helped identify instances of unequal exchange and patterns of dependence within particular networks. I will look at what is happening to the balance of flows and power in networks in the context of wider pressures later in this chapter and also in chapter seven.

Households varied in the geographical range of their networks of assistance. A few households had relatives abroad who sent them remittances. The majority of respondents in the network sample and ten per cent in the household survey had ongoing exchanges with rural areas, although the perception of the balance of flows with rural relatives and the motivations attributed to those relationships varied considerably, as will be discussed in chapter seven. The largest share of households in the survey and about half of the network cases had relations of assistance mainly in the neighbourhood. Those with relations in other parts of the city accounted for 17 per cent of the households in the survey. These usually had kin or wage work outside the neighbourhood or were part of casual work groups - in the last two instances, men were most numerous. This seems to suggest a certain gender structuring of social networks, with fields and areas of recruitment differing for men and women. Gendered network patterns have been disclosed in other studies, usually stressing the narrower social and spatial range of female networks. In this particular setting, however, as is the case in some other societies in West Africa, women have historically enjoyed considerable freedom of mobility, related to the trade careers in which they extensively engage (see chapter two)[205]. In Bissau, trade takes women to the opposite end of the city, to rotating markets in different parts of the country and even beyond national borders. Generally, a social network with a range beyond the neighbourhood seems to be an asset in times of crisis. Some people said that they avoided asking for help from those in their immediate proximity as they were usually experiencing equally difficult conditions and that they instead sought assistance from further a field[206].

An important dimension of networks of assistance pertains to spheres of recruitment. Firstly, "kin", as loosely and broadly understood by the respondents[207], is by far the most mentioned source of assistance – while this may

[204] Being in a better position included in several instances being in a position to get help from one's boss at the work place or having a central position in local redistribution systems by controlling rice fields and large surpluses of staple – the latter case pertains to the local ancestral group of the Pepel.

[205] See for example Dennis (1991) on the trading careers of Nigerian women.

[206] This became acutely true during the 1998-99 war, when urban residents were forced to search for their rural contacts.

[207] In the local understanding, "kin" is a vague category. It is used for consanguineous relatives and affines, but also used to describe distant affinities such as those among lineage members, but even

reflect the sampling strategy used it is also confirmed by the survey results (see above). This includes both ties stretched in space and exchange relations with neighbouring relatives as well as between households within compounds[208]. In several cases, meals and assistance were clearly exchanged only with kin neighbours and not with other neighbours. In at least two cases respondents expressed that they consciously avoided relationships with non-kin as "it creates problems". Others also considered it shameful to ask for the help of non-kin. More than one third of the respondents identified a relative as the most reliable social tie in his/her network. There is a general sense of obligation to help kin in distress as well as a recognition of certain norms pertaining to some kin categories. In addition, as discussed in chapter five, kin is also an important source of support for trade activities.

Secondly, non-kin neighbours and friends were two other important categories of exchange partners. Concerning the first of these, almost one third had developed assistance relations with their neighbours. Here, wider forms of affinity, such as the lineage and ethnic belonging, seem to sometimes have relevance. Several respondents justified not practising exchanges with neighbours because they belonged to different ethnic groups and thus had different "customs". Thirdly, market-based relationships appear as an important source of security in moments of need for one third of the respondents. This could take the form of help given by a market colleague. But this also includes credit from suppliers and participation in a rotating credit group, where the latter often allows switching turns in collecting the group's savings in case of unforseen difficulties. All of these were discussed in chapter five. In chapter five I discussed the various social arrangements by which participants gain access to income opportunities and attain a measure of stability in their businesses.

A share of the respondents had diversified networks in terms of social heterogeneity and geographical reach. Many of them developed relations of assistance in a variety of social settings, eventually drawing on the advantages of each sort. For example, both kin and market-based networks were often used for sustaining consumption and income strategies. But some people were not in a position to combine these various sources of support and seemed heavily reliant on one particular kind of relations. In eight cases, respondents

with other ethnic groups - as is the case with Pepel, Manjaco and Mancanha, who in the past had economic and political ties. People make a distinction however between close and more distant forms of "kinship", and used it often to explain differences in terms of the expectations and claims that could be placed on the two.

[208] It should be noted that among those whose neighbours were not relatives, several lived in large households congregating several siblings, their children and several generations. Thus a social network apparently poor in kin do not necessarily mean that kin ties are unimportant. They may instead take the form of assistance relations within extended families, not seldom the result of aggregating formerly separated household units. Some of those who seemed rather isolated seemed to rely instead on intra-household relations, for example with members loaning from each other when one's petty business suffered a downswing.

evaluated market-based support (rather than kin-based) as being their most secure or sole source of relief. However, as discussed in chapter five, social arrangements in the market are not equally accessible to all. In addition, as the case of rotating savings groups illustrated, such arrangements tend to work as long as participants fulfil their part of the deal and thus tend to exclude those in the most precarious conditions. This indicates the need for support bonds with a greater measure of durability, which in the study setting often means relying on obligations for assistance among relatives. But even kin assistance is not to be taken for granted as practice often deviates from norms and the pressures of economic crisis make for a selection of relatives eventually leaving some people to fend for themselves. These issues of exclusion and varying ability to combine and diversify relations of support are discussed at greater length in this and the next chapter. I return to the particular issue of how kin-based assistance is changing and how it relates to alternative sources of support in chapter seven.

6.2 Social connectivity as a variable of vulnerability

A concern of this study is with variations in social connectivity as a dimension of vulnerability, as I proposed in chapter one. I will begin this discussion with two cases, both of which also open the window for an analysis of the different social relations at work in networks.

Case 1: Luisa is in her thirties. Her household consists of her husband, her small child, one of her brothers and two of her husband's brothers. The males all had wage jobs in a foreign company but had not received any salary since the war broke broke out. Luisa sells different sorts of alcoholic drinks for a living. There are other households living in the same house. Luisa reports that she exchanges food with the one headed by her brother but not with the remaining two, who are neither relatives nor close relations to Luisa's household. Concerning neighbours in the nearby houses, except for one of her neighbours who lends her money and helps her with her baby daughter, Luisa has not developed relationships with them – she and her household have just moved in. However, in the house she lived in before, she and seven other neighbours had a weekly rotating savings group that functioned until the war started.

Luisa has been married once before. When her husband died two years earlier, she was left with an infant. The friends of her husband used to come to eat and drink at their house, "because her husband always had money", she says. After his death she "never saw them again". But during that crisis she got help from a wide range of people, including her own friends, kin and the relatives of her deceased husband. In less acute times she also benefits from the assistance of a variety of people. The relatives of her former husband have continued to visit her, even after she remarried. One who lives in a rural locality not far from Bissau has a rice field there and usually separates some rice from his harvest for her. Luisa's mother lives in Comura, a rural area in the proximity of the city, and makes cashew juice at a plot belonging to her ex-husband, Luisa's father. Luisa gives her money for food and medicine, and in her understanding, her mother is more dependent on her than vice versa.

But when Luisa cannot get hold of cashew wine in the city to sell, she travels to her mother and gets cashew wine for free from her. Luisa's father, besides working at a telecommunications firm in the city, also has two cashew plots from which he gets an abundant supply of rice, she says. When she 'falls off balance' in her business and is without money she goes to stay at her father's. He sometimes helps her with rice. When the war broke, Luisa's network dispersed. The household took refuge in Comura at her mother's house where they 'joined stoves', i.e. ate together from what the two households could get. Rice for the family came from the exchange of cashews collected at the plot tended by her mother and some came from her father.

Altogether, Luisa has one sister and seven brothers, all of whom are grown up. Most of her brothers have wage jobs and she considers them to be in a better economic situation than herself. Luisa reports to always be able to count on their help. Her eldest brother, who is part of her household at the time of the interview, provided her with rice after her husband died and allowed her to join his household. Another brother, who runs a taxi and resides in another urban district, also helps her with money. She describes the relationship between herself, her brothers and mother as a loving one. They visit each other every week and she feels free to ask any of them for help. If she would be forced to choose whom to help within her network of exchange, she says that she would give priority to them. Luisa's kin network of assistance does not end here. Two male cousins used to help her: one is in Portugal and sends her money every month; the other one is in Bissau, but because of the hardships caused by the war she has avoided asking him for help as she used to. Three female cousins who live in Comura and who were presently at the cashew plantation with Luisa's mother, also exchange help with Luisa. She considers that she gives these three cousins more than she receives from them.

I asked Luisa about other acquaintances or groups she participated in and the help she might expect from them. She attends a nearby catholic church where she has made many friends, but with whom she does not exchange any material help. They only visit each other at funeral ceremonies. Only the priest has offered her money for medicine. Luisa maintains contact with childhood friends residing in another urban district where she was born. They still visit each other, although she has lost contact with some of them for lack of time for visiting. One of them is from a better-off family and helps Luisa with "anything (she) might need" - in fact, Luisa says, this friend presented her with a large sum of money when her husband died. Luisa has no market acquaintances since she sells wine from her porch. But she buys palm wine on credit from rural producers with whom she has an agreement - although this does not work for cashew wine which she buys by the roadside in Bandim. It was her father's new wife, who is an experienced seller, who taught her the business.

When I asked her what was the secret for being able to get help from so many, Luisa answers that she gets along well with everyone and helps anyone who asks for help whenever she is able to do so. She also explains that she never feels exploited by people who ask for her help a lot, such as her cousins from Cumura, "because (her) turn to need help will also come".

Case 2: Segunda is in her thirties and a widow with two children. She used to clean and cook for a priest but at the time of our conversation she was deprived of that source of income because her employer had fled from the war. Additionally she used to prepare and sell peanuts and, later on, fried pastries as well. She has quitted this too because she 'fell off balance' and although she has asked many for help, she has not been able to get a small loan to restart her business. She used to sell by her doorstep or by the roadside, by herself, and thus had no "market friends". Her only income at the time is a modest 500 CFA Francs that she occasionally gets from the local evangelical church that she attends. Given the difficulties her niece, who lived with her while attending school in town, had to be sent back to her parents in the countryside.

When her husband died some years ago she had to leave the house where they lived because she could not afford the rent. So she decided to move close to her own kin. Her parents are dead so she now lives in a row of houses where her grandmother, eldest brother and cousins of her mother live. There are altogether eight households most of which are kin to Segunda. But she cannot count on any help from any of these relatives. "Each household struggles on its own", she adds. The children may occasionally get some food from the other households but that is not a habit. They have never offered her any food spontaneously when she has nothing to eat. The brother living next door, even when she asks him for help, always denies her help. She interprets this neglect from her neighbouring relatives as resulting from their lack of care for her, from economic hardship and her own inability to reciprocate help. She also considers her Christian affiliation to have isolated her from her kin.

She has three more siblings in the city who visit each other. But when they visit her they do not give her anything, even if they would have enough to share with her, she says. She has relatives in the village of her deceased father in the province of Biombo. But she only goes there for funerals and does not stay for long because, she explains, her relatives there have great economic difficulties, "they have nothing". They now visit each other less often than years ago, which she relates to the death of her husband and father and to her poor condition. When I ask her if she had anyone at all to turn to when she had difficulties, she says that she used to visit a Christian friend in another neighbourhood who used to share rice with her. But it has been a while since she visited her, given the difficulties everybody is facing. Since three years back she goes with her children to spend the days at the house of her Christian fiancé in another district in the city. Although at the moment he has no job and has to rely on casual work, he provides Segunda and her children with food. She spends the days there, she explains, because where she is living she gets no help and sometimes spent several days without any food.

The two cases above illustrate two people in very different situations in terms of the social networks on which they can depend for material assistance. Luisa has a large network comprising of close ties with a variety of kin and friends that have supported her through various crises. It is a heterogeneous one in that it includes persons in a better economic position than her own and with livelihoods differing from her own, as perceived by her. In this variety of overlapping dependencies, Luisa appears both as the dependent part and the giver, depending on the exchange partners being considered. It is also a wide range network in the geographical sense in that she receives considerable assistance from the countryside and even regular remittances from abroad.

Segunda, on the other hand, is a good example of a quite isolated person in terms of the help she can mobilise. Her network of assistance is clearly very narrow. Unlike Luisa, Segunda was faced with an unresponsive kin following the death of her husband and she came to feel marginalized by it. Indeed, at the time of the interview, while she was surrounded by kin in her house, had relatives in other parts of the city and in her father's village, she was unable to get help from any of these sources. At the time of the study, she could count upon only one person, her fiancé. But should his capacity or willingness to help her end, Segunda and her children would probably be forced to resort to less dignifying ways of finding food or else risk starvation. She appears to be extremely dependent on others for survival and is unable to reciprocate or materially nurture ties with others – she was even forced to break earlier commitments as illustrated by her sending her nice home.

Thus the two cases represent very disparate conditions in terms of the size, range, social heterogeneity and mutuality of exchange in the two networks. But they also show different types of relations at work. Luisa's network, described above, illustrates this. On the one hand, her network contained what she considered as relationships based on love with her brothers and mother which carried her through various hardships. On the other hand, it also included ties that she perceived as driven by egoistic motivations such as those represented by the friends of her former husband and who terminated their contact as soon as he died and the flow of food and wine in her house dried up.

In my understanding of *access to support* I am concerned not only with the relative number of sources one can count on for help but also the kinds of claims they can make on different people and the myriad of social relations, with differing forms of regulation, sanction and power balance. This requires 'unpacking' the conglomeration of social ties that constitute personal networks. The coexistence of these different types of ties and relations side by side and even in the same personal network is in itself a point worth making, as most analyses have chosen to show one side of the coin and neglect the other (see chapter one).

Significant differences in the *range* and *type* of social resources available to different people such as those illustrated by the introductory cases may be partly related to differences in personality and the particular social abilities of individuals to develop and maintain relationships with other people. While these differences have to be acknowledged, the driving motivation in this chapter is my belief that there are structural factors and wider frames that influence what individuals and households can attain in terms of mobilisation of support. For example, at least three aspects seem to be of relevance for understanding Segunda's rather isolated condition, the fact that she is very poor, her being a widow and her church affiliation. These are themes that will surface in this and the following chapter. In spite of structural constraints, one should not lose sight of the agency of individuals, i.e. their choices about who to affiliate with, which ties to nurture and discard, their efforts to influence rules, exert claims and informal rights in provisioning, and improve their position in redistribution systems.

6.3 Multifaceted social relations of assistance

Analyses of support networks have usually depicted them as being constituted by either benign relations or as driven by self-interested motives, as I discussed in chapter one. In this section I will attempt to go beyond these one-sided views and will explore the multifaceted nature of social relations of assistance. The discussion will illustrate how relations of assistance may include both mutual exchanges among social equals and unequal exchanges sometimes involving manipulations of power. The variety of motivations underlying support relations will be brought to light, including affection, self-interest and obligation.

Sahlins' notion of a variety of reciprocity forms is useful here (1984:193-6). Firstly, in transactions sustained by a social bond the expectation for return gifts is vague and flows can be one-way for a long period of time. This he calls "generalised reciprocity". Secondly, "balanced reciprocity" occurs where it is the material flow that sustains the social relationship, an equivalent return is expected within the shortest time possible, one-way flows are not tolerated and failure to reciprocate disrupts the relationship. Thirdly, in instances of "negative reciprocity" impersonal exchange dominates and the parties have opposing interests and each seeks to maximise returns at the expense of the other. The key aspects of the above model, such as the material balance and the time lapse of the exchanges, are a starting point to categorise different social ties according to respondents' own perceptions of the motivations underlying them. These perceptions are important to understand how people value different types of ties, make choices about them and strategize their use.

The significance of recognising a multiplicity of social relations for people's access to support lies in the apparent fact that the particular constellation of social ties and relations on which one relies for assistance is of relevance for people's access to support in critical times. It may also help to understand how vulnerable a person with a given set of ties is to being left to fend for him-/ /herself in a crisis. Let me present another case that is illustrative of this as well as some other aspects.

Case 3: José and Julia are a Balanta couple that live in a cluster of households of relatives. His father and uncle founded the cluster decades ago when they left their village in the south. They got land to settle on through acquaintances with Pepel men with whom they worked at the port. They are now dead and the eldest in the kin group is José's eldest brother. In this cluster of houses, likening a compound, live several of José's brothers and brothers in law with their families. José lost his job at the post office in 1990 and now lives from casual jobs that he gets through a variety of contacts with kin and friends. His wife earns an income mainly by roasting and selling peanuts as well as by making and selling wine during the cashew season. Their incomes are insufficient to feed themselves and their three children. When I first met them in 1992 they were already living in a very impoverished condition, eating only one meal a day.

José says that within the kin group some households are better off than his own. In fact some of them hire José for casual work. "But those who are better off do not give anything away because the situation now is difficult", he says. He further explains that ten years earlier all in the compound had work and food to eat. If money would end before payday, one could borrow from another in the compound and pay later. But now he has no work and cannot pay back, he adds. Thus when he asks for help his brothers usually say they have nothing to share with him. "Without work you cannot get any help". Even his eldest brother, who in José's opinion is in a position to help and should help, is tight-fisted. However, it has happened that others in the kin group occasionally lend them some money. But loans have to be returned since gifts seemed to be virtually out of the question. In general, José affirms that he cannot be sure of getting assistance from the others in the compound during times of need.

They have other relatives in the city that visit each other frequently. But José and Julia say that they are just as poor as themselves and they are therefore ashamed to ask them for help. However, Julia has a brother and a male cousin in Bissau who are in a better economic situation and they usually assist when she asks them for help. They do not expect her to pay back and have never turned her down, even during the war when she requested their assistance more often than usual. Particularly her cousin does all within his reach to help her, she says. Julia complains that she is not able to reciprocate their generosity and expressed feelings of shame for this.

Exchanges of assistance are more intense with the women heading the other household living in the same house. Besides exchanging meals, a close relationship exists particularly between Julia and this female neighbour. They have separate purses but help each other in the sale of peanuts and take turns in the selling so that they can take care of each other's children. When Julia 'falls off balance' she can borrow from this friend. But both also have the possibility of buying on credit from their steady supplier.

They have contact with relatives in the village of José's father but any help from there is rare, except when they travel there and ask for food. José usually goes there once or twice a year for such reasons or to attend funerals. Julia also travels to Boloma to harvest cashew on the land of a cousin of José. These places, together with other relatives living North of Bissau, became the refuge of José's family during the various episodes of the armed conflict in the preceding year. José explains that when he had a job at the post office, rural kin came to visit frequently. He had even looked after boys from the village who were studying in Bissau. But when he lost his job his family stopped visiting as frequently.

This case presents us with an interesting constellation of ties and particularly illuminates the varied nature of assistance relations among kin. The household could count with the help from two relatives in the city, Julia's brother and cousin. These ties seemed highly reliable as they survived the difficult test of the war, a period when most people had good reasons not to be generous with others. They are representative of the capacity that kin ties sometimes have to sustain one-way flows for considerable periods of time. This resilience is accounted for by feelings of affection or by a sense of obligation to assist relatives in distress, as prescribed by norms. I could find many examples of this in the studied cases. One example, Manuel, who had lost his job with the advent of the war, sustained his assistance to a narrower group of people, i.e. his close kin. He became the main provider for his four brothers and sister - all adult and some married - and their families. Like many others, they merged their households into one as a way of coping with the widespread scarcity. Although he expressed uneasy feelings about this situation, he felt forced to accept it. In the next chapter I will discuss instances of institutionalised one-way material flows within kin groups that follow specific sets of rights and duties.

However, the couple's exchange relations with close relatives in their residential cluster were quite different from those that Julia entertained with her brother and cousin. Here, any act of assistance generated strong expectations for return within a foreseeable future and was guided by a strict record of who gave what to whom. Relationships with rural kin too, at least as expressed in the frequency with which they interacted, seemed to be driven to a great extent by material motives. Luckily, the couple could count on the unconditional help of some of the members of their network. But there were other respondents whose networks completely collapsed when material conditions in their household suddenly worsened, as will be discussed below. Such networks which, in the perceptions of respondents, consisted mainly of instrumental ties, seem to be volatile. Those who rely heavily on this kind of assistance ties and live in a precarious material condition are particularly vulnerable to desertion in a moment of crisis.

The exchange relationship that Julia had with her brother and cousin however, was an unbalanced one with flows dominating in one direction. Julia experienced them as being demeaning for her. Like her, other respondents expressed their preference for relationships in which exchange is mutual and several affirmed not to address others with requests for help at all when they themselves lacked the ability to reciprocate. In other situations where unbalanced material exchanges implicate a loss of power for the receiving party, motivations for the latter to "disengage" from such a relationship may grow as may the potential for conflict (see chapter seven). At least in two cases, respondents mentioned that whilst they knew people who were in good positions, they did not approach them for help as they considered that this would have been humiliating. Another quite entrepreneurial woman also said that when she had approached better-positioned males for help, this ended with sexual requests by them. This issue of women approaching well positioned men to help them start or expand their businesses and the sexual concessions that they had to make as a consequence emerged in other interviews and conversations, even with men (see also chapter five). This seems to be a relevant aspect of the gendered politics of support mobilisation in the study setting. Refusal to engage in such relations, the costs implied and the alternatives that are devised are just as important. Because for some people, dignity and self-respect seem not to be easily traded for a cup of rice.

Julia and José possessed at least one mutual relationship, that with the neighbour living in the same house. This illustrates a type of relationship that I came across many times during my fieldwork in Bandim: two women, relatives or friends and usually neighbours, help each other daily in the running of their businesses, support each other when one experiences a temporary set-back and, if neighbours, they even exchange help in household work. These are usually long term friendships in which partners do not keep track of whose turn it is to help who, and a temporary exhaustion of resources usually does not jeopardise the exchange relationship. They usually involve a good deal of altruism, trust and affection. This type of partnership of a mutual and egalitarian nature usually occurs between social equals in the sense that they are often people with similar economic activities and material conditions. I will return to this kind of relationship later in the chapter.

In sum, this case illustrates some of the different motivations present in social relations of assistance, even cohabiting in one and the same network. This renders reductionist views inadequate.

6.4 Social networks in times of crisis

In this section I will address the issue of how social networks respond to crises. The first task in this exercise is to distinguish between different types of crises that may strike individuals and households, because this has implications for their ability to mobilise the support of others. Periods of crisis in a household may be triggered by events that pertain to the household alone, such as the death of an income earner. Alternatively, crises may have their origins outside the boundaries of the household and affect many households at the same time. Stresses of such of a generic nature also vary in their intensity and whether they are sudden or gradual processes. These distinctions are pertinent for the following analysis of the resilience of social networks in periods of stress as well as longer-term changes in their nature.

I will begin with crises that are internal to the household. One event that seems to trigger crises is the death of a husband[209]. This was not only followed by material hardship, particularly when the deceased contributed to household expenses, as the ratio of dependants to income earners increases. The event also seems to lead to a sudden narrowing of the networks of exchange of the household. Five widows among the respondents gave very similar accounts of this. Friends and workmates of the husband who used to visit the household and eat and drink there (sometimes food prepared by their wives or even purchased partly with their income) ceased visiting after his death and showed no concern for how the widow and her dependants were doing. But in two cases, women complained that their own blood kin had abandoned them when their husbands died and they fell into poverty. In most of these cases, the widows were indeed relatively isolated, i.e. had very small

[209] See chapter seven for the disadvantaged position of women in kin-based networks.

networks, and the turning point was identified by them as being the death of their husbands and their ensuing impoverishment. This is not to say that all widows are doomed to isolation, as Luisa's case at the beginning of the chapter clearly illustrates[210]. Her case is relevant in that, in spite of a withdrawal of a section of her contacts upon the death of her husband, a wide range of other relationships were not affected. However, at least a share of women whose husbands died or abandoned them seem to run the risk of becoming isolated, particularly for those that relied to some extent on the incomes and networks of their husbands.

Social networks are also affected by generic shocks. This is documented in the famine discourse where it has been reported that networks (usually meaning inter-household assistance in the form of food transfers) tend to break down at some stage following a sudden general shock such as a drought[211]. The 1998-9 war was of this sudden kind. Although material destitution did not reach desperate proportions for all, it displaced large numbers of Bissauans uprooting them from their usual social environment and daily acquaintances. People were repeatedly caught by surprise by new armed outbursts and forced to flee the city hastily. While some were able to join neighbours and others as they fled, in most cases there was a disbanding of urban social networks and even household members. Some networks were transferred from the city to the refugee areas - for example fishermen and fish sellers re-established their contacts at points of high refugee density. Others, in devising ways of earning an income, established new contacts in the refugee areas or borrowed some land, fishing nets and other resources from resident relatives with which they were able to get food or money. Indeed, as urban social networks split in all directions, it was the resilience at the rural end of these networks that was put to test. While this cannot be pursued here, it became obvious from my interviews that among those who did reach their rural kin, those who had good relations with them were often able to "join stoves" with them, i.e. pool resources and eat from the same pot, and in that way buffer their own shortage. The others had to fend for themselves.

The final phase of my fieldwork took place as people were returning to the city and their usual networks were slowly being reassembled. After a year of intermittent exile, uncertainty and hardship, many people had experienced an exhaustion of their material resources. Homes had been robbed, small stock gone astray and others reported to have been forced to sell whatever buffer assets they possessed in order to buy food[212]. People were thus drained of

---

[210] Indeed, in cases where husbands were more of a drain on household resources or where they were less than supportive of their wives' income activities and acquaintances away from home, their absence, caused by death or abandonment, may not necessarily have had a negative impact on the well-being and social networks of these women.

[211] See Corbet (1988), Davis (1996), Adams (1993), Campbell (1990), Drèze and Sen (1989), Sahlins (1984).

[212] In the study setting this often means woven-strips, stored for ceremonial purposes.

resources with which to rebuild their lives and assist others. It was common to encounter people sitting at home and unable to raise even a tiny loan from their usual sources to restart their petty businesses. The widespread nature and depth of the crisis seemed indeed to empty many networks of their resource bases and to leave many unable to gather any support. This poor capacity that many urban social networks exhibited in supporting recovery from the war crisis points to the limits of some of these networks in coping with crisis of such severity and widespread nature, in conditions of generalised scarcity. It should be pointed out however, that some were more affected than others[213]. Some people were able to call on the help of some of their relations who were not as drastically affected as they themselves were, as was the case of Julia and José. This suggests the importance of heterogeneous social networks in terms of income status for withstanding generic shocks and, conversely, the vulnerability of those persons who rely exclusively on ties with people of similar economic condition. This is similar to what Devereux (1999:36, 45) concluded in his analysis of informal safety nets in Blantyre town, Malawi. He emphasises the limitations of assistance among people who are equally poor for coping with a generic shock. Thus, the extent of the material resources commanded within the network needs to be considered. This theme will re-emerge later in the chapter.

Generic shocks of an economic kind, albeit possibly less traumatic in their effects than a war, are a more common source of affliction to urban populations in Africa, and thus will be discussed here in greater length. They can take the form of a sharp devaluation in local currency or of a steep price increase in basic foodstuffs[214]. While the opportunity for a similar study of the effects of such sudden shocks in Bissau did not present itself to me, I was concerned with the effects of general gradual deteriorating living conditions in the city on people's general ability to mobilise support and long-term changes in networks of assistance. In chapter three I described the problems that currency devaluations, sudden price hikes, increasing costs of living and basic necessities have posed to Bissauans, as well as the retrenchment and stagnation of salaries in the public sector, the shrinking opportunities for wage employment, the casualisation of work and the irregularity of incomes for a large share of the population. In chapter five it was argued that the increasing costs of production and decreasing purchasing power of many urbanites have led many small enterprises into involution and many small traders into a precarious

[213] Indeed, the generally greater diversity of ways of making a living and income levels in urban contexts as compared to rural areas means that, even in a severe crisis as the one described above, there will usually be a group that is in a position to withstand a generic shock without greater damage - if not to benefit from it. Thus there will probably be some food somewhere that can be claimed, begged for or even seized by illegal means, by those hit worst.

[214] See Devereux (1999) for a study of the role of informal safety nets in coping with 62 per cent devaluation in local currency and concomitant sharp increase in prices, in urban and rural southern Malawi.

existence and a harder working life. In the face of such trends, the pertinent question is thus how social networks that sustain consumption are responding.

I will begin with the impact of job redundancy, a problem that is affecting a large number of urban dwellers, on social networks, and the different types of relations within them. In the case of José, earlier in this chapter, the loss of his job meant a decreased possibility to borrow from his close kin in the compound and less exchanges with rural kin. His account echoes those of at least three other interviewees who reported abandonment by "friends" following the loss of a job and the consequent deterioration in their material conditions. Manuel for example, a car mechanic who used to have a permanent job, said that although he keeps contact with his former work colleagues, the freedom they used to have to borrow from each other has come to an end "because none of them has work". His relatives, likewise, ceased to visit as they did formerly because, he says, they know he has nothing. Now he limits his support to his closest relatives, i.e. his brothers and sister. Judging from these cases, it is reasonable to assume that the considerable extent of job redundancies in the city in the last one and a half decades may have caused a shrinkage of the exchange networks of former wage workers and their households.

The general deterioration of real incomes and worsened costs of living in the city has also had an impact on social networks of assistance. Many respondents affirmed that it had become more difficult to get help since ten or fifteen years back. They often attributed this to the change to the CFA Franc, to the impoverishment of exchange partners and their own. This deterioration of economic conditions seems to deny many the opportunity to reciprocate assistance, leading to a narrowing of the range of their networks or even to isolation. Some of my respondents seemed acutely aware of the impact of their poverty on their ability to get help. One poor and rather isolated woman expressed it in the following way: "nobody will want to associate with me because I am poor and cannot return others' assistance". Yet another respondent, João, complained that although he has many relatives in Bissau, "because I do not have a good life", he says, "they do not know me anymore", while they were keen to contact another relative that was well off.

From these repeated accounts it becomes obvious that one's material condition has significance for one's ability to get help – an idea that may seem obvious but largely ignored in the mainstream literature about social networks. Consequently, a deterioration of material conditions in the city must have affected that ability negatively. In addition, if people's perceptions of how their networks have evolved are correct, there seems to be a tendency for instrumentalisation of social ties, by which people increasingly act on the basis of a careful calculation of returns – a widening scope for "balanced reciprocity" in Sahlins' terms. Social ties of assistance are increasingly being put to the test under the current conditions of economic austerity. In the process, a share of those ties is obviously failing to pass the test and leaving some people in a fragile situation.

Still in connection to a narrowing of social networks of assistance, many of my respondents declared to avoid or to have ceased seeking help from other relatives, friends or neighbours who were as impoverished as themselves, as they would feel ashamed in doing so (see for example the cases of Segunda, and José and Julia)[215]. As with the case of Manuel, others said that they now restricted their help and exchanges to a smaller range of people. This implies a selection of which ties one is willing or can afford to discard and which ties one will go to considerable lengths to preserve. Underlying such choices are people's own perceptions of their various relationships, the meanings they attribute to them and the way they value their different ties - not merely economic calculations.

One type of association that seemed to be particularly valued by participants consisted of pairs of persons who exchanged mutual support daily in their market activities and beyond. This was the kind of relationship that Julia entertained with her neighbour, but in my interviews with traders I encountered many similar partnerships. In this type of collaboration two women in the same line of business help each other by pooling resources when needed, helping in the selling and supporting each other through their individual crises, such as when one of them 'falls off balance'. They often develop an affectionate relationship that goes beyond its market utility. It was mentioned above that this type of partnerships is often of a mutual and egalitarian nature, in the sense that they often associate people with similar economic activities and material conditions. In spite of the potentially benign nature of such relationships and the high value that participants seem to place on them, it is this same equality of conditions that constitutes the fragility of such relationships among poor partners. Occupying a similar niche in the urban economy, both are likely to be affected by the same shocks and the material assets at their disposal to cope with these shocks are identically low. Such seemingly strong relationships occasionally reach a point where both have exhausted their resources. However, a temporary mutual exhaustion of resources need not jeopardise such long-term affectionate relationships. Exchange may continue at other levels and collaboration in business may be resumed when the crisis has passed. The closeness of their association, the transparency of their finances to each other and their common history of withstanding frequent up and downswings probably facilitate this. The case of Ana illustrates the fragility of these relationships.

Case 4: Ana is a young mother and wife. She used to earn a living by selling fish together with a friend who she had met in business eight years ago. Ana says that exchange of help

---

[215] In some cases, this was connected to the event of the war but in other cases respondents were referring to a longer time period.

between them was mutual and that they were in a similar economic situation. When one of them 'fell off balance' she could borrow from the other. However, on one occasion they both 'fell off balance' and were unable to help each other. As none of them returned to the fish business their partnership in that activity ended, but they have kept contact and a concern for each other and frequently check up on one another to see if the other has enough to eat.

A few remarks can be made based on this case. Firstly, the impact of a shock on this relationship seems to be markedly different from that on more instrumental ties. Secondly, horizontal ties such as these have constraints of a material order. This suggests the importance of social heterogeneity in one's network in terms of economic level and differing livelihoods. While the importance of the "multiple modes of livelihood" of households in conditions of structural adjustment has been realised (Mustapha, 1992), the diversity of livelihoods within personal networks seem to also have significance for withstanding shocks that hit particular income activities.

Others have seen terms of exchange in their networks invert. José and Julia, who, in their own account, were once major givers, had become dependent on the assistance of others in later years. Impoverishment may turn once mutual and balanced relationships into unbalanced and dependent ones. These relations of a more vertical type, in which material flows are mainly in one direction, may take different forms. Relations of patronage, in which the giver is a person who is economically or politically well positioned, were rare in the non-market sphere but could be considered to exist in the market-place in the form of dependent relations between retailers and suppliers with powerful positions in the market (see chapter five). In a share of the cases, vertical exchanges were underwritten by ascribed claims and obligations, such as those between elders and juniors in local corporate kin groups, as will be analysed in chapter seven. Finally, they can be inscribed in affective relationships, motivated by empathy for the weaker party. These are important distinctions because while in the first two cases the unbalanced exchange relation implicates power differentials between the parties, in the latter case the giver has no obvious gains in continuing to disburse help to the dependent party and may be motivated by a genuine concern for the dependent party – this was the case of Luisa's brothers and Segunda's brother and male cousin, who according to local customs had no obligation in assisting them from the moment these women got married[216].

In general, while these more vertical relations of assistance seem to be of great importance for the poor because relations among social equals seem to be constantly under threat of exhaustion, two downsides should be considered. Firstly, they generally give the donor an upper hand in the relationship, inspiring in the recipient feelings of shame and lowered self-respect, as Julia

---

[216] Others do indeed follow the rule and are eager to strike out persons who can no longer have claims on their resources. See also chapter seven for inversions in obligations for assistance.

expressed about her generous better-off helpers. Secondly, whether they are regarded as an asset or as a constraint, such relations are not an alternative available to everyone. Among my respondents, several could only rely on social equals for assistance in a crisis and could not count with persons in a better off condition to assist them when resources among their poor partners became exhausted. While some are denied access to such ties, there were instances in which my respondents had acquaintances or relatives in useful positions but refused to call on that connection for purposes of assistance, for shame or fear of entering a subordinate position, of a sexual or another nature.

6.5 Conclusion

This chapter has described a variety of collaborative efforts devised by the poor in Bandim to cope with an insecure existence. The discussion highlights the important role that social networks have played in withstanding crises of different kinds. This is in line with other studies that have documented the importance of social networks in the context of economic crisis, retrenchment, narrowing of state provision and rising costs of living, in a variety of geographical settings[217].

However, the analysis sheds doubts on the current widespread use of social networks in the social capital literature as a panacea to solve the welfare problems of the poor under conditions of adjustment. Social relations of assistance seem to be generally under stress. Among organised groups, redistribution within casual worker groups bridging ethnic divisions and neighbourhoods in the city is being threatened by increasingly irregular work opportunities and declining incomes. The local evangelical church is providing some modest relief to some of its weakest members. But as it relies solely on its meagre internal resources, the church is incapable of assisting its large number of needy members. To these groups, one should add the social clubs of *manjuandades* whose costs of participation are prohibitive for many people, as well as rotating savings groups described in chapter five, which tend to exclude those with the most precarious conditions.

Concerning networks of personal ties, a share of the respondents appeared to be quite isolated and unable to mobilise support. These issues of access are often glossed over in the social capital discourse, as social capital is conceived as a property of communities and not of individuals. This renders invisible internal differentiation in access to support as well as the groups at risk, which in the study setting seem to consist of widows, redundant workers and the very poor. I have illustrated how some households who had experienced a sudden worsening of conditions often saw their networks narrow down. In other

[217] See for example: Loforte (2000) on Maputo; De Herdt and Marysse (1997) on Kinshasa; Moser (1996) on Lusaka and elsewhere.

instances balanced relations had turned into dependency ones and an instrumentalisation of ties is probably under way.

In sum, social resources are not something that the poor necessarily have. On the contrary, some are being left to fend for themselves. Evidence from elsewhere is not abundant. One exception is Deveraux's (1999) study of informal safety nets in urban and rural Malawi, where he reports an instrumentalisation and narrowing of ties. Another account is that by Benda-Beckmannn and Kirsch (1999), based on reports from five countries at a regional seminar on informal security systems in Southern Africa. They state that there is a tendency towards a shrinkage in the availability of resources for redistribution which is weakening informal security systems, at a time when structural adjustment policies are imposing considerable retrenchment and cost-saving schemes, thus increasing dependence on such systems (p. 30-1).

While economic hardship is generally undermining the collaborative efforts of the poor, some ties seem to be particularly vulnerable. In this chapter I have attempted a disaggregated analysis of networks that takes into account the different motivations underlying assistance and the degree of social heterogeneity contained in them. Different types of ties showed varying degrees of resilience in crisis situations. The cases illustrated how certain relationships of assistance were terminated during moments of hardship. Several respondents reported that, when the flow of food and wine in their houses was interrupted, some of their contacts vanished, which respondents interpreted as an unmotivated act of selfishness. On the basis of these perceptions, it seems that ties with the a focus on immediate material returns tend to easily dry up when one of the parties is hindered from reciprocating. Other relationships sustained one-way flows for considerable periods of time. This was the case with relationships involving better off people and those in which there were feelings of affection or a sense of obligation. In the case of vertical relations, the availability of resources to redistribute may account for their resilience. More egalitarian relations, often preferred by respondents, while usually sustained by affective bonds they were easily exhausted of their material resources. Finally, in some cases, the duty of assisting relatives in trouble explained persisting unbalanced assistance relations.

Unpacking social networks in this way proved to be a worthwhile approach. Firstly, it illuminates the multifaceted nature of relations of assistance instead of portraying them as fields of one-sided motivations. Secondly, it allows for a nuanced approach to the role and resilience of social networks in the context of economic crisis, rather than assuming a severance of all assistance ties and a collapse of social networks, as is often done. Thirdly, it reveals that the particular constellation of social ties in a poor person's network will matter for his/her ability to get help in a crisis. Not all respondents could count on a combination of assistance relations in which some resilient ties buffered the failure of others. Some networks were dominated by one type of relations and when that type was of the "wrong" sort, consequences were drastic when crisis came.

Indeed, people actively construct their networks by consciously nurturing acquaintances, selecting relatives and strategically investing in those types of ties that give the highest returns or that they value the most. But their ability to combine the most advantageous mixes of ties is not unconstrained. Clearly, a person's position in society and the current wider processes of impoverishment influence the extent and types of social resources at his/her disposal. In addition, conflicting interests within networks themselves may hamper individual choice about who to associate with. This latter aspect is discussed at length in chapter seven.

7 Kin-based networks of assistance

Kin was found to be an important category of assistance in Bandim. This is a very broad category that encompasses a variety of kin categories and configurations. These range from residential corporate kin groups and clusters of households related by kin, to interaction with relatives who do not reside in the immediate vicinity including those living in other parts of the city and in rural areas. These family relations were often found to be inserted into wider so-called "pre-capitalist" formations, such as the lineage and the chiefdom, which were evident both in the physical space of Bandim and in the extended relations that many migrants have with their communities of origin. This chapter includes reflections on these various kinds of relations. I will take a closer look at the nature of kin-based exchanges of assistance, both in their "moral" arrangements and the relations of subordination and dependence they entail. Patterns of expectations structuring claims on kin will be uncovered as well as how these may be changing in the current context of economic crisis and the social struggles involved.

The discussion will broach certain issues of social change, such as what happens to lineages, headmen, chiefs and commoners, kinship ties and extended families, and to the relations of assistance predicated upon these structures, with the advent of urbanisation, the penetration of market relations and Western values? In particular, how are such socio-cultural practices of assistance changing in relation to the current economic crisis? An awareness of the role of religious and traditional structures, ethnic forms of association, as well as of enlarging families in handling the stresses and challenges of contemporary urban life[218] has placed these issues high on current urban research agendas[219].

It should be emphasised, however, that this new concern with social change cannot be driven by the universalistic notions that inspired both the earlier modernisation paradigm and certain current discourses on globalisation. "Traditional" practices in urban Africa are not mere remnants of pre-capitalist orders doomed to extinction under the pressures of urbanisation, the market or

---

[218] Mabogunje (1990:41, 49); Rakodi (1997b:585); Hecht and Simone (1994:14-5, 150); Bangura (1994:82); Simone (1999:80); Attahi (1997). On informal enterprise related to ethnic based unions see Lugalla (1997); Macharia (1996); Meagher and Yunusa (1996); Onibokun (1994:263). On enlarging families see Moser (1996); Loforte (2000:112-113); Simone (1998:72-4).

[219] See for example Halfani (1994:158); Rakodi (1997b:563-7).

of globalizing Western culture. Such an understanding would deem both the direction of change and the ultimate outcome as predetermined. Rather, we need to consider the agency of local African societies, the diversity of paths and outcomes of change and how elements of continuity and change, tradition and modernity are combined in complex ways. These responses are highly locally specific and their contemporary configurations are the result of long historical processes of interplay between external forces and local agency (see chapter two). Furthermore, these "traditional" realms should be seen as major fields of struggle where external influences may induce a deepening of contradictions as well as struggles within these fields. These struggles, always indeterminate in their outcome, are part of how the informal livelihoods and support systemsare changing in urban Africa.

Let me more explicitly outline the research issues that will be pursued in this chapter. The general question concerns *how* exchanges of support and responsibilities in provisioning among relatives may be changing at a particular time-space intersection. Bissau shares with most other African cities the contemporary experience of deteriorating material conditions, increasing inequalities and the challenges presented by economic liberalisation. But the study area also has its own specificities. As mentioned in chapter four, this particular neighbourhood of Bandim is the seat of a pre-colonial kingdom. The ancient hierarchical structure of power and lineage organisation is still in place as is kin-based ascribed rank and duty. The analysis, inspired by the above perspective on social change, will highlight both continuity and change. I will begin by looking at shared norms in provisioning and assistance among kin which many people have been socialised into, but which have also been contested and undergone change. In relation to these changes, the discussion will concern three main issues.

Firstly, the relations of power and dependence in kin groups surrounding the reproduction and contestation of norms of assistance and provision will be reflected upon. Within these groups members may try to influence the reformulation of norms of assistance to their own advantage. In connection to this, it seems pertinent to look into eventual changes in the power structure within kin groups resulting from the intersection of various levels of contradiction and agency, between subordinate and dominant traditional groups and between the latter and the state. Secondly, I will examine how the changes in traditional norms of assistance impact upon the vulnerability of some groups. This is important because it can be expected that as traditional norms and hierarchies are contested, some groups may experience a decreasing ability to enforce their perceived rights.

Thirdly, I will consider the existing opportunities that are accessible to subordinate groups to allow "disengagement" from oppressive kin structures[220]. These include alternative forms of support, which are informed by other types of norms and forms of regulation, particularly the local church and groups and networks in the market. What are the structural constraints (at both the macro and micro levels) hampering the adoption and the viability of these alternative forms of support? Are these alternative forms accessible to the most vulnerable? Does the adoption of these alternatives compromise access to traditional sources of support or are they compatible with the latter? These various issues are at the heart of a politics of support mobilisation as outlined in chapter one. They are also of importance for understanding changes in the role of kinship as a major source of support for life in the city.

The chapter presents the various power games involved in the reformulation of traditional support systems in their complexity and inconsistency, as they presented themselves to me. By the end of the chapter the picture will not be complete - here I am not only referring to the indeterminacy of the game itself but also to the circumstances that hindered me from lengthier fieldwork. But the chapter may contribute to the growing body of knowledge that seeks to make sense of the complexities and unpredictable turns that social change in urban Africa can take.

The discussion is based on a variety of fieldwork methods. Firstly, the network method was a key tool in learning about kin-based relations of assistance. Qualitative interviews throughout my fieldwork with members of households and compounds, key informants and members of the local traditional nobility were equally important. Finally, the household survey was a useful tool for revealing some aspects of differentiation within compounds, which I was then able to follow up. As is evidenced in the following text, some parts of the discussion have a wider empirical basis than others. But the aforementioned combination of methods and sources proved to be a prolific fruitful one. The research methods are discussed at length in chapter one.

The chapter is structured in the following way. First, I begin by providing a description of generally recognised norms of assistance and provision among kin in order to later assess how they may be changing. Secondly, I will address changing relations of assistance within compounds and the host group in Bandim in relation to wider processes and the various layers of struggles involved. This is followed by a discussion of changing structures of expectations among relatives in general, i.e. those not living in compounds, particularly concerning resposibilities along gender and generational lines. Finally, I reflect upon exchange of support between urban and rural kin.

---

[220] The term "disengagement" is usually used by political scientists to describe popular strategies to circumvent state dominance. I find it legitimate to use the term in connection to people's strategies for disconnecting from local traditional power holders.

7.1 Households, compounds and networks

This chapter will address several facets of kin-based support which correspond to the variety of kin relations in which Bandim residents engaged. These include both interaction based on residential proximity and kin networks stretching across the city and beyond.

Firstly, there are exchanges within the traditional compounds among the "Pepel of Bandim", as members of the host group in Bandim call themselves - this is a branch of the wider ethnic group of the Pepel who have their ancestral roots in the area. These compounds are integrated into a local political hierarchy with a chief and heads of compounds at the top. There are material and other kinds of exchanges within this hierarchy. What I will refer to as "compounds" are residential and corporate groups based on lineage membership, with a common head whose authority is recognised by all members[221]. Within these groups there is a social hierarchy and a corresponding set of institutionalised, but evolving, rights and obligations, i.e. a set of entitlements that can be claimed.

Secondly, there are other large domestic groups or clusters of households related by kin among migrants, within which there is exchange of support[222]. Not usually being part of the host group, these groups hold no customary rights to farming land in Bandim and the corresponding hierarchical redistribution rules within them seem less elaborate. But many households do not reside within the close proximity of other relatives[223]. They may, however, exchange assistance with relatives in other parts of the city or in the rural areas. Both of these aspects are included in the analysis. Indeed, the uprooting of migrants from their rural areas of origin, and thus from their structured kin environments, has not necessarily put an end to their traditional obligations towards power holders and relatives in their villages.

I will use the expression "domestic group or domain" to generally refer to these various kinds of residential agglomerations of people sharing kin ties, ranging from households to large clusters of households related by kin. These various arrangements are seen as part of a domestic domain, a general field of struggle, in which they share certain features such as a patriarchal structure of authority - with the exception of some types of female heads of households. Analytically then, the household, generally understood here as a group of people who usually eat together, is treated here as one of such domestic groupings. Boundaries between these various kinds of kin arrangements seem to be

[221] Some compounds however contain some "strangers", i.e. persons allowed to settle in them in spite of lacking lineage credentials or marriage bonds.

[222] In the 1995 survey, in the majority of cases, gifts in food, meals or money to the household during the previous year were mainly among relatives and neighbours, particularly those living in the same house or compound.

[223] More than 40 per cent of the households inquired in 1995 stated that they had kin relations with other households cohabiting in the same house, while the remaining did not.

very fluid in the study setting. Different household units enjoying close ties of kinship sometimes temporarily join into one – which is locally called "joining stoves" - as a way of dealing with the absence of key household members (for example during temporary migration for the cashew harvest) or as a way of supporting a weaker household going through a difficult time. This may relate to similar examples of enlarging household units as observed in other African cities as a way of handling economic crisis (Moser, 1996; Loforte, 2000; Simone, 1998). However, "joining stoves" was not a possibility for some of my respondents. In at least one case this constituted a new source of vulnerability and tension as reshuffled responsibilities within the restructured household were not fulfilled, with the loosing party becoming extremely vulnerable. Further research could be carried out on this issue of "who is allowed to join in" and under what conditions, or, what one could call the politics of household restructuring.

The various configurations of domestic groups contain both relations of co-operation and conflict that facilitate or constrain the strategies of individual members in wider social fields. For, domestic groups are not bounded or self-contained, but are part of wider networks which they interact and overlap with. These different segments of social networks may complement each other and coexist in a functional balance or may embody tensions and rupture between contradictory kinds of affiliations and loyalties.

7.2 Traditional divisions of rights and obligations

Here I will present culturally specific sets of rules that are more or less generally recognised, and which regulate the rights and obligations for different social categories in local kinship structures and traditional social hierarchies. While these norms may help understand the rationale behind some exchange relations between relatives, people are certainly not mechanic performers of their ascribed roles. As will be suggested in the following sections, some are clearly eager to evade such norms if given the opportunity. Rules are not static but are subject to challenge, they are not given but are constructed (Epstein, 1981). As such, the concern here is not only with the shared norms and related redistributive mechanisms but also with non-conformity and "unruly" practices. This section is intended as a platform from which I will reflect upon what might be happening to traditional structures as units of redistribution in a particular place and historical context. This section is based on interviews with heads of compounds, the chief of Bandim and other key informants, as well as on my network interviewees and their expectations towards their relatives.

Traditional gender roles and expectations

Let me start with roles and responsibilities ascribed to the different genders in the domestic domain. Some features are common to most ethnic groups in the country[224]. Reproductive tasks are generally considered as female activities. Traditionally, men in all ethnic groups have the responsibility of providing the staple food, rice, for the household and women are expected to provide the other ingredients that are eaten with rice, locally called *mafe*. There are, however, signs that this division of responsibilities is changing (see "gender inversions" in section 7.4).

When women marry and move to their husbands, their provisioning becomes the responsibility of the husband and his kin. Her kin ceases to have any obligations towards her. Indeed, this issue surfaced occasionally in my network interviews. When they separate from their husbands, women loose some rights. In practice however, and depending on the circumstances surrounding the separation, these women may gain assistance either from their own family or the husband's family. Female-headed households living in a compound will still be subject to the patriarchal authority in the compound and cannot demand to be given a rice field for the sustenance of their households. It is only male heads who have the right to make such claims. The children of separated couples have the right to the contribution of their fathers for their sustenance. Access to such rights is, however, often denied and as will be illustrated below, may precipitate numerous forms of conflict.

Single mothers, i.e. mothers who did not go through the customary wedding ceremony, have no right to demand any contribution from the father towards the provisioning of the children. Unmarried fathers have no rights to their children. Single mothers and their children remain the responsibility of their parents until they marry. While this category is visibly on the increase in Bandim, elders report that the division of obligations in these cases is unclear. They regard childbirth outside of marriage as something new and thus not considered in Pepel law. In the old times, they explained, they exerted pressure on the future father to marry the pregnant girl or else he would die by way of sorcery. Today such threats have ceased.

There are other potentially weak groups who traditionally have rights to assistance. The sick and handicapped, for example, are to be catered for by their close relatives and members of the compound if they reside in one. Concerning the elderly, an aged man who has inherited has command over considerable land, labour and theoretically part of the cash incomes of his subordinates. An elderly female widow, on the other hand, is to be provided for by the inheritor of her deceased husband or her eldest married son, with the help of his wife and other members of the compound, if she lives in one. There

[224] For discussions of gender divisions of labour in Guinea-Bissau, see: INEP (1991), INEP (1991a) and PHROD (1991).

is a tacit understanding that, in or outside of the compound, the younger generation has responsibilities towards their elderly parents.

Chiefs and commoners

Given the fact that in Bandim there is a chief and a political hierarchy that is connected to collective forms of production and resource allocation, it is worthwhile briefly mentioning the specific provisioning duties and benefits that go together with important political offices. The chief should, in theory at least, be the last one to starve in a Pepel community. He is a collective symbol for his subjects, implying that it would be a collective shame if their highest prestige figure should starve. When he takes office he becomes the administrator of considerable assets such as land which ought to give him a well-supplied granary. Traditionally, the chief is entitled to contributions in the form of labour and kind, particularly from his subjects – in the study setting, the latter consist of the "Pepel of Bandim", with migrants usually having their obligations towards their own chiefs in their villages of origin. He benefits from food and animals offered to his *baloba* (i.e. his own ceremonial place) to which anyone in the neighbourhood may turn to for a variety of purposes. He also demands gifts when someone inherits rice fields in the chiefdom as well as part of the livestock sacrificed in customary funeral ceremonies, the *tchur*, a very important ceremony among the Pepel. While the various compounds were assisting the chief in recovering his rice fields[225] during my final fieldwork, according to one of the seniors they did it not out of compulsion but more out of respect and moral duty. The funeral "tax" on the other hand, continues to be enforced and even families in material distress are not excused from it, although in such cases the ceremony may be delayed until payment is possible.

There are also material flows in the opposite direction, i.e. from chief to commoners. Commoners may participate in food consumption at collective ceremonies that are the responsibility of the chief and which are 'financed' by him. Normally, if the chief has rice in store, he has the obligation to help those among his subjects who are experiencing shortage and who approach him for help. If he decides not to help despite being in a position to do so, commoners have no recourse to penalise him as Pepel chiefs are only deposed by death. The advice of his councillors - the *balobeiro*, a religious authority - and the male members of his compound - the so-called *ministros* – cannot however, simply be ignored by the chief. In the case of the chiefdom of Bandim, the depletion of the chief's material assets together with the unproductivity of his

---

[225] Rice is grown in swampland conquered from the mangrove. When the dikes brake down, salt water invades the fields ruining the harvest. Repairing the dikes requires large amounts of labour.

rice fields over the past few years have lead to a situation whereby there are few expectations of material support from him in the event of a food crisis.

Heads and members of compounds

Going down the traditional social hierarchy, we come to the division of rights and duties between heads of compounds and their members. In a similar manner to the chief, the head of a compound may also claim a share of the stock slaughtered at funeral ceremonies in the compound. He is also entitled to a share of the cash earned outside of the compound by his wives and sons[226]. Heads of compounds also control the largest rice fields and thus have the fullest granary in the compound. According to the heads of compounds interviewed, they traditionally have the moral obligation of assisting households in the compound who have run out of rice as long as they themselves have rice. This obligation, as perceived by elders themselves, does not cease at the compound's fence but may extend to members of other compounds and even to strangers who solicit their help. Between members of a compound there is also a general obligation of assisting households in distress. However, the extent of actual fulfilment of these obligations varies from one compound to another and some households within the same compound seem to enjoy greater assistance than others. Below, I discuss these inequalities.

Shared norms can be expected to vary along ethnic lines. The set of rights and responsibilities concerning chiefs and commoners, heads of compounds and their residents apply particularly to the host group, the "Pepel of Bandim". But elements of this set persist in the relations that some migrants keep with their home villages (see section on urban-rural links). Many of the other norms described also apply across ethnic boundaries[227].

7.3 Compounds as sites of support and inequality

I will now turn to the divisions of rights and obligations within compounds and their internal inequalities. This provides a basis from which to later discuss the politics these inequalities engender and how those divisions may be changing.

---

[226] This is still being done but, as the elders interviewed reported, sons increasingly tend to falter in this. Particularly, sons' lack of access to remunerative work may be a reason (if not an excuse) for the non-fulfilment of this duty.

[227] In this chapter, as in the preceding one, I exclude the Islamised groups, a minority in Bandim, as it was necessary to reduce the extent of cultural diversity included in the network study.

The contemporary livelihoods of households in compounds include a variety of activities[228]. A small share of households engaged in waged employment. Casual work, historically important among Pepel men in the city, was referred to more often. Trade, seen as being a female occupation, is the main source of income for women. In the last couple of decades cashew trees have been grown on customary land in Bandim as a response to a shift in international demand from groundnuts to cashew nuts. While women process and sell the cashew wine, men control these plantations, the cashew nuts and the rice, which the nuts are bartered for. Compounds also engage in subsistence production of the staple food, rice, which has been practised for centuries around Bandim and Bissau. The swampland where it is cultivated remained under customary tenure throughout the colonial and post-colonial periods and the lineage principle has remained important in the organisation of cultivation and in gaining access to land (see chapter two). Tasks in rice production continue to be organised according to age and gender and under the control of men and elders as was the case in pre-colonial times. They draw on the collective labour of compound members and on labour exchanges between different compounds according to age groups[229]. Labour recruited in this manner is "paid" with good meals and wine. Rice production is given priority by most compound members during the farming season.

Photo 7.1 Rice fields in Bissau

Aside from collective agricultural activities, the compound is a site of intense exchanges of various kinds. Considerable assistance in the form of food is often given when one household falls short of its needs and there are ex-

[228] The description of these activities is based on both my interviews and results of my household survey, filtered in a way as to isolate the group of compound households.

[229] Other types of collaboration between compounds pertain to the borrowing or giving away of seeds. These forms of co-operation between compounds, together with customs and ceremonies, help to hold together the host group and eventually the politico-religious hierarchy within it.

changes of meals between households. New houses are built and thatched roofs are replaced with the participation of the compound members. At least part of one's leisure time is spent with others in the compound, drinking, hairdressing, talking politics, gossiping, etc. The compound is also a platform for market-oriented strategies. Women may sell goods produced on land held by compound members and often find their business "partners" within the domestic group and receive support from co-wives or other women in caring for the children while they are away. Men may exchange information about casual work opportunities. Rotating saving clubs sometimes develop at the compound level, making sums of cash available to members for investing in businesses or for meeting urgent needs. But much as the compound is a site of co-operation and a locus of possibilities, it is also a site of inequality, division and constraint. Let us briefly look at these as they manifest themselves in the realm of food consumption.

In a particular compound where I spent a considerable amount of time, I realised that the quality of the food being cooked in the compound's collective kitchen varied for the different stoves. While some usually had a rich sauce with a variety of ingredients, others often cooked *cuntango*, i.e. boiled rice without any sauce. One Sunday I was given a saucepan containing a portion of meat sauce, something of a luxury, and was advised to take it discretely into my room in the compound so as not to awake any jealousy. This combination of obvious differences in quality of diet and the "public" cooking arrangements of the compound appeared somewhat paradoxical to me. To my outsider's eyes, the collective kitchen initially gave an impression of sharing, openness and co-operation while in fact under its roof I found a potential ground for envy, concealment and division. I was being introduced to the ironies of the compound and its evolving (i)morality. I found out later that households in the compound had ceased to exchange meals, as had been their earlier custom.

The results of my 1995 household survey also revealed significant intra-compound inequalities[230]. Within most of the compounds surveyed, and based upon the relative cost of the items usually consumed, most households had what I termed as being a "poor" or "very poor" diet. Some 20 out of a total of 85 compound households surveyed had a "non-poor" or "less poor" diet. In most cases these were male headed households, and often with combined wage work and self-employment. These findings suggest a degree of differentiation within extended domestic groups. Combined with the generally worsening economic climate for most people, this may be discouraging exchange of assistance between households. In addition to the above mentioned ending of meal exchange, difficulty in obtaining loans was referred to in more than one compound. The survey also showed intra-compound dif-

[230] I extended the survey to all households available in five compounds in Bandim in order to uncover eventual inequalities.

ferences in terms of access to farming land and food exchanges with other households. These various differences prompted me to select about ten households within several compounds who seemed to be at a disadvantage in these respects for further qualitative study in 1999, in order to understand the reasons for their condition.

Photo 7.2 A compound in Bandim (collective kitchen to the left)

In relation to access to farming land, younger heads of households are traditionally at a disadvantage in terms of size of rice plots and women have no claims to paddy fields, even if they are heads of households. Consequently, most of those interviewed lacked plots that were sufficiently large enough to provide them and their households with rice that would last until the following harvest. The head of the compound holds the largest paddy fields, which are transferred to him through matrilineal inheritance. He also controls the distribution of land for rice cultivation to male heads of households in the compound. Not surprisingly, the head of the compound also has the largest granary in the compound. In fact, it is only heads of compounds in Bandim (but not all) that appear to command a surplus of rice. Invariably, these surpluses are not sold. Firstly, rice is stored so that it can be consumed in large quantities during certain cultural ceremonies. This relates to a worldview common among the Pepel according to which accumulated surpluses or assets should be consumed or destroyed so that prestige is "accumulated" by the destroyer lineage[231]. An elderly woman described this tendency away from productive accumulation as "working for the grave", referring to the imperative of

[231] See Gomes (1989) on the Pepel in Biombo. See also Einarsdóttir (2000), who discovered that compounds in Biombo whose heads have large surpluses of rice may go hungry, because heads prioritise ceremonial consumption.

accumulating woven-strips to be displayed and destroyed at funerals, a very important lineage ritual among the Pepel[232].

Secondly, the rice surpluses controlled by the head of the compound are used for redistribution within the compound. This may be related to the symbolic qualities often attributed to staples in pre-capitalist societies of the sort described by Sahlins (1984:215-9). In such societies, she claims, food and staples in particular are imbued with too much social value to be exchanged for things (or money). Furthermore, she argues, in hierarchical societies, "the entire political order is sustained by a pivotal flow of goods, up and down the social hierarchy, with each gift not merely connoting a status relation but, compelling a loyalty" (p. 206). Where rank is ascribed, as among the Pepel, "to be noble is to be generous" (p.207). This generosity, which Sahlins sees as "the economic basis of primitive politics", implies unbalanced flows from high to low rank-orders. This seems to apply well to the principles of rice re-distribution within Pepel domestic groups in Bandim, where rice flows down the generation-gender rank seem to substantiate the relations between different positions in the social hierarchy. A disruption of these flows may thus have consequences for the stability of that hierarchy.

While the head of a compound has the generally recognised obligation of assisting households in need in the compound and these households theoretically have a claim on his surpluses, it became evident, however, that some households do not have acceptable levels of food consumption. In the section below I will discuss instances of isolation and discriminatory treatment of certain groups within compounds. The compound increasingly revealed itself as a site of considerable inequalities and contradictions. These inequalities may be widening in terms of members' ability to mobilise material support within their respective kin groups. I will proceed to analyse kin assistance as a major field of struggle.

7.4 Changes in kin assistance

Corporate kin groups

Let us take a closer look at how households in the compound may not enjoy equal protection and may not be equally integrated into its redistributive relations. I begin with a presentation of the accounts of two members of one particular compound in Bandim.

---

[232] This poses a major challenge to conventional entitlement theory which equates a direct relation between size of assets or stores and access to food. Woven stripe-cloths may serve as a buffer against extreme crisis - which they did for several of my interviewees during the 1998-1999 war - but poor diets and stored cloths are by no means incompatible.

Case 5: Joana, who is in her thirties, was allowed to settle together with her mother, brother and sisters in the compound. They used to live in a rural area. When Joana's father died some twenty years ago and his inheritor took over the rice fields and houses, Joana's mother left for Bissau with some of her children. Her mother's brother, who lived in the compound in Bandim, invited them to come to stay in the compound and he built a house for them. The head of that compound is also a close relative to her. Joana moved to another part of the city when she married but later left her husband and moved back to the compound. They have no rice field of their own but participate in the collective female tasks that are associated with rice cultivation. Her mother's brother and the head of the compound provision Joana's household with rice. This rice is enough to meet their cereal needs for half a year. When the rice is finished, and should they lack money to buy food, they can always turn to one of these two men for assistance. She says that they are always generous towards her. She enjoys living in the compound and does not want to move out as, in her view, that would result in greater hardship. In spite of her outside origin, Joana and her household seem very well integrated in the compound.

Case 6: Joaquim, in his fifties, has lived all his life in the same compound as Joana. Joaquim takes day jobs at the port of Bissau and has done so since 1963. In his opinion, it is now more difficult to get day work at the port than was the case a decade or so ago. He explains that he needs his day jobs in order to buy rice for the household since his paddy field is small. Joaquim tells me that his father was formerly the head of the compound. Back then, Joaquim was the administrator of his father's large granary but when his father died his situation changed drastically. The new head of the compound gave Joaquim a small rice field. The output from this plot does not give him and his household more than one month supply of rice. When I ask him what he thinks about this inheritance custom, he says that he is "merely following the tradition", but later on he expressed his dissatisfaction with his impoverished situation. He tells me that he does not feel supported in the compound, that he feels secluded and marginalised and that he is among those who receive the least support. Any material help within his compound, he says, is not voluntary, spontaneous or "from the heart", apart from exchanges with his brother, his last blood relative in the compound. The only advantage of living in a compound is, in his view, the help he gets for rice farming. Whenever he finds himself in difficulties he usually approaches not the head of the compound but other relations outside of the compound, namely one friend whom he grew up together with and the childhood friends of his age group who are now spread throughout the city. The latter meet frequently for recreation, to help each other with farm work and some of them also lend or give each other money.

These two contrasting accounts convey opposing experiences of one and the same compound. Joana, a well-integrated outsider who receives significant generosity, depicts the situation as a true "moral economy" without which she could not do. Joaquim, who has resided there for most of his life, finds himself almost dispossessed. This is a man in the autumn of life who has seen his situation worsen (both his market entitlements and his traditional claims) before it can eventually get any better – that is if his turn to inherit arrives during his life time[233]. His expectations for support lie largely outside of the compound. Before discussing these differences further, let me present a third

[233] Customary inheritance among the Pepel often occurs when men are already in their senior years.

case that illustrates another group that was found to often be in a disadvantaged position in the compounds.

Case 7: Quinta moved into the compound some twenty-five years ago when she married one of its members. Her husband died some years ago and none of his blood kin remain in the compound. She was, however, allowed to continue farming his small rice plot which provides her and her nine dependants with rice for three or four months. But she complains about the stinginess of the head of compound and how difficult it is to get any help from him, "in spite of (her) being a widow". She feels isolated in the compound and exchanges with other members are largely restricted to rice related work. Quinta has grown up sons in her household but she says that she has no authority over them. Not only do they refuse to share occasional incomes with her when she has nothing to eat but they also refuse to do their share of the collective work in the compound. This, in her opinion, contributes to the lack of generosity of her seniors towards her. When the 1998-99 war caused her to loose her job, things got very tough for Quinta and her children. But she avoids asking for help in the compound as she lacks the possibility to reciprocate. With the exception of one of her neighbours, assistance comes mainly from outside the compound, i.e. from the head of another compound who is a close relative to her, and from a brother of her deceased husband.

The roots of Joaquim's disadvantageous position stem partly from the age-old rules of inheritance and land allocation that dictate that a matrilineal relative and not the sons of a deceased head of compound inherit his assets. But upon moving into the compound, the new head also inherits responsibilities towards the sons and wives of the deceased. As the elders explained to me, it is expected that the new head treat these 'inherited' relatives well and in the same manner as he treated his own blood kin. However, this morality seems to be undergoing change, apparently to the detriment of certain groups within compounds, as these repeatedly expressed feeling discriminated. Joaquim, representing the condition of "inherited sons", felt unfairly treated since the death of his father. And, as was often related to me, issues of inheritance have become a source of conflict.

Quinta is representative of another group that seems disadvantaged in compounds and in the domestic domain in general, namely that of female heads of households and widows. Women in general have a structurally subordinate position in the domestic domain. They are dependent on male kin for access to the means of food production, particularly rice land, and access to the harvest. Inheritance rules dispossess them upon the death of their husbands thus making them particularly dependent on traditional norms of provisioning. Normally, and as is collectively recognised, the death of a husband should not pose a threat to the material security of the widow as her husband's kin has the responsibility of seeing to her needs. But Quinta's case, supported by at least two other studied cases, shows that in practice this is not necessarily so anymore. Several of the interviewed female heads of households residing in compounds complained, for example, about feeling isolated in the compound or discriminated against by their seniors[234] - while grown up sons may also falter in their duties towards their mothers (see section 7.4). This suggests that an erosion of responsibilities towards this category of women might be taking place. In addition, those living in extended domestic groups, in spite of their position as female heads of households, are invariably subjected to patriarchal authority.

A change in morality may be taking place whereby those in a structurally subordinate position in traditional Pepel society, i.e. women heads of households and inherited sons, seem to be increasingly vulnerable in terms of the claims they can make on seniors and of increasing isolation in the compound. Neglect by seniors of their responsibilities towards their dependants reached extreme proportions in a couple of instances. Let me present two cases to illustrate this.

Case 8: Madalena is a chronically sick middle-aged woman. She was born in her father's compound in Bandim. She left to marry but returned some years ago when she separated from her husband. In the meantime her father had died and a new head of compound settled in and provided for her mother. When that head of compound died some years ago, the new inheritor never bothered to move in and to assume the role of head of compound. He only took over the rice fields of the compound and did not give Madalena's brother any land to farm, as was his right. They reasoned with the inheritor but he nevertheless refused to concede. Madalena and her brother did not take any further action. "The elders in Bandim are aware of this situation but no one is willing to stand up for us", she explained. At the time I met her, Madalena was the only one providing for herself, her brother who was in ill health and two children. She related to me that she didn't expect to get any rice from the inheritor. The only assistance that she receives comes from another compound in the area, the head of which gives her rice, allows her to harvest cashew and to grow vegetables on his land.

Case 9: Natália is a woman in her sixties who has lived in the house of her deceased father in Bandim since she separated from her husband. Since her father died, the inheritor has not moved into the compound but he does farm the family's rice fields. Natália was resentful that she and her siblings were left without any rice fields and that they were never given any rice. In addition, she explained that because the inheritor had not performed the necessary ceremony connected to inheritance, it was the close family of the deceased that has the right to farm his land. She was planning to recover the land from the inheritor by taking the case to the highest customary Pepel authority in Bissau, at the kingdom of Djacal. She added that this chief has greater power than the chief of Bandim. If her problem was not solved there, she would then take it to the official courts. She also told me that one of her uncles had also tried to take one of Natália's two rooms to rent out for money, something that Pepel law does not entitle him to do. The situation lead to physical violence between them and the case was taken to the police. She was subsequently allowed to keep both of her rooms. Natália, who has been politically active in her neighbourhood for most of her life, is in a tenuous eco-

[234] Inherited wives may also feel discriminated in relation to earlier wives. This is an important cause for women to abandon compounds following the death of their first husbands. In rural areas this often drives them to the city. See section 7.6. Women who leave often loose their rights to provision in their domestic groups.

nomic situation and is dependent on the generosity of her daughter, her kin and her neighbours. Largely dispossessed from her investments in the political sphere in earlier days, her struggle continues for her perceived rights in the kin system.

A number of aspects struck me as being of particular importance in these cases. Firstly, that while some norms were being upheld, i.e. matrilineal inheritance rules that gave the inheritor access to the land (see below), other norms were being neglected, namely the inheritor's obligations towards his dependants[235]. In both cases, changes in norms were clearly working to the advantage of seniors whose powerful position allowed them to enjoy the benefits while defaulting on their obligations. In the process, subordinate groups stood to loose out and saw their traditional rights become threatened. The outcome of this struggle, however, is not predetermined, but is dependent upon how the loosing parties respond. In this respect, Natália differed from Madalena in her determination to fight back using the means at her disposal, which, in this case, was recourse to the traditional and official courts. Indeed, I did not find a lack of consciousness and will to change things among the interviewed disadvantaged persons within extended kin groups. And, over time, subordinate groups have certainly pressed for changes favourable to themselves (see below). The risks implied by a direct confrontation have possibly resulted in the resented compliance expressed by Joaquim and Madalena. A number of my respondents had invested in alternative networks of assistance outside the extended domestic group. Later in this chapter I assess the viability of available opportunities for these discontented groups to "disengage" from elders' support.

Variations between compounds

Changes in some traditional norms of assistance are not indicative of a general dissolution of the traditional social hierarchy or of traditional rights as a whole. Firstly, there are the above-illustrated inconsistencies in the direction of change. Secondly, extensive variations between compounds in Bandim make it difficult to generalise even at the level of the neighbourhood. The above cases of Natália and Madalena show one extreme of this variation, i.e. compounds in a state of apparent disintegration. In other compounds, rights and obligations in food transfers were being upheld (except for the discriminative allocations present in virtually all studied compounds), members reportedly fulfilled their assigned roles and the head seemed to enjoy an unabated level of authority. This is reflected in the persistent religious authority of heads of

[235] Changing inheritance practices and the fact that elders have sold most of the land in the neighbourhood mean that the benefits for matrilineal kin to inherit are increasingly restricted to the rice fields belonging to his lineage, which might work as a demotivating force for the latter to move into the inherited compound and take on the responsibilities of a head towards its members.

compounds as leaders of collective ceremonies of the domestic group. Also, in at least one case, one compound head was hindering teenage girls from attending school and girls were also being married away against their will, as I had the opportunity to witness[236]. In other compounds, the only thing that members seemed to share was collective agricultural arrangements. In two compounds that had not been able to cultivate their fields for several years, food exchanges were virtually non-existent and households seemed to mind their own businesses.

These variations between compounds concerning the operation of traditional hierarchies and traditional rights and duties should not be interpreted as different stages in an inexorable process of disintegration. An early generation of urban studies in Africa saw towns as an unfavourable environment to traditional family structures, corporate kin groups and descent as an organising principle for residence, access to land and the allocation of political rank[237]. These, it was thought, would gradually give way to modern institutions of law and order and to nuclear family forms, increasingly autonomous from the lineage and its system of obligations. Rights and obligations would be allocated by means of individualised contracts, rather than ascribed by descent. Exceptions to this general pattern were seen as "pockets of tradition" which would disappear with time. Later work came to document continuity in family norms and customary practices, the continued importance and adaptation of lineage and of traditional power offices such as the institution of chieftaincy in certain urban areas of West Africa (Gugler and Flanagan, 1978:70, 118, 129, 131; Peil, 1981:139-185; Barnes, 1986). The persistence of kin ties as a general category of social interaction and exchange of aid is well documented[238]. The vitality of traditional institutions in Bandim lends support to the latter stance. They are not merely the result of a "benevolent" or delayed process of urbanisation as it occurred in Bissau, but their persistence is also to be understood in the light of strategies of adaptation of these institutions to wider changes, as will be discussed in section 7.5.

Changing structures of expectations

Changes in norms of assistance among relatives seem to also be taking place outside extended domestic groups. I will focus on changes that are occurring along gender and generational lines as these repeatedly surfaced in my interviews.

---

[236] See Einarsdóttir (2000, chapter two) on similar problems among the Pepel in Biombo, although she also found a reduction of men's authority in these respects.

[237] See Basham (1978:125); Gugler and Flanagan (1978:121, 133-4); Little (1965:100); Southall (1961:31-5); Banton (1961:123); Boswell (1969); Epstein (1981).

[238] Idem. See also: Peil (1981); Rocha (1994); Devereux (1999).

Gender inversions

In context of structural adjustment, women's contribution to household expenses has been reported to be on the increase both in urban and rural areas[239]. My household survey and interviews suggested that the gender division of responsibilities is partly still in place in Bandim. In roughly half of the surveyed households the husband was the provider of rice for the household (usually by engaging in either rice production or cash work). But in many cases women took upon themselves partial or full responsibility for the provision of rice. Even when they were responsible for buying only the *mafe*, women often complained that they spent more money on food than their husbands did because *mafe* required more expenditure than rice. In addition, expenses for clothes, school and health were usually born by the women. One could say with considerable certainty that women's burden of providing for household needs has increased.

The retrenchment of public sector employment, the declining opportunities for wage work and the fall in real wages have affected men's formerly privileged access to wage work and to regular and sufficient incomes. Consequently, the ability of many to fulfil a major component of the established gender contract, that of the provision of rice for the family, has been jeopardised. The contribution of males could not always be counted upon and in several cases it was women's income that kept the household going. The reliance of increasing numbers of men on casual work has probably worsened whatever claims wives' may have had on the incomes of their husbands, as the latter may easily omit occasionally earned income from their wives if they wish to do so. In addition, men have usually retained the prerogative of not disclosing the size of their incomes. This possibly gives them room for deciding to keep a share for personal expenditure, irrespective of whether or not basic household needs have been met[240].

In the general context of a rigid sexual division of labour in both the family and the market, (based on both my field work and INEP 1991), the work load of women increases as they have to both fulfil domestic tasks and be the main or sole economic providers for the family. This increase in women's work burden and their increasing responsibility for managing the crisis has been reported elsewhere under conditions of structural adjustment (Dennis, 1991; Daines and Seddon, 1991). In the study setting, this is vividly illustrated by the following example: in one family that I met during my first fieldwork, the husband had lost his job in the public sector and the wife had become responsible

[239] See INEP (1991), based on a small sample in Bissau. See also Einarsdóttir (2000) particularly on Pepel women in Biombo - a rural area numerically dominated by the Pepel –, based on long anthropological fieldwork.

[240] The fact that the sale of cashew wine for local consumption has become virtually the most worthwhile business in the study setting, in the midst of widespread poverty and obvious diet insufficiencies, awakes suspicions that a good share of this personal expenditure is used for drinking.

for both domestic tasks and income generation. When I asked him whose responsibility it was now to provide for the family, he answered: "My wife's. It is *her* children." This was a striking remark in a society which otherwise ascribes to men extensive rights over the children born by their wives. When I visited them during my next fieldwork the couple had separated.

Men's incapacity to fulfil a fundamental part of the gender contract and to negotiate a new one seems to have had serious consequences for many families. The legitimacy of these men as heads of households is undermined and many women refuse to accommodate to new terms that they may perceive as unfair and oppressive. Not surprisingly, cases of and references to family rupture and domestic violence were common throughout my fieldwork[241]. Two local institutions of justice – a respected elder and a judge at the local Sectoral Court (an official court) – both reported to me that the most common grievances within families that were brought to their attention (and invariably by women) concerned food allowances (apart from inheritance matters)[242].

I heard, on numerous occasions, women say that the men in the household did not have a wage job as a means of explaining why men did not contribute to the household food needs. I got the impression that "not having a job" easily excused men from their responsibilities. The condition of being "out of work" seems to be attributable only to men. This condition legitimates men's evasion from their ascribed responsibilities in the provision and assistance of others. At a time when this is becoming the norm rather than the exception, and in the virtual absence of state provided security, a reshuffling of responsibilities is occurring. The burden is being shifted to those locally defined as not being afflicted by the problem of being "out of work", i.e. women (particularly wives and elderly women) who are expected to fill the gap by whatever means, supposedly by "non-work" activities, usually meaning petty trade.

Generational inversions

The widespread phenomenon of "out of work" men has implications not only for the provision of dependants in the household but also for the assistance given to other close relatives such as the elderly. The plight of elderly women in this context became quite evident in the interviews I had with several of them[243]. "Out of work" sons increasingly falter in their traditional duty to pro-

[241] INEP (1991) also reports a high number of references to divorce.

[242] At least until family matters were removed from the Sectoral Courts to a higher instance.

[243] The discussion in this section will be based on six cases out of my network studies in 1999, as well as on multiple encounters, namely with elderly women on the market place, during previous fieldwork.

vide for their elderly widow mothers[244]. The essence of the problem is well captured in a comment made by an elderly women, a fish seller for almost 40 years but now too ill and old to carry on: "I have four children, all male, and none has work!" This was her way of explaining why she went hungry. Here, we see how processes beyond the local level interplay with local notions of work and gender roles to increase the vulnerability of the elderly. But their plight does not end with being left to fend for themselves. Sons who are "out of work", sons and daughters that emigrate for a longer or shorter term, or simply the high mortality rates (where HIV plays a part), all contribute to burdening elderly women with the task of providing for large numbers of grandchildren. In some cases they reported to be the main providers of food in households where there were adult children and which included males who were idle. Rosa's case is illustrative of such a situation:

Case 10: Rosa is an elderly widow with a physical handicap and is very impoverished. From our conversation I concluded that, despite residing in a compound, she is quite isolated in terms of the support she can get. Her sons live with their own families in the same domestic group as their mother. But, "as they are out of work, they cannot help me", she says. "I have to work because nobody will give me anything". Her only security is to be found in the market where she can buy her merchandise on credit. On top of not being able to count on her children for help, she is the head of a household with seven grandchildren for whom she is the sole provider, on the basis of her petty trade. The children's parents, who live in villages in the nearby hinterland of Bissau, do not make any material contribution. She says that as they are in a very poor condition she could not refuse to take care of the children. She concluded our conversation by saying, "I only hope that God will give me a long life to raise my grandchildren".

It can be said that for Rosa, and for women in a similar situation, old age is no longer a phase of life characterised by rest and being cared for by younger generations. As Rosa's case shows, not only can elderly women not count on the help of their children, but they are also increasingly being burdened by the next generations[245]. As one of them chose to express this situation, "It is punishment until you hit the grave". Two other respondents expressed dissatisfaction with being economically unable to help their elderly parents. One of them regretted that she was instead dependent on her mother's help. In the case of another interviewee, the dependence of her grown up children and grandchildren on her petty trade hindered her from fulfilling her responsibilities towards her old father, "who has no sons alive"[246]. These repeated

[244] Possibly these responsibilities may be increasingly shouldered by daughters, as was the case of one female interviewee, who felt responsible for providing for her parents in the village," since her brother had no work".

[245] In the same logic, in several cases, respondents reported to have sent some of their children to stay with grandparents in rural areas, often as a result of a concern for their well-being.

[246] Her married son was an apprentice in a car repair shop and thus received no regular wage. Her sixteen-year-old daughter had just delivered a baby and the father, also a teenager, was out of the

references to unfulfilled obligations prompt me to speak of a generational inversion in the structure of provisioning. While poorly documented in other urban areas this is not exclusive to Bissau as a study by Brand et al (1995) of women informal sector workers in Harare has shown.

Another aspect of these gender and generational inversions in rights for assistance relates to the situation of an increasing number of single mothers and their children.

Teenage mothers

This is a somewhat recent category in Bandim which does not enjoy customary rights vis-à-vis other categories. The numbers of young girls giving birth outside of marriage is clearly increasing, although there are no statistics for this. I met many of them during my stays in Bandim. Often they were staying with their own mothers. One such case was the sixteen-year-old daughter of Maria who had just given birth when I met her in 1999. The father of the child was sixteen years old too. Maria contacted the mother of the boy to help provide for the baby but she answered that they had nothing to contribute with. This illustrates how the burden of providing for these children may be being placed on grandmothers, as this growing category of single mothers and their children cannot claim any responsibility from the father in the absence of a wedding sanctioned by customary rules. Obviously, this problem is not specific to the study setting but has been acknowledged in other urban areas in Africa and beyond. Rwebangira and Liljeström (1998) for example address the dynamics of this problem in Tanzania and the issue of young males being unable to assume the economic responsibilities of adulthood and parenthood has also been noted in Dakar by O'Brien (1996) and by Castells (1998) in the American ghetto.

In the study setting, this new and expanding group of teenage mothers may also be constructing new rights and making "unusual" claims. The case of Isabel illustrates this.

Case 11: Isabel was 21 years old when I met her. She had three children and had become pregnant for the first time at the age of fourteen. When she had her first child she moved in with the father but they did not get married. He promised her parents that he would marry her when his economic situation had improved. He later left Isabel with three children and married another woman instead. At the time of my visit I was told that he was not contributing to the expenses or even visiting the children. Isabel took her case to the highest court in Pepel land, the *cufet*, challenging the father of her children to assume his responsibility. By the time of the interview he had not yet responded to the challenge.

---

picture. She complained that this was not the first time this happened and that these events repeatedly frustrated her efforts to expand her business or to fulfil her duties towards her own father.

Although she had no customary legitimate rights to contributions from the father of her children, Isabel felt unfairly treated and took the serious decision of resorting to the most feared justice institution of the Pepel in order to defend her perceived rights. New claims were thus being pursued to their last instance, and interestingly, through customary institutions.

In sum, while food is being transferred and assistance is being exchanged intensively among relatives in Bandim, formerly established loyalties are in some cases being put to the test. Within extended domestic groups there seems to be a process of differentiation and selection whereby some households can count upon considerable support while others are falling from the safety net that the compound once provided them with. Among kin in general, roles and responsibilities seem to be shifting with the burden being placed disproportionately on women. This redefinition of norms or informal rights to assistance is to be understood in the light of both struggles at the micro level between the groups involved and of external processes shaping the conditions in which these struggles take place.

7.5 Wider processes, social struggles and traditional rights

Let me turn to the wider processes that might be having an effect on structures of authority and, directly or indirectly, on the rules of redistribution and on exchange relations within compounds. To begin with, natural processes are apparently leading to declining rice harvests. Rice farmers in Bandim consistently complained about faltering rains – crucial in this rain fed agriculture – and referred to more abundant rice harvests in the past. Farmers also complained that the soil is becoming less productive. One informant commented by making an association between two contemporary processes that were perceived to be eroding his subsistence basis: "the land is like money: what you get from both decreases all the time". Finally, farmers deplored the uncontrolled invasions of paddy fields by salt water and the difficulties in financing the reparation of dams which was resulting in abandonment of rice fields. This has probably impacted upon both the ability of rice farmers in Bandim to feed their dependants as well as the levels of generosity shown to others.

Processes of a political nature are also introducing new sources of material stress and tension to the Pepel community in Bandim. In chapters two and three I have referred to the changing position of the local Pepel and other traditional elites in relation to the wider political system. In this respect, the picture that emerges of the position of the local Pepel nobility in the last decade or so is contradictory. On the one hand, there seems to be a "revalorization" of neo-traditional powers manifested in official discourses and in the strategies of politicians in the context of multiparty politics as evidenced, for example, by the case of several elders in Bandim that claimed to have been contacted by politicians[247]. On the other hand, Pepel seniors in Bandim have been unable to mobilise the government in defence of their interests and those of their communities. Fifteen years earlier they had asked for help from the government to finance dam reparation in the paddy fields. They formed a committee through which they had contacted the President prior to the elections in1994 and again in 1996. According to one of its members, they had managed to get the President, the Minister of Agriculture and journalists to come to Bandim and promises had been made. These promises had, however, come to nothing and the seniors of Bandim related how they must simply rely on their own internal resources to solve production and other problems[248].

In addition to this, the local government has encroached extensively on customary land in Bandim, literally expropriating the Pepel of large shares of their land. This pertains particularly to land used for cashew production on Alto Bandim, an attractive location on the outskirts of the neighbourhood for house construction. Elders told me how the Municipal government at one point went in with machinery and started cutting down cashew trees without even contacting the customary holders. The "owners of Bandim", he explained, gathered to present their complaints to the President of the municipal council and were able to retain a fraction of their land. The major part was lost to the municipality without any compensation and later sold to private persons or turned into luxury residences, such as the recently built Ministers' Quarters on Alto Bandim. The several elders I interviewed had all lost land in this manner and some felt compelled to sell their remaining land for fear of being dispossessed of it later on. When I asked what action they had taken against this expropriation one interviewee burst into a bitter laughter, "Where should I turn to complain? The power of the state is nothing but abuse". However, elders are not as powerless as this statement may suggest. In the privacy of an elder's porch which I had visited many times before, I was told of an instance when witchcraft had been used against a certain government official who built a house on Pepel land in Bandim against the advice of the elders, reportedly resulting in his death[249]. Pepel elders have a reputation of being skilful performers in the sacred realm, and they may use this to defend their position both against the state and their own subordinates. Although they do not hold a

---

[247] See Einarsdóttir (2000) on similar trends among the Pepel nobility in Biombo.

[248] It is ironical that while in the 1942 famine local Pepel farmers received seeds from the colonial government for restoring rice production, several elders told me in 1999 that they would have to solve the seed shortages in the aftermath of the war by assisting each other.

[249] Members of the elite acquiring plots of land from these elders, although the land belongs to the Council, they not only pay the necessary dues to the traditional owner but also conduct the ceremonies that are supposed to accompany these transfers of land – according to local residents and the personal communication of an outsider, Helena Neves, a Guinean lawyer.

monopoly over these 'invisible' resources, there is a local consensus that their mystical powers continue to be feared[250].

The above does not simply expose the political inefficacy of this group in defending their interests in the city but also means a decline in the incomes resulting from the cashew nuts (in the form of bartered imported rice) and from the processing and sale of cashew wine by women – not to mention the withdrawal of local Pepel from the growing cashew export sector.

In sum, one could say that there is a general material squeeze on the host group in Bandim deriving from different kinds of processes that may be placing restraints on the "generosity" among rice farmers within extended domestic groups, at a time when demands are increasing for a redistribution of surpluses. The differential treatment that seniors and heads of compounds gave to different groups within the compound may be a result of their prioritising and selecting whom to be generous with. Others simply found themselves in a position to marginalise dependants traditionally entitled to their support, sometimes without penalty.

Alternative livelihoods and identities

There are other wider processes that may have impacted on pre-capitalist structures of authority and rights to provisioning and attendant struggles in Bandim. Here I am referring to general processes such as the impact of urbanization, modern institutions, commoditisation and of the mixing of ethnic groups on kin relations and to the issues of social and cultural change. As discussed above, these issues constituted a central focus in an earlier generation of studies on urbanization in Africa. But there has been a renewed interest in them in the current context of economic hardship. So let me consider how decades of urbanisation and related processes have influenced and continue to influence changes and continuities in kin relations among residents in Bandim. These relations pertain to both those of migrants and those of the host Pepel society. Changes in kin-based assistance are directly related to these wider changes.

Subordinate groups in local traditional societies have long been exposed to ideas and values that have sometimes been in conflict with the ideologies on which the authority of seniors rests. Modern education for example - although representing a post-independence opportunity for the vast majority of Bandim dwellers - has apparently been interpreted as a threat by Pepel seniors. According to the founder of a private-communitarian school in Bandim, in its first years the school met with hostility from the Pepel elders and considerable mobilisation was necessary to persuade them to let the youth attend "the

[250] On the modernity of witchcraft see: Comaroff and Comaroff (1999); Fisiy and Geschiere (1996) and Hecht and Simone (1994).

school of the whites". The chief of Bandim expressed his apprehension about the threat that city life poses to the "Pepel race". He complains that the youth nowadays cannot even speak the Pepel language and do not know about the defeats that the Pepel of Bissau inflicted on Portuguese troops before military conquest in 1915. He said that the elders try to tell them about the great deeds of the Pepel in the past - where resistance to colonialism has been a major shaper of their collective identity - at occasions such as initiation ceremonies. "But the young men are not interested, they prefer the discos and the cinema".

Religion is another realm of penetration of foreign values, and one with increasing significance in contemporary urban life in Africa (Bangura, 1994; Simone, 1998). The Evangelical Church of Bandim - the religious group I became most acquainted with – seems to provide alternative sources of material support, solidarity and social networks to traditional ones, as well as an alternative morality and basis for the construction of identities where women and youth have organised independently from traditional structures (and state) (chapter six). But the church also demands from their members a rupture with many traditional practices, particularly those connected to ceremonies involving the immaterial world. These include a variety of rituals related to agriculture or domestic affairs, marriage, funerals and consultation of traditional diviners. Conversion embodies the promise of liberation from witchcraft and the power of the ancestors and, in theory, a certain liberation from the domination from seniors as much of their power rests in their privileged positioning in the spiritual realm. On the other hand, it also means the cancellation of certain customary rights. Firstly, a break with the matrilineal inheritance practices common among the Pepel means that men are deprived of the rights of inheritance which might result in having to rely on a small rice field from that time on. Secondly, conversion may lead to ostracism from one's traditional group and eventually to a severing of assistance from that group, as at least four respondents who were church attendants reported having happened to them. Segunda's account in chapter six illustrates the serious consequences of her church membership for her material well being.

So there seems to exist an opposition between these and older sources of assistance and affiliation. This observation finds some support in studies carried out in other African cities where religious groupings have sometimes been found to be replacing traditional structures of clan and family (Espling, 1999; Loforte, 2000; Simone, 1998) This may appear to echo earlier arguments about the liberating effects on women and youth of thriving associational activity in West African cities (see for example Little, 1965). However, I also found instances where there was an overlapping of affiliations. Two of the local elders attending church and who had extensive rice fields responded to the needs of fellow churchgoers and also fulfilled their responsibilities as heads of compounds towards the members of their respective domestic groups. One of them had provided the land for the construction of the church and welcomed Sunday school in the premises of his compound. Nevertheless, he continued to be an important councillor to the chief of Bandim and was respected among the elders. These cases indicate the possibility of maintaining potentially contradictory identities and agendas in a functional balance, a situation so often referred to in postcolonial studies (Werbner, 1996; Hecht and Simone, 1994).

The fact remains that this kind of identity straddling in this particular context is neither open to everyone nor is it cost-free. The morality espoused by the church conflicts with the traditional one, and so individuals enjoying some material security proceeding from (non-Christian) kin groups may jeopardise that security by joining the church. The scarcity of the material resources commanded by this congregation further constrains it as a real alternative to disconnect from more traditional sources of support (see chapter six).

Traditional structures of power and provisioning are also confronted with the worldviews of other indigenous cultures in the city. Although ethnic relations have often been considered to be quite relaxed in Guinea-Bissau, the great inflow of people from all ethnic groups to the city, particularly since the colonial war, has turned Bissau into a melting pot. This has both contributed to tensions between groups and made available a wider variety of references for the construction of identities. In relation to the first of these issues, Islamised groups from the Eastern part of the country have moved in large numbers to the city to pursue trade careers since the liberalisation of commerce. In Bandim, where there has been an accelerated penetration of these groups since the 1980s, this has led to hidden tensions – as revealed to me during interviews with the chief, elders, key informants and residents. Firstly, these Eastern groups have formed residential clusters within Bandim and established important positions in the local market place of Caracol. In some instances they have encroached onto the physical and symbolic spaces of the local Pepel nobility. In addition to this, their increasing visibility in the urban economy, manifested not least in the prominent positions that these groups have attained in the supply of imported rice, is in contrast with the difficulties of the local Pepel community. As discussed above, the latter have been confronted with a generally shrinking resource base, a forced reduction in their participation in the production of the valuable export crop and declining rice harvests. They and have therefore become increasingly dependent on the purchase of imported substitute staples, controlled to a great extent by members of the Eastern groups, to close the cereal gap. This may lead to a certain hardening of ethnic identities currently occurring elsewhere, where the distribution of economic opportunities evolve along ethnic lines (Bangura, 1994; Simone, 1998).

At the same time, the ethnic mixture in the city accounts for a plurality of identities available to individuals. Again, the perceptions voiced by the Pepel chief, elders and residents in Bandim of groups with very different worldviews are illuminating in this respect. The "Pepel identity", as constructed by the chief and the elders that were interviewed, is related to being hard working farmers and feared warriors. This identity seems not to appeal to many Pepel, particularly the youth. A number of them have enamoured other worldviews that differ from the prestige oriented "destruction" of Pepel seniors (see section 7.3) and which instead value trade as prestigious work, a more promising alternative in the context of economic liberalisation. Ironically, this was hardly an identity one would aspire to in earlier times when the state regarded such private traders as immoral elements in society. I also heard references to Pepel individuals who, where the situation permitted, had negated their Pepel origin and opted instead to identify themselves as a Fula or a Mandinga (for example in the case of children of inter-ethnic marriages or of individuals living in or moving to neighbourhoods numerically dominated by those groups). Carrying such an identity rather than a Pepel one seems to be perceived as opening the possibility for penetrating prolific vertical connections and for entering the few channels of social mobility available to Bissauans in the current political economic context. If so, this suggests an instrumental and conscious use of identities, an idea so much in vogue in the current literature (Simone, 1999; Ferguson, 1999). Once again, however, I realised that the latter alternative was not a commonly available option and that this particular type of identity switching seems to be blocked for the majority – this is reflected for example in the frustrated efforts made by entrepreneurial Pepel individuals eager to penetrate those vertical networks (see chapter three).

Let me proceed by discussing what the penetration of market relations and the liberalisation of the economy have meant for kin-based sources of assistance in the study setting.

Market based livelihoods and networks

Cash income activities by local groups are as old as the city itself. In chapter two I described how, in the early times of colonial presence, the local Pepel were very keen to retain their share of international trade. With the advent of urbanisation, opportunities for earning cash income away from the direct supervision of the elders increased for the subordinate layers of the local Pepel society. Women engaged in market trade and men took work at the port outside of the agricultural season. However, as I discussed in chapter two, the conditions of their participation in the modern economy and the limited opportunities for social mobility away from the kin structures in the colonial period encouraged a continued dependence on subsistence production activities under the control of elders. Among Bandim dwellers, such cash income activities were combined with rice farming on ancestral lands and under the tutelage of the elders, facilitating continued lineage cohesion and allowing elders to withhold an important source of power. In addition, individual income activities away from the compound were at least partly "assimilated" into the traditional power structures, as seniors – who themselves were not involved in cash earning activities – established a claim on a share of those incomes[251].

Developments in the 1980s introduced some changes into this situation. Firstly, cashew cultivation in Bandim expanded in response to international demand. In connection to this, sons began putting pressure on their fathers to leave cashew plantations to them instead of transferring them through matrilineal descent. Several of the local Pepel declared to me that this has become a major source of conflict but that it has brought about concessions from elders[252]. At the same time, rice land has remained beyond negotiation and continues to be transferred within the matrilineage with deviations risking heavy punishment. This may be related to the important control that elders hold over rice production and the role that land plays in their control over others. Secondly, policy changes in the mid-1980s have changed conditions of participation in the market. The deterioration of material conditions in the city and the liberalisation of the economy encouraged an increase in participation of women in cash income activities, particularly in the trading of foodstuffs. Food trade by the women of coastal groups (including the Pepel) has pre-colonial roots and thus enjoys considerable legitimacy (see chapter two). These women are today experimenting with different commodities, supply sources and geographical locations. Some urban women have acquired a strong position in the urban food market. But many others are living hand to mouth and their small enterprises are permanently on the verge to collapse. This is resulting in a visible differentiation among market women (see chapter five).

There is a large literature on the evolving position of women in connection to urbanisation and income opportunities for them. Emphases and perspectives have changed through time but they seem to oscillate between two general positions. On the one hand, the early literature tended to focus on the opportunities that towns and the market opened for the autonomy of women. This was referred particularly for urban West Africa where women were reported to attain influential positions through trade, and, in the process, to gain autonomy from the control of husbands, their husbands' relatives and their own blood kin (Gugler and Flanagan, 1978:135-48; Little, 1965:118-137; Southall, 1961: :46-66; McCall, 1961). In a similar manner, in more recent contributions, some have argued that independent access of wives to income and their

[251] See for similar findings in rural Pepel villages by Gomes (1989) and Hochet (1985). At the rural end, some have interpreted migration, interaction with the city and the penetration of the cash economy as de-structuring for traditional rural Pepel society (Cardoso and Ribeiro, 1987:46). But others have seen it as a necessity to bridge the cereal deficit in the villages and a practice well integrated into the "traditional system of organisation of work in the compound" (Hochet, 1985:36).

[252] See Hochet (1985) for similar trends in rural Pepel communities. See Cissoko (1987) on Bissau.

contribution to feeding the family may raise questions about established male and female roles in the household (Cutrufelli, 1983; Young, 1992). Yet others have portrayed the market place as a crucial "liberating" space for women (The Win Document, 1985). In more recent times, this general argument has been translated into an emphasis on the variety of sources that towns offer for the construction of women's identities (Liljeström et al, 1998; Rosander, 1997). Others writers dwell on celebratory descriptions of the achievements of women informal traders in connection with economic liberalisation (Tripp, 1989; Sow, 1993). On the other hand, materialist and some strands of feminist research have forwarded critical assessments of the position of women in towns to illuminate the subordinate positions they came to occupy in the urban labour market and the "informal sector" and the persistence of patriarchal dominance both in the wider society and in the home[253].

Let me discuss how my findings fit into this general discussion. As was discussed above for the study setting, there has been an increase in women's participation in cash income activities, particularly trade, as well as in their contribution towards household cash expenses. Combined with the growing difficulties that many women face in selling their goods (chapter five), this has entailed that women generally spend an increasing number of hours at the market. The market activities of women seem in some ways to have come to be perceived as a threat by men and male seniors in the domestic field. The following statement by a male senior sums up my impressions in this respect. The greatest problem in Bandim, he said, was "women's disobedience to their husbands. Now they make their own decisions instead of their husbands', influenced by their colleagues at the market place". In some (but not all) compounds, the elders felt that they no longer controlled the labour of youth and women to the extent they once did[254].

In their market activities, women developed their own networks of support (chapter five) through which they may potentially carve out a space of autonomy from networks of assistance within the patriarchal familial. Many reach credit agreements with suppliers which guarantee them secure access to commodities; establish partnerships with market colleagues for mutual support and pooling of resources; or join rotating savings groups which keep businesses from collapsing. For several of my interviewees – including a couple of respondents who resided in corporate kin groups – their source of security seemed to lie almost completely in these and other market based networks. Their livelihoods were considerably anchored in the market – probably more

[253] See Bruce and Dwyer (1988); Chant and Brydon (1989). On the deterioration of women's position in the context of structural adjustment, see for example Sparr (1994) and Manuh (1994).

[254] They seem to have circumvented this problem by making recruitment arrangements more flexible, originally based on age groups, i.e. by drawing on a wide range of people in the neighbourhood willing to work a few days in exchange for food and wine, which should not be difficult nowadays when necessity is knocking at so many doors

because they were isolated from kin support rather than due to a conscious move on their part. As one of them summed it up, "my petty trade is my uncle's store". But is market-based support a viable alternative to kin-based assistance? As I discussed in chapter five, women's participation and position in networks and agreements in the market varied and there were instances of exclusion and subordination. In addition, a large share of my interviewees were dependent on the support of male kin for their businesses. Some of these seemingly autonomous market activities were anchored in traditional relations of production and resources governed by customary norms for the supply of commodities. To some extent, rice production on lineage land was sponsored by these market activities. Naturally, the varying domestic situation of market women needs to be considered here. For example, the situation of those embedded in corporate groups that are able to provide them with a sense of material security differs substantially from that of women that have exited the control of the extended family and head their own households as weel as from that of women who live with husbands unable to fulfil his share of the provisioning contract. The former have a lot more to loose and may reconsider before they rebel against patriarchal authority in the home.

The generally harsh economic conditions in the city, the insecurity of the market incomes of many women and their exclusion from supportive networks in the market may force them to comply with patriarchal authority at home. In this respect, the subordinate conditions that many market women experience in relation to the practices of both suppliers and local government may interact with domestic patriarchal structures to hamper a true empowerment of these women.

Dependence versus 'disengagement': a difficult equation

In the above section I have attempted to give a broad view of how wider processes and responses within local traditional groups have interacted as a basis to understand changes in kin based rights in provisioning and assistance and in the internal balance of power involving different levels of agency. Let me summarise.

In the study setting, traditional structures and power holders have faced a variety of challenges. Firstly, foreign values, a multiplicity of alternative worldviews and ethnic identities and modern types of solidarities have been perceived by traditional power figures as a threat and have challenged their monopoly over the local discourse on culture. Secondly, they have been facing a narrowing material base, namely through a decline in rice harvests and the expropriation of cashew land by the government, both of which are threatening their position as redistributors. Thirdly, the penetration of market relations made possible for subordinate groups to press for changes and to invest in alternative networks. This eventually broadened the platform of some for bargaining for a better position. Elders have made some concessions and some admitted having lost some control over the labour of youth and women.

However, the traditional hierarchy of power and provision have proven remarkably persistent in Bandim. They have not been frozen in time, locked in tradition or remained opposed to progress, as local stereotypes portray the local host group. Rather, traditional structures, affinities and norms have adapted to wider changes which have been used to readjust internal positions. Historically, the "Pepel of Bandim" have actively pursued emerging economic opportunities (from the slave trade to the cashew economy). Cash income activities, while carrying the 'danger' of increasing the autonomyof subordinate groups, have been largely carried out in combination with traditional obligations and have to some extent been functional to the preservation of power by elders. The emerging picture is one of a balancing of individual and collective interests and sometimes of different identities and affiliations.

The wider environment, while posing challenges, has also contributed to the reproduction of traditional structures and the informal rights associated with them. During colonial rule, the extremely limited opportunities for social mobility for members of local societies and their exclusion or subordinate participation in modern society contributed to such an outcome, while at the same time foreign capital was being relieved from the costs of social reproduction (see chapter two)[255]. Today, kin structures continue to fulfil crucial material (and other) functions in a context of austere living conditions. For many people they are an important source of capital for small trade enterprises, they provide a minimum of economic security and, among the host group, they are a source of staple food as well. Among other ethnic groups commanding important market niches in the city, kin affinities may even be facilitating social mobility, though this would require further research.

For the majority in Bandim however, current material insecurity works to perpetuate dependence on traditional systems of redistribution. Subordinate groups do engage in alternative networks of support – as is the case of rotating savings clubs, religious groups, redistribution groups among casual workers and networks of market colleagues and friends, all of which I have referred to. They may be complementary and be in functional balance with kin structures of support. But where these latter structures are experienced as oppressive, alternative networks could be considered as potential opportunities to disengage from them. However, as I have come to understand the situation, there are structural constraints which, to some extent, restrict these exit options and hold back the bargaining potential of subordinate groups. There has been a general decline in market-based entitlements, reflected for example in an

[255] See Keesing (1981:470), Gugler and Flanagan (1978:121-2) and Epstein (1981:191) on interpretations of the persistence of traditional forms of solidarity as a result of disadvantageous modern institutions, economic insecurity and as useful in the transition to a modern urban society.

erosion of real incomes making market incomes increasingly precarious and in the difficulty of getting casual work (see chapter five) which drains the potential of those alternative networks in the market. When business declines or fails, as is a common occurrence, people need their kin group. Most women appear not to be in a position to break with the compound. "Rebellious women", I was told, are "women who have money", who have the "economic strength" to stand on their own. The forms of resistance that are adopted are probably far subtler than a complete rupture with the domestic group and its authority structure. As one female compound resident told me in low voice, "women in the compound must keep low".

An obvious conclusion is that the question of whether traditional kin support is weakening or strengthening is an empirical one and cannot, as is often the case, simply be assumed. The same applies to whether old forms of solidarity are giving way to new forms and fields of struggle[256]. In the study setting, savings groups that exclude the poorest, casual worker groups on the verge to collapse, a church too poor to assist its members, and personal collaborations weakened by a lack of resources seem to be poor alternatives to those kin groups that guarantee a minimum of security (see chapters five and six). However, in the face of a generally declining production capacity among the host group, the kin redistribution system is also being put to the test. Some norms are being preserved (often through the manipulation of the sacred realm) while others are forgotten. In this process of norm reformulation, contradictions in the compound seem to be deepening and some people are falling outside of its safety net.

7.6 Urban-rural exchanges

Social networks with a wide geographical range are important at a time when mobility is playing an increasing role in the livelihoods of many urbanites in Africa (Baker, 1997; Andersson, 2002). Several of my respondents had relatives abroad and some could count on their remittances. Ties with rural areas were more common. In this section I will reflect upon what might be happening to urban-rural exchanges of assistance, as these are a part of urban livelihoods, in a wider context of change. The discussion is based to a great extent on my social network study with thirty respondents who were requested to tell me about their rural ties and the significance of these for their material security. The analysis is also based on interviews with elders, a few migration histories, my survey data to a limited extent and the general understanding I gained during my fieldwork of the links that Bandim dwellers maintain with their villages. I will focus the discussion on the Pepel ethnic group and the

[256] See on this: Lemarchand (1989); Benda-Beckmann (1999).

relations that they maintain with their rural areas of origin, particularly of Biombo, a rural area numerically dominated by the Pepel in the near hinterland of Bissau. Differences between ethnic groups and between geographical areas in the country justify this focus. A few other studies which have been conducted in Pepel rural areas will assist me in this effort[257]. This section is more of a reflection since a more conclusive analysis would require an in-depth study on these issues alone. Let me introduce the discussion with a migration history that I consider to be representative of a share of migrant dwellers in Bandim and of the ties that they maintain with their rural areas of origin.

Case 12: João identifies himself as a Pepel from Tór, a village some 40Km west of Bissau. He moved to Bissau in 1955 when he was 15 years old. Upon his arrival at Bandim he looked for one head of compound whom he heard also had origins in Tór and was thus "a relative". The latter sold him some land in his compound on which to build a house and João says that he practically became a "member" of that compound. He had no rights to a rice plot in Bandim but participated in the collective agricultural tasks of the compound and occasionally received some kilos of rice. Now that most in the compound are dead, João reminisces about the help and advise that the elder used to give him. João worked at the port of Bissau for many years but he continued going back to Tór for the agricultural season. In latter years, however, this has changed. His kin in Tór nowadays get their rice by growing cashew instead of producing it themselves. Also, they have started to sell cashew nuts for money instead of bartering it with rice. In his understanding, many people do not want to keep tons of rice at home because that will generate a lot of demands from kin. So, when João finds himself in difficulties, he avoids turning to his relatives in Tór. Other types of exchanges do nonetheless exist. His wife goes to Tór for the cashew season. She picks and presses the cashews at a plantation held by João's brother. Because João has certain rights to that land, he explains, she is able to keep both the juice and the nuts - this seems to be a good deal compared to many other women who usually are allowed to keep only the juice. The last cashew harvest gave a return of 500Kg of rice, normally sufficient to last five months in his household. He added, however, that this also depended on the number of guests coming from the village. Particularly during the cashew and tomato seasons, they bring their produce to sell in Bissau and sleep and eat in João's house for long periods without making any contribution to the household. This, he finds unreasonable. Finally, after almost 45 years in Bissau, João affirms he still has rights in his original compound in Tór. If his situation in Bissau becomes unbearable, he says he can move back and is certain that he will be given land to farm. He knows others that have moved back and he also has plans to do so at some point. But so far he is enduring in Bissau in order to get his children through school.

João's case illustrates the situation of many (male) migrants in Bissau, particularly those from Pepel rural areas. Many migrants continue to be connected to their rural areas of origin. Group identities related to the area of one's ancestors are widely used in the city, even among people born in Bissau. This

---

[257] These sources consist of Einarsdóttir's (2000) anthropological study based on years of residence and fieldwork in the area; as well as two other socio-economic appraisals of the area, by Hochet (1985) and Gomes (1989).

identification seems to imply some rights in the "home area", such as men's rights of inheritance and some of them do move back to inherit. The possibility of inheriting in the home village may be a motivation for many to nurture, or at least not to jeopardise, their rural ties. Residents in Bandim attend burial ceremonies in their villages, host rural kin who come to visit or to do business and many house their children who are studying in town. Indeed, permanence in the city does not necessarily cancel one's rights and obligations in relation to one's relatives and seniors in the village. Many migrants have continued to have access to rice fields in the village and to go back for the agricultural season[258]. The survey results also indicated such a situation as about one fifth of the total number of agricultural plots that households reported to hold were located in their rural area of origin. Other respondents sponsored rice production by sending food and wine. In the opposite direction, urban households receive rice grown in the village.

This persistent connection of urbanites in West Africa to their rural kin has been widely documented. An earlier generation of research reported, among other things, continued visiting in both directions and the exchange of gifts (Gugler and Flanagan, 1978:64; Peil, 1981:139-185), though emphasis was placed on remittances from urban to rural kin, as part of a pervasive concern at the time with a perceived gap between urban and rural incomes. But there was also recognition of the importance of transfers in the opposite direction for disadvantaged urban groups (Peil, 1981:164; Gugler and Flanagan, 1978:67). Gugler and Flanagan (1978:68), for example, stated that most urban dwellers in West Africa lived in a dual system because, with "Social security systems (...) still in their infancy", their "only social security (...) is provided by the solidarity of the village". More recent studies continue to discover the importance of rural links for many urbanites in the current context of economic crisis and declining urban conditions. It has been realised that "life in the dual system" was not merely a characteristic of a phase in the urban transition in West Africa (Gugler, 1997; Bouya, 1997; Tingbé-Azalow, 1997). Others have called attention to the continued importance of "multi-spatial households" and of obligations and reciprocal support across the urban-rural divide, with rural assets sometimes working as a safety net for the urban poor in times of crisis and political instability (Tacoli, 1998:6-7; Devereux, 1999:10, 22, 33; Andræ, 1992).

While rural ties seem to be a resource for many urbanites for dealing with the current crisis, these relations seem not to have remained unchanged under the impact of adjustment policies. I will discuss such eventual changes by

[258] See also Hochet's (1985:34) similar observations at the rural end. In this context, it is important to mention that in the rural areas of Guinea-Bissau a considerable share of land has remained in communal hands, facilitating the maintenance of land related claims. In this respect most migrants in Bissau differ from the landless proletariat that has been displaced by long established large-scale agriculture ventures in other African rural areas.

considering altered living conditions and opportunities in both the urban and rural areas – in the latter case focusing on the area of Biombo – as urban-rural ties may be affected by characteristics and dynamics in the two types of areas.

Consider first the effects of declining urban conditions on urban-rural exchange relations. Declining access to a regular income for many urban migrants and increasing dependence on casual work have most probably made it increasingly difficult for them to honour (or easier to evade) material obligations towards relatives in the village. In fact, one interviewee had been forced to send her nice back to her parents and in a couple of cases people had sent their own children to live with relatives in the countryside, decisions that were often connected to economic difficulties. One respondent affirmed that while he had a job at the post office his rural kin used to leave children in his care so that they could study in Bissau and he spent more on his rural relatives than he received from them. Since he lost his job, he receives more than he gives. Another respondent also reported that, contrary to earlier times, he was now dependent on the generosity of his rural kin. Others said they gave more to rural kin than they received. However, these rather general and subjective evaluations by respondents of the changes in their relations with rural kin may indicate far more complex patterns of transfers and dependence than those that were once believed to dominate, i.e. from the better-off urban relatives to the poorer and dependent rural kin. Furthermore, an issue for deeper research would be whether an inversion is occurring in the rural-urban flows of exchange[259].

These tentative findings find support elsewhere. It has been observed that as living conditions worsen in urban Africa, many urban residents face increasing difficulties in supporting rural kin (Potts and Mutambirwa in Tacoli, 1998:4, on urban Zimbabwe). Others have suggested a possible inversion in some aspects of the urban-rural relation, as an urban bias in urban incomes and security is no longer obvious. They refer to urban dwellers sending some children to live with rural kin and to trends of reversal in migration flows, either to settle permanently in rural areas of origin or for seasonal agricultural work (Tacoli, 1998:6; Amis, 1989:382; Gugler, 1997:69; Baker, 1997:14-5; Fergusson, 1999:150).

But wider changes have also altered conditions in the rural areas, with consequences for relations of assistance with urban kin. With the shift of exports from peanuts to cashew nuts Biombo has become a major cashew

---

[259]The alternative to collecting subjective judgements may not be a rigorous quantification of these material exchanges, given the complexity of the structure of obligations and expectations involved. Just to give an example, Manuela, resident in Bandim, houses and feeds two children that are not her own. They are the children of an aunt and her husband, who inherited her, in Prábis, some 20 km from Bissau. Manuela says she receives no compensation and that she does not ask the children's parents for rice either. The husband of her aunt has a cashew plantation in Prábis but Manuela says she has no right to go for the harvest there. During the 1998-9 war she consciously chose not to take refuge with them. But the house she lives in is her aunt's, to whom Manuela does not pay any rent.

producer (Einarsdóttir, 2000). Together with economic liberalisation, this has contributed to changes in urban-rural relations. Firstly, together with other factors, this has acted to discourage rice production in the area. This would deserve a systematic longitudinal study in its own right. But at least four of my respondents stated that the paddy fields of their rural kin were in a bad condition (probably due to lack of motivation to maintain the fields) to explain why they did not receive rice from the village anymore. Secondly, there has been a tendency in recent years to sell the cashew nuts instead of bartering them for rice, as was formerly more common. This may be partly a strategy of disguising assets or making stocks of food invisible on the part of rural producers to reduce expectations from (urban and other) kin to that rice, while demands on it are probably on the rise. These trends may be affecting the amount of rice that some urban dwellers can claim or expect to receive from their rural kin. This is not to be generalised and needs further study, as several of my respondents did receive rice from rural areas and even participated in farming or helped to finance its production in the village. But the choice to help an urban relative in distress may be becoming increasingly more optional for rural kin. The closeness of the kinship relationship seems to play a role here, as was indicated in several of the interviews. Those that were able to count upon help from rural kin usually had close kin in the countryside - usually parents and other close blood kin[260]. A severance of rural ties was often reported to occur when these relatives died. What is certain is that the conditions of exchange between urban and rural kin are undergoing important changes. Let us look at other aspects of this change.

The shift to cashew production, economic liberalisation and the improvement of transportation in the last one and a half decades have also provided the context for the emergence and possible intensification of other types of contacts and assistance between urban and rural dwellers. As both have been forced to diversify their income strategies by transgressing the urban and rural realms, they make use of contacts at both ends. Indeed, the current intensification of flows of goods and people between the two spatial realms - of which the new wholesale vegetable market "Caracol bus stop", described in chapter five, is the clearest manifestation - seems to be facilitated by these social networks stretching over the urban-rural divide. Firstly, the sale of cashew wine has become a high priority income activity for many urban women and this has provided the stimulus for a considerable female outmigration towards producing regions during the cashew season lasting from

[260] Not having close kin seems particularly disadvantageous for women, as shall be discussed. Respondents often distinguished between close kin and "lineage relatives". In the context of urban-rural links, lineage among the Pepel continues to be of importance in what concerns inheritance in the home village and attendance of funerals there but to be of little importance for material support in a hardship. As someone anecdotally explained, "when you are sick, nobody comes to visit you. But when you die, your yard will be full of people, only to show off". This refers in great part to the members of the lineage of the deceased.

April to June. The work agreements they reach with plantation holders vary. But those with the possibility of working on the plantations controlled by their own kin or husbands are often able to gain better deals, i.e. in addition to the pressed juice they are allowed to keep some of the cashew nuts which they can later exchange for rice or sell. This was the case of João´s wife who had brought home almost half a year of supply of rice in this way. Here, having close kin in production areas and good relations with them seems to play an important role. Those who do not, usually have to content themselves with the processed juice that they sell in town. Secondly, according to Einarsdóttir (2000) rural women in the villages of Biombo are facing an increasing burden in the provisioning of their families and have responded to changes by increasingly producing for the urban market, often travelling to Bissau themselves to market their fish, vegetables or cashew wine. Some return home the same day but others take advantage of lodging possibilities with their kin and acquaintances in town - the latter is even more the case for those coming from longer distances.

My interviewees reported constant or prolonged visits by rural relatives coming to the city to do business. This revealed itself to be a source of intensified strain between the two parties in at least five cases. Respondents complained that they could not count upon their visitors' contribution towards food expenses, while the latter pocketed the profits of sales. Their accounts consistently exhibited dissatisfaction, feelings of unfairness and even exploitation, as well as the, naturally subjective, judgement that they are loosing out or carrying the greatest burden in the current state of affairs. However subjective these judgements may be – particularly considering that exchanges in the opposite direction also exist and that I did not get the possibility of hearing the other side of the story - they do nonetheless raise questions. Is the type of urban-rural support becoming more orientated to making profits and moving from redistribution of resources towards facilitating market activities? Is the practice of giving good hospitality giving way to more instrumental, unbalanced and outright exploitative relationships, as was perceived by my interviewees? While answering these questions would require further research, the fact that urban hospitality to rural kin is being experienced as exploitative suggests that something may be changing in the morality and the terms of exchange between urban and rural kin.

In his study of Kitwe on the Zambian Copperbelt, Ferguson (1999:150-1) also found an intensification of antagonism between urban and rural kin as urbanites have been forced to turn to their rural relatives in order to survive the economic crisis. Many urban workers had neglected their rural kin and the latter utilised their new power to make new demands on the shrinking resources of their urban relatives. Urbanites, in turn, experienced these demands as unfair. He discusses how, in the context of economic decline, urban workers' imaginations of the rural changed from being a haven of reciprocity and solidarity to being "the locus of selfish, greedy, parasitic demands" and even of vindictive acts. Could a similar shift in the power balance between Bandim dwellers and their rural counterparts be taking place? While clearly dissatisfied with the terms of exchange, respondents seemed to accept them and had not taken measures so as to change them. The reported changes that have taken place over the past years seem to point to this possibility. These changes include rural people increasingly keeping stores in the form of cash rather than a full granary, the increasing (often experienced as unreasonable) demands that they place on urban hospitality in the pursuit of an income, to which one should add months of dependence forced by the war upon urban dwellers taking refuge with their rural kin and the consequent indebtedness. Further research is, however, required before any secure conclusions can be drawn.

In the context of the new opportunities and constraints that have emerged in connection to wider processes, different groups within the city (or the village) will be in different positions to utilise the urban-rural interface. A number of studies show how privileged groups located in either the city or the countryside have found new opportunities for accumulation, partly by investing in social networks crossing the urban-rural divide (see Nyassogbo, 1997; Tacoli, 1998:10; Gugler, 1997:70). Among urban dwellers, some will and some will not have contacts in rural areas, which means that *access* to urban-rural social networks becomes a key question to be pursued.

As Tacoli (1998:11) has argued, people marginalised from such networks may be unable to pursue multi-spatial strategies of assistance or income generation. Impoverished urban dwellers experiencing difficulties in fulfilling the expectations of rural relatives potentially risk such marginalization[261]. My respondents certainly varied in the degree of assistance they could expect from their rural kin, which in some cases was none at all. From my data it was evident that women who had left their husbands (or inheritors) in the countryside and come to the city usually lost some of their rights to provisioning from their rural kin, although, it should be noted, this also depended on the circumstances surrounding their reasons for leaving. Among female interviewees, those who had no blood kin remaining in the village often had weak rural ties and had few possibilities of returning home. Women have been found to be at a disadvantage in urban-rural ties elsewhere, even where they are major protagonists in the urban-rural connection[262].

---

[261] See Peil (1981:175, 181) on how size of incomes affects level of remittances to rural areas.

[262] See Peil (1981:165) and Bouya (1997) on West Africa and Tacoli (1998:11) for a general review.

7.7 Conclusion

The chapter has discussed how responsibilities in provisioning and assistance among kin are changing in the study setting. This is appreciated in the context of both longer-term processes that have unravelled through a long period of time, such as urbanisation and commoditisation, as well as more recent ones related to structural adjustment and economic crisis. These wider processes interplay with micro relations in the kinship field to giving rise to a multiplicity of social struggles fought from a variety of positions within kin groups and on a variety of fronts. Traditional power holders struggle both against their subordinates and modern political institutions to preserve their power and material interests. Subordinate groups in traditional structures struggle to keep those traditional norms that protect them and to improve their positions in those structures or seek alternative sources of support.

The outcome from these struggles reveals itself as far from clear or uniform. Rather, the emerging picture resembles a tug-of-war whose outcome is difficult to predict. The multiple forces at work, the complex interlacing of interests and strategies, the varying strength of the actors involved – a complexity which I do not claim to have fully portrayed but merely illustrated – may result in patterns of change whose direction is not only difficult to discern but is sometimes contradictory. I found great variations within the neighbourhood in terms of the extent of assistance that my interviewees could expect to receive from their relatives and seniors. I identified elements of both continuity and change in traditional norms of provisioning and assistance and in the power structures that underlie them. Some rules had lost strength while others were being preserved as a result of the power struggles involved in the reformulation of those rules. The complex picture that emerges is one that is at variance with simplistic interpretations that project change along a pre-determined and single path and that tend to neglect actors' ability to affect the course of events and even turn wider changes to their advantage[263].

Several elders among the host group continue to enjoy considerable religious authority and an unshakeable hold over lineage land, where staple food is produced. The latter places them in a central position as redistributors of cereal among their subordinates. Moreover, one could see these seniors as informal regulators who control both the redistribution of rice as well as access to important livelihood resources. In several cases they discriminated among their dependants in terms of the assistance they granted or even completely defaulted on their obligations towards them. This issue is of relevance at a time when traditional structures have been said to be undergoing revival in Africa and to increasingly intervene in governing urban relations (Simone, 1999; Bangura, 1994). Some have expressed concerns about what role they

[263] For reviews or critiques of views of socio-cultural change grounded on linear progressions see: Keesing (1981); Ferguson (1999); Werbner (1996); Bayart (1993); Mabogunje (1990); Berry (1985).

should play in 'urban governance' (Attahi, 1997; Halfani 1997; Piermay 1997). What is obvious from my material is that informal regulators are not necessarily accountable to their subordinates or perceived as fair in their roles.

In this context, I tried to assess the opportunities available in the neighbourhood for subordinate groups to 'disengage' from kin structures of support that they perceived as oppressed. Activities and collaborations outside the direct control of elders such as those taking place in the church, in the market place and among casual work groups, have offered opportunities for subordinate elements to organise for support outside the domestic domain and to construct new identities. I have discussed how these sources of support and affiliations interacted with kin-based ones. For example, casual work and rice farming under the control of elders seem to have been kept in a functional balance and to have allowed for combined rather than incompatible identities. This fits well with notions of actors as bearers of multiple and overlapping identities or "cultural styles" that are constructed, instrumentally deployed or "played like cards" in order to increase flexibility and opportunities in different social spaces (Simone, 1999; Ferguson, 1999).

However, other of these above mentioned fields of activity seemed particularly difficult to reconcile with ideologies legitimising traditional power. For example, becoming a member of the evangelical church was a potential source of ostracism and as such it was not a decision taken lightly and perhaps not even considered as a possible alternative by individuals who could not afford the risk of loosing kin-based support. In addition, the heavy constraints that structural adjustment has placed on the various above mentioned groups endanger the extent of assistance that they dispense and their viability in the longer run. An impoverished church, casual worker groups facing decreasing and increasingly irregular returns, declining incomes from petty trade for many and their consequent inability to participate in prolific social arrangements in the market such as rotating savings schemes, are all examples of the meagre alternatives available in the study setting. These structural constraints may be leaving subordinate persons in kinship groups with few exit options from these groups.

The above findings cast some doubts over perspectives that view the shifting or combination of identities as unconstrained or 'cost-free'. Rather, they suggest that we interpret it as a difficult balancing of different identities, responsibilities, risks and returns – or what I have compared to the skills of walking a tightrope.

Generally, in the current context of wider environment of material deprivation, kin-based assistance in Bandim seems to be under stress and to be undergoing a reconfiguration of the structure of claims of some social categories on others. While some groups continue to enjoy considerable protection, others seem to be becoming more vulnerable in contemporary processes of renegotiation and reconfiguration of rights and responsibilities. Some ceased to be able to count on formerly established sources of assistance. Others are increasingly shouldering the burden of provisioning and assistance to relatives, while their resource base is unlikely to have expanded. These groups pertain to women in general and to individuals structurally subordinate in traditional structures.

The material resources available for redistribution among kin are decreasing. I discussed this particularly in relation to redistribution practices among the Pepel host group. It should be recalled, however, that the same wider processes and external pressures might result in different outcomes for different groups. Sections of other ethnic groups in the city seem to have been able to capitalise on and revitalise old codes in the new policy environment in order to achieve dominant economic positions in Bissauan society. These codes seem to have been used to nurture networks of accumulation reaching far beyond national borders and controlling key international commodities (cashew and rice). My data here are limited, but similar cases have been documented for the sub-region and beyond, of parochial groups increasingly operating in the international arena (Diouf, 2000; Simone, 1999). In contrast, other cultural groups such as the Pepel of Bandim, burdened by various structural constraints, maintain with difficulty their cultural networks of survival. Different groups in the city seem thus to differ in their ability to appropriate the opportunities of deregulation and globalisation, with some expanding their economic and geographical horizons while many see them shrink.

8 Conclusions

The study has addressed processes of informalization of livelihoods in Bissau. At a wider level, I have analysed historical processes of evolving informality and illustrated their multifaceted nature by revealing the multiplicity of agents involved. The changing position and conditions of disadvantaged groups in these processes were a particular concern. At this level, one general goal was to explore the specific forms that contemporary informal activities, looming large in the world today, take in this particular city, deriving from its historical context and its position in the global economy. At a micro level, I explored the kinds of relations sustaining and pervading the informal livelihoods of the poor in the current difficult economic environment – both their income generating and redistribution components. I highlighted the kinds of social ties and networks created by disadvantaged people and showed how they differ in terms of the social resources on which they can draw for support and relief. I studied not only the extent of marginalization or participation but also the varying ability to exercise informal rights and the nature of the social relations involved. I illustrated the diversified nature of those relations, ranging from solidarity and egalitarian to unequal, exploitative and conflictual. This allowed me to show the multiplicity of power bases existing *within* the informal sphere with which people deal on a daily basis as they strive for survival. I explored how some of these loci of power influence the conditions of the poor and the complex webs of power relations involved in the negotiation of diverse claims. These micro processes are, in addition to the vertical relations with state and capital, part of the dynamics of informality.

A general goal of the study was to "unpack" informality[264] and social networks, both of which are often treated as black boxes with an undifferentiated content. One can go about a disaggregated analysis of the informal sphere by looking into the variety of actors and social relations at work, the coexisting modalities of exchange, the multiple sets of rules guiding informal activity and their varying degrees of institutionalisation. Unpacking social networks implies bringing to light the variety of sources of support for urbanites, the differing social relations and struggles involved, as well as

[264] By "informal" I mean activities that do not conform to at least one aspect of the written law or that are regulated by other kinds of "laws". This does not necessarily imply the absence of the state in these activities. For a more elaborate discussion of the concept, see chapter one.

patterns of participation and marginalization. The contents of this last chapter will be structured in the light of this general goal.

I will begin by reviewing overarching processes of informalization in this particular area in a historically informed manner, which explain how informal livelihoods have come to look as they do in Bissau. Attention is given to the multiplicity of agents that have been involved in these processes. Then I will proceed with a discussion of the constellations of social ties and the way in which they are woven into social networks of assistance, the internal power games that take place within networks and to what extent they are withstanding the crisis. At the end of the section I propose a set of parameters for the analysis of a politics of support mobilisation, as an alternative to the mainstream "social capital" discourse. In the last section in the chapter I reflect upon the variety of ways in which the informal sphere is regulated, including informal kinds of regulation, on the basis of my observations in Bissau.

The chapter summarises the findings and arguments displayed throughout the thesis and brings together the different threads of analysis pursued in the various empirical chapters in order to provide a composite picture of patterns and processes in the study setting. This picture builds on my understanding of those patterns and processes, on the basis of qualitative fieldwork with a small share of the households, traders and food producers residing in the neighbourhood and complemented by interviews with a variety of informants and a household survey encompassing some ten per cent of the population. The resulting data do not represent the full diversity and complexity of cultures and relations present in Bandim and the wider city. But they illustrate how a share of Bissauans is faring under the contemporary conditions.

8.1 Social processes of informalization in historical context

There seems to be little doubt that Guinea-Bissau and its capital city have been experiencing an extensive informalization, on the basis of both my fieldwork material and the analyses that other commentators have made of developments in the country (see chapter three). This is a trend that is not exclusive to Guinea-Bissau but is being witnessed both across much of the continent and in the world at large, as I discussed in chapter one. The forms that informality takes in this particular place however, are shaped by particular historical processes and the specific geographical positioning of the study area in Africa and the world. Contemporary informality in Bissau contains both novel sides and deep historical roots. In chapters two and three I discussed how the historical evolution of the conditions of production and social reproduction have allowed for a perpetuation of informal relations in both domains.

While informal activities in Bissau and the country are far from new, changes in policies since the mid-1980s seem to have provided new stimuli for their expansion. Since that time, international agencies have pressed for deregulation and liberalisation of the economy and for setting free the energies of the "informal sector", as became clear from the analysis of documents of some influential agencies. In this sense, they have themselves become actors of informalization. These changes are analogous to policy shifts in other African countries under the guidance of international institutions and can be seen as the local variant of current global-wide trends towards deregulation and state withdrawal. A deterioration of real incomes and of conditions of social provision for many urbanites has followed the implementation of adjustment policies in Guinea-Bissau, a trend which is also widely documented for other developing countries and finds correspondence in the marginalization of sections of urban populations in core areas of the world economy (see chapter one). As a result, impoverished Bissauans seem to have intensified their informal strategies in both the spheres of production and reproduction.

Informality in Bissau, however, is not simply the result of the strategies of popular groups hit by adjustment austerity or the exclusive domain of the "working poor". Significantly, merchant capital has used informal relations in order to take advantage of the opportunities opened by economic liberalisation. This resembles trends looming large in global economic space (namely the flexibilization and informalization strategies of global capital) but assumes specific local guises, deriving from the historical context and the position of the country and the city in the global and regional economies. In the face of the absence of any significant investment by overseas capital, related to the extremely peripheral position of Guinea-Bissau in the world economy, it is African capital (Guinean and from neighbouring countries) that has become the hegemonic economic actor. A handful of firms have come to thrive in a growing and voluminous trade in international commodities, particularly in rice and cashew nuts. This process which has seen Bissau become the stage for considerable accumulation, has reportedly acted to more deeply internationalise and integrate the country into sub regional trade networks, along paths that are reminiscent of pre-colonial traditions. This accumulation is apparently being facilitated by informal modes of operation.

In Guinea-Bissau, capital has always relied to some extent on informal relations for accumulation, as discussed in chapter two on the basis of available historical analyses. But with the advent of economic liberalisation, the informal strategies of merchant capital seem to have expanded or become more visible. Increasing numbers of urbanites have been drawn into subordinate relations with capital and work in conditions that do not enjoy the protection of state laws. Firstly, the sale of cashew wine has become a major income activity for many women in the studied neighbourhood. These women seasonally migrate to work under informal conditions in cashew farms supplying export firms, thus giving continuity to the historical reliance of capital on informal relations in cash crop production in Guinea and in other parts of the sub region. Secondly, casual work appears to be the only source of income for an increasing pool of urban men as formal wage opportunities shrink. This is a kind of labour that merchant capital has been historically keen to employ in Guinea but can also be said to constitute one type of "flexible labour", the kind of jobs being created by global capital in cities of the developing world today. Thirdly, and perhaps a more novel category in the city, rice retailers selling imported rice operate sometimes under conditions similar to subcontracting.

These subordinating forms of informal labour and outlets being used by capital are crucial to understand the extremely precarious conditions that I found among the latter two groups, discussed at different points in the thesis. These groups have been excluded from the benefits of the accelerated economic growth taking place. Indeed, while Bissau would certainly qualify as an "engine of growth" by World Bank standards (2001) – given the accelerated growth reported prior to the 1998-99 war -, these groups could be seen as the "human diesel" being literally consumed for the sake of that growth. In addition, the majority of Bissauans are not only excluded from this growth but are also victims of hoarding and speculation in the prices of imported rice, the staple food consumed in the city. As has been noted before, this kind of growth in which capital is given such free hands is clearly not sustainable.

Let me now focus on the informal strategies of popular groups. Concerning income activities, small-scale trade emerged from my survey data as being the most common of these. Small-scale trade has, according to a variety of informants and some studies by others, expanded greatly as a means of earning a living in the city since trade was liberalised. The forms that these activities take today – i.e. the practices and groups involved - reflect long indigenous trade traditions in Guinea and the sub region (see chapter two). This is the case of the *Djilas*, male itinerant traders from the Eastern groups who have seemingly flocked into Bissau in the last one and a half decades, most probably to pursue trade careers. Women, particularly of the coastal groups, also have ancient trade traditions. They participated in pre-colonial rotating markets, which I found to continue to be an important component of the diversification strategies of a share of the interviewed women urban traders in the city today (see chapter five). Since the colonial period women have been pivotal in supplying Bissau with fresh foods. This historical tradition probably accounts for the considerable freedom of movement and the legitimacy that women traders enjoy, as indeed women in many West African societies do, which are at variance with the negative reputation of women traders in other parts of the continent[265]. These historical specificities both inform the local

[265] However, this does not preclude gender conflicts in the domestic domain, under the stresses imposed by the current economic hardship (see chapter seven).

responses of Bissauans to adjustment policies and explain the ethnic-gender segmentation that we find in trade activities in contemporary Bissau.

These trade traditions never died, even though the colonial state is said to have attempted to strictly control them and the early post-colonial state to have accused the groups involved of being "immoral elements" in society. On the contrary, they reportedly gained increasing space from the state and their growing numbers probably came to constitute a pressure from below for a relaxation of controls. The liberalisation policies of the mid-1980s seem to have merely intensified trends that were already in place. The available accounts suggest that elements of the disengagement perspective, referred to in chapter one, may have been involved in the expansion of informal trade in Guinea-Bissau and its capital. But we need to look at the conditions of these informal traders to see whether the contemporary expansion of these activities is synonymous with the empowerment of these groups, as argued in that perspective. Some groups are said to have been able to develop viable trade businesses – and here, the historically rooted segmentation of the market along ethnic-gender lines may have grown into an axis of differentiation. But a large share of food traders seems to be confined to low-income activities, as revealed by my household survey in two neighbourhoods. Qualitative interviews with retailers further revealed that many retailers have experienced a worsening of conditions, squeezed as they have been between the declining purchasing power of urban consumers and rising input costs, or by the exploitative practices of powerful agents in the market. Many were spending an increasing number of hours at the market place in an attempt to sustain former levels of consumption. Others reported loosing their working capital frequently and some had been forced to decrease the volume of their operations (see chapter five).

The above trends are not specific to the Bissauan context. Other studies indicate an increase in intra-urban economic polarisation and in differentiation within the informal economy, as well as rising levels of exploitation and marginalization of large sections of informal actors in other African cities in the context of "deregulation" policies (Lugalla, 1997; Meagher and Yunusa, 1996). This study joins this emerging evidence that challenges celebratory views and the populist discourses of development institutions that assume that the "informal sector" in its current guise is able to provide sufficient levels of income to the poor and to reduce poverty (chapter one). Supposedly "equitable" policies to promote informal sector growth such as those of "deregulation" are most likely to have served the rich rather than the poor. The large number of people I met that were living hand to mouth would most probably disagree with the neo-liberal rhetoric that small informal actors are being "empowered" or "liberated" by these policies. That rhetoric suffers from a lack of attention to how resources are unequally distributed in the local and international economies and a neglect of the various social relations (class, gender, generational, ethnic) pressing down upon certain groups. What can be expected is a rise in social contradictions and tensions within Bissau and other cities sharing this experience.

Turning now to non-market components of informal livelihoods, one of their most visible features in the study setting is the important role of kin-based forms of assistance and the considerable resilience of traditional structures in provisioning and assistance (see chapter seven). Particularly the latter is to be interpreted in the context of West Africa, where traditional structures have preserved considerable vigour. As discussed in chapters two and three, ancient local power hierarchies strongly opposed effective colonial occupation in Bissau and have survived both the penetration by capitalist relations and a variety of modern political regimes, and shifting responses towards them. Traditional structures and cultural practices reportedly remained the only option for the majority of Guineans during colonialism. Partly as a reflection of the marginal position of the colony in the interests of Portuguese colonialism, levels of investment in social infrastructure and in the development of the economic base remained extremely modest as did the level of modernisation and proletarianization, compared to some other urban areas in Africa (such as the industrial towns in Nigeria or the mining towns of the Zambian Copperbelt). Opportunities for social mobility were thus restricted and reliance on traditional relations was a necessity for the majority.

In fact, the colonial state formalised by law a dual system of rights that left the majority of Guineans with virtually no rights in modern society and effectively perpetuated sets of customary rights. In the city, this duality was also very marked. The majority of Africans, lacking a "civilised" or "assimilated" status and living in indigenous quarters like Bandim, worked in the colonial centre under heavily monitored conditions but did not enjoy any social security benefits and even lacked work contracts. I illustrated this with the cases of dockworkers and women market traders in chapter two. Their exclusion from formal rights and their subordinate participation in the modern urban economy contributed to keep customary rights alive and forced many to rely for their social reproduction on kin-based assistance and traditional forms of provision, including subsistence activities on lineage land controlled by elders. Although this was convenient to colonial interests, elements of cultural resistance may have also contributed to the persistence of traditional practices, particularly in Bandim where there is a collective memory of resistance to colonialism.

The failure of the early post-independence state to deliver goods and services and to allow for political participation seemingly contributed to the continued importance of traditional structures and practices. Given their historical continuity, these structures and practices continue to inform and shape contemporary livelihoods in the study area, producing highly specific responses to general processes such as adjustment related hardship in recent times. I found that they constitute particular frames of reference for structuring obligations of assistance and provisioning, rights of access to land and food, among historically evolved social groups. In this way, they appear to provide a modicum of social security for a share of urbanites (see chapter seven). These traditional relations of support can take the form of exchanges between urban and rural kin, between relatives residing in town or of daily interactions within residential clusters of relatives, including corporate kin groups structured along lineage lines. The latter is probably a particular feature of the study setting and not very common in most African urban contexts. Exchanges among kin have come to be combined with newer forms of assistance, though the role of a formal voluntary sector in social provision is still modest in the city.

Reflecting upon the deeper historical origins of contemporary configurations of informality as I attempted to do in chapter two proved to be a rewarding exercise. It helped me understand how certain actors have achieved their powerful positions in the informal realm and by what rules they legitimise those positions. This historical dimension of informality has remained in the shadow in perspectives that see informality merely as a response to the state or as a strategy of capital.

This section has attempted to summarise the processes by which informality has come to look as it does in a place like Bissau in terms of both their generalizeable features and specificities. Bissau shares with many other places the experiences of colonialism, structural adjustment and of worsening conditions for large segments of the population. But it also has particular features that derive from specific historical processes and the position of this place in wider geographical contexts. This is a place that throughout its history has always occupied a particularly peripheral position in the international economy – global, regional and sub regional. It has experienced a negligible level of industrialisation and has an economy strongly biased towards trade and services. The role of informal relations in the economy has been historically important and traditional structures and practices in both trade and provision have retained some of their vigour. This city has a particular mixture of ethnic and gender relations and a locally specific market segmentation along these lines. Furthermore, it has a deeply rooted culture of political activism (particularly in Bandim). Finally, one should mention its small size as well as the accelerated economic growth it has experienced in the last years which probably makes social contradictions all the sharper. The result is an informality whose configuration is both locally specific and historically contingent.

One way of approaching these variations in the configurations of informality across time and space could be by looking at the agents involved in the production of informality. Indeed, in my longitudinal discussion of this process in chapters two and three a variety of agents emerged, ranging from popular groups to capital and international agencies. Realising the multifaceted nature of this social process is important in that existing theoretical approaches tend to explain the dynamics of informality as driven by one or another agent – as the disengagement and the informalization perspectives tend to do (see chapter one). Clearly, particularly the complexity of contemporary informalization processes require a broader model of understanding that encompasses this multiplicity of agents and agendas that constitute the informal realm. I have limited my analysis to an illustration of this multiplicity – given my data gaps and considerable reliance upon secondary sources for historical material, possibly with their own biases. And while some aspects of the Bissauan configuration are specific to that place, other aspects seem to hold potential for generalisation and comparison. The latter could be the case with the pressures exerted by popular groups during phases of state-centred development, the prominent role that international institutions have achieved and the current use of informal strategies by capital in Africa and beyond. So let me suggest a simple model for further work and development. Figure 8.1. represents the diversity and potential constellation of agents involved in the negotiation of the boundary between the formal and the informal spheres, based on what I learned from Bissau.

Figure 8.1 The multiplicity of agents involved in the production of informality

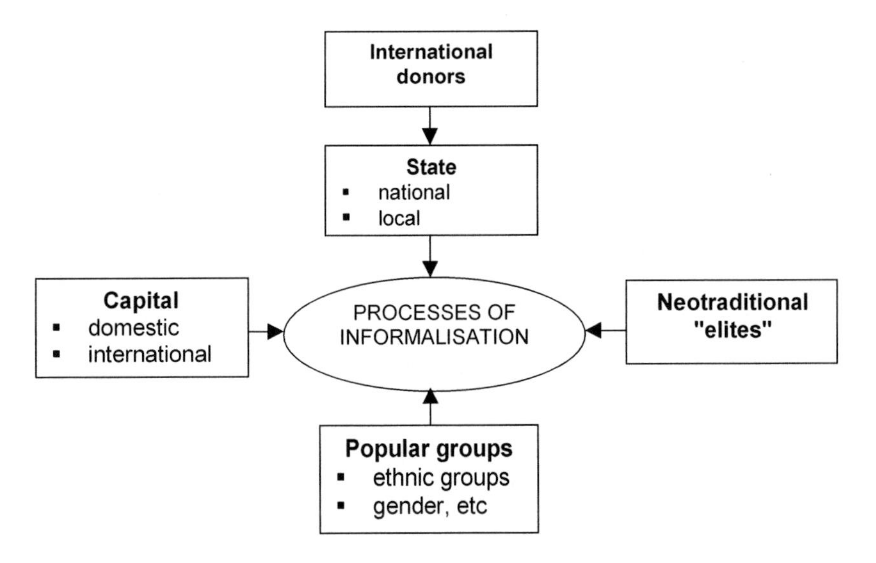

More systematic work could be done in mapping the constellations of actors involved in contemporary informalization processes and in understanding how these constellations have varied through time so as to produce changing mixes of formality/informality. This would allow, for example, a probing of whether different agents attain a prominent role under different historical conditions. This implies looking at the relations between these agents, rather than taking them for granted, as these relations may entail both alliances, straddling of formerly assumed divisions and various forms of opposition. Together these relations could be said to account partly for the politics of informalization[266].

8.2 'Unpacking' social networks

A large share of city dwellers seem to live hand to mouth and in the uncertainty of whether or not their daily basic needs will be met. This I have compared to walking a tight rope, i.e. an endless effort in making do and continuously being on the verge of loosing that precarious balance. This is expressed in the local expression "falling off balance". And yet, the poor achieve what in the eyes of an affluent audience would appear to be close to an impossibility - they endure. A driving question in the study was *how* is life sustained in the city under such harsh conditions. Much of this resilience can be attributed to the protection offered by "safety nets" that tightrope walkers build in order to sustain them through the exercise and assist in case of a fall. The nature of these social networks for survival, sustaining livelihood activities both in and outside the market, is the subject of this section. As part of my effort to move beyond aggregate approaches to informality, I have tried to "unpack" these networks of assistance in ways that differ from those that I have found in the current mainstream literature. Using social networks as a reshaped tool along the lines proposed in chapter one facilitated this task. It uncovered the varying constellations of ties and social relations of assistance, how different sets of relations interact with each other as well as patterns of marginalization and inequality. It also revealed the power relations involved. In this way, a multiplicity of loci of power came to light within the informal sphere, which have been largely invisible to many interpretations of informal activities and social networks, including the more fashionable "social capital" discourse. Indeed, networks presented themselves to me as a field of possibility and constraint and as a reflection of both inventiveness and subordination. This prompted me to look at networks as intertwined with social process, as manifesting both structure and agency. The patterns of relations involved are what I have called the 'politics of support mobilisation' (see chapter one).

In this second part of the chapter I would like to summarise my findings on relations of assistance and address the interweaving of different sources and relations of assistance, including relations sustaining income activities and those supporting consumption which were discussed in separate chapters. The discussion will address the multifaceted nature of assistance relations, how they are responding to crisis, how norms of assistance are changing and the

---

[266] I say partly, because in my view the politics of informality also include the micro-processes taking place among informal actors at the bottom, of which my "politics of support mobilisation" is an example.

power relations involved. The section concludes by bringing together the various dimensions that have emerged as being of relevance in understanding the politics surrounding the mobilisation of assistance.

I begin with a summary of the various kinds of networks of survival found in the study setting. Kin and neighbours were important sources of food and money for the studied households. According to my survey, these transfers came mainly from other households sharing the same house or compound. But a share also received help from people living in other parts of the city and a tenth had ongoing exchanges with relatives in the countryside. Among various recruitment categories, relatives in particular were regarded as those with the obligation to assist, even though practice often deviated. Kin relations supporting consumption took a variety of forms, ranging from dyadic exchanges between two relatives to a complex system of reciprocities within corporate kin groups (existing within the neighbourhood or split between town and countryside). But kin support also pertained to market activities, for example by being a major source of start up capital, skills and even goods, and by assisting in recovery when traders lost their working capital.

Other relations of assistance developed at the market place. Through interviews with traders I found a variety of forms of co-operation at work. There were also partnerships between sellers in the same trade who assisted each other throughout the working day, sometimes pooling resources and contacts, and sometimes even exchanging help in domestic activities. A share of traders could count on credit from suppliers, with the great advantage of not needing to have capital up front to get access to merchandise. Rotating savings groups - a long tradition in the city and common in other West African contexts – constituted, for some traders, a way of expanding their businesses and a security in case of unforeseen material difficulties (at home or the market), as the turn of participants to collect the group's savings could often be anticipated. Another kind of co-operation that I found in the study setting consisted of organised groups among day workers, a labour category that is as old as Bissau itself. In these groups, men share job opportunities and redistribute incomes. Finally, a share of Bandim residents participated in local religious groupings, particularly catholic and evangelical congregations (since Islamised groups are a minority in this neighbourhood). The evangelical church, the one I became more acquainted with, seemed more important in terms of recruitment of personal acquaintances for co-operation in other social settings such as the market, than in terms of the volume of material assistance it dispensed to its needy members.

The above forms of support often straddle the divide between consumption and redistribution on the one hand and market and income activities on the other. This renders it difficult to separate relations supporting consumption from those assisting income activities. Thus, I treat them generally as networks of survival, as these pertain mainly to relations sustaining survival activities. The forms they take include both those that are common in other African cities and those that are guided by locally and culturally specific sets of norms.

Social networks and relations of assistance did not only vary in their configurations and spheres of recruitment. They also varied in the kinds of claims that could be made, the social relations and the motivations they contained. Concerning the latter, I found that a variety of motivations and rationalities were at work, based on the characterisation that respondents made of the nature of their various support relations. First, there were exchange relations that seemed to be driven by culturally specific obligations, such as those governing assistance between particular categories of kin or within corporate kin groups in Bandim (see chapter seven). Secondly, ties where failure to reciprocate was reported to terminate the relationship and that were perceived as being driven mainly by material motives (what I have usually referred to as 'instrumental ties') seemed to pervade many relations in the market but were not absent from support exchanges outside the market (see chapter six). Finally, there were also relations that were described by respondents as being altruistic in content and based on affection, where there was no careful account of debts[267]. This latter kind of ties was usually referred to in relation to relatives and friends. Although it differs markedly from a market rationality, this kind of relation was also found to support market activities, as was the case of many partnerships between women traders (see chapters five and six). On the basis of this kind of data, I would like to suggest that a variety of motivations and rationalities are present in support networks. In the light of this material, views that tend to focus on either the moral economy components or the maximising principles in informal support systems appear reductionist and insufficient to capture the multifaceted nature of relations of relations of assistance. I found these varied motivations to be important in understanding differences in resilience and manoeuvrability in the networks of my respondents, as will be discussed below.

In addition to the variety of motivations at work, support relations were differentiated in terms of the power balance they appeared to exhibit. On the one hand, I encountered relations of exchange and co-operation between social equals, i.e. people in fairly similar material conditions, where the flow of exchange was perceived as more or less balanced and where no one had the upper hand – one of many examples is the above-mentioned egalitarian and mutual exchange between pairs of women in trade activities. On the other hand, a share of respondents reported to be involved in unequal relations of exchange with people in better off or more powerful positions. This was the case of one way assistance from relatives enjoying better living standards in the city (see chapter six) as well as the flows of food downward in the social

[267] This is inspired by Sahlins' model of reciprocity (1984), as discussed earlier in the thesis.

hierarchy within corporate kin groups in Bandim - in the latter case with clear linkages to positions of power and subordination (see chapter seven). In the market, I found instances of unequal relations in the informal agreements involving powerful agents in the market - as was the case of those between rice wholesalers and fish suppliers - who were in a position to decide the terms of the exchange and often to exploit retailers (see chapter five). Some of these agents had ascended to the position whereby they could dictate the rules governing access to merchandise, thus themselves becoming informal regulators. In the respective chapters I presented the uneasy feelings of people in disadvantaged positions in these various kinds of unequal relations and their efforts to circumvent them.

This distinction between equal and unequal relations that emerged from my fieldwork material may seem an obvious point. But the acknowledgement of both takes us beyond the usual one-sided interpretations of informal support systems. In the light of my data, views lending networks exclusively positive attributes, such as the moral economy perspective and the newer social capital discourse, seem particularly inadequate. These views render invisible the power relations at work, directly implicated in considerations of the sustainability of such networks, and foreclose conflict as a driving force in their dynamics. This clashes with my view of social networks as manifestations of social processes (see chapter one).

Throughout my fieldwork I discovered how people actively constructed their own networks within the opportunities within their reach. They created and nurtured links to others, entered agreements, selected ties, manipulated norms and invested in some networks to break free from others. A share of my respondents often combined different kinds of relations (kin and market based, instrumental and altruistic, hierarchical and egalitarian etc), possibly drawing on the advantages of each kind. However, participants were differently positioned in these various constellations of assistance relations and this seemed to have consequences for their vulnerability as well as manoeuvrability. First, respondents varied in their access to support and thus were not equally "insured" against misfortune. Some people were quite isolated. They reported a very small number of sources which they could turn to for help and traders differed in their access to credit given by suppliers or to savings groups. This group often expressed that they were not certain that they would be able to mobilise assistance during times of need (see chapter six). On the basis of these findings, I would like to suggest that current widespread notions that social networks are a resource that the poor *do* have or that "social capital" *does* provide sufficient welfare to the poor are unrealistic (see chapter one).

Secondly, a share of my respondents seemed not to be in a position to combine different kinds of networks. While reported to have diversified networks in terms of the nature of ties, social settings, social composition, geographical reach etc, others seemed heavily reliant on one particular type of relations, such as instrumental ties or market-based support. Indeed, some people seemed not to be entirely free to combine networks, to select those ties that they preferred and to disconnect from those they deemed oppressive or disadvantageous. This suggests that what can be achieved through networks needs to be related to a variety of constraints, including both wider processes and relations in society and power relations within networks, both of which I will now address. Let me begin by considering the first set of constraints, that is, how and whether social networks are coping with economic hardship, how different kinds of assistance relations are responding and what changes seem to be taking place in social relations within networks.

Networks in times of crisis

Contemporary economic hardship seems to be eroding the collaborative efforts among the poor and the material basis of their support networks (see chapter six). Many respondents declared a narrowing of their networks of assistance in connection with job redundancies, death of an income earner or a general worsening of their living conditions. Some households came to rely only on their own resources, as they perceived their former sources of assistance to be as impoverished as they themselves were. Redistribution groups among casual workers were, according to respondents involved in this kind of work, struggling with irregular work and declining incomes. Welfare practices by the local evangelical church were reported as insufficient to reach the large number of needy members (see chapter six). For other respondents, participation in collective arrangements such as rotating savings groups had ceased to be an option often because they became unable to make regular contributions due to lower and variable incomes or ill health in the household (see chapter five). Taken together, these sets of data give a picture that differs substantially from common assumptions in the mainstream literature about social networks being able to withstand the crisis and to buffer the poor against the effects of adjustment policies.

While social relations of assistance seem to be generally under stress, I have also argued for a disaggregated analysis of networks to see how different ties are responding, instead of lumping them together and assuming that they all behave in the same way, as is usually done. Ties that were perceived by respondents as being driven mainly by material interests were often reported to terminate when the household had lost its ability to keep up the material flows, at times such as when a household earning member died or lost his/her job (see chapter six). Ties perceived as being based on affection, on the other hand, were the ones often reported to endure through crises. Indeed, relations that appeared to be based on strong affective bonds or on deeply institutional-ised norms seemed to have a greater tolerance for unequal flows for long periods – indeed, as discussed in chapter seven, among compounds in Bandim traditional hierarchies seemed to be premised upon the maintenance of such unequal relations of exchange. The picture that emerged from this collection of characterisations by respondents of their ties of assistance was that people were differently exposed depending on the particular combination of ties they relied upon. Respondents that relied heavily on instrumental ties appeared to run a greater risk of being left to fend for themselves at critical moments. I would like to speculate that assistance relations are most probably becoming increasingly instrumentalized, judging from the general evaluations of respondents about the evolving nature of their support networks. They often declared that their exchange partners had become more calculating in the help they dispensed. If this is so, this could mean a trend towards increased vulnerability in the current context of severe economic conditions.

Formerly mutual relations had, in several instances, reportedly turned into one-direction flows when one of the parties lost the ability to reciprocate. Unbalanced relations of assistance with persons in a better-off economic condition showed, in several instances, considerable resilience during crises, thus pointing to the advantage of having a heterogeneous network from the socio-economic point of view. But one could assume that these relations also risk introducing power differentials into the relationship. Dependent parties often expressed feelings of shame and a preference for mutual kinds of ties with balanced flows in both directions and therefore potentially more egalitarian in nature. The latter seemed, however, more easily exhausted in their material resources. A few examples illustrate the limitations that deteriorating economic conditions place on horizontal, egalitarian kinds of assistance relations. The first one concerns partnerships among women sharing the same market niche and a similar economic situation. They assisted each other in their trade activities but, given the poverty of both partners, that ability sometimes collapsed when market conditions for their particular niche suddenly worsened or continuously deteriorated (see chapter five). Another example concerns the fragility of casual worker groups and rotating savings groups (see chapter five). As mentioned above, some respondents had ceased to ask for the assistance of others that they thought were just as badly off as themselves.

A share of traders and households reported that their material security and that of their dependants relied exclusively on market based networks – that is, that they could not count on assistance from kin for either their income activities or their consumption (see chapters five and six). One may consider that, compared to some forms of kin-based assistance, market based networks seemed to offer wider scope for flexibility and manoeuvrability in terms of who one chose to associate with. This flexibility was a necessity, given the great fluidity of trade activities themselves which was reflected in the temporary character of many activities, the continuous search for cheaper supply sources and better selling sites and the short-lived location of some market places (see chapter five). But one may also assume that most market anchored relations of assistance have an inbuilt form of vulnerability considering that, with a few exceptions, they tended to be less tolerant of repeated failure to reciprocate or of prolonged one-way flows. As savings groups illustrate, market-based relations seemed to work as long as participants fulfilled their share of the deal, and indeed, as mentioned above, a share of traders were being marginalised from this and other prolific kinds of assistance in the market. (In addition, the exploitative nature of some credit agreements with suppliers and the fragility of partnerships among poor retailers are also sources of vulnerability). The income squeeze that many traders were experiencing was probably decreasing their range of options and the elasticity of these social arrangements in the market. Interviewed traders with the most precarious levels of income seemed to be particularly exposed. Not surprisingly, a large share of small traders were involved in relations of assistance with longer staying power - often based on kinship bonds, particularly the support of husbands and male relatives - to back up those market relations. This may have implications for the balance of power in the kinship field, as discussed below.

To be sure, some groups seem to have seen their "social capital" increase in the market in the contemporary context of adjustment. This is most probably the case with well-positioned participants in the vertical networks of accumulation headed by import-export firms – although I only interviewed a handful of persons involved in such networks. These networks seem to differ substantially from networks of survival in the amount of resources they command, in their relations with state actors and in their direct links into the international space. In addition, networks of accumulation appear to derive a share of their profits from the exploitation of groups such as rice retailers and casual workers. This exploitation seems to be draining the resources and energies of horizontal networks among these latter groups and to be threatening their viability. One could assume that networks of survival may to some extent be subsidising networks of accumulation thereby indirectly contributing to reproducing inequalities and power relations in the wider society. But I also identified instances where networks among small actors were subversive of the interests of capital and were used in circumventing them (chapter five). And indeed, one could interpret some horizontal networks among small actors as representing spaces of autonomy from a variety of dominant actors in society. However, the sustainability and potential of support networks are to be seen as interwoven with wider processes and distribution of power and as conditioned by the structural position of actors in society. These crucial differences have been overlooked in the neo-liberal literature about social networks.

The above paragraphs suggest that economic hardship seems to be contributing to changes in social relations within networks, concerning for example the patterns of dependence and the balance of motivations within them. I will now focus on the power games unravelling within kin-based networks in the context of wider changes.

Negotiating norms and networks

The potential of networks for personal improvement and empowerment is not solely constrained by policy decisions taken at the national and international levels and the actions of hegemonic actors on the national or international scene. Networks constitute in themselves a realm of possibility and constraint in that they may contain resources for improvement or for cushioning against the crisis but may also restrain individual freedom. Conceptualising networks as 'structures' in Giddens' sense, as I suggested in chapter one, makes visible the internal power games and the agency of members in their efforts to stretch the limits of those networks, circumvent their rigidities and negotiate better positions within them. In this respect, it is of interest to highlight the nature of kin-based networks and how they interact with other networks in the study setting, an issue discussed at length in chapter seven. In some instances, kin-based assistance appeared to be more resilient than market networks in its ability to sustain people unable to return assistance. But in those instances obligations also seemed difficult to discard. Deeply institutionalised rules of assistance and the power positions connected to them seemed to account for this durability, as discussed in chapter seven. This has not precluded considerable manoeuvring of those norms by participants.

One could expect that one potential source of expanding one's room for manoeuvre in kin-based support systems comes from alternative material bases and social networks in the city. As mentioned earlier, most of my respondents combined kin support with other sources of assistance. The involvement of women and youth in income generating activities and associated alternative forms of social organisation is not novel in the city and seems to have been to some extent functional to, and compatible with, the maintenance of traditional hierarchical structures of support. Today they continue to participate in a variety of networks for a variety of purposes, thereby cultivating a variety of positions and identities "making them easy to be reached from different angles and for different purposes" (Hecht and Simone, 1994:150), as this is required for survival. But I would maintain that this juggling with different identities is not always unproblematic, contrarily to the views of some writers who insist on the complete fluidity of identities. The allegory of tightrope walking also applies to this seemingly difficult balancing of affiliations, as a wrong step could conceivably have drastic consequences for one's well-being. For there were ways in which activities carried out away from the domestic kin group were reported to conflict with the interests of powerful persons in that domain and potentially endangered the traditional claims that subordinates could have on them. Church attendance emerged as one such potential area of conflict, judging from the accounts of several church members (see chapter seven). The increasing number of hours that women were spending at the market was also perceived by male seniors as a threat to the labour needs of the compound and the authority of men (see chapter seven). On the basis of these accounts, there seem to exist rigidities and limits to the choices of individual members.

Where kin structures of support are perceived as oppressive and constraining, it could be expected that subordinated categories in kin groups would try to disconnect from them and to invest in alternative sources of support. And here it is important to identify the available alternative forms of support and to consider their viability as alternatives to kin support. As far as I understood, the locally available alternatives - the evangelical church, casual worker groups, rotating credit groups and other market-based networks -, as mentioned earlier, either tended to marginalise the poorest or lacked sufficient resources. From a material point of view, they seemed to be poor alternatives for low-income people willing to disengage from senior and male authority in kin groups. (In addition, it should be recalled that the market activities of women were in many cases dependent upon the support of male relatives for credit or even other resources for production). On the basis of my data, it would seem that deteriorating incomes are draining the potential of these alternative networks and restricting the exit options and the bargaining strength of subordinate persons within kin structures. One could assume that those that lack the resources to establish viable livelihoods independently from kin assistance and that can count on the support of male and senior relatives will probably think twice before they directly challenge the authority of the latter.

Thus, one could see the wider material insecurity as contributing to the reproduction of power hierarchies in the kinship and domestic fields among the studied groups. But I would not interpret this as a general and unambiguous return to tradition. For these hierarchies are also experiencing a variety of pressures, as I discussed in chapter seven. The emerging picture is one of a complex interweaving of struggles and of layers of agency involving both powerful and subordinate groups in these hierarchies, whose outcome seems to be far from unequivocal or unilinear. For example, I identified wide variations between compounds and found elements of both continuity and change in terms of the extent to which redistribution obligations were being fulfilled and of the position of compound heads as redistributors of food and resources. Judging from the accounts of seniors and members in several compounds, some norms were being upheld while others were being discarded, seemingly as a result of the intersection between manipulations from both subordinate and powerful members. Some instances of tension and change in norms of assistance surfaced repeatedly in my interviews, which had consequences for the well being of my respondents.

But within compounds, some people expressed resentment over their subordinate positions in these kin groups and complained about being neglected and discriminated against by heads of compounds in their redistribution practices. I also found a couple of more extreme instances where new heads of compounds simply took over the compounds' resources and simply refused to assume their responsibilities towards their members. In the accounts of the latter, they had become unaccountable to their dependants by simply denying them their legitimate rights. Here it is important to ask who is breaking which rules and at the expense of whom. In these particular cases, powerful persons in traditional structures were breaking the rules, with drastic consequences for their dependants. This contrasts with the limited options of the subordinate categories who, usually lacking viable alternatives, could not afford to default on their obligations towards seniors. I interpreted these cases as being instances of norm reformulation "from above", in which members of subordinate groups were becoming increasingly vulnerable.

When considering the wider group of kin relations of assistance beyond those taking place within compounds, exchange of support among relatives also showed signs of on-going change (see chapter seven). Concerning exchanges between urban and rural kin, a handful of cases suggested that a reformulation of the terms of exchange between urban and rural relatives might be underway, in a context of altered general conditions for interaction between city and countryside. More generally, and on the basis of the limited number of cases studied, I could decipher shifting structures of expectations among certain kin categories, by which some groups seemed to be becoming more vulnerable. This was often the case of women and the elderly. Not only were many women responsible for feeding the household, as the responsibilities of males "out of work" were easily being written off, but they also seemed to increasingly bear the burden of assisting other relatives. Young single mothers often could not claim the assistance of the father of their child. Older women often could no longer count on assistance with provisioning by the younger generation, and were instead increasingly burdened with assisting the latter or imposed with the responsibility of providing for grandchildren. I referred to these signs of change as potential gender and generational inversions in responsibilities for provisioning and assistance. Violation of one's legitimate rights was not always accepted with passivity. In some cases action was taken to correct these perceived injustices, including by resorting to customary courts.

The above findings suggest a need to re-evaluate the assumptions pervading various celebratory and romanticising views of informal support systems, among which the social capital discourse is the most recent[268]. In this discourse, it is assumed that social capital facilitates performance in the market and is capable of providing a minimum of welfare and services. In the light of my findings, there are at least two major problems with this discourse. The first refers to the neglect of issues of exclusion and marginalization from support networks, as documented here. Directly connected to this is a lack of consideration of structural limitations on what networks of survival can achieve. This includes the viability of networks in an environment of adjustment-led austerity. My empirical material suggests that the immiseration imposed by adjustment policies was undermining the collaborative efforts of many and that some people were falling off the various networks available in the neighbourhood, whether kin or market-based. Among the group of my respondents, these people were often the income poor, subordinate members of kin groups and notably women. Take the typical case of many elderly women who were unable to rely on their offspring and, because they were usually segregated to the lowest income niches in the market, they were too poor to participate in savings groups and some other market arrangements. The limits of the "communitarian spirit" are also visible in other large African cities being subjected to similar pressures, where new groups of people excluded from support networks are swelling the numbers of street children and are inflating rates of crime (see Piermay, 1997; Halfani, 1994). In its present rhetoric, the social capital discourse accounts for little more than passing the whole burden of social reproduction onto the poor and releasing the state from any responsibilities towards them. As it looks in my data, the weak economic viability of many networks among the poor suggests that prospects that this "social capital" will be able to replace the state in taking care of the weak are quite slim.

A serious consideration of the role of social networks or social capital in the creation of sustainable cities requires not loosing sight of how networks are inserted in the wider society. This takes us to the second major problem with social capital and similar discourses. This consists of a blindness to the inequalities that social capital may contain and reproduce and the attendant struggles. My data suggest that support systems may be held together by both bonds of solidarity and relations of dependence and unequal power. Indeed, relations of assistance seemed to be as much a source of relief and success as they were of subordination and marginalization. They represent a whole range

[268] The degree of its novelty should, however, not be exaggerated as it partly reproduces some of the weaknesses of earlier perspectives on these matters, such as the moral economy and economy of affection.

of possibilities and constraints and a variety of fronts of struggle to be discovered analytically. Clearly the governing of the informal city must be anchored in the social fabric of urban society, the practices, values and affiliations created by urbanites, as failure to do this in the past has contributed the current urban crisis[269]. But the representation of African values and traditions as something inherently good and democratic and the romanticising of voluntary or ascriptive groups in urban society need to be replaced by critical assessments of existing modes of organisation in concrete empirical situations in order to judge their content and sustainability. Among the studied cases there were egalitarian forms of collaboration but I also found a variety of informal agreements and relations of assistance that involved differences in power, as mentioned above. Indeed, as incomes and the range of options declined, some groups were apparently being pushed into, or forced to remain in, subordinate relations - whether with well positioned agents in the market or with powerful people in traditional groups - to make ends meet. Ignoring these loci of power (within the informal sphere and in networks of assistance) also renders invisible the efforts of disadvantaged groups to circumvent them. It thus also obstructs the promotion of a sustainable social city that builds on such efforts.

In this study I have attempted to look at social networks in a different light. I have approached social networks as a conflictual terrain where informal rights and rules of assistance are fought over and where divisions may be both reproduced as well as challenged. The intention is to conceive of networks as resulting from social processes, which I have tried to capture in the expression 'the politics of support mobilisation' (see chapter one). Throughout my study of social networks conceived in this way, a number of dimensions emerged as important for understanding the politics of assistance and which are potentially of relevance in other contexts. Figure 8.2. attempts to sketch a framework that assembles these various dimensions. This could be of assistance in future comparative work, for example on how informal support systems among the poor are changing in contemporary cities. These dimensions are not entirely mutually exclusive and discerning how they may relate to each other is one possible path for development. I suggest that they be considered as components of network relations influencing access to support and what can be attained through and within networks. Each box or component represents, at one time, a set of constraints and a potential source of contradiction and struggle, and thus to be constantly subjected to the possibility of change. This implies looking at relations and change within each of the components.

[269] Simone (1999) and Halfani (1997). See also Bangura (1994).

Figure 8.2 Dimensions of a politics of support mobilisation

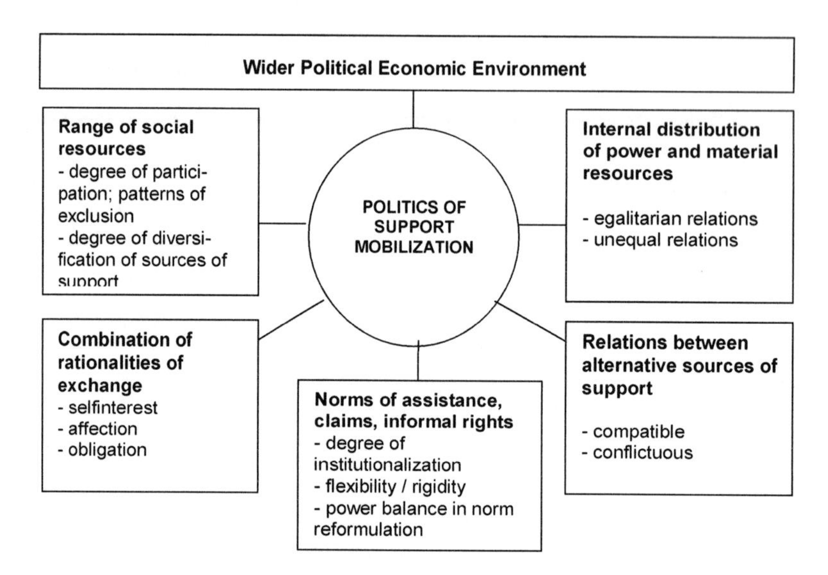

To begin with, the political economic environment and the structural position of participants in it are crucial to understanding what is happening to the networks of the poor. Then, their positioning within social networks may be considered on the basis of the several dimensions. First, the range of their sources of support needs to be considered, including processes marginalizing people from networks. Secondly, the kinds of rationalities pervading assistance relationships seem to have implications for the resilience of assistance ties in crises. Thirdly, and related to the latter aspect, the kinds of claims that people can make on others in their networks, their perceived rights to assistance and the characteristics of the norms pervading exchange of assistance are of importance. Some of these characteristics are the degree of institutionalisation, where a high degree may guarantee a minimum of security; the degree of rigidity or flexibility contained in these rules, for example to what extent they can be manoeuvred or discarded without serious consequences; and the instances of rule reformulation and the power relations involved, i.e. who is pushing the changes and their consequences. Fourthly, the power balance in the relationships pertains to the terms of participation and to members' ability to exercise their rights to assistance. This may vary between egalitarian and unequal relations. Finally, particularly where relations of assistance entail subordination, it is important to identify what are the alternatives available to the subordinate partners and the viability of these alternatives.

Opening these various windows into social networks possibly facilitates venturing into the politics of support mobilisation and equips us to understand change in relations of assistance taking into consideration both the internal dynamics of networks and wider processes in society.

8.3 The informal as *regulated*

The highly diverse nature of the informal sphere has been recognised before. And yet, aggregate conceptions of the informal sphere have prevailed that render invisible its content in a variety of ways. Related to this is the wide-spread notion of the informal as being "unregulated". By doing so, informal sector writers adopt the written law of the state as the only parameter of significance for understanding changes in the informal realm and leave outside an entire universe of internal boundaries and informal rules and the power relations involved in their negotiation. Examples of this great variety of rules, actors and social relations contained in the informal realm have surfaced throughout the book. Here, I would like to bring together those dispersed threads and elaborate a little on the issue of a differentiated informal domain from the point of view of regulation.

Alternatively to seeing regulation as being the exclusive domain of the state, one may look at regulation as encompassing: (a) a variety of rules, written or unwritten, which are recognisable by groups of people and govern economic activities and social interaction and access to a variety of resources ranging from productive ones to general assistance; (b) a corresponding multiplicity of power relations and struggles involved in defining and redefining those rules; and (c) a wide range of agents that may be involved, including a variety of regulatory agents beside the state and different forms of sanction. The intention is to uncover the variety of ways in which relations in the informal sphere are regulated. Figure 8.3. tries to depict how one may dissect this variety.

Figure 8.3 Components of multifaceted forms of regulation in the informal sphere

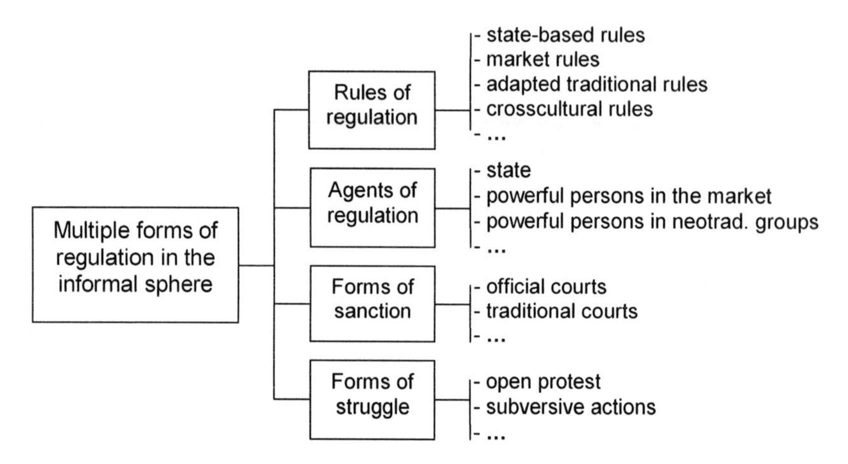

One could expect that such a complex constellation of rules and agents is both historically contingent and place specific. So let me attempt to roughly sketch how this constellation looks like in contemporary Bissau, as I understand it. There is no ambition of being exhaustive, given the spatial and sectoral delimitation of the study. I will focus on forms of regulation governing activities in the informal food sector, in both its market and non-market components, as these activities have been the focus of the study. The rules of regulation that I found as being of significance in this particular spatial-historic intersection could be grouped in the following way: state-based rules (a), market rules (b), adapted traditional rules (c) and cross-cultural rules (d). State-based rules (a) encompass both written laws that could be sanctioned by formal means such as courts of law as well as unwritten rules imposed by informal means of exerting pressure and existing laws not being enforced or enforced in an inconsistent or biased fashion. Forms of struggle may take a variety of forms, ranging from open protest to non-compliance. Market rules (b) consist basically of the laws of supply and demand and characterise depersonalised exchange. They differ in this respect from the remaining two, in which exchange takes place in the context of a longer-term bond of some kind. Regulatory agents are usually powerful agents in the market. Attempt to circumvent their power may range from looting to subversive actions (for examples of such actions, see chapter five). Adapted traditional rules (c) refer to pre-colonial norms that have evolved and been modified to suit contemporary purposes. Persons of power in traditional hierarchies are usually the ones in a position to be regulators of access to important livelihood resources. Traditional courts, witchcraft and manipulation of traditional rules for one's advantage are some of the ways in which conflicts may be handled. Finally, cross-cultural rules (d) govern relations between people of different ethnic backgrounds, where no shared cultural norms exist that can be resorted to. They pertain to recurrent kinds of personal agreements between actors in the market and to rules of operation in collectivities of different kinds. They may be unequally or collectively defined.

These sets of rules differ in terms of regulatory agents and the kinds of social relations involved. Each set of rules may generate its own kinds of divisions as well as power struggles. But the idea is not to insist on exclusive categories of rules working in isolation from each other or on clear divisions between for example state and market or between market and non-market kinds of rules[270]. Though they may dominate in particular interaction contexts, these various sets of rules often merge into each other and may sometimes be difficult to distinguish. How different sets of rules and agents may relate to each other requires further work. Although I occasionally hinted about it in my empirical chapters, theorising about it requires a discussion relating to several parallel debates – such as those dealing with relations between state and traditional elites or between state and market – which would take me too far at this point.

The scope for market rules in Bissau has certainly increased with deregulation policies over the last number of years, as in other places[271]. But the market seldom remains the abstract entity of neo-classical theory. Rather, its laws are distorted for particular ends. And indeed, most of the traders that I interviewed sought protection from those laws by engaging in relations regulated by rules other than the pure market ones. But as mentioned above, not all were equally protected. As market rules seem to account for some of the fluidity of market activities and the ephemeral nature of market places in Bissau, one wonders *who* is being 'fluid' (i.e. frequently switches selling sites, supply sources and merchandise). For this fluidity is not unlimited, as this would in some instances compromise advantageous agreements with suppliers (see chapter five). It could be that what appears as an extreme flexibility to adapt to market conditions simply reflects a desperate chase for customers by "unprotected" traders. This would be an interesting avenue for further research.

The increased terrain that market rules have gained has partly been at the expense of some of the earlier areas of state regulation or direct intervention but does not necessarily correspond to a decrease in the influence of the state. As discussed in chapter three, the state has been reported to continue to intervene in both direct and indirect ways. To begin with, the Guinean state has historically been keen to consciously choose what spheres were and were not to be subjected to the rule of the written law, and in this sense the supposedly

[270] See chapter one where I suggest a continuum rather than a sharp division between market and non-market exchange. See also chapter six on examples of a market rationality outside the market.

[271] As noted above, a market rationality may also be gaining terrain in spheres of provision outside the market, as ties of assistance show signs of undergoing an instrumentalization.

"unregulated" sphere has in fact sometimes corresponded to a conscious and convenient absence on the part of the state. There have been instances of state backed informal relations, particularly where these relations have suited the interests of the modern state and capitalist accumulation (see chapter two). For example, export crop production in rural areas and the sphere of social provisioning were areas that the colonial state deliberately left to be regulated by customary rules, at a time when a battery of modern laws was being produced to regulate other spheres of activity.

In the contemporary era, the division between the supposedly state-"regulated" and "unregulated" spheres seems to have become further blurred. First, "deregulation" (i.e. the minimisation of whatever state laws that may hamper the forces of the market) has become a part of mainstream development policy and one that has actively contributed to the expansion of a realm where large numbers of people lack the protection of labour legislation[272]. Secondly, the attitude of the state towards informality is ambivalent as it entertains different relations with different kinds of informal actors. On the one hand, small informal entrepreneurs have continued to be the object of oppressive practices by the local state and its agents – ranging from zoning prohibitions to arbitrary fee charging in the market places (see chapter five). On the other hand, large informal actors, particularly import-export firms, have been found to be dependent on connections to the Guinean state and state actors have been reported to mix bureaucratic positions and informal entrepreneurial ventures (if not openly, then secretly). This straddling by a number of well-positioned actors suggests a sort of selective permeability between the formal and the informal. It suggests that instances of both "engagement" and "disengagement" seem to have been implied in the construction of the informal realm. In this respect, the "disengagement" perspective on the dynamics of informality is clearly insufficient (see chapter one). Likewise, conceptualisations of the informal sphere as the realm of the "unregulated" tend to put it in opposition to the state and thus render invisible the state's participation in it[273].

Certain spheres of interaction are mainly governed by rules other than those of the state. Among these, in the study setting, adapted traditional rules (c) play a role in meeting contemporary needs and challenges. Their purposes may range from accumulation - such as the ancient kinds of affinities that seemingly cement the accumulation networks of merchant capital mentioned in chapter three – to provisioning and assistance among kin and lineage members, documented in chapter seven. These rules have deep historical roots and are thus deeply institutionalised (see chapter two). The positions from which the distribution of resources could be regulated were ascribed among the studied group, but in other groups and societies they may be acquired, not least through market means. Some have noted the intervention of neo-

---

[272] For a general discussion of this, see Meagher (1995:277).

[273] See Kiondo (1994) and Beckman (1997) for such an argument on civil society and the state.

traditional power groups in the regulation of urban relations (Simone, 1999:80; Attahi, 1997; Piermay, 1997). Considering the general revival of traditional structures in Africa and its cities, this form of regulation could be on the increase – though subordinate groups may have a say in this.

Finally, there are cross-cultural rules (d) governing relations between actors in the market and within collectivities of different kinds. Cross-cultural relations include informal agreements in the market, which may be egalitarian or exploitative in nature. The latter was the case of agreements between merchant firms and wholesalers on the one hand and small retailers or groups of casual workers on the other. Another example was the relations between fish suppliers and retailers (see chapter five). Cross-cultural rules could include those governing the life of collectivities such as the so-called "grassroots organisations". Non-governmental and voluntary organisations still have but a modest role in Bissau and Bandim, although they might be prominent agents of regulation in other African cities (see Aina, 1997 and Tostensen et al., 2001). In the studied neighbourhood, other kinds of collectivities are a lot more common, such as religious groups, rotating savings groups and redistribution groups among casual workers. In the latter two cases, the rules at work are most probably decided on a collective basis.

Cross-cultural rules of assistance are fundamentally different from traditional kinds of rules, in that they may provide a counterbalance to a reported increase in parochialism in Africa and its cities. There is a hardening of boundaries between different religious and ethnic affiliations as well as around neighbourhoods and economic and social networks that are structured along ethnic and kinship lines, a development which contributes to social fragmentation and threatens the social cohesion of cities (Onibokun, 94:263; Bangura, 1994:804; Simone, 1998:76, 1999:81, Rakodi, 1997b:572). However, some writers have also referred to the practices and networks that link neighbourhoods, ethnic and religious groups into larger networks that serve to integrate the city (Simone, 1999:82; Kharoufi, 1994:94). I became aware of these practices and networks in Bissau as I studied the commercial networks of traders and became interested in casual worker groups. As discussed in chapter six, these groups are typically composed of men from a variety of ethnic groups and living in different parts of the city. In this sense, they are cross-cultural networks, bridging over parochial and ethnic divisions as well as worldviews. In a manner of speaking they could be said to be integrating the fragmented city from below[274]. Also worth mentioning is a more recent creation, the National Movement of Civil Society, which congregates associations and groups from a variety of positions and creeds. These various integrative initiatives and widely spread networks that urbanites develop for survival and

[274] This echoes a usual perception of Guineans, whereby they are often said to be able to get along across ethnic boundaries, given a history of close interaction and senses of belonging above one's own ethnic group, forged not least during a decade of armed struggle against colonialism.

the juggling of different identities they require, may be the starting platform on which to build a new social consensus that takes into account the competing agendas and aspirations of different groupings within the city (Simone, 1998).

The fact that each of the above sets of rules combine and blend in complex ways, prompts me to proceed by illustrating these combinations of regulation rules in different sub-spheres of the informal domain. The first example refers to the sphere of entrepreneurial and accumulation activities, which is crossed by an interesting mixture of forms of regulation. Import-export and wholesale firms have been reported to have a particular position in relation to state regulation, i.e. they comply with a number of state decreed regulations (hold licenses etc.) but evade others. A few of them have also been said to have been supported in their ascension by an alliance with the state, suggesting that a less visible kind of regulation has possibly been at work. Hierarchical relations between import-exporters and their middlemen seem to be predicated either on market rules or on "traditional" rules based on kinship, ethnic and religious affinities. Relations between merchant capital and small actors, such as retailers and casual workers, were seemingly governed by supply-demand rules or by rules of a cross-cultural type when longer duration agreements were reached, though in the context of an exploitative relationship.

Relations among small actors in the market also reveal an interweaving of a variety of rules. Firstly, while most marketers may lack licenses required by law, they pay daily fees to local government. Secondly, they are subjected to the laws of supply and demand, and when lacking agreements that cushion the impact of those laws, this is certainly a source of vulnerability. In an attempt to counter the ups and downs of the market, traders often seek the assistance of relatives and enter personal relationships with other agents in the market. Here too there may be some recurrent sets of rules pervading such relationships. One example concerns the agreements between a share of the fish retailers and their suppliers where the latter were in the position of informal regulators, from which they could influence the "fate" of retailers. Sexual subordination was often reported as being implied in these agreements. The efforts of those in disadvantaged situations to circumvent the power of those regulators were also mentioned in chapter five. Other relations of support were based on more egalitarian and apparently collectively determined forms of regulation. This was the case of rotating savings groups and redistribution groups among casual workers. Both types had explicit rules of functioning that were of the cross-cultural type as they gathered people of various ethnic backgrounds.

In the sphere of consumption, relations of assistance draw on a variety of affinities, such as those between friends, neighbours and relatives. Kinship based assistance and provisioning regulated by "traditional rules" emerge as particularly important, as they have historically been in the city and beyond.

There are recognisable general sets of obligations and rights for different kin categories as well as group specific norms determining the responsibilities and rights of members of corporate kin groups (see chapter seven). In corporate kin groups, seniors are the distributors of food and productive resources and enjoy considerable power of sanction. This type of regulation revealed itself as a source of subordination of women and youth and sometimes of great vulnerability when seniors twisted norms to their own advantage. One may speculate that the way norms are formulated and enforced may assume more democratic forms among traditional societies with less hierarchical structures. Judging from the accounts of seniors, the state, while seemingly absent from this sphere of regulation, acts in ways that interfere with it. On the one hand, the state occasionally seeks contact with elders in Bandim while on the other hand it expropriates them of a share of their land (see chapter seven). These historically deeply rooted forms of regulation lend strength to the notion of geographically specific forms of regulation.

From the point a view of hegemonic development agendas, one of the main implications of these findings is that the assumption that "deregulation" will suffice to put things right is unrealistic. My empirical material revealed instances of unaccountable and discriminatory forms of informal regulation. The same could be said of naïvely over-enthusiastic views of informal governance that imbue it with positive attributes. For example, Halfani (1997:25) praises informal modes of governance (comparing these to state centred modes) as socially robust, rooted in local culture and traditions and as emanating from and for the poor. They may currently be indispensable for providing a minimum level of predictability in transactions. But the findings here suggest that it is unlikely that all forms of informal regulation will lead to equitable development. The study has shown instances where informal regulatory agents used discrimination and unaccountability, inspiring feelings of resentment among those affected negatively. I found this to be the case of seniors in kin groups and of fish suppliers. The potential of informal forms of urban governance needs to be analysed in concrete situations and in the light of criteria similar to those used for more formal types of governance, such as accountability, internal democracy etc. Here, there is clearly scope for further work.

The current emphasis on the multiplicity of governance regimes in Africa has highlighted the importance of forging links and partnerships between different actors and of the quality of the interrelationships (Halfani 1997:33; Swilling 1997:11). In this context mutual scrutiny and counter-checks between formal and informal institutions are important to hold both accountable and to ensure that they are working for the common good. In this equation, the state has a role to play. Overarching norms have been considered to be important for keeping informal loci of governance under check (Bangura, 1994:821), to bridge the various modes of regulation and to regulate relations between groups with few cultural affinities. As people constantly move between different socio-economic settings in the city, there is a need for accountability in various social contexts (ibid. p. 817-9).

The conditions of small informal actors and the sustainability of their efforts depend upon progress in these directions. The multiplication of power bases influencing their informal livelihoods means that they increasingly have to strive for empowerment on a variety of fronts. This requires novel ways of looking at informal politics. An excessive focus on readily identifiable collectively organised actors as is usual in the urban governance debate may give modest results in some contexts, given that such forms of organisation are often limited in the informal sphere (Gibbon, 1995; Sanyal, 1991). So we need to search beneath the apparent chaos for the more diffuse and less visible networks, actors and forms of regulation of the sort that this study has illustrated. In addition, the virtual absence of visible forms of organisation should not distract from the political potential of such a rapidly growing number of small informal actors. They are today a social and political force to be reckoned with, capable of influencing urban change (Swilling, 1994:346; Stren 1994: :15). Some writers have begun to envisage a global future where these "post-modern economies" will gradually coalesce to overcome the constraints weighing upon them (Burbach et al, 1997:8). In the meantime, where organised and confrontational means are perceived as having drastic consequences, subtle forms of resistance may be making progress. For the majority who are walking on a tightrope, small steps may be safer than bold moves.

References

Achtinger, G., 1993: "Os efeitos do programa de ajustamento estrutural sobre as condições económicas e sociais das mulheres da zona rural". In Imbali, F. (coord.), op. cit..

Acioly, C., 1993: *Planejamento urbano, habitação e autoconstrução: experiências com urbanização de bairros na Guiné-Bissau*. Delft: Publikatieburo Bouwkunde.

ACOBES (Associação do Consumidor de Bans e Serviços), 1997. *Estatutos* (internal document). Bissau.

Adams, A., 1993: "Food insecurity in Mali: exploring the role of the moral economy". *IDS Bulletin*, 24:4, pp.41-51.

Aguilar, R., and Zejan, M., 1991: *Guinea-Bissau: a fresh start?*. Gothenburg: University of Gothenburg.

Aguilar, R., and Zejan, M., 1992: *Guinea-Bissau: getting off the track*. Gothenburg: University of Gothenburg.

Aguilar, R., and Zejan, M., 1994: "Ajustamento estrutural na Guiné-Bissau". *Soronda*, 17, pp. 79-106.

Aguilar, R., and Stenman, Å., 1993: *Guinea-Bissau: facing new temptations and challenges*. Gothenburg: University of Gothenburg.

Aguilar, R., and Stenman, Å., 1994: *Guiné-Bissau: na véspera de amanhã*. Gotemburgo: Universidade de Gotemburgo.

Aguilar, R., and Stenman, Å., 1996: Guinea-Bissau: missing the beat. Stockholm: SIDA.

Aguilar, R., and Stenman, Å., 1997: *Guinea-Bissau: looking for new development paths*. Stockholm: SIDA.

Aguilar, R., 1998: *Guiné-Bissau: entrando em alta velocidade*. Estocolmo: ASDI.

ALC (Análise da legislação comercial), 1994: *O impacto de leis e regulamentos no comercio e no investimento do sector privado*. Documento Base do workshop, 1-3 Março 1994, Bissau (unpublished).

Almeida, I. and Drame, M., 1993: "Projecto de seguimento do programa de ajustamento estrutural no sector da saude". In Imbali, F. (coord.), op. cit..

Amis, P., 1989: "African development and urban change: what policy makers need to know". *Development Policy Review*, 7:4, pp. 375-391.

Andersson, A., 2002: *The bright lights grow fainter: livelihoods, migration and a small town in Zimbabwe*. Stockholm Studies in Human Geography 10. Stockholm: Acta Universitatis Stockholmiensis.
Andræ, G., 1992: "Urban workers as farmers: agro-links of Nigerian textile workers in the crisis of the 1980s". In Baker, J. and Pedersen, P., *The rural-urban interface in Africa, expansion and adaptation*. Uppsala: Nordiska Afrikainstitutet.
Anwar, M., 1995: "Social networks of Pakistanis in the UK: a reevaluation". In Rogers, A. and S. Vertovec (ed), op. cit..
Appadurai, A., 1995: Introduction: commodities and the politics of value". In Appadurai, A. (ed.), *The social life of things: commodities in cultural perspective*. Cambridge: Cambridge University Press.
Appadurai, A., 1996: *Modernity at large: the cultural dimensions of globalisation*. Minneapolis and London: University of Minnesota Press.
Attahi, K., 1997: "Decentralisation and participatory urban governance in Fracophone Africa". In Swilling, M., (ed.), op. cit..
Augel, J. 1996: "Bissau: autoprivilegiamento e luta pela sobrevivência". In Augel, J. and Cardoso, C., *Transição democrática na Guiné-Bissau e outros ensaios*. Bissau: INEP.
Azarya, V. and Chazan, N., 1987: "Disengagement from the state in Africa: reflections on the experience of Ghana and Guinea". *Comparative Studies in Society and History*, 29, pp.106-131.
Azarya, V., 1988: "Reordering state-society relations: incorporation and disengagement". In Rothchild and Chazan (eds), op. cit..
Baker, J., (ed), 1997: *Rural-urban dynamics in Francophone Africa*. Uppsala: Nordiska Afrikainstitutet.
Baker, J., 1997: "Introduction". In Baker, J., (ed), op. cit..
Bangura, Y., 1992: "Authoritarian rule and democracy in Africa: a theoretical discourse". In Gibbon and Bangura (eds), op. cit..
Bangura, Y. and Gibbon, P., 1992: "Adjustment, authoritarianism and democracy in Sub-Saharan Africa: an introduction to some conceptual and empirical issues". In Gibbon, P.; Bangura, Y. and Ofstad, A. (eds.), op. cit..
Bangura, Y., 1994: "Economic restructuring, coping strategies and social change: implications for institutional development in Africa". *Development and change*, 25:4, pp. 785-827.
Banton, M., 1961: "The restructuring of social relationships". In Southall, A., (ed), op. cit..
Barnes, J., 1969: "Networks as political processes". In Mitchell, J., op. cit..
Barnes, S., 1986: *Patrons and power: creating a political community in metropolitan Lagos*. Manchester: University Press.
Barr, A., 1998: *Enterprise performance and the functional diversity of social capital*. Working Paper Series 98-1. Oxford: Centre for the Study of African Economies.

Barr, A., 2000: *Collective action and bilateral interaction in Ghanaian entrepreneurial networks*. Working Papers No. 182. Helsinki: World Institute for Development Economics Research.

Barry, B., 1990: "A Senegâmbia do séc. XV ao séc. XX: em defesa de uma história subregional da Senegâmbia". *Soronda*, 9, pp. 3-21.

Basham, R., 1978: *Urban Anthropology: The cross-cultural study of complex societies*. Palo Alto: Mayfield Publishing Company.

Bayart, J-F., 1993: *The state in Africa: the politics of the belly*. London and New York: Longman.

Bayart, J-F., 2000: "Africa in the world: a history of extraversion". *African Affairs*, 99, pp. 217-267.

Beal, J., 1997: "Social capital in waste – a solid investment?". *Journal of International Development*, 9:7, pp. 951-961.

Beckman, B., 1992: "Empowerment or repression? The World Bank and the politics of African adjustment". Gibbon, P. et al. (eds.), op. cit..

Beckman, B., 1997: "Explaining democratization: Notes on the concept of civil society". In Özdalga, E. and Persson, S. (eds), *Civil society, democracy and the Muslim world*. Istambul: Swedish Research Institute.

Benda-Beckmann, F. And Kirsch, R, 1999: "Informal security systems in Southern Africa and approaches to strengthen them through policy measures". *Journal of Social Development in Africa*, 14:2, pp.21-38.

Bernstein, H., 1988: "Labour regimes and social change under colonialism". In Crow, B. et al., *Survival and change in the Third World*. Oxford: Polity Press.

Berry, S., 1985: *Fathers work for their sons: accumulation, mobility and class formation in an extended Yoruba community*. Berkeley, Los Angeles, and London: University of California Press.

Berry, S., 1989: "Social institutions and access to resources". *Africa*, 59:1, pp. 41-55.

Bigman, L., 1993: *History and hunger in West Africa: food production and entitlement in Guinea-Bissau and Cape Verde*. London: Greenwood Press.

Bigsten, A. et al., 2000: "Contract flexibility and dispute resolution in African manufacturing". *The Journal of Development Studies*, 36:4, pp. 1-37.

Booth, W., 1994: "On the idea of the moral economy". *American Political Science Review*, 88:3, pp. 653-67.

Bouya, A., 1997: "The roles of women in urban-rural interaction: the case of Sokone, Senegal". In Baker, J., (ed), op. cit..

Brand, V.; Mupedziswa, R.; and Perpetua, G., 1995: "Structural adjustment, women and informal trade in Harare". In Gibbon, P. (ed), *Structural adjustment and the working poor in Zimbabwe: studies on labour, women informal sector workers and health*. Uppsala: Nordiska Afrikainstitutet.

Bridge, G., 1993: *People, places and networks*. Bristol: School for Advanced Urban Studies Publications.

Brown, E., 2000: "Social movements, the state and civil society". In Mohan, G. et al, op. cit..
Bruce, J. and Dwyer, D., 1988: "Introduction". In Dwyer, D. and Bruce, J. (eds), *A home divided: women and income in the Third World.* Stanford: Stanford University Press.
Bryceson, D., 1990: *Food insecurity and the social division of labour in Tanzania*, 1919-85. Oxford: The Macmillan Press Ltd.
Burbach, R.; Nuñez, O.; Kagarlitsky, B., 1997: *Globalization and its discontents: the rise of postmodern socialisms.* London, Chicago, Illinois: Pluto Press.
Cabral, A., 1974: "Brief analysis of the social structure in Guinea". In *Selected texts by Amilcar Cabral. Revolution in Guinea: an African people's struggle.* London: Stage 1.
Cabral, A., 1980: *Unity and struggle: speeches and writings.* London: Heinemann.
Campbell, D., 1990: "Community-based strategies for coping with food scarcity: a role in African famine early-warning systems". *GeoJournal*, 20:3, pp. 231-241.
Cardoso, B. 1989: "A produção popular e o desenvolvimento económico e social da Guiné-Bissau: uma reflexão". *Boletim de Informação Sócio-económica*, 4/89, pp.1-6.
Cardoso, C. and Imbali, F., 1993: "As questões institucionais e o programa de ajustamento estrutural na Guiné-Bissau". In Imbali, F. (coord.), *Os efeitos socio-económicos do programa de ajustamento estrutural na Guiné-Bissau.* Bissau: INEP.
Cardoso, C. and Imbali, C., 1996: "A família". In Monteiro, A. (coord.), op. cit..
Cardoso, C., 1992: "A ideologia e a prática da colonização Portuguesa na Guiné e o seu impacto na estrutura social, 1926-73. *Soronda*, 14, pp 29-63.
Cardoso, C. 1994: "A transição democrática na Guiné-Bissau: um parto difícil". *Soronda*, 27, pp. 5-30
Cardoso, C. and Ribeiro, C., 1987: "Considerações sobre as estruturas socio-económicas das sociedades agrárias e a sua evolucão histórica – um estudo de caso". *Soronda*, 3, pp. 5-20.
Carreira, A., 1960: "Populacão autóctone segundo os recenseamentos para fins fiscais". *Boletim Cultural da Guiné Portuguesa*, 15:58, pp. 277-289.
Carreira, A., 1967: "Manjacos-Brames e Balantas: aspectos demográficos". *Boletim Cultural da Guiné Portuguesa*, 22:85-86, pp. 41-92.
Castells, M. and Portes, A., 1989: "World underneath: the origins, dynamics and effects of the informal economy". In Portes, A.; Castells, M.; and Benton, L., (eds.), op. cit..
Castells, M., 1998: *The information age: economy, society and culture.* Vol. III: End of Millenium. Blackwell Publishers Inc.

Castro, A., 1980: *O sistema colonial Português em África*. Lisboa: Editorial Caminho.

Chabal, P., 1984: "Socialismo na Guiné-Bissau: problemas e contradições no PAIGC desde a independência". *Revista Internacional de Estudos Africanos*, 1, pp. 139-168.

Chabal, P. and Daloz, J-P., 1999: *Africa works: disorder as political instrument*. London : International African Institute.

Chambers, R., 1989: "Editorial introduction: vulnerability, coping and policy". *IDS Bulletin*, 20:2, pp. 1-7.

Chambers, R., 1995: "Poverty and livelihoods: whose reality counts?" *Environment and Urbanization*, 7:1, pp. 173-204.

Chambers, R., 1995a: *Poverty and livelihoods: whose reality counts?* IDS Discussion Paper no. 347.

Chant, S., 1989: "Gender and urban production". In Brydon, L. and Chant, S., *Women in the third World: gender issues in rural and urban areas*. Hants: Edward Elgar.

Cheal, D., 1988: *The gift economy*: London: Routledge.

Cissoko, M. et al, 1987: *A realidade social e o sistema educativo em Bunau*. Bissau: INDE (unpublished).

Colónia da Guiné, 1948: *Foral da Câmara Municipal de Bissau e Plano de urbanizacão da cidade de Bissau*. Diplomas Legislativos 1:415 e 1:416. Bolama.

Corbet, J., 1988: "Famine and household coping strategies". *World Development*, 16, pp. 1099-1112.

Comaroff, J. and Comaroff, J., 1993: "Introduction". In Comaroff, J. and Comaroff, J., *Modernity and its malcontents: ritual and power in Postcolonial Africa*. Chicago and London: The University of Chicago Press.

Comité information Sahel, 1974: *Qui se nourrit de la famine en Afrique? Le dossier politique de la faim au Sahel*. Paris: Maspero.

Cornia, G., 1987: "Adjustment at the household level: potentials and limitations of survival strategies". In Cornia, G.; Jolly, R. and Stewart, F., *Adjustment with a human face*. Vol. I. Oxford: Clarendon Press.

Costa, L. and Silva, V., 1996: "Despesas orçamentais correntes". In Monteiro (coord.), op. cit..

Costa, F.; Moreira, A. and Proença, C., 1994: *Estudo da evolução dos niveis de vida, Bissau 1986/1991*. Bissau: INEC (unpublished).

Crowley, E., 1993, *Guinea-Bissau's informal economy and its contributions to economic growth*. The Hague: USAID (unpublished).

Cutrufelli, M., 1983: *Women of Africa: roots of oppression*. London : Zed Press.

Daines, V. and Seddon, D., 1991: *Survival struggles, protest and resistance: women's responses to "austerity" and "structural adjustment"*. Gender Analysis in Development No. 4. Norwich: School of Development Studies.

Davies, S., 1996: *Adaptable livelihoods: coping with food insecurity in Malian Sahel*. London: Macmillan Press.
Davila, J., 1987: *Shelter, poverty and African revolutionary socialism: human settlements in Guinea-Bissau*. Buenos Aires, London and Washington DC: International Institute for Environment and Development.
Dávila, J., 1991: "Planeamento urbanistico e territorial na Guiné-Bissau". *Soronda*, 12, pp. 91-120.
De Herdt, T. and Marysse, S., 1996: *L'économie informelle au Zaïre: survie et pauvreté dans la période de transition*. Paris: L'Harmattan.
De Herdt, T. and Marysse, S., 1997: "Against all odds: coping with regress in Kinshasa, Zaïre". In Kay, C. (ed), *Globalisation, competitiveness and human security*. London and Portland: Frank Cass.
De Soto, H., 1989: *The other path*. New York: Harper and Row.
Delgado, A., 1989: "Mobilização feminina em Bissau: o caso das vendedeiras dos mercados". *Boletim de Informação Sócio-económica*, 4/89, pp. 7-18.
Delgado, A., Fernandes, R., and Handem, D., 1989: *Relatórios do seminário UNESCO/INEP sobre: As mulheres na economia nacional*. INEP: Bissau (unpublished).
Dennis, C., 1991: "Constructing a "career" under conditions of economic crisis and structural adjustment: the survival strategies of Nigerian women". In Afshar, H. (ed), *Women, development and survival in the Third World*. London and New York: Longman.
Devereux, S. 1999: "*Making the less last longer: informal safety nets in Malawi*". IDS Discussion Paper 373.
Dhemba, J., 1999: "Informal sector development: a strategy for alleviating urban poverty in Zimbabwe". *Journal of Social Development in Africa*: 14:2, pp. 5-19.
Dias, E., 1992: "Ser Mandinga e Muçulmano, um modo de ver o mundo". *Forum Sociológico*, 1, pp. 95-104.
Dias, E., 1993: "A Guiné-Bissau e as dinâmicas sociais da sub-região". In Cardoso, C. e Augel, J. (coord.), *Guiné-Bissau: vinte anos de independencia: desenvolvimento e democracia, balanco e perspectivas*. Bissau: INEP.
Dias, N., 1992: *Produção e comercialização dos productos agrícolas na Guiné-Bissau*. Colóquio sobre a modernização da agricultura Guineense. Bissau (unpublished).
Diouf, M., 2000: "The Senegalese Murid trade diaspora and the making of a vernacular cosmopolitanism". *Codesria Bulletin*, 1, pp. 1930.
Downing, T., 1990: *Assessing socioeconomic vulnerability to famine*. Paper 2.1, USAID FEWS Working Paper.
Drakakis-Smith, D., 1991: "Urban food distribution in Asia and Africa". *The Geographical Journal*, 157:1, pp. 51-61.

Drakakis-Smith, D., 1993: "Food security and food policy for the urban poor". In Dahl, J.; Drakakis-Smith, D. and Närman, A. (eds), *Land, food and basic needs in Developing Countries*. Gothenburg: Kulturgeografiska Institutionen.

Drèze, J. and Sen, A., 1989: *Hunger and public action*. Oxford: WIDER:

Duarte, A. and Gomes, A., 1996: "O sector informal". In Monteiro, A. I. (coord.), op. cit..

Einarsdóttir, J., 2000: *Tired of weeping: child death and mourning among Papel mothers in Guinea-Bissau*. Stockholm: Stockholm Studies in Social Anthropology.

Ellis, F., 2000: *Rural livelihoods and diversity in Developing Countries*. Oxford: Oxford University Press.

Embaló, F., 1993: "Os desajustes do programa de ajustamento estrutural". *Soronda*, 16, pp. 51-72.

Epstein, A., 1969: "The network and urban social organization". In Mitchell, C (ed), op. cit..

Epstein, A., 1981: *Urbanization and kinship: the domestic domain on the Copperbelt of Zambia 1950-1956*. London and New York: Academic Press.

Espinosa, M., 1994: "Ponteiros na Guiné-Bissau: o processo de concessão de terras, 1879-1991". *Soronda*, 18, pp. 15-38.

Espling, M., 1999: *Women's livelihoods strategies in processes of change: cases from urban Mozambique*. Series B, No. 94. Gothenburg: University of Gothenburg.

Fafchamps, M., 1996: "The enforcement of commercial contracts in Ghana". *World Development*, 24:3, pp. 427-48.

Faro, J., 1958: "Os problemas de Bissau, Cacheu e suas dependências vistos em 1831 por Manuel Antonio Martins". *Boletim Cultural da Guiné Portuguesa*, 13:50, pp. 203-216.

Ferguson, J., 1999: *Expectations of modernity: myths and meanings of urban life on the Zambian Copperbelt*. University of California Press.

Fernandes, R., 1993: "Partido unico e poderes tradicionais". *Soronda*, 16, pp. 39-50.

Fernandes, R. M., 1994: "Processo democrático na Guiné-Bissau". *Soronda* 17, pp. 31-43.

Fine, B., 1999: "The Developmental State is dead – long live social capital?" *Development and Change*, 30, pp. 1-19.

Fisiy, C. and Geschiere, P., 1996: "Witchcraft, violence and identity: different trajectories in postcolonial Cameroon". In Werbner, R. and Ranger, T. (eds), op. cit..

Fox, J., 1997: "The World Bank and social capital: contesting the concept in practice". *Journal of International Development*, 9:7, pp. 963-971.

Frej, L. et al., 1984: *Saúde e nutriçāo infantis na Guiné-Bissau*. Estocolmo: SAREC.

Funk, U., 1993: "Labour, economic power and gender: coping with food shortage in Guinea-Bissau". In Downs, R.; Kerner, D.; and Reyna, S., (eds), *The political economy of African famine*. Philadelphia : Gordon and Breach Science Publishers.

Galaskiewicz, J., 1979: *Exchange networks and community politics*. Beverly Hills: Sage Publications, Inc..

Galli, R. and Jones, J., 1987: *Guinea-Bissau: politics, economics and society*. London: Frances Pinter.

Galli, R., 1990: "Liberalisation is not enough: structural adjustment and peasants in Guinea-Bissau". *Review of African Political Economy*, 49, pp.52-68.

Garcia, C., 1993: *O impacto de leis e regulamentos no comércio e no investimento do sector privado*. Bissau: USAID (unpublished).

Gaughan, J. and Ferman, L., 1987: "Towards an understanding of the informal economy". *The Annals of the American Academy of Political and Social Science*, 493, pp. 15-25.

Ghai, D., and Alcantara, C., 1990: *The crisis of the 1980s in Africa, Latin America and The Caribbean: economic impact, social change and political implications*. DP 7. Geneva: UNRISD.

Gibbon, P. and Bangura, Y., 1992: "Adjustment, authoritarianism and democracy in Sub-Saharan Africa: an introduction to some conceptual and empirical issues". In Gibbon, P.; Bangura, Y. and Ofstad, A. (eds.), op. cit..

Gibbon, P.; Bangura, Y. and Ofstad, A. (eds.), 1992: *Authoritarianism, democracy and adjustment: the politics of economic reform in Africa*. Uppsala: Nordiska Afrikainstitutet.

Gibbon, P., 1993: "Introduction: economic reform and social change in Africa". In Gibbon, P. (ed), *Social change and economic reform in Africa*. Uppsala: Nordiska Afrikainstitutet.

Gibbon, P., 1995: "Introduction". In Gibbon, P. (ed), *Structural adjustment and the working poor in Zimbabwe*. Uppsala: Nordiska Afrikainstitutet.

Gibbon, P., 1995a: "Merchantisation of production and privatisation of development in Post-Ujamaa Tanzania: an introduction". In Gibbon, P., (ed), *Liberalised development in Tanzania*. Uppsala: Nordiska Afrikainstitutet.

Gibbon, P., 1996: "Structural adjustment and structural change in Sub-Saharan Africa: some provisional conclusions". *Development and Change*, 27, pp. 751-784.

Giddens, A., 1999: *The constitution of society: outline of the theory of structuration*. Cambridge: Polity Press.

Giddens, A., 1999: *Runaway world: how globalization is reshaping our lives*. London: Profile books.

Gifford, P., 1998: *African Christianity: its public role*. London: Hurst.

Gomes, A., et al, 1989: *Étude socio-economique de Biombo*. Vol. I Bissau: INEP (unpublished).
Gomes, P., 1993: "O financiamento externo e a liberalização comercial durante o PAE". In Imbali, F. (coord.), op. cit..
Gomes, A. and Duarte, A., 1996: "O sector informal". In Monteiro, A. (coord.), op. cit..
Gomes, J., 1998: *Polón di Brá: Um documento de reflexão sobre uma guerra devastadora, desnecessária e injustamente imposta ao povo da Guiné-Bissau*. Bissau: INACEP.
Gore, C., 1993: "Entitlement relations and "unruly" social practices". *The Journal of Development Studies*, 29:3, pp. 429-460.
Gough, K. and Yankson, P., 2000: "Land markets in African cities: the case of peri-urban Accra, Ghana". *Urban Studies*, 37:13, pp.2485-2500.
Governo da Colónia, 1946: "Aspectos da cidade de Bissau". *Anuário da Guiné Portuguesa*. Lisboa.
Governo da Colónia, 1948: *Anuário da Guiné Portuguesa*. Lisboa.
Governo da Guiné, 1968: *Boletim official da Guiné Portuguesa*. Número 31. Bissau.
Gregory, C., 1982: *Gifts and commodities*. London: Academic Press.
Grey-Johnson, C. 1992: "The African informal sector at the crossroads: emerging policy options". *Africa Development*, 17:1, pp. 65-91.
Gugler, J. and Flanagan, W., 1978: *Urbanization and social change in West Africa*. Cambridge: Cambridge University Press.
Gugler, J., 1997: "Life in a dual system revisited: urban-rural ties in Enugu, Nigeria, 1961-1987". In Gugler, J. (ed.), *Cities in the developing world: issues, theory and policy*. Oxford: Oxford University Press.
Halfani, M., 1994: "Urban research in Eastern Africa". In Stren, R., (ed.), op. cit..
Halfani, M., 1997: "The challenge of urban governance in Africa: institutional change and knowledge gaps". In Swilling, M., (ed), op. cit..
Halfani, M., 1997a: "The governance of urban development in East Africa". In Swilling, M., (ed.), op. cit..
Handem, D., 1987: "A Guiné-Bissau a adaptar-se à crise". *Soronda*, 3, pp. 77-100.
Hannerz, U., 1980: *Exploring the city: inquiries toward an urban anthropology*. New York: Columbia University Press.
Harriss, J. and Renzio, P, 1997: "Missing link or analytically missing?: The concept of social capital". *Journal of International Development*, 9:7, pp. 919-937.
Hashim, Y. and Meagher, K., 1999: *Cross-border trade and the parallel currency market – trade and finance in the context of structural adjustment: a case study from Kano, Nigeria*. Research Report No. 113. Uppsala: Nordiska Afrikainstitutet.

Health Project, 1994: *Crowding and health in low-income settlements: case study report, Bissau*. Preliminary draft. Bissau (unpublished).
Hecht, D. and Simone, M., 1994: *Invisible governance: the art of African micropolitics*. New York: Autonomedia.
Hochet, A-M., 1985: *Les ex-royaumes Pepel du Tor et du Biombo*. Bissau (unpublished).
Hydén, G., 1983: *No shortcuts to progress*. Berkeley and Los Angeles: University of California Press.
Hyden, G., 1990: "Creating an enabling environment". In World Bank: *The long-term perspective of Sub-Saharan Africa*. Washington: The World Bank.
ICMU (*Inquérito de consumo de cereais no meio urbano*), 1991. Bissau: GAPLA, MRDA (unpublished).
Iheduru, O., 1999: *The politics of economic restructuring and democracy in Africa*. Westport and London: Greenwood Press.
Imbali, F. (coord.), 1993: *Os efeitos socio-economicos do programa de ajustamento estrutural na Guiné-Bissau*. Bissau: INEP.
Imbali, F. and Cardoso, C., 1996: "A familia". In Monteiro, A. I. (coord.), op. cit..
INEC (Instituto Nacional de Estatistica e Censo), 1991: *Recenseamento geral da populacão e habitacão*. Bissau.
INEP, 1991: *Sobre a integração da mulher no processo de desenvolvimento da Guiné-Bissau*. Relatório preliminar. Bissau. (unpublished).
INEP, 1991a: *La promotion du role des femmes dans le processus du developpement de la Guinée-Bissau*. Bissau. (unpublished).
Jenkins, P., 2000: "Urban management, urban poverty and urban governance: planning and land management in Maputo". *Environment and Urbanization*, 12:1, pp. 137-152.
Kapferer, B., 1969: "Norms and the manipulation of relationships in a work context". In Mitchell, C. (ed), op. cit..
Keesing, R., 1981: *Cultural Antropology: a contemporary perspective*. Fort Worth, New York and London: Harcourt Brace College Publishers.
Kiondo, A., 1994: "The new politics of local development in Tanzania". In Gibbon, P. (ed.), *The new local level politics in East Africa: studies on Uganda, Tanzania and Kenya*. Research report no. 95. Uppsala: Nordiska Afrikainstitutet.
Koudawo, F., 1996: "Sociedade civil e transição pluralista na Guiné-Bissau 1991-6". In Mendy, P. and Koudawo, F. (eds), *Pluralismo politico na Guiné-Bissau: uma transição em curso*. Bissau: INEP.
La Mettrie, D., 1992: *Rapport Technique diagnostic sur le commerce de cereales en Guinée-Bissau*. Rome: FAO (unpublished).
Lemarchand, R., 1988: "The state, the parallel economy, and the changing structure of patronage systems". In Rothchild and Chazan (eds), op. cit..

Lemarchand, R., 1989: "African peasantries, reciprocity and the market: the economy of affection reconsidered". *Cahiers d'Études Africaines*, 113:29-1, pp 33-67.
Lemarchand, R., 1991: "The political economy of informal economies". *Africa Insight*, 21:4, pp. 214-221.
Levi, M., 1996: "Social and unsocial capital: a review essay of Robert Putnam's Making democracy work". *Politics and Society*, 24:1, pp. 45-55.
Liljeström, R. et al., "Cultural conflicts and ambiguities". In Rwebangira, M. and Liljeström, R. (eds), 1998: *'Haraka, haraka, look before you leap': youth at the crossroad of custom and modernity*. Uppsala: Nordiska Afrikainstitutet.
Little, K., 1965: *West African urbanization: a study of voluntary associations in social change*. London and Colchester: Cambridge University Press.
Lobban, R., 1979: *Historical dictionary of the Republics of Guinea-Bissau and Cape Verde*. London: The Scarecrow Press, Inc.
Loforte, A., 2000: *Género e poder entre os Tsonga de Mocambique*. Maputo: Promédia.
Lomnitz, L.,1977: *Networks and marginality: life in a Mexican shantytown*. New York: Academic Press.
Lopes, C., 1987: *Guinea-Bissau: from liberation struggle to independent statehood*. London: Zed Books.
Lopes, C., 1988: *Para uma leitura sociológica da Guiné-Bissau*. Lisboa e Bissau: INEP.
Lopes, C., 1990: "Relações de poder numa sociedade malinké: o Kaabu do séc. XIII ao séc. XVIII". *Soronda*, 10, pp. 17-26.
Lourenço-Lindell, I., 1993: *Informal food production, distribution and consumption in a peripheral quarter of Bissau. Master thesis*. Stockholm: Stockholm University (unpublished).
Lourenço-Lindell, I., 1995: "The informal food economy in a peripheral urban district: the case of Bandim district, Bissau". *Habitat International*, 19:2, pp.195-208.
Lourenço-Lindell, I., 1996: "How do the urban poor stay alive? Modes of food provisioning in a squatter settlement of Bissau". *African Urban Quarterly*, 11:2, 3 pp. 163-168.
Lourenço-Lindell, 2001: "Coping with urban vulnerability: the role of social networks". In Tvedten, I.; Torstensen, A.; and Vaa, M. (eds), op. cit..
Lugalla, J., 1997: "Development, change and poverty in the informal sector during the era of structural adjustment in Tanzania". *Canadian Journal of African Studies*, 31:3, pp. 424-516.
Mabogunje, A., 1990: "Urban planning and the post-colonial state in Africa: a research overview". *African Studies Review*, 33:2, pp. 121-203.
Mabogunje, A., 1994: "Overview of research priorities in Africa". In Stren, R., (ed.), op. cit..

Macharia, K., 1997: *Social and political dynamics of the informal economy in African cities: Nairobi and Harare.* Lanham, New York, Oxford: University Press of America.

MacGaffey, J., 1988: "Economic disengagement and class formation in Zaire". In Rothchild and Chazan (eds), op. cit..

MacGaffey, J., and Bazenguissa-Ganga, R., 1999: "Personal networks and trans-frontier trade: Zaïrean and Congolese migrants". In Bach, D. (ed), *Regionalisation in Africa: integration and disintegration.* Oxford: James Currey.

Manuh, T., 1994: "Ghana: women in the public and informal sectors under the Economic Recovery Programme". In Sparr, P. (ed), op. cit..

Massey, D., 1999: Imagining globalization: power-geometries of time-space. In Brah, A.; Hickman, M.; and Ghaill, M., 1999: *Global futures: migration, environment and globalization.* New York: S. Martin's Press Inc.

Mauss, M., 1967: *The gift.* New York: W. W. Norton and company.

Mbembe, A., 2000: "At the edge of the world: boundaries, territoriality and sovereignity in Africa". *Public Culture,* 12:1, pp.259-284.

McCall, D., 1961: Trade and the role of wife in a modern West African town". In Southall, A., (ed), op. cit..

McCarney, P; Halfani, M.; and Rodriguez, A., 1995: "Towards an understanding of governance". In Stren, R. and Bell, J. (eds.), *Perspectives on the city.* Toronto: Centre for Urban and Community Studies.

Meagher, K. and Yunusa, M-B., 1991: *Limits to labour absortion: conceptual and historical background to adjustment in Nigeria's urban informal sector.* UNRISD Discussion Paper 28.

Meagher, K., 1995: "Crisis, informalisation and the urban informal sector in Sub-Saharan Africa". *Development and Change*, 26:2, pp. 259-284.

Meagher, K. and Yunusa, M-B., 1996: *Passing the buck: structural adjustment and the Nigerian urban informal sector.* UNRISD Discussion Paper 75.

Mendy, P., 1990: "A economia nacional da Guiné-Bissau: "nacionalização" e exploração, 1915-1959. *Soronda*, 9, pp. 23-51.

Mendy, P., 1994: *Colonialismo Português em África: a tradição da resistência na Guiné-Bissau (1879-1959).* Bissau: INEP.

Mhone, G., 1996: "Conceptual and analytical issues". In Mhone, G. (ed), *The informal sector in Southern Africa: an analysis of conceptual, research and policy issues.* Harare: Sapes Books.

Mitchell, J. (ed), 1969: *Social networks in urban situations: analysis of personal relationships in Central African towns.* Manchester University Press.

MNCS (Movimento Nacional da Sociedade Civil para a Paz, Democracia e Desenvolvimento), 1998: *Resoluções finais.* (Internal document).

Mohan, G., 2000: "Contested sovereignty and democratic contradictions: the political impacts of adjustment". In Mohan, G. et al., *Structural adjustment: theory, practice and impacts*. London and New York: Routledge.
Monteiro, A. (coord), 1996: *O programa de ajustamento estrutural na Guiné-Bissau: análise dos efeitos sócio-económicos*. Bissau: Instituto Nacional de Estudos e Pesquisa.
Monteiro, J. and Silva, D., 1993: "Exame longitudinal do comportamento dos indicadores do sistema educativo durante o programa de ajustamento estrutural". Imbali, F. (coord), op. cit..
Monteiro, H. and Martins, G., 1996: "Os efeitos do PAE no sector da educação". In Monteiro, A. (coord.), op. cit..
Monteiro, H. (ed), 2001: *Bandim: subsídios para uma política de apoio ao pequeno negócio*. Colecção Lala Kema No. 2. Bissau: INEP.
Moser, C., 1996: *Confronting crisis: a comparative study of household responses to poverty and vulnerability in four poor urban communities*. Washington: The World Bank.
Mota, A., 1954: *Guiné Portuguesa*. Vol. I and II. Lisboa: Agência Geral do Ultramar.
Moustier, P., 1993: *Systemes Maraichers approvisionnant Bissau: enquete exploratoire*. Montpelier: CIRAD-CA (unpublished).
Mustapha, A., 1992: "Structural adjustment and multiple modes of livelihood in Nigeria". In Gibbon and Bangura, (eds), op. cit..
Nabuguzi, E., 1994: *Structural adjustment and the informal economy in Uganda*. CDR Working Paper 94.4. Copenhagen: Centre for Development Research.
Narayan, D. and Pritchett, L., 1997: *Cents and sociability: household income and social capital in rural Tanzania*. Policy Research Working Paper 1796. Washington: The World Bank.
Narayan, D., 2000: *Voices of the poor: can anyone hear us?* Washington: The World Bank.
Ndiaye, F., 1998: "L'impact de la vie familiale sur l'activité entrepreneuriale des femmes au Sénegal". *Africa Development*, 23:3, 4, pp. 149-161.
Nsarhaza, K., 1997: *Au-delà de la régulation étatique: la gouvernance du marché informel de la santé: cas des médicaments au Zaïre*. DP 84. Genève: UNRISD.
Nyassogbo, G., 1997: "Urban-rural interactions in Sub-Saharan Africa: the case of Palimé and its hinterland in South-West Togo". In Baker, J., (ed), op. cit..
O'Brien, D., 1996: "A lost generation? Youth identity and state decay in West Africa". In Werbner, R. and Ranger, T., (eds), op. cit..
O'Laughlin, B., 1996:"From basic needs to safety-nets: the rise and fall of urban food-rationing in Mozambique". *The European Journal of Development Research*, 8:1 pp. 200-223.

Onibokun, A., 1994: "Urban research in Anglophone West Africa". In Stren, R., (ed.), op. cit..
Padovani, F. and Delgado, A. M., 1993: "O sector informal e o ajustamento na Guiné-Bissau". In Imbali, F. (coord.), op. cit..
Parecer da Câmara do Comércio, Industria e Agricultura da Guiné-Bissau, 1995: *Memorandum*. Bissau (internal document).
Paulo, A. and Jao, A., 1996: "Saude". In Monteiro, A. (coord.), op. cit..
PCGB (*Plan cerealier de la Guinée-Bissau*), 1991. Paris: MDRA et CILSS (unpublished).
Peattie, L., 1987: "An idea in good currency and how it grew: the informal sector". *World Development*, 15:7, pp. 851-860.
Pelissier, R., 1997: *História da Guiné: Portugueses e Africanos na Senegâmbia*. Lisboa: Editorial Estampa.
PHROD (Population and Human Resources Operations Division), 1991: *Guinea-Bissau: WID assessment and strategy paper* (draft). Bissau: The World Bank (unpublished).
Piel, M., 1981: *Cities and suburbs: urban life in West Africa*. New York: Africana Publishing Company.
Piermay, J-L., 1997: "Kinshasa: a reprieved megacity?" In Rakodi, C (ed.), op. cit..
Platteau, J-P., 1991: "Traditional systems of social security and hunger insurance: past achievements and modern challenges". In Ahmad, E. (ed), *Social security in Developing Countries*. Oxford:Clarendon Press.
Portes, A., 1981: "The informal sector: definition, controversy and relation to national development". *Review*, VII, 1, pp. 151-174.
Portes, A.; Castells, M.; and Benton, L., (eds.), 1989: *The informal economy: studies in advanced and less developed countries*. London: The John Hopkins Press Ltd..
Portes, A. and Schauffler, R., 1993: "Competing perspectives on the Latin American informal sector". *Population and Development Review*, 19:1, pp. 33-60.
Portes, A., 1998: "Social capital: its origins and application in modern sociology". *Annual Review of Sociology*, vol. 24, pp. 1-24.
Potter, R. and Lloyd-Evans, S., 1998: *The city in the developing world*. Essex: Addison Wesley Longman Limited.
Potts, D., 1997: "urban lives: adopting new strategies and adapting rural links". In Rakodi, C (ed.), op. cit..
Putzel, J., 1997: "Accounting for the 'dark side' of social capital: reading Robert Putnam on democracy". *Journal of International Development*, 9:7, pp. 939-949.
Quintino, F., 1969: "Os povos da Guiné". *Boletim Cultural da Guiné Portuguesa*, 24:96, pp. 861-915.

Rakodi, C., 1995: "Poverty lines or household strategies? A review of conceptual issues in the study of urban poverty". *Habitat International*, 19:4, pp. 407-426.
Rakodi, C., (ed) 1997: *The urban challenge in Africa*. Tokyo, New York and Paris: United Nations University Press.
Rakodi, C., 1997a: "Global forces, urban change and urban management in Africa". In Rakodi, C (ed.), op. cit..
Rakodi, C., 1997b: "Conclusion". In Rakodi, C (ed.), op. cit..
Rakodi, C., 1999: "A capital assets framework for analysing household livelihood strategies: implications for policy". *Development Policy Review*, 17, pp. 315-342.
República da Guiné-Bissau, 1988: Decreto 29/88. *Boletim Official*, No. 37. Bissau.
República da Guiné-Bissau, 1994: Decretos 29/94 and 30/94. *Boletim Official*, No. 32. Bissau.
Ribeiro, C., 1989: "Causas da queda da produção do arroz na Guiné-Bissau". *Revista Internacional de Estudos Africanos*, 10-11, pp. 227-265.
Ribeiro, C.; Delgado, A. and Padovani, F., 1990: *Estudo de pre-viabilidade da promoção e fomento da microempresa e sector informal em Bissau*. Bissau: INEP (unpublished).
Rocha, M., 1994: *The resources of poverty: women and survival in a Mexican city*. Oxford and Cambridge: Blackwell.
Rodney, W., 1970: *A history of the Upper Guinea Coast, 1545-1800*. Oxford: Clarendon Press.
Rogers, A. and Vertovec, S., 1995: "Introduction". In Rogers, A. and Vertovec, S. (eds), op. cit..
Rogers, A. and Vertovec, S. (eds), 1995a: *The urban context: ethnicity, social networks and situation analysis*. Oxford and Washington: Berg Publishers.
Rogerson, C., 1993: "Urban agriculture in South Africa: policy issues from the international experience". *Development Southern Africa*, 10:1 pp. 33-44.
Rogerson, C., 1997: "Globalization or informalization? African urban economies in the 1990s". In Rakodi, C (ed), op. cit..
Roitman, J., 1990: "The politics of informal markets in Sub-Saharan Africa". *The Journal of Modern African Studies*, 28:4, pp. 671-696.
Rosander, E., 1997: "Introduction". In Rosander, E. (ed), *Transforming female identities: women's organizational forms in West Africa*. Uppsala: Nordiska Afrikainstitutet.
Rothchild, D. and Chazan, N. (eds), 1988: *The precarious balance. State and society in Africa*. Boulder: Westview Press.
Rudebeck, L., 1988: "Kandjadja, Guiné-Bissau: Observações sobre a economia politica do desenvolvimento de uma aldeia africana". *Soronda*, 5, pp. 61-82.

Rudebeck, L., 1990: "Ajustamento estrutural numa aldeia oeste-africana". In *Nas encruzilhadas: alianças politicas e ajustamento estrutural*. Uppsala University: AKUT.

Rudebeck, L., 1997: *'Buscar a felicidade': democratização na Guiné-Bissau*. Colecção Lala Kema No. 1. Bissau: INEP.

Rudebeck, L., 2001: *On democracy's sustainability: transition in Guinea-Bissau*. Stockholm: SIDA.

Liljeström, R. et al, 1998: "Cultural conflicts and ambiguities". In Rwebangira, M. And Liljeström, R., (eds), *Haraka, Haraka... Look before you leap: youth at the crossroad of custom and modernity*. Uppsala: Nordiska Afrikainstitutet.

Sahlins, M., 1984: *Stone age economics*. New York: Aldine de Gruyter.

Santos, N., 1971: "As fortalezas de Bissau". *Boletim Cultural da Guiné Portuguesa*, 26:103, pp. 481-519.

Sanyal, B., 1987: "Urban cultivation amidst modernization: how should we interpret it?". *Journal of Planning, Education and Research* 6, pp. 197-207.

Sanyal, B., 1991: "Organizing the self-employed: the politics of the urban informal sector". *International Labour Review*, 130:1, pp. 39-56.

Sarrazin, C. and Gjerstad, O., 1978: *Sowing the first harvest: national reconstruction in Guinea-Bissau*. Oakland: LSM Information Center.

Sassen-Koob, S., 1989: New York City's informal economy. In Portes, A.; Castells, M. and Benton, L. (eds), op. cit..

Sassen, S., 1998: *Globalization and its discontents: essays on the new mobility of people and money*. New York: The New Press.

Sassen, S., 2000: *Cities in a world economy*. Thousand Oaks and London: Pine Forge Press.

Scholte, R.; Cá, T.; Sandström, A. and Aaby, P., 1997: *Indicadores sócio-demográficos e sanitários, Bandim e Belém, 1990-1995*. Bissau: Projecto de Saude de Bandim (unpublished).

Scott, J., 1976: *The moral economy of the peasant*. New Haven: Yale University Press.

Sen, A., 1981: *Poverty and famines: an essay on entitlement and deprivation*. London: Oxford University Press.

Short, J. and Kim, Y-H., 1999: *Globalization and the city*. Essex: Longman.

Silveira, J., 1989: "La spatialisation d'un rapport colonial: Bissau, 1900-1960". In Coquery-Vidrovitch, C. and Cahen, M., (eds), *Bourgs et villes en Afrique Lusophone*. Paris: L'Harmattan.

Simon, D., 1992: *Cities, capital and development: African cities in the world economy*. London: Belhaven Press.

Simon, D., 1997: "Urbanization, globalization and economic crisis in Africa". In Rakodi, C (ed.), op. cit..

Simone, A., 1998: "Urban social fields in Africa". *Social Text,* 56, 16:3, pp. 71-89.

Simone, A., 1999: "Thinking about African urban management in an era of globalization". *African Sociological Review*, 3:2, pp. 69-98.
Simone, A., 2001: "Between Ghetto and globe: remaking urban life in Africa". In Tostensen, A.; Tvedten, I. And Vaa, M. (eds), op.cit..
Sjögren, A., 1998: *Civil society and governance in Africa - an outline of the debates*. Working Paper no. 1. Uppsala: Nordiska Afrikainstitutet.
Sobral, J., 1994: *Revisão da legislação comercial, regime de preços, acesso à actividade e licenciamento*. Trade and Investment Promotion Support Project. Bissau: USAID (unpublished).
Southall, A., (ed), 1961: *Social change in modern Africa*. London: Oxford University Press.
Southall, A., 1961: "Introductory summary". In Southall, A., (ed), op. cit..
Sow, F., 1993: "Les initiatives féminines au Sénegal: une réponse à la crise?" *Africa development*, 18:3, pp. 89-115.
Sparr, P., 1994: *Mortgaging women's lives: feminist critiques of structural adjustment*. London: Zed Books.
Sparr, P., 1994: "Feminist critiques of structural adjustment". In Sparr, P. (ed.), op. cit..
SSP (*Síntese do sector privado na Guiné-Bissau*), 1990. Bissau (unpublished).
Stren, R. and White, R. (eds), 1989: *African cities in crisis: managing rapid urban growth*. Boulder, San Francisco and London: Westview Press.
Stren, R., 1989: "The administration of urban services". In Stren, R. and White, R. (eds), op. cit..
Stren, R., 1992: "African urban research since the late 1980s: responses to poverty and urban growth". *Urban Studies*, 29:3/4, pp. 533-555.
Stren, R., (ed), 1994: *Urban research in the developing world*. Vol. Two: Africa. Toronto: Centre for Urban and Community Studies.
Sundberg, A., 1999: *God's princess in Congo: women's strategies in a disintegrating society*. Paper presented at the conference "Nordic Africa Days", Uppsala 29-31 October.
Swift, J., 1989: "Why are rural people vulnerable to famine?" *IDS Bulletin*, 20:2, pp. 8-15.
Swilling, M., 1994: "Towards an urban research agenda for Southern Africa". In Stren, R., (ed.), op. cit..
Swilling, M., 1997: "Introduction". In Swilling, M., (ed.), op. cit..
Swilling, M., (ed.), 1997a: *Governing Africa's cities*. Johannesburg: Witwatersrand University Press.
Tacoli, C., 1998: *Bridging the divide: rural-urban interactions and livelihood strategies*. Gatekeeper Series No. 77. International Institute for Environment and Development.
Tevera, D., 1995: "The medicine that might kill the patient: structural adjustment and urban poverty in Zimbabwe". In Simon, D.; Spengen, W.;

Dixon, C. and Närman, A. (eds), *Structurally adjusted Africa: poverty, debt and basic needs*. London and Boulder: Pluto Press.
Texto final do diploma sobre licenciamento comercial, 1995. Bissau: Ministério do Comércio (unpublished).
The Win Document, 1985: *The conditions of women in Nigeria and policy recommendations to 2.000 A.D.*. Samaru: WIN.
Tingbé-Azalou, A., 1997: "Cultural dimensions of urban-rural relations in Benin: the case of Abomey and its hinterland". In Baker (ed), op. cit..
Tokman, V., 1992: "Synthesis and conclusions". In Tokman, V. (ed), *Beyond regulation: the informal economy in Latin America.* Boulder and London: International Labour Organisation.
Tostensen, A; Tvedten, I.; and Vaa, M., 2001: *Associational life in African cities: popular responses to the urban crisis.* Uppsala: Nordiska Afrikainstitutet.
Trager, L., 1987: "A re-examination of the urban informal sector in West Africa". *Canadian Journal of African Studies*, 2:2, pp. 238-255.
Tripp, A., 1989: "Women and the changing urban household economy in Tanzania". *The Journal of Modern African Studies*, 27:4, pp. 601-623.
Tripp, A. M., 1997: *Changing the rules: the politics of liberalisation and the urban informal economy in Tanzania.* Berkeley and Los Angeles: University of California Press.
Tvedten, I., 1991: "Programas de ajustamento estrutural e implicações locais: o caso dos pescadores artesanais na Guiné-Bissau". *Soronda*, 11.
United Nations, 1996: *Informal sector development in Africa.* New York: United Nations.
United Nations, 1996a: *Urban agriculture: food, jobs and sustainable cities.* New York: UNDP.
Vaa, M.; Findley, S. and Diallo, A., 1989: "The gift economy: a study of women migrants' survival strategies in a low-income Bamako neighbourhood". *Labour, Capital and Society*, 22:2, pp. 234-60.
Viegas, L., 1936: *Guiné Portuguesa.* A Colónia da Guiné. Lisboa.
Watts, M., 1984: "The demise of the moral economy: food and famine in a Sudano-Sahelian region in historical perspective". In Scott, Earl (ed), *Life before the drought*. London: George Allen and Unwin.
Watts, M. and Bohle, H., 1993: "The space of vulnerability: the causal structure of hunger and famine". *Progress in Human Geography*, 17:1, pp. 43-67.
Werbner, P., 1995: "From commodities to gifts: Pakistani migrant workers in Manchester". In Rogers, A. and S. Vertovec (ed), op. cit..
Werbner, R. and Ranger, T., (eds), 1996: *Postcolonial identities in Africa.* London and New Jersey: Zed Books Ltd.
Werbner, R., 1996: "Multiple identities, plural arenas". In Werbner, R. and Ranger, T., (eds), op. cit..

Jorge Sobral and Anildo Cruz: consultants working on new legislation concerning small enterprises.
Júlia Silva: official at the local office of World Food Program.
Filipe Reis: medium-rank official at the Ministry of Commerce.
Alió Camará: City Council representative at Bandim market.

November – December 1992:
Marcelino Martins: director of the Green Belt Project in Bissau.
Agostinho Silva: National Institute of Statistics and Census (INEC), department of markets.
Idrissa Djaló: director of a fishing enterprise.
(Anonymous): director of the department of markets at Bissau City Council.
Adolfo Ramos: 'director of urbanism', at the Ministry of Public Works.
Fernanda Tavares: official at the Ministry of Promotion of Women.
Isabel Almeida: nutricionist at the Ministry of Public Health.
Siraio Seidi: agronomist at the Department of Agricultural Research.
Yves Tencalla: director of the local office of The World Bank.

(among others)

4579

List of interviews with officials and members of organisations

May – June 1999:

Rafael Barbosa: Co-founder of the PAIGC. Head of the political party The Social Democratic Front. Resident in Bandim.

Fernando Saldanha: vice-president of the Movement of the Civil Society for Peace, Democracy and Development. President and vice-president of two other national and international organisations. President of a local NGO. Journalist.

Pinto Marques: vice-president of the Guinean Alliance for Human Rights. Active within the Movement of the Civil Society. Former vice-president of the City Council in Bissau. Former president of the PAIGC's neighbourhood committee (Comité de Bairro). Resident in Bandim for two decades.

Pinto Vieira e Silva: general-director at the Ministry of Justice. Resident in Cupilon.

Filomeno Veiga: judge of the Sectoral Court of Bandim.

Domingos Nanque and João Baptista: former judges in the local PAIGC's 'Popular Court' (Tribunal Popular).

Tiago Sampaio: co-ordinator of the projects of the Evangelical church in Guinea-Bissau.

Martinho Nanque: director of a private school in Bandim.

Rosa Mendes: director of the health centre in Bandim.

Luis Baptista and Zinho Nanque: leaders of Bandim's Evangelical church.

Fodé Sanhá: president of the national Consumer Association with headquarters in Bandim.

Leaders of the *manjuandade* (social club) "Esperança de Bandim".

Sátiro Almeida: vice-president of a Youth Association in Bandim.

Moreira Indi: member of the board of the Evangelical Youth of Guinea-Bissau. Resident in Bandim.

Peter Aaby: director of the Health Project of Bandim.

January – April 1995:

Sérgio Mané: Department of Markets at Bissau City Council.

Adulai Djamanca: Section for the Inspection of Markets, Bissau City Council.

Rogério Dias: Chamber of Commerce in Bissau.

Wheeldon, P., 1969: "The operation of voluntary associations and personal networks in the political process of an inter-ethnic community". In Mitchell, J. (ed), op. cit..

White, R., 1989: "The influence of environmental and economic factors on the urban crisis". In Stren, R. and White, R. (eds), op. cit..

World Bank, 1987: *Guinea-Bissau: a prescription for comprehensive adjustment*. A World Bank country report. Washington.

World Bank, 1991: *Urban policy and economic development: an agenda for the 1990s*. Washington: The World Bank.

World Bank, 1997: *The state in a changing world.* Washington: The World Bank.

World Bank, 2000: *Entering the 21st century*. Washington: The World Bank.

World Bank, 2002: *Building institutions for markets*. Washington: The World Bank.

Yan, Y., 1996: *The flow of gifts: reciprocity and social networks in a Chinese village*. Stanford University Press.

Young, K., 1992: "Household resource management". In Ostergaard, L. (ed), *Gender and development: a practical guide*. London: Routledge.

Zack-Williams, A., 1993: "Crisis, structural adjustment and creative survival in Sierra Leone". *Africa Development*, 18:1, pp. 53-65.

Zack-Williams, A., 2000: "Social consequences of structural adjustment". In Mohan, G. et al (eds), op. cit..